Human Spatial Memory

Remembering Where

Human Spatial Memory

Remembering Where

Edited by

Gary L. Allen
University of South Carolina

LEA

LAWRENCE ERLBAUM ASSOCIATES, PUBLISHERS

2004   Mahwah, New Jersey   London

Lawrence Erlbaum Associates, Inc., Publishers
10 Industrial Avenue
Mahwah, New Jersey 07430

Cover design by Sean Trane Sciarrone

Library of Congress Cataloging-in-Publication Data

Human spatial memory : remembering where /edited by Gary L. Allen.
     p. cm.
   Includes bibliographical references and index.
ISBN 0-8058-4218-7 (cloth : alk. Paper)
   1. Space perception—Congresses. 2. Spatial behavior—Congresses. 3.
Spatial ability—Congresses.   I. Allen, Gary L.

BF469.H86 2003
153.1′3—dc21   2003048854
                                               CIP

Books published by Lawrence Erlbaum Associates are printed
on acid-free paper, and their bindings are chosen for strength
and durability.

Printed in the United States of America
10 9 8 7 6 5 4 3 2 1

To the family,

with a smile.

Contents

Contributors

Gary L. Allen, Department of Psychology, University of South Carolina, Columbia, SC 29208, USA.

Mark Blades, Department of Psychology, University of Sheffield, Sheffield S10 2TP, UK.

Cynthia Chiong, Department of Psychology, Northwestern University, Evanston, IL 60208, USA.

Edward H. Cornell, Department of Psychology, University of Alberta, Edmonton, Alberta T6G 2E9, Canada.

Sarah Creem-Regehr, Department of Psychology, University of Utah, Salt Lake City, UT 84112, USA.

Kathryn Desmond, Department of Psychology, University of Sheffield, Sheffield S10 2TP, UK.

Stephanie Fraone, Department of Psychology, Boston College, Chestnut Hill, MA 02467, USA.

Daniel B. M. Haun, Max Planck Institute for Psycholinguistics, Wundtlaan 1, PB 310, 6500 AH Nijmegen, The Netherlands.

Mary Hegarty, Department of Psychology, University of California—Santa Barbara, Santa Barbara, CA 93106, USA.

C. Donald Heth, Department of Psychology, University of Alberta, Edmonton, Alberta T6G 2E9, Canada.

Roy P. C. Kessels, Psychological Laboratory, Helmholtz Instituut, Utrecht University, Heidelberglaan 2, 3584 CS Utrecht, The Netherlands.

Timothy P. McNamara, Department of Psychology, Vanderbilt University, Nashville, TN 37203, USA.

Daniel R. Montello, Department of Geography, University of California—Santa Barbara, Santa Barbara, CA 93106, USA.

Robin G. Morris, Neuropsychology Unit, Department of Psychology, Institute of Psychiatry, King's College London, De Crespigny Park, London SE5 8AF, UK.

Nora S. Newcombe, Department of Psychology, Temple University, Philadelphia PA 19122, USA.

David M. Parslow, Neuropsychology Unit, Department of Psychology, Institute of Psychiatry, King's College London, De Crespigny Park, London SE5 8AF, UK.

Beverly Plester Psychology Subject Group, Coventry University, Coventry CV1 5FB, UK.

Albert Postma, Psychological Laboratory, Helmholtz Instituut, Utrecht University, Heidelberglaan 2, 3584 CS Utrecht, The Netherlands.

Anthony E. Richardson, Department of Psychology, University of California—Santa Barbara, Santa Barbara, CA 93106, USA.

Ruth Schumann-Hengsteler, Lehrstuhl Psychologie, Katholische Universität Eichstätt. Ostenstraße 26-28, D-85072 Eichstätt, Germany.

Amy Lynne Shelton, Department of Psychological and Brain Sciences, Johns Hopkins University, Baltimore, MD 21218, USA.

M. Jeanne Sholl, Department of Psychology, Boston College, Chestnut Hill, MA 02467, USA.

Julia Sluzenski, Department of Psychology, Temple University, Philadelphia PA 19122, USA.

Christopher Spencer, Department of Psychology, University of Sheffield, Sheffield S10 2TP, UK.

Martin Strobl, Lehrstuhl Psychologie, Katholische Universität Eichstätt. Ostenstraße 26-28, D-85072 Eichstätt, Germany.

David H. Uttal, Department of Psychology, Northwestern University, Evanston, IL 60208, USA.

Christine M. Valiquette, Department of Psychology, Vanderbilt University, Nashville, TN 37203, USA.

Marieke van Asselen, Psychological Laboratory, Helmholtz Instituut, Utrecht University, Heidelberglaan 2, 3584 CS Utrecht, The Netherlands.

David Waller, Department of Psychology, Miami University, Oxford, OH 45056, USA

Christof Zoelch, Lehrstuhl Psychologie, Katholische Universität Eichstätt. Ostenstraße 26-28, D-85072 Eichstätt, Germany.

Preface:

Routes of Human Spatial Memory Research

The study of spatial memory is innate to contemporary cognitive psychology. Historical routes from psychology's origins to today's study of spatial cognition are marked with familiar landmarks. At the time psychology differentiated itself from philosophy in the late 19th century, the concept of space had status similar to that of time and causality as central concerns of classical epistemology. There is clear evidence of early scientific interest in spatial memory as a phenomenon (Trowbridge, 1913). A few decades into the 20th century, spatial memory proved to be the definitive issue when competing groups of American learning theorists debated whether response hierarchies could satisfactorily explain complex phenomenon such as maze learning in rodents. With experimental evidence seasoned with good humor, Tolman (1948) presented a convincing case that even rats acquired an internal representation of place. The cognitive map was born, and in that catchy expression, cognitive psychology and space were linked for the long run.

While learning theorists were thusly engaged, other traditions on both sides of the Atlantic assumed mind's existence rather than debated its validity and proceeded to study its structure and ontogeny. The psychometric enterprise, typified by Guilford (Guilford & Zimmerman, 1941), began to map the spatial domain. Developmental theories, such as Piaget's (Piaget & Inhelder, 1956), addressed the matter of how the ability to represent spatial relations internally evolved over the course of childhood. By the time human information processing became cutting edge in American experimental psychology, spatial tasks derived from both the psychometric and cognitive-developmental traditions were available to yield the requisite accuracy and response time data. Chronometric analysis of performance on tasks derived from psychometric tests led to a rejuvenation of mental imagery study (Shepard & Metzler, 1971) and provided the foundation for process-based accounts of spatial abilities (Just & Carpenter, 1985). From this enterprise came some of the methods and materials used in the contemporary study of spatial working memory (e.g., Shah & Miyake, 1996).

After key writings were translated, disseminated, and ingested, Piaget's (Piaget & Inhelder, 1956) theory began to have a revolutionary impact on the experimental study of children's cognition, including spatial memory. The 1970s saw an explosion of activity, motivated by dissonance among Piagetian genetic structuralism, Gibsonian perceptual learning, and traditional American associationism (Liben, 1978; Pick & Rieser, 1982; Siegel & White, 1975). The result was an exciting eclecticism, with advances on methodological and conceptual fronts as shown in Liben, Patterson, and Newcombe's (1981) *Spatial Representation and Behavior Across the Life Span: Theory and Application,* which sprang from the touchstone Pennsylvania State conference in 1979, and later in Robert Cohen's (1985) *The Development of Spatial Cognition.* In the long run, the critical developmental questions are more or less as Piaget and his epistemological predecessors had laid them out. Are there different cognitive means for internally representing spatial relations, and if so, what are the conditions and timing of their emergence? Genuine progress in addressing these questions takes effort, care, and time, but clearly advances have been forthcoming, as seen in Newcombe and Huttenlocher's (2002) *Making Space: The Development of Spatial Representation and Reasoning.*

The search for the neural basis of memory is another historical route leading to the contemporary study of spatial memory. From the mid-20th century, it was clear even to ardent empiricists that if place were represented internally, there might well be a discernable relation between environmental structure and neural structure. Evidence began to accrue from ablation and electrophysiological recording studies in rats. Integrating these findings into an eloquent and challenging framework, O'Keefe and Nadel's (1978) published *The Hippocampus as a Cognitive Map,* one of the most readily identifiable landmarks on this historical route. Reaction and repartee infused what was then known as physiological psychology with intellectual vitality. As alternative views of the hippocampus and memory were presented (Olton, 1979) and other mechanisms of spatial orientation explored (Potegal, 1982), the entire field of physiological psychology began a transformation into what is now known as behavioral neuroscience. However, cognitive mapping theory was meant to apply to human brains in addition to rodent brains. The study of brain–cognition relations in humans began in basic neuropsychology (Benton, 1969; DeRenzi, 1982). Experimental analysis of cognitive performance in individuals with brain damage was one source of substantial progress in this undertaking (Morrow & Ratcliff, 1988). The implementation of brain imagining techniques was, quite obviously, the other. By the late 1990s, cognitive neuroscience had arrived in full force, with spatial memory playing an important role. Twenty years after *The Hippocampus as a Cognitive Map* came *The Hippocampal and Parietal Foundations of Spatial Cognition* (Burgess, Jeffery, & O'Keefe, 1999).

Yet what of mainstream cognitive psychology? Curiously, for years the study of human spatial memory had little in the way of a unique niche within the field. Perhaps the computer, which played servant to information-processing researchers, also played master by limiting the problems studied and the approaches used. Nonetheless, some investigators, such as Tommy Gärling, Janellen Huttenlocher, Clark Presson, and Jeanne Sholl, focused specifically on the matter of the representation of spatial relations. They were always accompanied by now-central figures in this area who came to study spatial memory per se as a consequence of working in areas otherwise labeled, such as visual (Dennis Proffitt), auditory (Jack Loomis), or haptic (Roberta Klatzky) perception; discourse processing and graphic comprehension (Barbara Tversky); and associative memory (Tim McNamara). The contributions of these experts in cognition and perception paved the way for linking the study of spatial representation to the study of human memory in general. However, this research area would not have evolved as it did without other major influences, principally from geography, information science, and ethology.

In the 1960s, behavioral geographers, environmental psychologists, and urban designers attempted to forge a new vision of human–environment relations firmly grounded in principles of human cognition and behavior. The classic edited volumes *Image and Environment* (Downs & Stea, 1973) and *Environmental Knowing* (Moore & Golledge, 1976) stand in testimony to this vision. As a consequence of this energetic and stimulating movement, geography and psychology had joint intellectual custody of the terms *cognitive map, spatial cognition,* and *spatial behavior* from the 1970s onward. It was geographers who invested heavily in nurturing intellectual interest in human spatial cognition in the final decade of the 20th century. The biennial Conference on Spatial Information Theory, sustained by Andrew Frank, Werner Kuhn, David Mark, Max Egenhofer, Dan Montello, and others, established a tradition of multinational and multidisciplinary inquiry in spatial representation. The National Center for Geographic Information and Analysis at the University of California—Santa Barbara sponsored a series of workshops, including outstanding sessions concerned with scale and detail in the spatial cognition (hosted by Reg Golledge and Dan Montello in May 1998) and multiple modalities and frames of reference in spatial representation (hosted by Holly Taylor and Scott Freundschuh in February 1999), which featured lectures and brainstorming sessions by experts from geography, psychology, information science, and mathematics.

Information science as a driving force in the study of spatial representation was evident in a variety of other contexts as well. During the 1990s, the *Deutsche Forschunggemeindschaft* (comparable to the National Science Foundation in the United States) began a priority program in Germany focusing specifically on spatial cognition. This emphasis resulted in a series of meetings such as the Shloss Tutzing conference hosted by Christian Freksa, Christopher Habel, Wilfried Brauer, and Karl Wender in May 2002. It also brought about the establishment of the international Spatial Cognition Research Center by universities in Bremen, Freiburg, and Hamburg, Germany. In the same time frame, the journal *Spatial Cognition and Computation* came into being with Stephen Hirtle, from information science, as a major organizer and editor.

Research in ethology has historically provided a stimulus to investigators interested in human spatial memory. From the 1970s onward, programs of research concerned with bird (Wiltschko & Wiltschko, 1987), insect (Wehner & Menzel, 1990), and mammal (Etienne, 1980) navigation stimulated a great deal of interest in mechanisms of spatial memory, as did studies of food cache retrieval in birds (Shettleworth, 1995). As always, separate traditions and literatures initially prevented a great deal of cross talk, but events such as the marathon NATO Advanced Studies Institute "Cognitive Processes and Spatial Orientation in Animal and Man" organized by Paul Ellen and Catherine Thinus-Blanc in Aix-en-Provence, France, in July 1985 served to develop mutual awareness and closer ties among cognitive, developmental, ethological, and neuropsychological traditions. Relatively recent work to integrate the animal behavior literature from ethology and the learning literature from psychology has paid substantial dividends. *The Organization of Learning* (Gallistel, 1990) provides an excellent case in point, as it appears consistently in the reference sections of contemporary cognitive work on human spatial orientation and wayfinding. By the mid-1990s, it was possible for geographers, ethologists, neuroscientists, developmental psychologists, cognitive psychologists, and perception psychologists to sit around a table and do a pretty good job of communicating about spatial cognition, as occurred at a small seminar sponsored by the Borchard Foundation at Chateau de la Bretesche in France July 1996 (Golledge, 1999).

Thus, pushed, pulled, and otherwise motivated by a variety of forces, the study of human spatial memory found its identity within psychological science by the beginning of the 21st century. Ultimately, that is what this volume is all about—providing a survey representation of this research area at this point in time. The various routes leading here are clearly evident in the authors and topics included in this volume. The flow of topics begins with general theoretical and conceptual concerns from cognitive (Timothy McNamara & Christine Valiquette, chap. 1, and Gary Allen & Daniel Haun, chap. 3, this volume) and developmental (Nora Newcombe & Julia Sluzenski, chap. 2, this volume) perspectives. Thereafter comes a series of chapters concerned primarily with object-location memory as a problem of remembering where. These include a review of working memory in small-scale and prospectus for working memory in large-scale space from cognitive psychology (Jeanne Sholl & Stephanie Fraone, chap. 4, this volume); two chapters examining developmental change in location memory from sequences to patterns of objects (Ruth Schumann-Hengsteler, Martin Strobl, & Christof Zoelch, chap. 5, and David Uttal & Cynthia Chiong, chap. 6, this volume), and a neuropsychological analysis of object-location memory processes (Albert Postma, Roy Kessels, & Marieke van Asselen, chap. 7, this volume). Continuing with the issues of large-scale space raised by Jeanne Sholl, the next group of chapters is concerned with traveler orientation as a problem of remembering where. These include analyses of spatial updating (Sarah Creem-Regehr, chap. 8, this volume) and dead reckoning (Ed Cornell & Don Heth, chap. 9, this volume) and a neurocognitive examination of these and other issues related to place memory in large-scale spaces (Robin Morris & David Parslow, chap. 10, this volume). The final group of chapters is concerned with memory for spatial relations as derived from experience other than a traveler's normal view of the environment. This intriguing collection includes a comparison of spatial knowledge acquired from real, virtual, and cartographic displays (Dan Montello, David Waller, Mary Hegarty, & Tony Richardson, chap. 11, this volume), a developmental examination of aerial photographs as representations of environmental relations (Mark Blades, Christopher Spencer, Beverly Plester, & Kathryn Desmond, chap. 12, this volume), and neuroscientific investigation of the memory consequences of different perspectives during spatial learning (Amy Shelton, chap. 13, this volume).

The novice to this research area will benefit from the breadth and depth represented in these chapters, as well as from the inevitable feeling that these scientific issues are outstanding vehicles for linking laboratory to life. Learning and memory experts may well enjoy the opportunity to make links between cognitive psychology, developmental psychology, and cognitive neuroscience without having to switch between volumes or even switch between sections within the same volume. The discerning eye will detect signs of the various routes that led to this point—both obvious and subtle influences of cognitive mapping theory, associative memory theory, Piagetian theory, psychometric testing, working memory, visual perception, neuropsychology, behavioral geography, information science, and ethology. Chapters from cognitive psychologists are alongside chapters by developmentalists and neuroscientists, results from field studies are just pages away from those based on functional magnetic resonance imaging during observation of virtual displays, and contributions from 25-year veterans of this area are alongside those from promising newcomers. All in all, it is a fitting and informative way to provide an overview of human spatial memory.

ACKNOWLEDGMENTS

Assembling an edited volume of this type is a challenging task. Recovering from a serious health crisis is a challenging task. Assembling an edited volume of this type while recovering from a serious health crisis is a challenging task squared. Shortly after organizing this book project, I proceeded pell-mell from diagnosis to surgery to treatment to convalescence. The only chance this project had of coming to fruition hinged on the convergence of three factors. First, in the high pressure, publish-or-perish, time-sensitive world of contemporary science, the authors had to be patient. Fortunately, the list of authors include 29 names of scholars who, despite inevitable and understandable frustration, showed compassion and understanding as days turned to weeks and weeks turned to months. Second, I had to have local emotional, intellectual, and administrative support. My colleagues Robin K. Morris, Doug Wedell, Sandra Kelly, Tom Cafferty, David Clement, Bob Deysach, Scott Huebner, and Rich Nagle at the University of South Carolina, along with my spouse and colleague K. C. Kirasic, provided emotional and intellectual support. The administrative effort came from Daniel Haun, an enthusiastic and capable scientist-in-training who earned a master's degree in my laboratory during his "break" between undergraduate work at Trier, Germany and his PhD training at the Max Planck Institute at Nijmegen, The Netherlands. Without his help, the project would have collapsed. Third, there had to be a publisher willing to endure the delay and uncertainty. Bill Webber of Lawrence Erlbaum Associates, Inc. demonstrated this willingness and in so doing integrated humanity with professionalism seamlessly in a manner that seems so very rare.

A number of scholars contributed commentary on chapters and chapter components in their formative stages, among them the intrepid Daniel Haun, K. C. Kirasic, Jack Loomis, Tim McNamara, Robin K. Morris, Nora Newcombe, Sandra Kelly, and Doug Wedell. It was especially enlightening and enjoyable to discuss each chapter with Eleanor Gibson in person, who of course struggled to tolerate an important role for memory and had no use whatsoever for the construct of spatial representation. Such discussions were a good way to say "goodbye." She will be missed.

A number of the authors in this volume participated in the symposium on "Spatial Memory: New Developments, New Directions" that I organized for the Third International Conference on Memory, Valencia, Spain, in July 2001. Robin G. Morris was central to a different symposium based on a cognitive neuroscience approach to spatial memory at the same conference, and, much to the advantage of this volume, he expressed interest in participating in this project. I am grateful to these authors who made the Valencia symposia a success and to those who responded positively to the invitation to make this a more interesting and intellectually stimulating collection of readings through their written contributions.

—*Gary L. Allen*

REFERENCES

Benton, A. L. (1969). Disorders of spatial orientation. In P. Vinken & G. Bruyn (Eds.), *Handbook of clinical neurology* (Vol. 3, pp. 212–228). Amsterdam: North-Holland.

Burgess, N., Jeffery, K. J., & O'Keefe, J. (Eds.). (1999). *The hippocampal and parietal foundations of spatial cognition.* New York: Oxford University Press.

Cohen, R. (Ed.). (1985). *The development of spatial cognition.* Hillsdale, NJ: Lawrence Erlbaum Associates, Inc.

DeRenzi, E. (1982). *Disorders of space exploration and cognition.* Chichester, England: Wiley.

Downs, R., & Stea, D. (Eds.). (1973). *Image and environment: Cognitive mapping and spatial behavior.* Chicago: Aldine.

Etienne, A. S. (1980). The orientation of the golden hamster to its nest-site after the elimination of various sensory cues. *Experientia, 36,* 1048–1050.

Gallistel, C. R. (1990). *The organization of learning.* Cambridge, MA: MIT Press.

Golledge, R. G. (Ed.). (1999). *Wayfinding behavior: Cognitive mapping and other spatial processes.* Baltimore: Johns Hopkins University Press.

Guilford, J. P., & Zimmerman, W. S. (1941). *Guilford–Zimmerman aptitude survey, Part V: Spatial orientation.* Beverly Hills, CA: Sheridan Supply.

Just, M. A., & Carpenter, P. A. (1985). Cognitive coordinate systems: Accounts of mental rotation and individual differences in spatial ability. *Psychological Review, 92,* 137–172.

Liben, L. S. (1978). Performance on Piagetian spatial tasks as a function of sex, field dependence, and training. *Merrill-Palmer Quarterly, 24,* 97–110.

Liben, L. S., Patterson, A. H., & Newcombe, N. (Eds.). (1981). *Spatial representation and behavior across the life span: Theory and application.* New York: Academic.

Moore, G. T., & Golledge, R. G. (Eds.). (1976). *Environmental knowing.* Stroudsburg, PA: Dowden, Hutchinson, & Ross.

Morrow, L., & Ratcliff, G. (1988). Neuropsychology of spatial cognition: Evidence from cerebral lesions. In J. Stiles-Davis, M. Kritchevsky, & U. Bellugi (Eds.), *Spatial cognition: Brain bases and development* (pp. 5–32). Hillsdale, NJ: Lawrence Erlbaum Associates, Inc.

Newcombe, N., & Huttenlocher, J. (2002). *Making space: The development of spatial representation and reasoning.* Cambridge, MA: MIT Press.

O'Keefe, J., & Nadel, L. (1978). *The hippocampus as a cognitive map.* Oxford, England: Clarendon.

Olton, D. S. (1979). Mazes, maps, and memory. *American Psychologist, 34,* 583–596.

Piaget, J., & Inhelder, B. (1956). *The child's conception of space.* London: Routledge & Kegan Paul.

Pick, H. L., Jr., & Rieser, J. J. (1982). Children's cognitive mapping. In M. Potegal (Ed.), *Spatial abilities: Development and physiological foundations* (pp. 107–128). New York: Academic.

Potegal, M. (1982). Vestibular and neostriatal contributions to spatial orientation. In M. Potegal (Ed.), *Spatial abilities: Development and physiological foundations* (pp. 361–387). New York: Academic.

Shah, P., & Miyake, A. (1996). The separability of working memory resources for spatial thinking and language processing: An individual differences approach. *Journal of Experimental Psychology: General, 125,* 4–27.

Shepard, R. N., & Metzler, J. (1971). Mental rotation of three-dimensional objects. *Science, 171,* 701–703.

Shettleworth, S. J. (1995). Memory in food-storing birds: From the field to the Skinner box. In E. Alleva, A. Fasolo, H. Lipp, L. Nadel, & L. Ricceri (Eds.), *Behavior-brain research in naturalistic and semi-naturalistic settings* (pp. 159–192). Dordrecht, The Netherlands: Kluwer.

Siegel, A. W., & White, S. H. (1975). The development of spatial representations of large-scale environments. In H. W. Reese (Ed.), *Advances in child development and behavior* (Vol. 10, pp. 9–55). New York: Academic.

Tolman, E. C. (1948). Cognitive maps in rats and men. *Psychological Review, 55,* 189–208.

Trowbridge, C. C. (1913). On fundamental methods of orientation and 'imaginary maps.' *Science, 38,* 888–897.

Wehner, R., & Menzel, R. (1990). Do insects have cognitive maps? In W. Cowan, E. Shooter, C. Steverns, & R. Thompson (Eds.), *Annual review of neuroscience* (Vol. 13, pp. 403–414). Pal Alto, CA: Annual Reviews.

Wiltschko, W., & Wiltschko, R. (1987). Cognitive maps and navigation in homing pigeons. In P. Ellen & C. Thinus-Blanc (Eds.), *Cognitive processes and spatial orientation in animal and man* (Vol. 1, pp. 201–216). Dordrecht, The Netherlands: Martinus Nijhoff.

I

Theoretical Issues in Remembering Where

This collection of three chapters provides an eclectic look at theory in spatial memory. In chapter 1 (this volume), Timothy McNamara and Christine Valiquette present an overview of previous theoretical perspectives on spatial memory and then introduce a new theory that incorporates ideas from Irving Rock's theory of form perception. This new theory, a work in progress, raises interesting and eminently testable questions. In chapter 2 (this volume), Nora Newcombe and Julia Sluzenski delve into the realm of developmental theory, covering new conceptual ground in the ongoing scientific struggle to delineate the ontogenetic roots of spatial memory. Their considerations point to important steps toward developing a new consensus in this area. In chapter 3 (this volume), Gary Allen and Daniel Haun examine the question of how many systems humans have for remembering spatial relations, focusing on the abundance of two-system accounts. Although firm conclusions are elusive, some issues are raised to stimulate additional studies and perhaps provide closure in the future.

1

Remembering Where Things Are

Timothy P. McNamara
Christine M. Valiquette

The title to this chapter might give the reader the impression that we have found a solution to a problem that has long plagued American households (or at least one household the first author, Timothy McNamara, knows well): How to prevent loved ones from misplacing their keys and wallets. Unfortunately, we do not have anything quite so grand to report.

What we do want to report are some new ideas that have emerged in our laboratory about how people remember the locations of objects in their environments. The evolutionary success of our prehistoric ancestors depended, at least in part, on abilities to navigate in unfamiliar territory, to locate sources of food and water, and to be able to return to those sources and to home at a later time. In contemporary societies, people rely on their spatial memories for activities as mundane as reaching out in the morning darkness to shut off an alarm and as consequential as escaping from an office building during a raging fire. How is the spatial structure of the environment represented in memory and how are remembered spatial relations used to guide action in space? These questions guided the research summarized in this chapter.

The plan of the chapter is as follows. We begin by presenting a new theoretical framework for understanding spatial memory and showing how it accounts for the results of several recent experiments. We then review theories and models of spatial memory proposed by other scholars. In the third section, we examine the relations between spatial memory and locomotion. We close with a summary of our findings and a brief discussion of some unresolved puzzles.

A NEW THEORY OF HUMAN SPATIAL MEMORY

The theory of spatial memory that we have been developing finds its conceptual roots in principles of form perception proposed by Rock (1973). Rock wanted to know why the perceived shape of a figure depends on its orientation (e.g., square vs. diamond). Rock was especially interested in whether a change in orientation with respect to the observer or a change with respect to the environment was the primary cause of differences in perceived shape.

Rock's (1973) experiments indicated that for unfamiliar figures, changing egocentric orientation had little effect on perceived shape. However, when the orientation of a figure with respect to the environment was changed, the figure was seen as different and often not recognized at all. For example, Rock and Heimer (1957) had upright observers view novel figures during a training session and then discriminate those figures from new figures in a test session. In the test session, the observer's head was tilted 90°, and each old figure was presented twice, once in the environmentally upright orientation and once tilted by the same amount as the observer's head. Because the observer's head was tilted at test, the tilted test figures actually matched the egocentric orientation of the study figures. The results showed that the environmentally upright figures were recognized better than the environmentally tilted figures; indeed, the environmentally upright figures were recognized as well in this experiment as they were in a control experiment in which the observer maintained an upright head orientation at both study and test.

Rock (1973) concluded that the perceptual interpretation of an object or a figure depended on which part was determined to be the "top." Perceived shape could be altered dramatically by a change in the assignment of this direction. Rock's experiments led him to conclude that top was normally assigned so as to correspond to the perceived direction of "up" in the environment, where up could be determined by gravity or another salient environmental frame of reference. Rock acknowledged that other sources of information could also be used to determine the top of a figure, including intrinsic properties of the object, orientation with respect to the observer, familiarity, and instructions, but he argued that these sources were typically less salient than environmental sources. Rock's experiments also showed that when there was no salient environmental frame of reference, perceived shape was determined by the figure's orientation with respect to the observer. For example, if a figure was viewed on a horizontal surface through a circular aperture, the egocentrically uppermost region was typically perceived as the top (Rock & Heimer, 1957). The results of more recent studies (e.g., Friedman & Hall, 1996; McMullen & Jolicoeur, 1990) indicate that Rock (1973) probably underestimated the importance of egocentric orientation in the perception of form. These findings, however, do not contradict Rock's fundamental principle, which is that the perception of form involves the assignment of directions based on a spatial reference system.

According to the theoretical framework we are developing (Mou & McNamara, 2002; Shelton & McNamara, 2001; Werner & Schmidt, 1999), when people learn the locations of objects in a new environment, they interpret the spatial structure of the layout in terms of a spatial reference system. We conceive of this process as being analogous to determining the top of a figure or an object; in effect, conceptual north is assigned to the layout, creating privileged directions in the environment. Our working hypothesis is that reference systems intrinsic to the collection of objects are used (e.g., rows and columns formed by chairs in a classroom). Intrinsic directions or axes are selected using cues such as viewing perspective and other egocentric experiences (e.g., instructions), the structure of the layout (e.g., it may appear to be square from a given perspective), aspects of the surrounding environment (e.g., geographical slant), and properties of the objects (they may be grouped based on similarity or proximity). An important difference between form perception and spatial memory is that whereas figures in the frontal plane are oriented in a space with a powerful reference axis, namely gravity, the locations of objects are typically defined in the ground plane, which does not have privileged axes or directions (e.g., there is no compelling evidence that humans can perceive magnetic fields). We therefore propose that the dominant cue in spatial memory is egocentric experience. The intrinsic reference system selected at the initial learning position establishes the interpretation and hence, the memory of the layout. This reference system appears to be updated or changed only if a subsequent viewing position is aligned with more natural axes in the surrounding environment.

The theory is perhaps best understood in the context of a specific experiment. In one experiment (Shelton & McNamara, 2001, Experiment 7), participants learned the locations of objects in a cylindrical room from three points of view (in the order 0°–90°–225° or 225°–90°–0°; see Fig. 1.1). Participants were given the same amount of study time at each view. They were then taken to a different room and made judgments of relative direction using their memories ("Imagine you are standing at the book and facing the wood. Point to the clock."). The surprising result was that only the first study view (0° or 225°) appeared to be mentally represented: Pointing judgments were quite accurate for the imagined heading parallel to the first study view but no more accurate for the second and third study views than for novel headings (see Fig. 1.2).

According to the theory, when observers studied the layout from the first viewing position, they interpreted its spatial structure in terms of an intrinsic reference system aligned with their viewing perspective. For example, an observer who started at 0° in Fig. 1.1 might have organized the layout into "columns" formed by jar-clock, shoe-lamp, and so forth, whereas an observer who started at 225° might have organized the layout into columns formed by lamp-clock, wood-shoe-jar, and so forth (these are only examples of possible intrinsic organizations and are not meant to exclude other possibilities). When participants were taken to the second

and the third points of view, they continued to interpret the spatial structure of the layout in terms of the reference system selected at the first point
of view just as if they were viewing a familiar object at novel orientations.
The initially selected reference system was not changed or updated because subsequent views were not aligned with more natural axes in the
environment (the room was round). We do not know why performance
was relatively good on the unfamiliar heading of 45° in the 225°-first
group, but good performance on the heading 180° away from a familiar
heading sometimes occurs in these experiments.

An example of a situation in which the initially selected reference system
seems to have been updated can be found in Shelton and McNamara's
(2001) third experiment. They required participants to learn the locations of
objects in a room from two points of view; one view was aligned and the
other was misaligned with a mat on the floor and the walls of the room (0° &
135° in Fig. 1.3).

Performance in judgments of relative direction indicated that the
aligned view was represented in memory, but the misaligned view was not
(see Fig. 1.4). There was no behavioral evidence that participants had even
seen the misaligned view, even for participants who learned the misaligned
view first! According to the theory, participants who first learned the
aligned view represented the layout in terms of a reference system aligned
with their viewing perspective, the edges of the mat, and the walls of the
room. When they moved to the misaligned view, they still interpreted the
layout in terms of the reference system selected at the aligned view. Observers who first learned the misaligned view must have interpreted the
layout in terms of a reference system aligned with that view. This conclu-

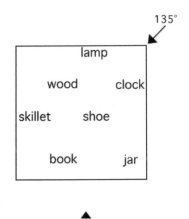

FIG. 1.3.   Diagram of a layout
used by Shelton and McNamara
(2001) in their "aligned-misaligned
view" experiment. Both views
were learned; order was counterbalanced across participants.

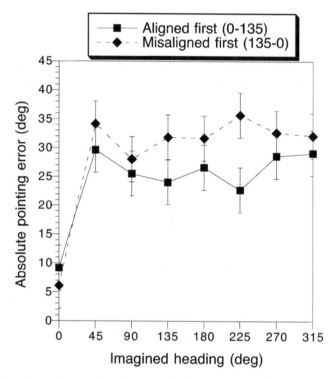

FIG. 1.4.   Angular error in judgments of relative direction as a function of imagined heading and learning order in the aligned-misaligned view experiment.

sion follows from the results of an experiment in which participants learned the same layout but only from the misaligned view (i.e., only 135° in Fig. 1.3; Shelton & McNamara, 2001, Experiment 2). The results of this experiment showed that participants represented the layout from this single familiar view. What happened to this mental representation of the layout when participants learned a second, aligned view? Our hypothesis is that when participants were taken to the second, aligned view, they reinterpreted the spatial structure of the layout in terms of a reference system defined by the aligned view because it was aligned with salient axes in the environment (e.g., the edges of the mat and the walls of the room) and with egocentric experience (albeit a new experience). After moving from the misaligned study view to the aligned study view, observers changed the definition of "north." A new spatial reference system—one that was aligned with the environment and with egocentric experience—was selected and the spatial layout was reinterpreted in terms of it.

Evidence that location and orientation are defined in intrinsic reference systems was presented by Mou and McNamara (2002). They required participants to learn layouts like the one illustrated in Fig. 1.5. Objects were placed on a square mat oriented with the walls of the room. Participants studied the layout from 315° and were instructed to learn the layout along the egocentric 315° axis or the nonegocentric 0° axis. This manipulation was accomplished by pointing out that the layout could be seen in "columns" consistent with the appropriate axis (e.g., clock-jar, scissors-shoe, etc. vs. scissors-clock, wood-shoe-jar, etc.) and by asking participants to point to the objects in the appropriate order when they were quizzed during the learning phase. All participants studied the layout from the viewpoint of 315° in Fig. 1.5.

After learning, participants made judgments of relative direction using their memories of the layout (see Fig. 1.6). One important result is the crossover interaction for imagined headings of 0° and 315°: Participants who were instructed to learn the layout along the nonegocentric 0° axis were better able to imagine the spatial structure of the layout from the 0° heading than from the 315° heading (which is the heading they actually experienced), whereas the opposite pattern was obtained for participants who learned the layout along the egocentric 315° axis. A second important finding was that there was no apparent cost to learning the layout along a nonegocentric axis. Overall error in pointing did not differ between the two groups. A third important finding is the different patterns of results for the two groups: In the 0° group, performance was better on novel headings orthogonal or opposite to 0° (90°, 180°, and 270°) than on other novel headings, producing a sawtooth pattern, whereas in the 315° group, performance on

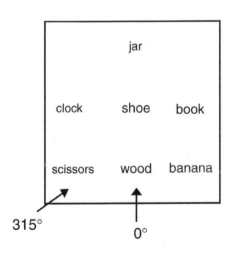

FIG. 1.5. Diagram of the layout used by Mou and McNamara (2002) in one of their experiments. Participants viewed the layout from 315° and were instructed to learn it along the egocentric 315° axis or the nonegocentric 0° axis.

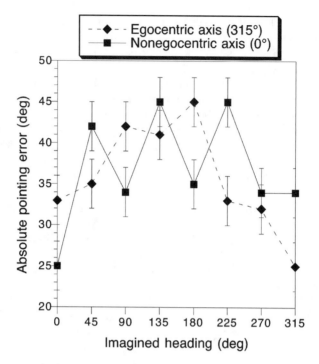

FIG. 1.6. Angular error in judgments of relative direction as a function of imagined heading and learning axis in Mou and McNamara's (2002) experiment.

novel headings depended primarily on the angular distance to the familiar heading of 315°. The sawtooth pattern in the 0° group also appeared when the objects were placed on the bare floor of a cylindrical room, which indicates that this pattern was produced by the intrinsic structure of the layout, not by the mat or the walls of the enclosing room.

We believe that the sawtooth pattern arises when participants are able to represent the layout along two intrinsic axes (e.g., 0°–180° and 90°–270°). Performance may be better on the imagined heading of 0° because this heading was emphasized in the learning phase. We suspect that the sawtooth pattern did not occur in the condition in which participants learned the layout according to the 315°–135° axis because the 45°–225° axis is much less salient in the collection of objects. Indeed, we suspect that participants did not recognize that the layout could be organized along "diagonal" axes unless they actually experienced them because the "major" axes were much more salient; for example, the layout is bilaterally symmetric around 0°–180° but not around 315°–135° or 45°–225°.

Several aspects of this theoretical framework have been discussed or demonstrated by others. In particular, Tversky (1981) showed that errors in remembered spatial relations could be explained in terms of heuristics derived from principles of perceptual organization. Tversky also argued that spatial memory was influenced by how a map or environment was interpreted when it was learned and discussed how intrinsic reference systems might be induced from features of the environment (Tversky, 1981, p. 420). Experimental evidence that the geometry of the surrounding environment plays an important role in spatial memory has been documented by Hermer and Spelke (1994); Learmonth, Newcombe, and Huttenlocher (2001); Montello (1991); and Werner and Schmidt (1999).

ALTERNATIVE MODELS OF SPATIAL MEMORY

Models of spatial memory have addressed a number of different issues. Kosslyn's (1987) categorical-coordinate model distinguished between two types of spatial information and attempted to explain how these sources of information are represented and processed. The category-adjustment model developed by Huttenlocher, Hedges, and Duncan (1991) was designed to explain patterns of bias in reports of location from memory (see also Lansdale, 1998). The spatial framework model developed by Bryant, Franklin, Tversky (e.g., Bryant & Tversky, 1999; Franklin & Tversky, 1990) and their colleagues was developed to explain the representation of space around a central character or object. Sholl's (e.g., Easton & Sholl, 1995; Sholl & Nolin, 1997) model was designed to explain the relationship between egocentric self-to-object spatial relations and allocentric object-to-object spatial relations. Finally, a class of models has been proposed to explain the representation and processing of spatial information in the brain (e.g., Milner & Goodale, 1995; Ungerleider & Mishkin, 1982). In this section of the chapter, we briefly review each of these models in turn.

Categorical-Coordinate Model

Kosslyn (1987; Kosslyn, Andersen, Hillger, & Hamilton, 1994) proposed that the spatial relations between objects or parts of objects were computed by two separable subsystems. One subsystem, referred to as the *coordinate system*, calculated spatial relations in metric terms (e.g., "The book is three inches from the edge of the table."). The other subsystem, referred to as the *categorical system*, calculated nonmetric spatial relations (e.g., "The book is on the table."). Calculations of coordinate spatial relations were proposed to be performed best by the right hemisphere of the human brain, whereas calculations of categorical spatial relations were proposed to be performed best by the left hemisphere. One or the other subsystem would be preferentially involved in any given task depending on the specific constraints of the task. For instance, knowing that the book is on the table greatly narrows one's search for the book. Merely knowing that the book is on the table, however, does not allow one to successfully reach for and grasp the book. According to Kosslyn (1987), the categorical system, housed in the left hemisphere, would be responsible for perceiving that the book is on the table, whereas the coordinate system, housed in the right hemisphere, would be responsible for perceiving the book's exact location so that it could be successfully grasped. Experimental evidence has provided modest support for this theory (e.g., Hellige & Michimata, 1989; Kosslyn et al., 1989; but see Bruyer, Scailquin, & Coibion, 1997; Sergent, 1991).

Category Adjustment Model

Huttenlocher et al. (1991; see also Lansdale, 1998) proposed an elegant mathematical model of positional uncertainty and bias in memory of the location of a single object. Building on the assertions of Bartlett (1932) and of Brewer and Nakamura (1984) that when memory is inexact, memory reports are reconstructions influenced by schematic or category information, Huttenlocher et al. proposed a model of category effects on the retrieval of an object's location. This model shows that bias in the remembered location of an object is not necessary for bias to appear in the reporting of an object's location from memory.

According to the category adjustment model, location is encoded at a fine-grained level and at a categorical level. Encoding at both levels varies in precision but is unbiased. If the mental representation is exact, the two sources of information match perfectly, and no bias in reporting is predicted. If the mental representation is inexact, the two sources of information are combined to produce an estimate. Bias in the recall of location occurs for two reasons. One source of bias arises from the manner in which fine-grain and categorical information are combined. Recall of location is a weighted average of the fine-grain value and the prototype, or average value, of the category. The relative magnitudes of the weights depend on the relative precision of the two sources of information: As the precision of the fine-grain value decreases relative to the precision of the prototype, the fine-grain value is weighted less relative to the prototype. Hence, greater bias toward the prototype occurs as the fine-grain values become less precise relative to the prototype. The second source of bias arises because reports of the locations of objects are constrained to lie within a category, and consequently, the distribution of memory reports will be truncated at category boundaries. This fact implies that the retrieved location of an object near a category boundary will be biased toward the center of the category. These two sources of bias are referred to as *prototype effects* and *boundary effects,* respectively.

Huttenlocher et al. (1991) tested the model with a task requiring participants to remember the location of a single dot in a circle. The categories corresponded to the quadrants of the circle created by implicit vertical and horizontal axes centered on the circle. Huttenlocher et al. showed that the model provided an excellent account of quantitative properties of bias in this task. This model is important because it demonstrates how general principles of spatial memory (e.g., categorical representation, exact and inexact encoding) can be implemented formally. However, the model does not speak to the representation of interobject spatial relations and is not easily scaled up to large-scale spaces.

Spatial-Framework Model

The spatial-framework model (e.g., Bryant & Tversky, 1999; Franklin & Tversky, 1990) was designed to explain the relative accessibility of spatial information in various directions from a central character or object. Although the model was originally proposed to explain spatial representations constructed from narratives, it has been extended to spatial representations constructed from perceptual experiences. In particular, Bryant and Tversky (1999) had participants study two-dimensional (2D) diagrams or three-dimensional (3D) models of six objects surrounding a central character in the canonical directions front, back, right, left, head (e.g., above an upright character) and feet (e.g., below an upright character). In the test phase, the participants identified the objects in cued directions. Across trials, the central character was described as rotating to face different objects and as changing orientation (e.g., from upright to reclining).

For diagrams, the retrieval times were ordered head/feet < front/back < right/left regardless of whether the character was upright, reclining, or upside down. In contrast, for models, the retrieval times were ordered head/feet < front/back < right/left for upright and upside down characters but front/back < head/feet < right/left for reclining characters. Bryant and Tversky (1999) argued that the diagrams (and other 2D interpretations of the scenes) were represented using an intrinsic reference system centered on the character and that retrieval times reflected the relative salience of the intrinsic axes. The models (and other 3D interpretations of the scenes), however, were represented with an egocentric spatial framework in which participants mentally adopted the orientation and the facing direction of the central character. The retrieval times reflected an interaction between asymmetries of the body, which are dominated by the front/back axis, and asymmetries of the environment, which are dominated by the up/down axis. When the head/feet axis is aligned with the up/down axis (upright or upside down characters), the environmental axis confers an advantage to head/feet relative to front/back; however, when head/feet and up/down are unconfounded (reclining observers), the front/back asymmetry of the body dominates.

The use of an intrinsic reference system for 2D scenes is broadly consistent with our theoretical framework. As Bryant and Tversky (1999) used the term, it refers to an object-based reference system centered on objects that have intrinsic asymmetries, such as people and vehicles. In our theoretical framework, it refers to a reference system in which reference directions or axes are induced from the layout of the environment to be learned. The fundamental notion is similar, however. The egocentric spatial framework used for 3D scenes would seem to be inconsistent with our model. We believe, however, that the two are complementary. Bryant and Tversky's experiments examine situations in which the observer has adopted an orientation in imagination and then is asked to retrieve objects in cued directions. The difficulty of retrieving or inferring the spatial structure of the layout from novel versus familiar orientations is not measured. Our experiments, in contrast, have focused on effects of orientation, not on the efficiency of retrieval of objects in cued directions. The results of experiments in which both effects have been measured indicate that they may be independent (e.g., Sholl, 1987; Werner & Schmidt, 1999).

Sholl's Model

The model proposed by Sholl and her colleagues (e.g., Easton & Sholl, 1995; Sholl & Nolin, 1997) is designed to explain the representation and retrieval of egocentric spatial relations between an observer and objects in the environment and allocentric spatial relations among the objects. The model contains two subsystems. The *self-reference system* codes self-to-object spatial relations in body-centered coordinates using the body axes of front–back, right–left, and up–down (as in the spatial-framework model). This system provides a framework for spatially directed motor activity, such as walking, reaching, and grasping. The *object-to-object system* codes the spatial relations among objects in environmental coordinates. This system is formalized as a network of nodes, each representing a different object, interconnected by vectors. Interobject distance is represented by vector magnitude; relative direction is represented by angles between vectors emanating from a common node. Spatial relations in this system are specified only with respect to other objects (i.e., an intrinsic reference system is used). Relative direction is preserved locally among the set of objects but not with respect to the surrounding environment, and there is no preferred reference direction. The representation is therefore orientation independent. These two systems interact in several ways. For example, the heading of the self-reference system fixes the orientation of the object-to-object system such that the front pole of the front–back axis determines "forward" in the object-to-object system. As the self-reference system changes heading by way of actual or imagined rotations of the body, the orientation of the object-to-object system changes as well.

Our theoretical framework does not currently address self-to-object spatial relations, although we recognize that such spatial relations must be represented, at least at the perceptual level, for the purpose of guiding action in space (e.g., Anderson, 1999) and seem to play an important role in the spatial-framework paradigm. An important similarity between Sholl's model and ours is the use of intrinsic reference systems to represent interobject spatial relations. A major difference, though, is that the object-to-object system is orientation independent in Sholl's model but orientation dependent in ours.

There may be situations in which people are able to form orientation independent spatial representations (e.g., Evans & Pezdek, 1980; Presson, DeLange, & Hazelrigg, 1989; Richardson, Montello, & Hegarty, 1999, real-walk condition; Sholl & Nolin, 1997, Experiments 3 and 4), but these situations seem to be the exception rather than the rule; moreover, attempts to replicate many of these findings have not been successful (e.g., McNamara, Rump, & Werner, in press; Roskos-Ewoldsen, McNamara, Shelton, & Carr, 1998; Valiquette, McNamara, & Smith, 2003). In our opinion, the balance of evidence shows that spatial memories are orientation dependent (in addition to the studies cited above, see Christou & Bülthoff, 1999; Easton & Sholl, 1995; Levine, Jankovic, & Palij, 1982; Presson & Montello, 1994; Richardson et al., 1999, map and virtual-reality conditions; Rieser, 1989; Rieser, Guth, & Hill, 1986; Sholl & Nolin, 1997, Experiments 1, 2, and 5; Simons & Wang, 1998). Orientation dependence typically takes the form of better performance on familiar views and orientations than on unfamiliar views and orientations, but in Mou and McNamara's (2002) experiments, performance was better on orientations aligned with the intrinsic axis of learning than on other orientations. (For a more detailed analysis of the literature on orientation dependence, see McNamara, 2003).

The Ventral-Dorsal Dissociation

There is compelling evidence that the human visual system comprises two processing streams, ventral and dorsal (Milner & Goodale, 1995; Ungerleider & Mishkin, 1982). Ungerleider and Mishkin (1982) proposed that the ventral stream was involved in the processing of visual information necessary for object recognition and therefore constituted a "what" system, whereas the dorsal stream was involved in the processing of visual information necessary for spatial localization and therefore constituted a "where" system. Milner and Goodale (1995) argued that both systems process information about what and where but differ in the transformations they carry out. The ventral system processes perceptual and cognitive representations of an object's enduring properties and significance, whereas the dorsal system processes transient and egocentric features of objects needed to control goal-directed actions (see also, Creem & Proffitt, 1998, 2001; Proffitt, Bhalla, Gossweiler, & Midgett, 1996).

Recent investigations using functional neuroimaging indicate that a similar dissociation may exist in spatial memory (e.g., Aguirre &

D'Esposito, 1997; Mellet et al., 2000). For example, Aguirre and D'Esposito (1997) required participants to learn a virtual environment and then measured brain activity with functional magnetic resonance imaging while the participants made judgments about the appearance and the locations of landmarks in the virtual town. The appearance task involved judging whether a name matched a pictured place. In the location task, the participant's position was specified by a view of the town, and the participant had to indicate the direction of a target location (forward, backward, left, right). This task is therefore similar to judgments of relative direction. Direct comparisons of the two tasks revealed more activity in ventral areas (e.g., fusiform gyrus, parahippocampus) in the appearance task than in the location task but more activity in dorsal areas (e.g., posterior parietal cortex) in the location task than in the appearance task.

SPATIAL MEMORY AND LOCOMOTION

Spatial memories are often, if not typically, acquired during navigation and other forms of locomotion. Moreover, an important function of spatial memories is to allow humans to find their ways in familiar environments. There is therefore an intimate connection between spatial memory and locomotion (see chap. 8 by Creem-Regehr, chap. 9 by Cornell & Heth, and chap. 10 by Morris & Parslow, this volume).

In one line of research (Valiquette, McNamara, & Smith, 2003), we have examined whether locomotion at the time of learning affects the orientation dependence of spatial memory. Several researchers have suggested that spatial memories may be orientation independent if people are allowed to move freely during learning, experiencing the layout from many orientations and views (e.g., Evans & Pezdek, 1980). Valiquette et al. (2003) tested this hypothesis in three experiments. In the first experiment, participants learned the locations of seven objects placed on the bare floor of an otherwise empty, rectangular room (e.g., Fig. 1.3 but without the square mat). Participants learned the locations of objects by alternately studying them from a viewing position that was parallel to the walls of the room (e.g., 0° in Fig. 1.3) and then attempting to place the objects on their correct locations. Participants were required to maintain a fixed heading during the learning phase, stepping side to side and backward to locomote through the collection of objects. Participants therefore experienced many views of the layout but only one heading or orientation. Valiquette et al.'s Experiment 2 differed from Experiment 1 in that participants were not required to maintain a fixed heading while replacing the objects, thus allowing them to experience many views and headings. In Experiment 3, participants were not instructed to learn the locations of the objects; instead, they gathered all of the objects to one object location, replaced all of the objects, gathered them to a second location, replaced them again, and so on until they had gathered and replaced the objects seven times (once for each object). These procedures forced the participants to have approximately equal experience with the layout from a number of different headings. When the learning phase was completed in each experiment, participants' memories were tested by having them make judgments of relative direction in a separate room. These pointing judgments were made using a mouse and a simulated pointer and dial (e.g., Shelton & McNamara, 1997).

The results from the Valiquette et al. (2003) experiments indicated that locomotion alone could not be responsible for the orientation-independent results reported in other studies. The angular error of pointing judgments differed across headings in all of the experiments, indicating that participants in all three experiments had formed orientation-dependent mental representations (see Fig. 1.7).

In Experiment 1 (Fig. 1.7A), performance was best on the heading of $0°$, which corresponded to the study view, and there was no evidence that participants represented the layout in terms of another intrinsic axis or direction. In Experiment 2 (Fig. 1.7B), performance was also best for the heading of $0°$, which corresponded to the initial study perspective, but in addition, a dramatic sawtooth pattern was obtained. Recall that in this experiment participants were allowed to move freely through the layout during learning. In Experiment 3, participants learned the layout incidentally, interacted with the objects extensively, and experienced many views and headings. To analyze these data, we identified the best imagined heading (in terms of least angular error in pointing) for each participant individually and then aligned the functions so that $0°$ corresponded to the best heading, $45°$ corresponded to the heading $45°$ counterclockwise from the best heading, and so on. Visual inspection revealed sawtooth patterns for the 12 participants whose best heading was $0°$ or $90°$. The other 12 participants' data revealed a pattern more similar to that obtained in Experiment 1, although more "M" shaped. Results are plotted separately for these two groups in Fig. 1.7C.

Our explanation of these findings relies heavily on the theoretical framework developed earlier. Participants in Valiquette et al.'s (2003) Experiment 1 were required to maintain a fixed body orientation during learning. We hypothesize that this feature of the learning context highlighted the intrinsic direction parallel to the learning view and body orientation and that only this direction was used as a reference direction in memory. As discussed previously, we interpret the sawtooth pattern obtained in Experiment 2 as evidence that participants represented the layout in terms of orthogonal intrinsic axes ($0°–180°$ & $90°–270°$). Our conjecture is that participants were more likely to notice and to use the $90°–270°$ axis in this experiment because they were allowed to move freely in the room and therefore presumably experienced the layout from these directions (unlike participants in Experiment 1). We believe that similar principles can explain the two patterns of data obtained in Experiment 3, although we cannot explain why different groups of participants represented the layouts differently.

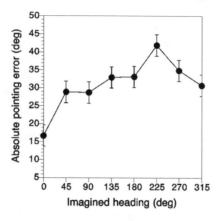

A.

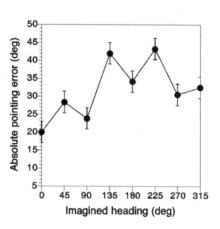

B.

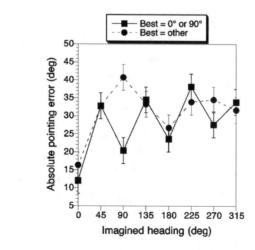

C.

FIG. 1.7. Angular error in judgments of relative direction as a function of imagined heading. A. Experiment 1: Participants were required to maintain a fixed body orientation during learning. B. Experiment 2: Participants were allowed to move freely through the layout during learning. **C.** Experiment 3: Participants learned the layout incidentally by repeatedly picking up and replacing the objects.

The different patterns of results might have been caused by different patterns of movement in the room. Unfortunately, Valiquette et al. did not record participants' patterns of locomotion in the room.

Another important result of the Valiquette et al. (2003) experiments is that performance in the pointing task did not get better as participants had greater opportunities to interact with the objects and to experience the layout from multiple views. The average angular error in pointing judgments was 31°, 32°, and 31° in Experiments 1, 2, and 3, respectively. This level of performance is comparable to that obtained in experiments in which participants have learned one, two, or three stationary views (e.g., Shelton & McNamara, 2001). Collectively, these findings indicate that locomotion and interaction with objects at the time of learning do not seem to improve the overall fidelity of spatial memories, at least as assessed by judgments of relative direction.

SUMMARY AND PROSPECTUS

The theoretical framework we are developing can be summarized in four principles:

1. When people learn a new environment, they interpret the spatial structure of that environment in terms of a spatial reference system.

2. Our working hypothesis is that reference systems intrinsic to the layout are used.

3. Intrinsic directions or axes are selected using various cues. These cues include the experiences of the observer, properties of the objects, the "shape" of the layout itself, and the structure of the surrounding environment. The dominant cue is egocentric experience because the environments in which humans navigate rarely have directions as salient as those established by point of view.

4. The intrinsic reference system selected during the first learning experience is not usually updated with additional views or as the observer moves through the environment. The initial reference system is updated only if the first view is misaligned but a subsequent view is aligned with salient axes in the environment.

Framed in this manner, the theory raises several interesting research questions. For example, according to the theory, egocentric experience is the dominant cue for selecting an intrinsic reference system because environments rarely have axes or directions as salient as those defined by point of view. Would it be possible to find or to create an environment that had an internal structure so salient that it would dominate the usual tendency for intrinsic organization to be selected based on egocentric point of view? Suppose participants learned the locations of objects on a steep hill, from a viewpoint looking across, rather than up or down the hill, or they learned, from an oblique viewing direction, the layout of objects split by a river or a fence. It is possible that in these or similar situations participants would select an intrinsic reference system parallel to the geographical feature rather than one parallel to their egocentric point of view.

Another important issue concerns principle Number 4 (previously). The theory predicts (and the data indicate) that an initially selected reference system is not changed or updated unless a more natural one is experienced at a later time. For example, in Shelton and McNamara's (2001) cylindrical room experiment (Figs. 1.1 and 1.2) participants studied the layout of objects from three points of view. Participants spent the same amount of time at all views, and they walked (blindfolded and guided by the experimenter) from study view to study view. Even so, they were able to retrieve spatial relations efficiently only from perspectives parallel to the first view they had learned. This pattern of results indicates that participants did not update the reference axes as they locomoted. If participants had updated their mental representations, one might expect performance to have been best on perspectives parallel to the last study view or perhaps on perspectives parallel to all three study views.

Research on spatial updating, however, indicates that as participants rotate without vision, they update the reference axes used to represent the spatial structure of the layout (e.g., Farrell & Robertson, 1998; Rieser, 1989). Rieser (1989), for example, showed that after rotating without vision to a new heading, people were able to point to objects as quickly and as accurately from the new heading as from the original learning perspective. These results are not necessarily inconsistent with Shelton and McNamara's (2001) because experiments on spatial updating have required participants to point to target objects from their actual location in the room (e.g., "You are facing the book. Point to the clock.") and therefore may depend on self-to-object spatial relations, whereas Shelton and McNamara's experiments have required participants to point to target objects from imagined locations and facing directions ("Imagine you are standing at the book and facing the wood. Point to the clock.") and therefore depend on object-to-object spatial relations. It is possible that the self-to-object system but not the object-to-object system is updated with observer movement (e.g., Sholl & Nolin, 1997). It is also possible, however, that both tasks tap a common memory system and that efficient updating is limited to simple arrays of objects, which have typically been used in experiments on spatial updating. Ongoing experiments in our laboratory are testing these explanations.

Another promising line of research is stimulated by Shelton and McNamara's (2001) finding that a misaligned study view seemed not to be represented in memory when it was learned at the same time as an aligned study view (e.g., Figs. 1.3 and 1.4). Shelton and McNamara (2001) also showed, however, that a misaligned study view was represented in memory when it was the only view experienced. Given that participants in the two-view experiment did not know they would be learning a second view, they must have represented the misaligned study view when it was learned first. So what happened to this representation? As discussed previously, our interpretation of these findings is that when participants moved from the misaligned to the aligned study view, they reinterpreted the spatial structure of the layout in terms of a new intrinsic reference system. Although there was no evidence in judgments of relative direction that participants had even seen the misaligned study view, the possibility exists that misaligned study views might be revealed if memory were probed with a different task, such as visual scene recognition.

In a preliminary experiment (Valiquette & McNamara, 2003), we repeated Shelton and McNamara's (2001) aligned–misaligned view experiment but tested participants using visual scene recognition in addition to judgments of relative direction. The results replicated previous findings for judgments of relative direction (i.e., best performance on the aligned view and equivalent performance on the misaligned view and novel views, as in Fig. 1.4) but also showed that visual recognition performance was equally good for both study views. These preliminary data suggest that two representations may be formed during spatial learning: One preserves interobject spatial relations in an intrinsic reference system and the other is a visual memory of the layout. Future experiments will explore the extent to which these two representations are interconnected and their relative importance in navigation.

The theoretical perspective we have arrived at is quite different from the visual-spatial "snapshot" model proposed several years ago by the first author and his colleagues (e.g., Diwadkar & McNamara, 1997; Shelton & McNamara, 1997). As an example, consider a situation in which the editor of this volume, Gary L. Allen, takes a walk through an unfamiliar city park, following a path that leads through the entrance gate straight into the park, takes a 90° turn to the right, takes a second obtuse turn to the right, and then returns straight to the entrance gate (a triangular "loop"). Formerly it was theorized that Allen's memory of the spatial layout of the park would consist of egocentric representations of familiar views and orientations, and therefore, he would be better able to retrieve (or infer) the layout of the park from the three familiar orientations than from unfamiliar orientations. According to our new theory, however, Allen (or more precisely, Allen's memory system) would use his experiences in the park, as well as properties of the path and the park's geography, to establish a reference direction for representing the spatial layout of the park. In the absence of very strong geographical cues (e.g., a steep hillside), one of the path segments would probably be used to establish a reference direction; the first segment is a strong candidate because of the salience conferred by novelty. In this case, Allen would find it easier to imagine the layout of the park from points of view parallel to the direction he walked on the first segment of the path than from points of view parallel to other directions, including the two familiar ones corresponding to the second and third segments of the path. It is also possible that one or more of the other segments of the path might be used to establish a reference system (based on our experimental results, we would not expect all three segments to be used). The crucial prediction is that, in terms of Allen's ability to retrieve or infer the layout of objects in the park, some familiar directions will be privileged relative to other, equally familiar directions, and these latter familiar directions will be roughly equivalent to unfamiliar directions.

We emphasize that this theoretical framework is still in its infancy. We are confident that future research along the lines suggested previously, and critical experiments by other researchers, will lead to further development of the theory, to an even better understanding of how interobject spatial relations are represented in memory, and clearer insight into how remembered spatial relations are used to guide action in space.

REFERENCES

Aguirre, G. K., & D'Esposito, M. (1997). Environmental knowledge is subserved by separable dorsal/ventral neural areas. *Journal of Neuroscience, 17*, 2512–2518.

Andersen, R. A. (1999). Multimodal integration for the representation of space in the posterior parietal cortex. In N. Burgess, K. J. Jeffery, & J. O'Keefe (Eds.), *The hippocampal and parietal foundations of spatial cognition* (pp. 90–103). Oxford, England: Oxford University Press.

Bartlett, F. C. (1932). *Remembering: A study in experimental and social psychology.* New York: Macmillan.

Brewer, W. F., & Nakamura, G. V. (1984). The nature and functions of schemas. In R. S. Wyer & T. K. Srull (Eds.), *Handbook of social cognition* (Vol. 1, pp. 119–160). Hillsdale, NJ: Lawrence Erlbaum Associates, Inc.

Bruyer, R., Scailquin, J. C., & Coibion, P. (1997). Dissociation between categorical and coordinate spatial computations: Modulation by cerebral hemispheres, task properties, mode of response, and age. *Brain and Cognition, 33*, 245–277.

Bryant, D. J., & Tversky, B. (1999). Mental representations of perspective and spatial relations from diagrams and models. *Journal of Experimental Psychology: Learning, Memory, and Cognition, 25*, 137–156.

Christou, C. G., & Bülthoff, H. H. (1999). View dependence in scene recognition after active learning. *Memory & Cognition, 27*, 996–1007.

Creem, S. H., & Proffitt, D. R. (1998). Two memories for geographical slant: Separation and interdependence of action and awareness. *Psychonomic Bulletin and Review, 5*, 22–36.

Creem, S. H., & Proffitt, D. R. (2001). Grasping objects by their handles: A necessary interaction between cognition and action. *Journal of Experimental Psychology: Human Perception and Performance, 27*, 218–228.

Diwadkar, V. A., & McNamara, T. P. (1997). Viewpoint dependence in scene recognition. *Psychological Science, 8*, 302–307.

Easton, R. D., & Sholl, M. J. (1995). Object-array structure, frames of reference, and retrieval of spatial knowledge. *Journal of Experimental Psychology: Learning, Memory, and Cognition, 21*, 483–500.

Evans, G. W., & Pezdek, K. (1980). Cognitive mapping: Knowledge of real-world distance and location information. *Journal of Experimental Psychology: Human Learning and Memory, 6*, 13–24.

Farrell, M. J., & Robertson, I. H. (1998). Mental rotation and the automatic updating of body-centered spatial relationships. *Journal of Experimental Psychology: Learning, Memory, and Cognition, 24,* 227–233.

Franklin, N., & Tversky, B. (1990). Searching imagined environments. *Journal of Experimental Psychology: General, 119,* 63–76.

Friedman, A., & Hall, D. L. (1996). The importance of being upright: Use of environmental and viewer-centered reference frames in shape discriminations of novel three-dimensional objects. *Memory & Cognition, 24,* 285–295.

Hellige, J. B., & Michimata, C. (1989). Categorization versus distance: Hemispheric differences for processing spatial information. *Memory & Cognition, 17,* 770–776.

Hermer, L., & Spelke, E. S. (1994). A geometric process for spatial reorientation in young children. *Nature, 370,* 57–59.

Huttenlocher, J., Hedges, L. V., & Duncan, S. (1991). Categories and particulars: Prototype effects in estimating spatial location. *Psychological Review, 98,* 352–376.

Kosslyn, S. M. (1987). Seeing and imagining in the cerebral hemispheres: A computational approach. *Psychological Review, 94,* 148–175.

Kosslyn, S. M., Anderson, A. K., Hillger, L. A., & Hamilton, S. E. (1994). Hemispheric differences in sizes of receptive fields or attentional biases? *Neuropsychology, 8,* 139–147.

Kosslyn, S. M., Koenig, O., Barrett, A., Cave, C. B., Tang, J., & Gabrieli, J. D. E. (1989). Evidence for two types of spatial representations: Hemispheric specialization for categorical and coordinate relations. *Journal of Experimental Psychology: Human Perception and Performance, 15,* 723–735.

Lansdale, M. W. (1998). Modeling memory for absolute location. *Psychological Review, 105,* 351–378.

Learmonth, A. E., Newcombe, N. S., & Huttenlocher, J. (2001). Toddlers' use of metric information and landmarks to reorient. *Journal of Experimental Child Psychology, 80,* 225–244.

Levine, M., Jankovic, I. N., & Palij, M. (1982). Principles of spatial problem solving. *Journal of Experimental Psychology: General, 111,* 157–175.

McMullen, P. A., & Jolicoeur, P. (1990). The spatial frame of reference in object naming and discrimination of leftright reflections. *Memory & Cognition, 18,* 99–115.

McNamara, T. P. (2003). How are the locations of objects in the environment represented in memory? In C. Freksa, W. Brauer, C. Habel, & K. Wender (Eds.), *Spatial cognition III: Routes and navigation, human memory and learning, spatial representation and spatial reasoning* (pp. 174–191). New York: Springer.

McNamara, T. P., Rump, B., & Werner, S. (in press). Egocentric and geocentric frames of reference in memory of large-scale space. *Psychonomic Bulletin & Review.*

Mellet, E., Bricogne, S., Tzourio-Mazoyer, N., Ghaëm, O., Petit, L., Zago, L., Etard, O., Berthoz, A., Mazoyer, B., & Denis, M. (2000). Neural correlates of topographic mental exploration: The impact of route versus survey perspective learning. *NeuroImage, 12,* 588–600.

Milner, A. D., & Goodale, M. A. (1995). *The visual brain in action.* Oxford, England: Oxford University Press.

Montello, D. R. (1991). Spatial orientation and the angularity of urban routes: A field study. *Environment and Behavior, 23,* 47–69.

Mou, W., & McNamara, T. P. (2002). Intrinsic frames of reference in spatial memory. *Journal of Experimental Psychology: Learning, Memory, and Cognition, 28,* 162–170.

Presson, C. C., DeLange, N., & Hazelrigg, M. D. (1989). Orientation specificity in spatial memory: What makes a path different from a map of the path? *Journal of Experimental Psychology: Learning, Memory, and Cognition, 15,* 887–897.

Presson, C. C., & Montello, D. R. (1994). Updating after rotational and translational body movements: Coordinate structure of perspective space. *Perception, 23,* 1447–1455.

Proffitt, D. R., Bhalla, M., Gossweiler, R., & Midgett, J. (1996). Perceiving geographical slant. *Psychonomic Bulletin and Review, 2,* 409–428.

Richardson, A. E., Montello, D. R., & Hegarty, M. (1999). Spatial knowledge acquisition from maps and from navigation in real and virtual environments. *Memory & Cognition, 27,* 741–750.

Rieser, J. J. (1989). Access to knowledge of spatial structure at novel points of observation. *Journal of Experimental Psychology: Learning, Memory, and Cognition, 15,* 1157–1165.

Rieser, J. J., Guth, D. A., & Hill, E. W. (1986). Sensitivity to perspective structure while walking without vision. *Perception, 15,* 173–188.

Rock, I. (1973). *Orientation and form.* New York: Academic.

Rock, I., & Heimer, W. (1957). The effect of retinal and phenomenal orientation on the perception of form. *American Journal of Psychology, 70,* 493–511.

Roskos-Ewoldsen, B., McNamara, T. P., Shelton, A. L., & Carr, W. (1998). Mental representations of large and small spatial layouts are orientation dependent. *Journal of Experimental Psychology: Learning, Memory, and Cognition, 24,* 215–226.

Sergent, J. (1991). Judgments of relative position and distance on representations of spatial relations. *Journal of Experimental Psychology: Human Perception and Performance, 17,* 762–780.

Shelton, A. L., & McNamara, T. P. (1997). Multiple views of spatial memory. *Psychonomic Bulletin & Review, 4,* 102–106.

Shelton, A. L., & McNamara, T. P. (2001). Systems of spatial reference in human memory. *Cognitive Psychology, 43,* 274–310.

Sholl, M. J. (1987). Cognitive maps as orienting schemata. *Journal of Experimental Psychology: Learning, Memory, and Cognition, 13,* 615–628.

Sholl, M. J., & Nolin, T. L. (1997). Orientation specificity in representations of place. *Journal of Experimental Psychology: Learning, Memory, and Cognition, 23,* 1494–1507.

Simons, D. J., & Wang, R. F. (1998). Perceiving real-world viewpoint changes. *Psychological Science, 9,* 315–320.

Tversky, B. (1981). Distortions in memory for maps. *Cognitive Psychology, 13,* 407–433.

Ungerleider, L. G., & Mishkin, M. (1982). Two cortical visual systems. In D. J. Ingle, M. A. Goodale, & R. J. W. Mansfeild (Eds.), *Analysis of visual behavior* (pp. 549–586). Cambridge, MA: MIT Press.

Valiquette, C. M., & McNamara, T. P. (2003). Unpublished data.

Valiquette, C. M., McNamara, T. P., & Smith, K. (2003). Locomotion, incidental learning, and the selection of spatial reference systems. *Memory & Cognition, 31,* 479–489.

Werner, S., & Schmidt, K. (1999). Environmental reference systems for large scale spaces. *Spatial Cognition and Computation, 1,* 447–473.

Starting Points and Change in Early Spatial Development

Nora S. Newcombe and Julia Sluzenski
Temple University

In the first century of the systematic study of psychology, roughly 1875 to 1975, there was clear agreement on the nature of infants. William James thought they inhabited a state of confusion, Jean Piaget portrayed them as having only simple sensory and motor skills without the ability for abstract internal representation, and Freudian theorists spoke of a state of primary narcissism and lack of differentiation between the self and the world. However, the next quarter century of research has produced a remarkable change in this consensus. Finding after finding has emerged pointing to infant capability and competence. Infants have been argued to be capable of imitation of other people at birth (e.g., Meltzoff & Moore, 1977), to have a concept of a permanent object (e.g., Baillargeon, 1987; Baillargeon & DeVos, 1991), to be endowed with core principles of physical knowledge (e.g., Spelke, Breinlinger, Macomber, & Jacobson, 1992), to engage in causal reasoning (e.g. Leslie & Keeble, 1987), and to have mathematical ability that includes not only a cross-modal concept of number (e.g., Starkey, Spelke, & Gelman, 1983, 1990) but also the competence to add and subtract (Wynn, 1992, 1995).

The domain of spatial representation and reasoning took longer than other domains to come under the sway of the "competent infant" movement. Although Landau, Gleitman, and Spelke proposed as early as 1981 that metric representation and reasoning were available early in life (even in a blind child who lacked visual input; see Landau et al., 1981), other researchers at that time were actively pursuing studies that seemed to indicate a profound change in spatial coding toward the end of the 1st year of life (e.g., Acredolo, 1978) and subsequent transformations in the ability to judge distance (Kosslyn, Pick, & Fariello, 1974) and to represent space (Liben, Moore, & Golbeck, 1982). In the end, however, spatial competence has ended up being added to the array of abilities claimed for infants; the numerically competent infant who reasons about physical principles and causal connections is now thought to have impressive spatial abilities as well.

The trend toward an emphasis on early spatial competence got underway initially with findings suggesting that key spatial abilities emerge in the preschool age range rather than at Piaget and Inhelder's (1948/1967) hypothesized age of 9 or 10 years. For instance, preschoolers were shown to be not as susceptible to spatial egocentrism as Piagetian theory postulated (e.g., Flavell, Shipstead, & Croft, 1978) and, in fact, to be capable of the systematic computation of spatial location from various vantage points under the right task conditions (Newcombe & Huttenlocher, 1992). Preschoolers were also found to be able to reason more sensibly about distance than hypothesized by Piaget (Bartsch & Wellman, 1988; Fabricius & Wellman, 1993).

The emphasis on early spatial competence strengthened as researchers began to examine toddlers and even infants. Demonstrations that toddlers could use distance to locate objects (Bushnell, McKenzie, Lawrence, & Connell, 1995; Huttenlocher, Newcombe, & Sandberg, 1994) were followed by data suggesting that even infants could code distance in continuous space (Newcombe, Huttenlocher, & Learmonth, 1999; Wilcox, Rosser, & Nadel, 1994) and imagine the unseen rotation of a turning object (Hespos & Rochat, 1997; Rochat & Hespos, 1996). Of late, there have been stronger claims. Investigators have argued that not only do infants and toddlers seem to reason about space with surprising competence but also that they do so using an innate geometric module impervious to nonspatial information (Hermer & Spelke, 1994, 1996).

The findings on early spatial competence are remarkable, and all of them probably tell investigators something about the starting points of spatial development. However, the purpose of this chapter is to draw in the reins on the galloping trend of emphasis on infant spatial competence. We do not doubt that infants and toddlers are far more spatially gifted than was imagined by early investigators. However, we also believe that there is good reason to think that their gifts are less impressive than was imagined in the first flush of enthusiasm over discovering infant capabilities, and we doubt that there is any such entity as an innately specified geometric module impervious to other relevant influences. Accordingly, we review the evidence on spatial endowment in the first few years of life with an eye to pointing out limitations of infant ability and stressing the importance of subsequent transformations with development. Such a review points the way to fascinating new avenues for research that hold the potential for strengthening understanding of the nature of development and the mechanisms of developmental change. We begin with the first year of life.

SPATIAL CODING IN THE FIRST 12 MONTHS

Adult humans use four major systems for encoding spatial location: a *response learning* system in which objects are noted as at the disposal of certain actions (e.g., "The cup is to my right"); a *cue learning* system in which objects are noted as being under, on, over, or next to a landmark (e.g., "The cup is on the coffee table"); a *dead reckoning* system in which objects' locations with respect to the body are updated as one moves in the world (e.g., "The cup is on my left now that I've moved to the other side of the coffee table"); and a *place learning* system in which the distance and direction of objects from landmarks are noted (e.g., "The cup is 4 feet from the fireplace and 6 feet from the door;" Gallistel, 1990; Newcombe & Huttenlocher, 2000). The first two systems have the virtue of simplicity. However, this virtue comes attached to obvious drawbacks. In the case of response learning, movement causes errors because the old response will now lead to an incorrect location. In the case of cue learning, no contiguous cues may be available. Dead reckoning is a more sophisticated form of body-referenced coding than response learning because it updates location following movement. Place learning is a more sophisticated form of environment-referenced coding than cue learning because it can code location using distal cues when contiguous ones are unavailable.

Dead reckoning and place learning normally converge on the same location (for discussion, see Cornell & Heth, chap. 9, this volume). However, each system has advantages and drawbacks. Dead reckoning is usable even in the dark or in unfeatured environments (as when at sea), whereas place learning is not. However, place learning, unlike dead reckoning, does not cumulate error. (See Table 2.1 for this way of conceptualizing spatial representation.)

When is each of these systems available to the developing infant? Piaget and Inhelder (1948/1967) emphasized response learning as the earliest form of spatial coding, calling it *sensorimotor* or *egocentric coding*. The domi-

TABLE 2.1

Types of Spatial Coding

Type of Coding	Self-Referenced	Externally Referenced
Simple, limited	Sensorimoter learning (also called egocentric learning, response learning)	Cue learning
Complex, powerful	Dead reckoning (also called inertial navigation)	Place learning

nance of response learning seemed to be confirmed by experiments (Acredolo, 1978; see summary in Acredolo, 1990) in which infants learned that they should turn to their left (or right) to see an interesting visual display—and continued to make such a turn even after they had been moved to the opposite side of a room. Responses in this situation seemed only gradually to begin to take account of movement (dead reckoning) or to use cues as to which way to turn (cue learning). Infants did not fully and easily take account of their own movement or cues in the environment until after the 1st year of life. Observations such as these gave rise to the hypothesis of an egocentric-to-allocentric shift.

The egocentric-to-allocentric shift hypothesis, although not entirely wrong, is probably not quite right either as a description of early spatial development. Its problem lies in the fact that it describes development, in Piagetian fashion, as involving a qualitative shift. Thus, it is undermined by several kinds of evidence suggesting overlap in modes of spatial functioning. Cue learning is evident as early as 6 months, at least when the cues are salient and not in conflict with response learning (Rieser, 1979). Infants can take account of their motion by 5 or 6 months as long as the motion is simple and the kind that infants naturally perform by that point in development, such as trunk rotation (McKenzie, Day, & Ihsen, 1984). Furthermore, infants who are emotionally secure are more likely to use cues (Acredolo, 1979, 1982).

Overall, the evidence suggests that response learning, cue learning, and dead reckoning are all available in the first 6 months of life, although response learning predominates. Experiences in the world correct the excessive reliance on response learning as infants gain experience with finding or not finding objects using different coding systems (Newcombe & Huttenlocher, 2000). Such a reweighting hypothesis suggests that motion in the world is necessary to acquire experiences that lead to reweighting. Crawling has long been known to influence developments in spatial coding (see Campos et al., 2000, for an overview), but earlier developments such as sitting and trunk rotation are likely also important, as well as later developments such as walking (Clearfield, 2001).

This description of spatial development could be taken to be a competent infant argument because it claims that infants have three of the four adult coding systems virtually from the start of life. However, emphasizing the presence of early competence would be to ignore other vital aspects of the description. The approach is deeply developmental in its emphasis on the reweighting of reliance on the three systems as a function of experience. Furthermore, it is deeply developmental in that a central fact to be remembered and explained is that the most powerful of the four systems does not seem to be present at the start.

We move on to examine the origins of place learning, arguably the most important of the four spatial coding systems. One prerequisite for place learning is coding of distance in continuous space. There is evidence that infants can perform such coding by 5 months of age (Newcombe et al., 1999).

When shown an object hidden repeatedly in one location in a long rectangular sandbox, infants react with increased looking time, relative to a control group, when they see the object emerging from a location 8 or 12 in. away. They react in this way even when they have been watching a sequence of two objects being hidden, one in one location and one in another, and thus have to remember which location most recently had an object hidden in it.

As with the claim that three of the four coding systems are present in the first half of the 1st year, the data showing coding of distance in continuous space could be cited as evidence for the spatial competence of infants. However, although the abilities revealed are indeed noteworthy, they need to be interpreted in a wider context. For one thing, coding distance is only one component ability required for place learning, which also requires the coding and integration of two or three distances and/or directions to fix a location in space uniquely. As we discuss in the next section, there is reason to think that place learning does not emerge until a year and a half after we first have evidence of distance coding. In addition, a claim of mature distance coding would require more evidence than presently available. Indeed, there are at least two reasons to think that early distance coding is distinctly different from that shown by adults.

First, consider the fact that the sides of the sandbox provide a perceptually present reference standard against which to measure distance by eye. In a somewhat different paradigm than that used in the sandbox hiding studies, Huttenlocher, Duffy, and Levine (2002) showed that infants may not appreciate distance or length without such a standard. They showed babies a dowel in one of three contexts: in a clear container in which the sides provide a reference standard much like the sandbox, with a container beside the dowel to provide a reference standard that did not enclose the stimulus, and with no reference standard present at all. They found that infants reacted with increased looking times to seeing dowels of different lengths when a reference standard was available, either surrounding the dowel or beside it, but not when the dowel was presented alone. Such difficulties suggest that encoding distance in an absolute form, as might be needed in an "open field," could be a much later developing accomplishment than encoding distance in a relative form, with a referent (such as the sides of the sandbox) continuously perceptually present.

A second way in which early distance coding may be immature was suggested by one of the experiments reported in Newcombe et al. (1999). Infants saw two objects hidden in each of two locations, first one then the other, for a total of three familiarization trials each. On a test trial, one object was hidden in its usual spot, but then the other object emerged from that spot—that is, from a location in which it had never been hidden. Infants did not react. They acted as if they had followed the spatial trajectory of an object without linking this information to its static perceptual characteristics such as shape and color. This phenomenon echoed a finding of Xu and Carey (1996) who showed infants two objects (e.g., a rabbit and a ball) appearing in alternation from behind a screen. Twelve-month-olds, but not 10-month-olds, reacted with increased looking when the screen was dropped to reveal only one object. In the Xu and Carey study, the younger babies acted as if they thought that there was only a single object—as if an object was defined by having a coherent spatiotemporal trajectory rather than also in terms of its static perceptual characteristics (i.e., all the shape, color, and texture differences that differentiated the rabbit and the ball).

Adults code the location of specific objects (e.g., "The large black-and-white-striped cup with the chip in the handle is on the coffee table;" see Postma, Kessels, & van Asselen, chap. 7, this volume). They define the object by its static perceptual attributes ("what" information to use the terminology of Ungerleider & Mishkin, 1982) and regard its location ("where" information) as a linked attribute of the object. Clearly, if the infant data just discussed are correct, infants have a very different coding of objects and of spatial location. They define objects as entities that trace out coherent spatiotemporal trajectories and regard static perceptual attributes as incidental. In this view, infants do not possess a system in which objects have spatial location as just one of their attributes but rather use a system in which spatial location is the very essence the object. A change in the definition of an object between 10 and 12 months of age would be a qualitative developmental change indeed.

Postulating a sharp qualitative shift may, however, overstate the case. Just as the egocentric-to-allocentric shift hypothesis was neither exactly right nor exactly wrong, the hypothesis that infants move from defining objects by spatiotemporal trajectory to defining them by "what" information may be only partially correct. There is abundant evidence that infants attend to "what" information, using it, for example, to define the boundaries between adjacent objects such as a cup and a saucer (Needham, 1998). There is also evidence that they react to changes in "what" information in some kinds of displays (Kovacs, Maguire, & Newcombe, 2002; Wilcox & Baillargeon, 1998a, 1998b).

One way to reconcile the various findings is to postulate that infants may have difficulty in linking two types of information so that they focus on either "what" information or on "where" information, depending on the pull of the situation. Studies showing dominance of "where" information have involved very strongly marked, even rhythmic trajectories, drawing attention to spatiotemporal information (Newcombe et al., 1999; Xu & Carey, 1996). Studies showing coding of "what" information have not involved movement at all (e.g., Needham, 1998), or have involved movement of a simple kind (e.g., Wilcox & Baillargeon, 1998b). Movement may also be regarded as irrelevant if it seems random and unpredictable. Kovacs et al. (2002) recently gathered evidence that random jiggling movement leads to the coding of "what" information in a situation very similar to one in which Newcombe et al. (1999) previously found that "where" information was coded but not "what" information.

In summary, infants either begin life with or quickly develop several essential elements of spatial coding, including response learning, cue learning, dead reckoning, and the ability to code distance in certain situations. These abilities are far from an indication of mature competence, however. In the 1st year of life, infants engage in a reweighting of the reliance they place on different coding systems as they explore their environments. They may also become able to link "what" and "where" information rather than focus on simply one or the other, although this hypothesis is still under investigation. Later, although not until 4 years of age, they develop the ability to code distance when no perceptual standard is present (Huttenlocher et al., 2002).

SPATIAL CODING IN THE 2ND YEAR OF LIFE

We now turn to the 2nd year of life to continue to chart some additional ways in which initial abilities are changed in the course of development. As noted earlier, place learning involves coding the locations of objects with respect to distal landmarks. A *distal landmark* is one that is not perceptually available when viewing the location in question, whereas a *coincident landmark* is perceptually available and in this way directly cues the location (thus, the term *cue learning* in spatial language). Importantly, place learning involves coding direction and distance between a landmark and an object's location, whereas cue learning does not. Also, because place learning involves coding spatial information that is environment based (thus, independent of one's body position), by definition it must be an ability that is robust to movement and even to possible disorientation. No matter what the position of observers, if they can see known landmarks they should be able to infer the position of a target object. Thus, place learning is the spatial coding system that predominates when other coding systems are uninformative (Newcombe & Huttenlocher, 2000).

By the 2nd year of life, children are demonstrating at least the rudiments of spatial abilities necessary for place learning. Huttenlocher et al. (1994) showed that toddlers could code distance in continuous space. The paradigm used by Huttenlocher et al. (1994) went beyond the demonstrations possible with infants in several ways. First, children performed searches for objects hidden in a sandbox (i.e., acted on the environment) rather than showed a passive reaction to a situation displayed by an experimenter. The child watched as an experimenter hid a small toy in the sandbox (which was 5 feet in length and 1 foot in width and could be treated as a one-dimensional search space along its length axis). The child turned around briefly (so that visual fixation on or straining toward the location was not possible) and then was asked to retrieve the toy from one of several locations in the box. Children ages 16 to 24 months were highly accurate in their searches, with mean errors for all of the nine locations tested being very small. In fact, there was no developmental improvement on this task for the ages studied. Additionally, no age differences were found when children were required to watch the hiding from one end of the box and move laterally before searching. Although this task involved only a brief delay between hiding and search and only one object, the results clearly demonstrated that even children as young as 16 months could gain information about extent and use that information to guide them in successful searches for desired objects. Furthermore, the lack of any developmental trend indicates that this ability is fairly robust from close to the start of the 2nd year of life, at least in the experimental conditions used.

What does the Huttenlocher et al. (1994) study tell us about place learning abilities in the 2nd year of life? Infants as young as 16 months are demonstrating one of the necessary components of this mature spatial coding, namely, the ability to find objects using coded distance information (in this case, the extent between the edge of the sandbox and the point at which the toy was last seen). However, excellent performance on the specific task used in the Huttenlocher et al. (1994) study does not require place learning because, as already discussed, the search was performed using a framework that lay within the infant's field of vision while searching. Essentially, no coding of distal landmarks was needed for the search.

In a later study (Newcombe, Huttenlocher, Drummey, & Wiley, 1998), the issue of place learning was specifically examined. Using the same sandbox as in the Huttenlocher et al. (1994) study, Newcombe et al. (1998) had children ages 16 to 36 months search for an object in the sand after walking $180°$ around the sandbox. Half of these children performed the search with a surrounding white curtain forming the periphery of the room (thus with no visible external landmarks) and the other half with the curtain removed (thus with landmarks available in the periphery of the room). In this case, children could still do pretty well in finding the toy based on its position in the frame of the sandbox, but their performance was somewhat worse than in the case in which they did not move or only moved laterally. Going around the box did not create right–left confusion, but it did seem to increase uncertainty and lead to wider margins of error. In this situation, it is possible to see if toddlers do or do not use distal landmarks to reduce uncertainty.

The data seen in Fig. 2.1 show that children ages 21 months and older performed significantly better without the curtain than they did with the curtain, indicating that they were able to use landmark information in the room to reorient to the location in the sandbox. However, younger children performed at the same level with or without the presence of the curtain. Thus, although children of 16 to 20 months had demonstrated the ability to code distance (Huttenlocher et al., 1994), they seemed to have difficulty combining multiple distal cues such as distances and relations among objects. A similar transition at a similar age using a different paradigm was demonstrated by Mangan, Franklin, Tignor, Bolling, and Nadel (1994). The dramatic transition to place learning at around 21 months of age suggests the existence of a crucial transition in spatial development.

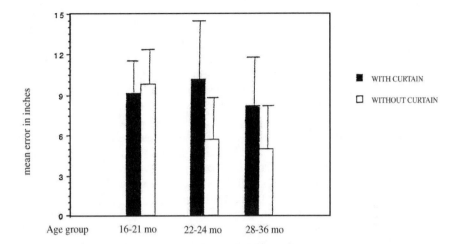

FIG. 2.1.   Emergence of place learning at 18 months. *Note.* From "The Development of Spatial Location Coding: Place Learning and Dead Reckoning in the Second and Third Years," by N. Newcombe, J. Huttenlocher, A. B. Drummey, and J. G. Wiley, 1998, *Cognitive Development, 13,* p. 194. Copyright © 1998 by Elsevier. Reprinted with permission.

Inspired by this discovery, we have recently been investigating other ways in which the early spatial competence of toddlers may be limited in scope, generality, and power. Both the Huttenlocher et al. (1994) and the Newcombe et al. (1998) work deliberately involved a very simple situation in order to ascertain whether there was any early spatial competence at all. First, these prior studies involved search after only a brief delay (sometimes of only a few seconds, depending on how quickly the child began the search, and never exceeding about 15 s). However, successful coding in the adult world clearly would require durable memory for spatial location—people need to find their papers the next morning or their glasses hours after they put them on the coffee table. Second, the Huttenlocher et al. (1994) and Newcombe et al. (1998) work involved memory and search for only one object. Yet successful coding in the adult world involves the ability to find multiple objects—people need to locate both their papers and their glasses. Additionally, successful searches often involve making inferences about the locations of objects based on relations to known locations of other objects—if a person's glasses are on the coffee table, then the papers may be there too.

The focus then of the next part of the discussion is the development of separate components of *functional* spatial abilities, that is, basic abilities that are necessary to successful searches. We argue here that for spatial knowledge to be functional or useable for successful searching, there are at least three fundamental components that must be in place. First, the searcher must be able to retain spatial information across some substantial delay. For instance, learning the location of a food source is not very useful unless that location is remembered at a later time when one is hungry. Second, the searcher should be able to form and utilize spatial relations. Forming a spatial relation requires the ability to remember the locations of multiple objects (see both Schumann-Hengsteler, Strobl, & Zoelch, chap. 5, and Uttal & Chiong, chap. 6, this volume). Utilizing a spatial relation requires the ability to use a spatial relation between two objects in a search.

To examine memory for spatial location across a delay, Sluzenski, Newcombe, and Satlow (2003) recently had 18-, 24-, 30-, 36-, and 42-month-olds participate in the following task. The experimenter hid a small toy in front of each child in the same sandbox used in the studies mentioned previously. Both the child and the experimenter then immediately left the room for approximately 2 min, and when they returned, the experimenter asked the child to retrieve the buried object. Results indicated that 18-month-olds performed significantly worse than did the older age groups, although the older age groups did not differ from each other. In fact, the 18-month-olds performed at chance—their searches were not systematically related to where they had seen the toy buried but were simply concentrated in the center of the box. These results indicate that a shift occurs from 18 to 24 months of age in the ability to withstand a delay between the time of learning an object's location and the time of searching for that object. Also note, however, that the searches of the older children were not perfect. The average error was around 9 in. Adults would likely do considerably better in a task of this kind.

Sluzenski et al. (2003) used two tasks to investigate two logically related abilities: the development of search for multiple objects and the development of retention of a spatial relation between objects. To examine memory for multiple objects, children in each of the same five age groups observed as an experimenter hid two identical objects in the sandbox. After briefly looking away from the sandbox, children were allowed to search immediately for the objects. Although there were no age differences in the search for the first object uncovered, 18-month-olds performed worse than all older age groups (who did not differ from each other) on the search for the second object, with a tendency to return to the location of the first successful search in trying to find the second object. There are several possible explanations for the relative difficulty of the youngest children in searching for the second object. It is possible that the children were simply unable to retain location information about two objects simultaneously. Another (perhaps more likely) possibility was that they initially coded the locations of both objects, but there was substantial decay in memory for the second object during the time in which the child was searching for the first object. Although no data on time were collected, it was observed by the experimenters that sometimes minutes had passed between the initial hiding and the child's attempt to retrieve the second object. Yet another possibility, which may perhaps work in conjunction with the second mentioned explanation, is that there was some sort of interference from the first search that hindered the second search. In line with this latter argument is the fact that, when asked to find the second object, the youngest infants often continued to search at the location where they had retrieved the first object. However, regardless of the reasons underlying the transition, the existence of a difference between 18 and 24 months in the search for multiple objects suggests that there is substantial improvement in this fundamental ability throughout the 2nd year of life.

To examine the development of the use of relations among objects, Sluzenski et al. (2003) taught children ages 18 to 42 months the following relation: that two different toys, no matter where they were located in the sandbox, were always in a fixed position with respect to each other (more specifically, always 18 in. apart and each always on the same side relative to the other). After the training, the toys were hidden while the child was not looking; one toy was then revealed and the child was asked to find the other. Essentially, he or she had to infer the position of the second object based on the learned fixed relation. There are two kinds of data that are important to report here: the proportion of children who completed the training (and thus made it to the actual test trials) and subsequent performance of children who did pass the training. In terms of the first issue, there was a clear age-related difference: 18- and 24-month-olds were much more likely than older children to drop out—to appear unable to learn the task at all. Specifically, 60% of the 18-month-olds and 45% of the 24-month-olds could not be trained on the basic relation, whereas only 8% of the 30-, 36-, and 42-month-olds showed such difficulty. In terms of the second issue, the performance of children who did complete the training, although not perfect, was not random either. Overall, children searched on the correct side more often than on the incorrect side and were on average about 8 in. away from the correct location. Furthermore, there was no improvement across the ages tested (at least not for children who made it to the test trials).

Overall, the data on place learning (Newcombe et al., 1998), memory over delay, memory for more than one location at a time, and ability to learn relative spatial location (Sluzenski et al.) are all in agreement in showing that there are fundamental differences between the spatial coding abilities of 18- and 24-month-olds. It is possible that hippocampal changes could underlie this transition. The fact that the hippocampus is responsible for place learning is one of the best documented facts in psychology (Nadel, 1990). There is recent data suggesting that the hippocampus is also necessary for the retention of spatial information over a delay longer than a few seconds (Kesner & Hopkins, 2001) and for the retention of the location of two or more locations at once (Angeli, Murray, & Mishkin, 1993). However, it is important to note that hypothesizing that changes at the behavioral level have associated changes at the level of the brain is not to say, necessarily, that brain maturation causes behavioral change. There is excellent evidence that the hippocampus is a plastic structure showing neurogenesis even in adults (Gould, Tanapat, Rydel, & Hastings, 2000). In particular, spatial activity seems to lead to increased hippocampal volume (Maguire et al., 1999). It may be that the increased mobility of children toward the end of the 2nd year and their greater willingness to venture further afield from attachment figures both lead to demands on their spatial system that stimulate hippocampal change.

AN INNATE GEOMETRICAL MODULE?

In the preceding two sections, we have shown many ways in which the spatial abilities of infants and toddlers are limited, falling rather short of adult competence and of what is required to survive in the spatial world. These limitations are evident even in fairly simple abilities. Differences between younger and older children are even more apparent if we consider more complex spatial abilities, such as use of spatial symbols, spatial reasoning and transformation, or spatial planning (see Newcombe & Huttenlocher, 2000, for a full discussion). Rather than continue discussion of the multitude of ways in which spatial development transforms developing children, in the remainder of this chapter we discuss one prominent view on spatial knowledge that is at odds with this developmental perspective.

Specifically, Hermer and Spelke (1994, 1996) have claimed that, early in life, humans rely on a geometric module to locate objects. They have shown that toddlers of 18 to 24 months can reorient after movement by using remembered metric information concerning the shape of the surrounding space. Specifically, Hermer and Spelke (1994, 1996) observed search for an object hidden in one of four identical containers located in the corners of a rectangular room, 6 × 4 feet in dimensions, after children were disoriented so that they could not use body information to find the hidden toy. The children searched equally often in the two geometrically identical corners (e.g., corners where the short wall is to the left) but very seldom in the other two corners. However, an additional finding makes this reorientation behavior evidence of a module rather than merely of an early competence. Reestablishment of position with respect to surroundings seemed to involve solely this geometric information; it was not aided by information from landmarks such as a blue wall that serve to differentiate the corners for adults.

However, a recent set of studies by Learmonth, Newcombe, and Huttenlocher (2001) shows that this conclusion was premature. Young children are able to combine landmark information with geometric information to assist them in more efficient searching. To examine this issue, Learmonth et al. (2001) had children aged 17 to 24 months search for an object in a room that was 12 feet × 8 feet in its dimensions. Children had to perform this search after they were disoriented (accomplished by having them close their eyes and spin in several circles with their mothers). In the absence of any landmarks, children searched equally as often in the correct corner as they did in the incorrect but geometrically equivalent corner (with very few errors made in the other two corners), replicating this aspect of Hermer and Spelke (1994, 1996). However, when a bookshelf was available as a landmark, children then searched significantly more often in the correct corner than they did in the geometrically equivalent corner, and they did so whether the bookshelf was coincident with one of the corners or was centered on one of the short walls. Additionally, it did not matter in which of the four corners the object was hidden (i.e., whether it was close to or far away from the landmark). Importantly, children did not show this behavior only with furniture but also with a colored wall. Collectively, these results indicate that children this age are able to combine other types of spatial information with geometric information (casting doubt on the view of toddlers relying on a geometric module).

What accounted for the contrast between the results of Hermer and Spelke (1994, 1996) and those of Learmonth et al. (2001)? It turns out that a very simple factor is crucial, namely, the size of the room (Learmonth, Nadel, & Newcombe, 2002). Although the ratio of the short to the long wall was constant in the two sets of studies, the Hermer and Spelke work was done in a tiny space, 24 square feet in area. By contrast, Learmonth et al. (2001) worked in a room that, although still small at 96 square feet, was large enough to allow for children and adults to fit comfortably and still have space in which to move. Thus, the larger room was more likely to engage the child in a navigational task and reveal the child's spatial competence. The results from the larger space can be argued to be more important for the question of a geometric module because the larger space seems more ecologically valid than the smaller one. In addition, any module that only operates under a severely restricted set of circumstances seems unlikely to be very important to spatial functioning in the real world.

Questioning the existence of a geometric module does not, of course, show that a nativist approach to spatial development cannot work at all. For instance, there might be other relevant spatial modules yet to be formulated. However, science can only test specific proposals. Therefore, until another specific nativist hypothesis is advanced, the preponderance of the evidence favors the idea that infants are born with certain spatially relevant abilities but that there are no encapsulated modules. In addition, we have seen that these early abilities undergo considerable change in the course of development, in response to environmental input (see Newcombe, 2002, for further discussion).

SUMMARY AND CONCLUSION

The competent infant movement has been good for developmental psychology. We as psychologists know far more than we did a few decades ago about the capabilities infants bring to bear on the task of understanding their world. However, the excitement about how much infants can do needs to be tempered with an understanding of what they cannot do. In the 1st year of life, as they acquire a variety of motor capabilities and move more in the world, they learn to rely less on response learning than they initially do. They also learn to coordinate information about the static perceptual characteristics of objects with information about spatiotemporal trajectories of objects. In the 2nd year of life, they acquire a set of spatial coding abilities that form the foundation for effective interaction with the spatial world: place learning, spatial coding that is durable, spatial coding of more than one object at a time, and spatial coding that is flexibly relational. During the preschool years and beyond, they will build on these developments to become able to code distance in a fashion that is not dependent on the physical presence of a referent or "yardstick," as well as to acquire competence in spatial symbolization and reasoning. All of these capabilities depend on the starting points we see in infants. However, there is no evidence that these starting points are also ending points.

ACKNOWLEDGMENT

Preparation of this chapter was supported by grant BCS-9905098 from NSF.

REFERENCES

Acredolo, L. P. (1978). Development of spatial orientation in infancy. *Developmental Psychology, 14*, 224–234.

Acredolo, L. P. (1979). Laboratory versus home: The effect of environment on the 9-month-old infant's choice of spatial reference system. *Developmental Psychology, 15*, 666–667.

Acredolo, L. P. (1982). The familiarity factor in spatial research. *New Directions for Child Development, 15*, 19–30.

Acredolo, L. (1990). Behavioral approaches to spatial orientation in infancy. *Annals of the New York Academy of Sciences, 608*, 596–612.

Angeli, S. J., Murray, E. A., & Mishkin, M. (1993). Hippocampectomized monkeys can remember one place but not two. *Neuropsychologia, 31*, 1021–1030.

Baillargeon, R. (1987). Object permanence in 3½- and 4½-month-old infants. *Developmental Psychology, 23*, 655–664.

Baillargeon, R., & DeVos, J. (1991). Object permanence in young infants: Further evidence. *Child Development, 62*, 1227–1246.

Bartsch, K., & Wellman, H. M. (1988). Young children's conception of distance. *Developmental Psychology, 24*, 532–541.

Bushnell, E. W., McKenzie, B. E., Lawrence, D. A., & Connell, S. (1995). The spatial coding strategies of one-year-old infants in a locomotor search task. *Child Development, 66*, 937–958.

Campos, J. J., Anderson, D. I., Barbu, R., Marianne, A., Hubbard, E. M., Hertenstein, M. J., & Witherington, D. (2000). Travel broadens the mind. *Infancy, 1,* 149–219.

Clearfield, M. W. (2001). The role of locomotor experience in the development of navigational memory. *Dissertation Abstracts International: Section B: The Sciences and Engineering, 62*(2–B), 1114.

Fabricius, W. V., & Wellman, H. M. (1993). Two roads diverged: Young children's ability to judge distance. *Child Development, 64,* 399–414.

Flavell, J. H., Shipstead, S. G., & Croft, K. (1978). Young children's knowledge about visual perception: Hiding objects from others. *Child Development, 49,* 1208–1211.

Gallistel, C. R. (1990). *The organization of learning.* Cambridge, MA: The MIT Press.

Gould, E., Tanapat, P., Rydel, T., & Hastings, N. (2000). Regulation of hippocampal neurogenesis in adulthood. *Biological Psychiatry , 48,* 715–720.

Hermer, L., & Spelke, E. S. (1994). A geometric process for spatial reorientation in young children. *Nature, 370,* 57–59.

Hermer, L., & Spelke, E. (1996). Modularity and development: The case of spatial reorientation. *Cognition, 61,* 195–232.

Hespos, S. J., & Rochat, P. (1997). Dynamic mental representation in infancy. *Cognition, 64,* 153–188.

Huttenlocher, J., Duffy, S., & Levine, S. (2002). Infants and toddlers discriminate amount: Are they measuring? *Psychological Science, 13*(3), 244–249.

Huttenlocher, J., Newcombe, N., & Sandberg, E. H. (1994). The coding of spatial location in young children. *Cognitive Psychology, 27,* 115–148.

Kesner, R. P., & Hopkins, R. O. (2001). Short-term memory for duration and distance in humans: Role of the hippocampus. *Neuropsychology, 15,* 58–68.

Kosslyn, S. M., Pick, H. L., & Fariello, G. R. (1974). Cognitive maps in children and men. *Child Development, 45,* 707–716.

Kovacs, S., Maguire, M., & Newcombe, N. (2002, April). *Young infants' ability to use "what" information when the source of "where" information is reduced.* Poster session presented at the annual meeting of the International Society on Infant Studies, Toronto, Ontario, Canada.

Landau, B., Gleitman, H., & Spelke, E. (1981). Spatial knowledge and geometric representation in a child blind from birth. *Science, 213*(4513), 1275–1278.

Learmonth, A. E., Nadel, L., & Newcombe, N. S. (2002). Children's use of landmarks: Implications for modularity theory. *Psychological Science, 13*(4), 337–341.

Learmonth, A. E., Newcombe, N. S., Huttenlocher, J. (2001). Toddlers' use of metric information and landmarks to reorient. *Journal of Experimental Child Psychology, 80,* 225–244.

Leslie, A. M., & Keeble, S. (1987). Do six-month-old infants perceive causality? *Cognition, 25,* 265–288.

Liben, L. S., Moore, M. L., & Golbeck, S. L. (1982). Preschoolers' knowledge of their classroom environment: Evidence from small-scale and life-size spatial tasks. *Child Development, 53,* 1275–1284.

Maguire, E. A., Gadian, D. G., Johnsrude, I. S., Good, C. D., Ashburner, J., Frackowiak, R. S. J., & Frith, C. D. (1999). Navigation-related structural change in the hippocampi of taxi drivers. *Proceedings of the National Academy of Sciences, 97,* 4398–4403.

Mangan, P. A., Franklin, A., Tignor, T., Bolling, L., & Nadel, L. (1994). Development of spatial memory abilities in young children. *Society for Neuroscience Abstracts, 20,* 363.

McKenzie, B. E., Day, R. H., & Ihsen, E. (1984). Location of events in space: Young infants are not always egocentric. *British Journal of Developmental Psychology, 2,* 1–9.

Meltzoff, A. N., & Moore, M. K. (1977). Imitation of facial and manual gestures by human neonates. *Science, 198*(4312), 75–78.

Nadel, L. (1990). Varieties of spatial cognition: Psychological considerations. In A. Diamond (Ed.), *The development of neural basis of higher cognitive functions* (pp. 613–636). New York: New York Academy of Sciences.

Needham, A. (1998). Infants' use of featural information in the segregation of stationary objects. *Infant Behavior and Development, 21*, 47–75.

Newcombe, N. S. (2002). The nativist–empiricist controversy in the context of recent research on spatial and quantitative development. *Psychological Science, 13*(5), 395–401.

Newcombe, N., & Huttenlocher, J. (1992). Children's early ability to solve perspective-taking problems. *Developmental Psychology, 28*, 635–643.

Newcombe, N. S., & Huttenlocher, J. (2000). *Making space: The development of spatial representation and reasoning.* Cambridge, MA: MIT Press.

Newcombe, N., Huttenlocher, J., Drummey, A. B., & Wiley, J. G. (1998). The development of spatial location coding: Place learning and dead reckoning in the second and third years. *Cognitive Development, 13*, 185–200.

Newcombe, N., Huttenlocher, J., & Learmonth, A. (1999). Infants' coding of location in continuous space. *Infant Behavior and Development, 22*, 483–510.

Piaget, J., & Inhelder, B. (1967). *The child's conception of space* (F. J. Langdon & J. L. Lunzer, Trans.). New York: Norton. (Original work published 1948)

Rieser, J. J. (1979). Spatial orientation of six-month-old infants. *Child Development, 50*, 1078–1087.

Rochat, P., & Hespos, S. J. (1996). Tracking and anticipation of invisible spatial transformation by 4- to 8-month-old infants. *Cognitive Development, 11*, 3–17.

Sluzenski, J., Newcombe, N. S., & Satlow, E. (2003). *Knowing where things are in the second year of life: Implications for hippocampal development.* Manuscript submitted for publication.

Spelke, E. S., Breinlinger, K., Macomber, J., & Jacobson, K. (1992). Origins of knowledge. *Psychological Review, 99*, 605–632.

Starkey, P., Spelke, E. S., & Gelman, R. (1983). Detection of intermodal correspondences by human infants. *Science, 222*(4620), 179–181.

Starkey, P., Spelke, E. S., & Gelman, R. (1990). Numerical abstraction by human infants. *Cognition, 36*, 97–127.

Ungerleider, L. G., & Mishkin, M. (1982). Two cortical visual systems. In D. J. Ingle, M. A. Goodale, & R. J. W. Mansfield (Eds.), *Analysis of visual behavior.* Cambridge, MA: MIT Press.

Wilcox, T., & Baillargeon, R. (1998a). Object individuation in infancy: The use of featural information in reasoning about occlusion events. *Cognitive Psychology, 37*, 97–155.

Wilcox, T., & Baillargeon, R. (1998b). Object individuation in young infants: Further evidence with an event-monitoring paradigm. *Developmental Science, 1*, 127–142.

Wilcox, T., Rosser, R., & Nadel, L. (1994). Representation of object location in 6.5-month-old infants. *Cognitive Development, 9*, 193–209.

Wynn, K. (1992). Addition and subtraction by human infants. *Nature, 358*, 749–750.

Wynn, K. (1995). Infants possess a system of numerical knowledge. *Current Direction in Psychological Science, 4*, 172–177.

Xu, F., & Carey, S. (1996). Infants' metaphysics: The case of numerical identity. *Cognitive Psychology, 30*, 111–153.

Proximity and Precision in Spatial Memory

Gary L. Allen
University of South Carolina

Daniel B. M. Haun
Max Planck Institute for Psycholinguistics

Almost 50 years ago, George Miller's (1956) survey of the literature on human information-processing capacity resulted in his being persecuted by an integer, specifically the number 7, which at that time had magical properties (see Miller, 1956). Today, our consideration of the literature on human spatial memory has led to similar vexation. We too have been visited repeatedly by an integer, in our case the number 2. Miller's troublesome number came in a variety of disguises, but none of these was so opaque as to make the intrepid integer unrecognizable. Similarly, we see significant diversity in the context of spatial cognition, but dual systems or processes are a consistent theme. Repeatedly, we have encountered accounts of two means of coding spatial relations, one related to precision and one to proximity. Rather than ignore this intriguing phenomenon, we elected to address this dauntless digit directly in this chapter.

Our approach is straightforward. First, we describe select dual-processing accounts that make clear distinctions and hence hold theoretical promise. These descriptions conclude with consideration of types of evidence that are used to differentiate between systems or types of processing. Second, we present some experimental findings that muddy the conceptual waters a bit by showing what happens when two different dual-processing accounts are examined in the context of a single procedure. Third, we tread well beyond evidence from these studies to present some musings that might serve to link current efforts to past approaches and to stimulate future research on how people remember "where."

Before proceeding further, we engage in the courtesy of providing general definitions for our terms. For our purposes, *memory* is simply a record of experience, the existence of which is inferred from a change in capability, behavioral or cognitive, afforded by that experience. Accordingly, *spatial memory* is basically a record of geometric relations involving observers, objects, and surfaces. The term *system* in this context connotes a distinct assemblage of components and accompanying principles dedicated to a particular function. Dual-system accounts of spatial memory, then, involve a distinction between different components and principles dedicated to providing the observer with information about spatial relations after encounters with objects, surfaces, and events. Concomitant with the idea of distinct spatial memory systems is the assumption that, although a record of spatial experience is formed, each system's components and principles regularly delimit and perhaps modify the information to which it is dedicated This selectivity and assimilation are referred to as *coding*. Thus, to hypothesize that spatial memory systems involve different means of coding information is to predict different consequences from the same spatial experience. Used in this manner, coding is a type of process, that is, another way of referring to system components and principles doing their job. Thus, when the term *processing* is used in this discussion, it is a synonym for coding.

DUAL CODING ACCOUNTS OF SPATIAL MEMORY

One of the intriguing aspects of dual coding treatments of spatial memory is that although none of the accounts corresponds directly to another, there is enough conceptual similarity among them to motivate efforts to integrate them into a common framework. In the descriptions that follow, we emphasize components of various dual coding accounts that yield both proximity and precision in memory for spatial location. From the outset, we acknowledge that these accounts are principally, if not exclusively, concerned with spatial information acquired through vision. This fact may facilitate efforts to integrate them into a common framework, but simultaneously it may limit the generalizability of conclusions regarding spatial memory.

Perception-Action Versus Cognitive Systems

This dual-system account contrasts the rapid, unconscious processing of spatial location to support immediate action with slower, conscious processing that creates an enduring record of spatial experience. Through conceptual analysis and a series of informative and straightforward experimental studies, Proffitt and his colleagues (Creem & Proffitt, 1998, 2001a, 2001b; Proffitt, Bhalla, Gossweiler, & Midgett, 1995; Wraga, Creem, & Proffitt, 2000) developed a well-articulated version of this theory. Although this distinction is supported by evidence from a variety of experiments, its foundation was laid out in a series of studies involving perception of and memory for geographic incline.

It is widely understood that observers in situ typically overestimate the slant of hills. Yet, the stepping behavior of hill climbers does not reliably suggest such inaccuracy. This contrast was demonstrated simply and elegantly in a series of studies by Creem and Proffitt (1998) in which observers indicated perceived or remembered incline by either estimating it verbally or matching it motorically using a manual response board. Participants significantly overestimated the incline of hills with verbal judgments, but motor estimates were highly accurate. When they relied on memory for the incline, even with a brief delay, observers' verbal overestimates reliably increased. In contrast, their motor estimates were not affected by very brief delays. However, these responses were context sensitive. Given a delay of 1 day or when taken to a different location, error in participants' motor responses began to resemble those in their verbal responses.

Creem and Proffitt (1998, 2001a) interpreted their findings as support for two different systems for processing spatial information. With minimal delay and no change in an observer's position, motor responses are the product of a perception-action system, which provides spatial information relevant for visually guided action implicitly, that is, without the observer's awareness or conscious intent. This system enables an observer to perform known actions (such as stepping or reaching) immediately within the environment, updating changes in observer–environment relations such as viewer relative location, orientation, and movement. Because this system is grounded in an observer's point of view and his or her response potential, it may be said to incorporate an egocentric (or relative) frame of reference. The spatial information within the perception-action system is characterized by rapid availability and high precision. Furthermore, once an action is performed, the record of the precise information that supported that response would be expected to decay rapidly, especially when the perception supporting the action is altered (i.e., when the context is changed). Rapid decay and context specificity free the system for ongoing activity. However, it need not be a case of "out of sight, out of mind" if there is a record of experience from a second system.

The second system posited by Creem and Proffitt (1998) is a cognitive system dedicated to the development and maintenance of multipurpose internal representations of experience. It is this system that is theoretically involved in the production of verbal estimates of geographic slant and other spatial properties; specifically, the estimate is a symbolic manifestation of the hill's incline. The functioning of this system is explicit, meaning that it is in the realm of awareness, judgment, and contemplation. The representation resulting from this system is flexible, and thus, it can accommodate different frames of reference. Nevertheless, because the representation identifies or describes an object or event, the system involved in developing it is highly compatible with object-based (intrinsic) and global (absolute) reference frames. Such representations apparently work on a sufficiency principle in terms of spatial determinacy; they supply spatial gist sufficient for general purpose. Coding is relatively slow compared to coding location for action, but the payoff in terms of longevity of the representation is quite significant.

To enhance their theory with neural plausibility, Creem and Proffitt (2001a) linked the perception-action and cognitive systems to the two anatomical pathways projecting from the primary visual cortex. Fully cognizant of the fact that information from the two streams are interactive at some point, they associated the cognitive system with the ventral stream, referred to functionally as the "what" system because it is intimately involved in object identification by means of vision (Goodale & Milner, 1992; Ungerleider & Mishkin, 1982). Consistent with the scheme, they associated the perception-action system with the dorsal stream, referred to functionally as the "where" system because of its involvement in providing object location independent of identity (Ungerleider & Mishkin, 1982) or the "how" system because of its support of visually guided action (Goodale & Milner, 1992).

Categorical Versus Fine-Grain Spatial Memory

In this dual coding account, categorical processing involves a rapid, virtually automatic coding of location relative to a spatially defined region, whereas fine-grain processing entails a more time-consuming, effortful process that specifies a particular location relative to the entire range of spatial possibilities. This contrast between coding processes is the essence of the category adjustment model developed by Huttenlocher and her colleagues (Huttenlocher, Hedges, & Duncan, 1991; Huttenlocher, Hedges, & Vevea, 2000) and expanded into a developmental theory by Newcombe and Huttenlocher (2000).

Basically, the category adjustment model is designed to achieve a theoretical rapprochement between two well-established facts: First, spatial locations are often remembered with considerable accuracy without much effort (Anooshian & Seibert, 1996; Hasher & Zacks, 1979), and second, bounded regions have a distorting effect on memory for direction and distance (Acredolo & Boulter, 1984; Allen, 1981; Stevens & Coupe, 1978). The category adjustment model accommodates these findings by positing the memory for location is a joint function of fine-grain processing, which yields precision, and categorical processing, which yields proximity.

A fundamental assumption of the model is that internal representations of spatial location are unbiased; no doubt, a system that provides a veridical record of location had certain evolutionary advantages over a system that includes inherent distortion. However, even unbiased representations are characterized by a degree of uncertainty, which in the case of fine-grain coding is reflected in a distribution of potential locations dispersed around the true value. When that representation is referred to in the act of estimating a location, the fine-grain value that is retrieved is one sample from that distribution of potential locations.

Categorical coding is a story of boundaries and prototypes. A category is defined by the range of fine-grain values within its boundaries and is assumed to be perceived effortlessly by the observer. The prototype is the center or middle of the distribution of fine-grain values within the boundary-defined category. As with fine-grained information, boundaries may be ill defined, and in such cases, they may be represented as a distribution of possible values. Ill-defined boundaries necessarily result in uncertain prototypes, which also may be conceived of as a distribution of potential values. Again, it is assumed that these distributions are sampled during retrieval.

According to the model, when an individual produces an estimate of a previously experienced location, faster decaying fine-grain memory and more robust categorical memory act as a dynamic duo in a somewhat compensatory fashion. The more uncertain the fine-grain information, the greater the adjustment of estimated location consistent with categorical information. The literal adjustment is a matter of truncating at category boundaries and weighting the fine-grain value with the prototypic value. With unbiased representations, such truncation and prototypical weighting will inevitably reduce response variance and therefore constrain overall error.

Although the model has been applied in a variety of experimental studies, its foundation was laid by a series of studies employing the simple laboratory task of remembering the location of a dot in a circle (Huttenlocher et al., 1991). In this task, it was hypothesized that observers impose implicit horizontal and vertical boundaries that divide the circular field into quadrants. The quadrants serve as categories, and the center of these quadrants are considered the prototypic values. Thus, the basic prediction of the model was that observers' memory-based estimation of dot location would be displaced slightly toward the middle of quadrants. The model provided an excellent fit to the data. In other words, memory for a single location in the circle was systematically shifted so that remembered location was biased toward the center of imaginary quadrants of the circle.

As originally posited, the distinction between categorical and fine-grain coding was not associated with corresponding neural structures. However, Newcombe and Huttenlocher (2000) entertained the idea that these two means of coding location might map onto the theory of hemispheric differentiation originally put forth by Kosslyn (1987).

Categorical Versus Coordinate Spatial Memory

This account of spatial memory originally included separate systems, although in its current incarnation as a computational model it involves dual processes that regulate attention toward specific task demands (Chabris & Kosslyn, 1998). Similar to the category adjustment model, the theory contrasts a rapid, automatic process for categorical coding with a more deliberate, effortful process for coordinate coding (Kosslyn, 1987, 1994; Kosslyn, Chabris, Marsolek, & Koenig, 1992). Processing involving spatial classification or categorization is considered to have consequences that are more robust and longer lasting than those involving precise information about the magnitude of spatial properties (such as size, distance, and direction).

However, unlike the category adjustment model, this theory is firmly grounded in visual system neurophysiology. Categorical coding is predominantly the domain of the left hemisphere with a bias toward information processed along the ventral pathway, which mainly receives input from small, nonoverlapping retinal receptive fields. In contrast, coordinate coding information is mainly processed in the right hemisphere with a bias toward information processed along the dorsal pathway, which mainly receives input from large, overlapping retinal receptive fields.

The theory is supported by results from experiments in which observers made either categorical or coordinate judgments about a stimulus display (Kosslyn et al., 1989). For example, in a task involving a horizontal bar and a dot, observers had to respond whether the dot was above or below the bar (i.e., a question about categorical relations) or whether it was greater or less than a specific reference distance (2 cm) from the bar (i.e., a question about coordinate relations). The matter of hemispheric specialization was addressed by comparing speed and accuracy of responding when the display was presented in the right visual field for left hemispheric processing versus the left visual field for right hemispheric processing (Hellige & Michimata, 1989; Kosslyn et al., 1989). Consistent with the theory, categorical judgment was facilitated by initial left hemisphere processing, whereas coordinate judgment was facilitated by initial right hemisphere processing.

Taxon Versus Locale Systems

Although the terminology is from the cognitive mapping theory of O'Keefe and Nadel (1978), this distinction involves a convergence of various frameworks and theories, each positing a fundamental distinction in the structure of two types of memory. In various guises, this distinction has been referred to as involving route versus survey memory (Shemyakin, 1962; see also Shelton, chap. 13, this volume), route versus configurational memory (Siegel & White, 1975), route versus place learning (O'Keefe & Nadel, 1978), and network versus vector memory (Byrne, 1982).

A route representation is posited as a series of stimulus-response associations in which the stimuli are proximal environmental objects or features, and the responses are locomotor maneuvers. Unidimensional representations of this type have been described as products of an associative-serial learning process (Siegel & White, 1975) mediated by mechanisms referred to by O'Keefe and Nadel (1978) as taxon (stimulus-response) systems. Thus described, route memory may be considered spatial in its consequences but not in its content. In contrast, a survey representation is posited as a cognitive map, that is, as knowledge of a set of places systematically related by spatial rules (O'Keefe & Nadel, 1978). Multidimensional representations of this type are posited to be the product of a pattern-learning process (Siegel & White, 1975) mediated by a locale (mapping) system (O'Keefe & Nadel, 1978). Thus, survey memory is spatial in both content and consequence.

Considerable advances have been made in the study of spatial memory since the modern instantiation of these distinctions. In particular, cognitive mapping theory has inspired 2 decades of neuroscientific research focusing on the role of the hippocampal formation and related structures in memory, spatial and otherwise (see Burgess, Jeffery, & O'Keefe, 1999; Burgess, Maguire, & O'Keefe, 2002). Although the "taxon versus locale system" terminology is not all that common currently, the distinction itself remains a fundamental one in that it has found contemporary expression in several forms, as, for example, in Easton and Sholl's (1995) distinction between the self-reference system, which codes self-to-object spatial relations in body-centered coordinates, and the object-to-object system, which codes spatial relations among objects in environmental coordinates (see McNamara & Valiquette, chap. 1, this volume).

In neuroscientific studies, the distinction between systems is supported by evidence demonstrating the behavioral dependence of place learning—but not associative learning—on hippocampal function in rats and by evidence showing the differential activation of hippocampal and medial temporal lobe areas in neuroimaging studies of humans who are processing place information (Burgess et al., 2002). In cognitive studies with humans, the distinction between self-reference and object-to-object systems is supported by data showing different response accuracy and latency patterns when research participants must point to a set of locations after imagined movement (Easton & Sholl, 1995). Specifically, with regularly structured arrays of objects (e.g., objects arranged in a circle or square), observers' pointing behavior shows that they preserve object-to-object memory as they imagine moving without changing direction; with irregularly structured arrays, in contrast, their pointing behavior shows that they rely on memory for self-to-object relations as they imagine moving without changing direction (Easton & Sholl, 1995; Rieser, 1989).

Differentiating Between Systems or Processes

According to the preceding accounts, different systems or processes for spatial memory can be distinguished from each other in a variety of ways. Given the emphasis on brain-cognition relations over the past decade, it is inevitable that distinctions based on brain structures or neural systems come to mind. Nevertheless, behavioral measures provide powerful and sensitive means of distinguishing between systems as well.

Neurally Based Distinctions. Neurally grounded distinctions between systems or processes involved in spatial memory can be based on traditional behavioral measures or, presumably, on indicators of differential neural activity. As mentioned previously, Kosslyn et al.'s (1989) tests of hemispheric specialization involved examining speed and accuracy of categorical versus coordinate responding following stimulus presentation to either the right visual field (and left hemisphere) or the left visual field (and right hemisphere). Similarly, the tendency to distort remembered location toward category prototypes, which is characteristic of categorical coding in the category adjustment model, has been compared after right versus left visual-field presentation. Although it may prove rather challenging because multiple means of coding occur simultaneously, it seems feasible to test predictions about hemispheric specialization in fine-grained or coordinate versus categorical processing using techniques for assessing differential neural activity, such as functional magnetic resonance imaging and especially high-density event-related potentials (see Morris & Parslow, chap. 10, this volume; Shelton, chap. 13, this volume).

Of course, the distinction between taxon systems and the locale system is built on a neural foundation (O'Keefe & Nadel, 1978). Yet in truth, much of the research generated by cognitive mapping theory has focused on the role of the hippocampus rather than on distinguishing between taxon and locale systems. Ablation and electrophysiological recording studies in animals have firmly established that the hippocampus is involved in place memory (e.g., Bures et al., 1999), and neuropsychological and neuroimaging studies with humans (e.g., Maguire, Frith, Burgess, Donnett, & O'Keefe, 1998) have substantiated and elaborated on that conclusion.

Behaviorally Based Distinctions. As with most memory research, the behaviorally based dependent measures typically used for this purpose reflect the accuracy and speed of responding. The perception-action system in Creem and Proffitt's (1988) theory, the taxon system in O'Keefe and Nadel's (1978) theory, and categorical coding in Huttenlocher et al.'s (1991) model and in Kosslyn et al.'s (1992) model are characterized by more rapid processing than are the cognitive system, locale system, fine-grain coding, or coordinate coding, respectively. Thus, exposure time to spatial stimuli should have more of an impact on the accuracy of verbal estimates compared to that of motor estimates, more of an influence on fine-grain information relative to categorical information, and more of an influence on the accuracy of coordinate judgments than on that of categorical judgments.

In addition, the two means of representing spatial relations are posited as differing in robustness, referring to both the effort required for coding and the decay rate of the resulting representation. The perception-action system, taxon system, and categorical coding are described as automatic or, at least, requiring less attention and effort than the cognitive system, locale system, fine-grain coding, or coordinate coding. Thus, the influence of reduced attention through some manipulation such as a dual-task procedure should be much more in evidence with the cognitive system, fine-grained coding, or coordinate coding than with the perception-action system or categorical coding. With respect to decay or degradation rate, in general it is proposed that the perception-action system, fine-grain coding, and coordinate coding are characterized by more rapid loss of information. Thus, the products of these memory processes should be more affected by delay between exposure and responding than should be products of the cognitive system or categorical coding.

Central to yet another possibility for distinguishing between the two means of coding spatial relations is the predicted contrast between remembered or estimated values as a function of actual metric values. Plotting estimated location, incline, direction, or size as a function of actual location, incline, direction, or size across a range of stimulus values provides a relational gradient that can serve as a signature function for a particular system or process. The contrasting functions predicted by Creem and Proffitt (1998) for the perception-action and cognitive systems are clearly laid out. The perception-action system should produce a tight-fitting linear relation with the function's intercept at zero. Generally, estimates produced by the cognitive system should also be linear but with the functions' intercept above zero, thus reflecting constant overestimation. However, if extreme values were included (e.g., estimates of flat ground or of a vertical cliff in the estimation of incline), the function would reflect quadratic curvature at the extremes, as these values would, no doubt, be estimated with metric accuracy. Huttenlocher et al. (1991) predicted different signature functions for fine-grain and categorical coding. Estimates based on fine-grain coding should yield an essentially linear function with intercept near zero and variability reflecting the uncertainty involved in the representation. Estimates based on categorical coding should yield a cubic function (per category), with low values overestimated and higher values underestimated toward the prototype. Clearly, at first blush the predictions made by Creem and Proffitt's (1998) model are not altogether compatible with those made by Huttenlocher et al.'s (1991) model. We turn our attention to this matter in the next section.

COMPATIBILITY OF DUAL CODING ACCOUNTS

In the best of all academic worlds, each of these two-system or two-process accounts of spatial memory would be readily compatible with the others, given a touch of sharpening here and a bit of broadening there. Some alignment among dichotomies is apparent. In terms of basic description, the perception-action system in Creem and Proffitt's (1998) dichotomy can be matched with a taxon system (visually based) described by O'Keefe and Nadel (1978). Likewise, the metric accuracy of Huttenlocher et al.'s (1991) fine-grained coding, Kosslyn et al.'s (1989) coordinate system, and O'Keefe and Nadel's (1978) locale system offers the promise of formal similarity, as does the predictable bias in categorical processing characteristic of Huttenlocher et al.'s (1991) and Kosslyn et al.'s (1989) categorical processing.

Yet, despite this alignment, some apparent lack of correspondence remains. Ideally, in this situation 2 + 2 = 2, that is, if the conceptual and empirical basis for one dichotomy were combined with the conceptual and empirical basis for another dichotomy, the outcome would be a single dichotomy. However, if we simply begin with the two dichotomies mentioned initially in the preceding section, some problems appear rather quickly. As we pointed out at the conclusion of the last section, Creem and Proffitt's (1998) model predicts very accurate, unbiased motor estimates of incline reflecting the precision-based functioning of the perception-action system and biased verbal overestimations of incline reflecting the proximity-based functioning of the cognitive system. Although Huttenlocher et al.'s (1991) category adjustment model has not been applied to incline estimation, its predictions are clear. Bias associated with categorical coding would lead to the overestimation of small angles and the underestimation of large ones (with "small" and "large" referenced to the categorical prototype).

We assumed that the systems or modes of processing described in the Creem and Proffitt (1998) model and the Huttenlocher et al. (1991) model were sufficiently robust to apply to laboratory versions of field situations and sufficiently general to encompass a range of visually based estimation tasks (e.g., estimation of azimuth, height, and distance in addition to estimation of incline). Using these assumptions, we conducted experimental studies in search of the signature functions predicted by the models.

A preliminary study provided a very simple test of whether small angles and heights would be overestimated and large angles and heights underestimated in verbal estimation tasks (Allen, unpublished). Based on evidence that observers automatically tended to subdivide circular regions into 90° categories (Huttenlocher et al., 1991), we assumed that a 45° angle would serve as the prototype in incline estimation and in the azimuth estimation tasks. By logical extension, we also assumed that the middle of an 8-foot-tall wooden board would serve as the prototype in the height estimation task. Participants estimated from memory two inclines, two azimuths, and two heights, one assumed to be greater than the prototype and one to be smaller than the prototype in each case. To parallel the conditions in Creem and Proffitt's (1998) studies, all estimates of spatial properties in this study were incidental to the intentional task of memorizing letter strings that served to demark the target angles or heights. Although it is not clear how critical incidental learning remained in subsequent studies by Proffitt and his colleagues (e.g., Wraga et al., 2000), it was posited as playing an important role in yielding unbiased motor estimates in the early studies.

Results from the incline and azimuth estimation tasks were very similar. When the target incline was small (6°), verbal estimates were higher than motor estimates (14° overestimation vs. 7° overestimation, respectively, on average). However, when the target incline was extreme (53°), verbal estimates were lower than motor estimates (20° underestimation vs. 5° underestimation, respectively, on average). Similarly, when the target azimuth deviated from straight ahead by a small angle (10°), verbal estimates were higher than motoric estimates (15° overestimation vs. 2° overestimation, respectively, on average). Yet when the target azimuth was more discrepant from the participant's heading (55°), verbal estimates were lower than motoric estimates (13° underestimation vs. 2° underestimation, respectively, on average). The height estimation data varied from this pattern. Verbal estimates were significantly lower than motoric estimates for both the 36-in. target (18.5 in. underestimation vs. 7.8 in. underestimation, respectively, on average) and the 72-in. target (12.2 in. underestimation vs. 5.0 in . underestimation, respectively, on average).

These findings supported three important conclusions. First, the similarity between the incline and azimuth estimation data supported the idea that the similar underlying visually based estimation processes apply to each. Second, the pattern of overestimation of small target values and underestimation of large ones in incline and azimuth estimation tasks were perfectly compatible with the categorical biasing effects described by Huttenlocher et al.'s (1991) model. Third, the data showed bias in motor estimates in all three tasks, which according to the Creem and Proffitt (1998) model should be unbiased.

Bolstered by these findings and those of Franklin, Henkel, and Zangas (1995); Montello, Richardson, Hegarty, and Provenza (1999); and Newcombe and Huttenocher (2000) showing categorical bias in a variety of spatial memory tasks, we embarked on a model-based examination of verbal and motor estimates from incline, azimuth, height, and distance estimation tasks. The category adjustment model provided a way of determining the interplay of both fine-grained information, hypothetically from the perception-action system of Creem and Proffitt (1998) or the coordinate system of Kosslyn et al. (1989), and categorical information, hypothetically from the cognitive system of Creem and Proffitt (1998) or the categorical system of Kosslyn et al. (1989). In this study, we obtained participants' estimates from memory to multiple targets along the target dimension, which are necessary to evaluate the fit of the model. Thus, in this study participants made verbal and motor estimates to five inclines (4°, 24°, 43°, 68°, and 86°), five azimuths (2°, 24°, 49°, 71°, and 88° to the left or right), five heights (distributed around each participant's eye height), and five tabletop distances (distributed within each participant's reach). As before, we assumed 45°

would be the prototypic value for the two angle-estimation tasks; we took eye height to be the prototype for the height estimation task and half the participant's reach as the prototype for the distance estimation task. A subset of incline estimation trials were implicit so that we could subsequently determine whether implicit versus explicit estimates differed. Comparisons revealed that they did not.

The category adjustment model posits that estimated location (i.e., $E[R]$) is a weighted average of fine-grained and categorical information expressed as follows:

$$E[R] = \lambda\mu + (1 - \lambda)p. \tag{1}$$

In this statement, μ is the true location of the object, p is the expected prototype location, and λ represents the relative weight of the fine-grained information.

The central idea expressed in the model is that uncertainty with regard to fine-grained information results in greater reliance on categorical information, referring to the "pull" of the prototypic value in the category. Here are the specifics. The variable M represents the memory recollection on any given trial; it is assumed to be normally distributed about μ, with standard deviation, S_M, corresponding to the uncertainty of the information encoded into memory. Likewise, the category prototype is signified by the random variable P, with mean, p, and standard deviation, S_P, representing the uncertainty of recollection of the prototype. If only the fine-grained information were used in computing an estimate, that estimate would be unbiased because M is centered on the actual value m. However, uncertainty typically creeps into memory, leading to the integration of categorical information (p) into the estimate, thus yielding bias.

Consistent with Huttenlocher et al.'s (1991) original model, we assumed that λ, or the weight of the fine-grained information, is an increasing function of S_P/S_M. Given this relationship, λ should be close to 1.0 when uncertainty about fine-grained memory values is small, and λ should be close to 0 when uncertainty about fine-grained memory values is large.

At this conceptual juncture, our colleague Doug Wedell (personal communication, April 2002) brought to light an important point about uncertainty pertaining to prototype information and uncertainty pertaining to fine-grained information. Specifically, he pointed out that although it is reasonable to assume that certainty about prototypic information is unaffected by where the target falls along the relevant dimension, certainty about fine-grained information may well be influenced by target magnitude. In psychophysical tasks, uncertainty is typically reduced at the endpoints of the range of values (Luce, Nosofsky, Green, & Smith, 1982). The increase in uncertainty toward the middle of a linear series (or conversely, the decrease in discriminability at the endpoints of a series) indicates that stimulus discriminability, and hence weighting of fine-grained memory (λ), should be maximal at the endpoints of the natural category (i.e., $0°$ and $90°$).

With this point in mind, we fashioned a Wedell–Haun–Allen modification (WHAM) of the category adjustment model. We used a simple quadratic function to approximate the aforementioned affect, predicting fine-grained memory weight as a function of the distance between the true angle and the protoype:

$$\lambda = a + b(\mu - p)^2, \tag{2}$$

where a and b are constants. When b = 0, then the relative weighting of fine-grained and protoype information does not vary with stimulus value. Positive values of b would then capture the increased weight given to fine-grained information when values are extreme. Increases in the value of a would reflect generally greater weighting of fine-grained memory.

In the category adjustment model, the focus is on bias or how the estimates deviate from the actual values. Substituting the expression for λ from Equation 2 into Equation 1 and solving for bias yields the following equation that we used to fit the data:

$$\text{Bias}(R) = (\mu - p)(a + b(\mu - p)^2 - 1). \tag{3}$$

Three values are free to vary in Equation 3: p, representing the location of the prototype, a, representing the general weighting of fine-grained information, and b, representing how the weighting of fine-grained memory information changes as a function of distance from the prototype.

Motivated by curiosity, we decided first to apply this model to the incline estimation data from Creem and Proffitt's (1998) Experiment 1 and from our own preliminary study (Allen, unpublished). All estimates had been made without vision shortly after viewing the incline without instructions to remember the angle. As shown in Fig. 3.1, the model provided a good fit to the data ($R^2 = .980$ for the verbal estimates and .955 for the motor estimates). This outcome provided ample motivation for us to proceed with fitting the data from our incline, azimuth, height, and distance estimation tasks.

Consistent with expectations based on our preliminary study, the model provided a good fit to the data from the incline and azimuth estimation task. For example, we obtained a fit of $R^2 = .939$ for all 20 data points simultaneously, with the same prototype for three conditions and a unique prototype for motor estimates of incline. The incline and azimuth estimation data are shown in Fig. 3.2. Thus, verbal and motor estimates of incline and azimuth in our studies showed effects of both fine-grained and categorical coding.

We were a little surprised to find that motor and verbal estimates of height and distance could not be modeled using the category adjustment model (with or without WHAM), principally because a prototypic value re-

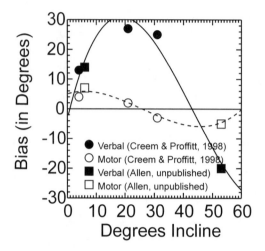

FIG. 3.1. The Wedell–Haun–Allen modification version of the category adjustment model fit to verbal and motor estimates of incline from Creem and Proffitt's (1998) Experiment 1 (three target values) and Allen (unpublished) preliminary study (two target values).

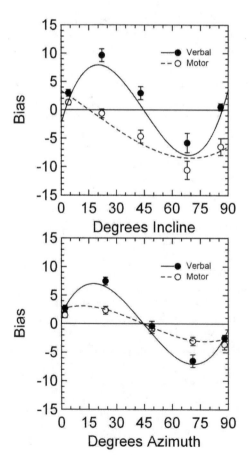

FIG. 3.2. The Wedell–Haun–Allen modification version of the category adjustment model fit to verbal and motor estimates of incline (top panel) and azimuth (bottom panel) to five target values.

mained elusive. Although this outcome was consistent with results involving height estimation from our preliminary study, we understand that it stands in contrast to results in a comparable distance estimation task reported by Newcombe and Huttenlocher (2000). We are uncertain as to what aspects of method led to the disparate results, although our attempt to base prototypic values on each individuals height and reach may well have had a lot to do with it. Nevertheless, it is clear that both data sets show bias, and in our case, the bias is apparent in verbal and motor estimates (see Fig. 3.3).

Because we had originally expected motor estimates to be unbiased, we did an additional study to establish the reliability of the categorical bias effects in motor estimates of azimuth. Participants were asked to estimate azimuth to nine targets distributed in a 180° response field. Additionally, memory load, delay between presentation and estimation, and interference between presentation and estimation were varied. Results showed predictable categorical bias in all conditions. Contrary to our expectations, memory load and interference had very little influence. Our WHAM variation of the category adjustment model provided a respectable fit to these data (Table 3.1).

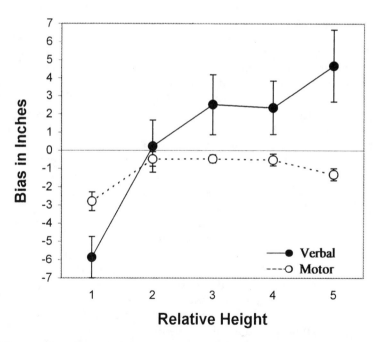

FIG. 3.3.   Bias for verbal and motor estimates in a height estimation task as a function of five target values. Values were selected for each participant individually based on eye height (which is portrayed as relative height).

TABLE 3.1

Fit of WHAM Version of the Category Adjustment Model to Motor Estimates of Azimuth (Nine Target Values) under Various Conditions of Processing Load

	Low Processing Load			High Processing Load		
Model Fit	No Delay	Delay	ASL Task	No Delay	Delay	ASL Task
R^2	.857	.907	.837	.818	.538	.879

Note. WHAM = Wedell–Haun–Allen modification; ASL = American Sign Language task during delay.

Taken together, the results from our experimental studies suggest an uncomfortable marriage between the two models we set out to examine. On one hand, neither the unbiased motor estimates that Creem and Proffitt (1998) attributed to the perception-action system nor the consistent verbal overestimates that they attributed to the cognitive system were in evidence. Hence, it could be argued that their dual-system account was not supported. On the other hand, the interaction between fine-grained and categorical information that was observed is consistent with the interaction (Bhalla & Proffitt, 2000) between the perception-action and cognitive systems that Proffitt and his colleagues (e.g., Creem & Proffitt, 2001) have posited. Thus, despite the failure to obtain the signature functions predicted by distinction between perception-action and cognitive systems, we did indeed find the estimates were influenced by two factors: fine-grained and categorical influences. Basically, our data must be interpreted as showing rapid influence of categorical bias on location coding.

In the final analysis, the chief source of conceptual incompatibility between the models we examined is not to be found in the data we presented showing categorical influences on both verbal and motor estimates. Instead, it is found in the characterization of the fine-grained information that yields precision in spatial memory. In Creem and Proffitt's (1998) model, the perception-action system is the source of precision, exactness that is lost as the vividness of perception fades and the biasing influence of the cognitive system grows. In Huttenlocher et al.'s (1991) model, fine-grained coding consistent with a coordinate system is the source of precision, exactness that is gained only as additional time and effort reduce uncertainty and concomitant reliance on categorical information. These descriptions do not suggest the same two-system or two-process account of spatial memory.

DUAL-CODING ACCOUNTS RECONSIDERED

At this point, the number 2 has successfully retained its intriguing qualities, especially if we examine various models two by two. With its differentiation between fine-grained and categorical coding, the category adjustment model of Huttenlocher and colleagues (Huttenlocher et al., 1991; Newcombe & Huttenlocher, 2000) is a prime candidate for providing common ground for all dual-coding accounts. The model provides a theoretically potent and empirically valid means of examining fine-grained and categorical influences on spatial memory. However, it does not provide an unambiguous conceptual umbrella for all of the two-system accounts simply because, as originally put forth, it does not discriminate between potential sources of fine-grained information. It can be used to model the interplay of rapidly degrading perception-for-action information with more enduring categorical information as readily as it can be applied to model the interplay of categorical information with more slowly discerned coordinate information.

Thus, closure is elusive on the issue of a unifying two-system scheme. Are there viable alternatives to the dual-system account? In response to this question, we the authors are of two rather disparate views, both of which involve some unusual mathematical expressions.

2 + 2 = 1.　It is never wise to dismiss a parsimonious account prematurely. Is it possible that there is a single spatial memory system? First, consider that reliance on comparisons between verbal and motor estimates of spatial properties may not be ideal for resolving the one- versus two-system question. A line of thinking that can be traced back to the 18th-century philosopher George Berkeley (Luce & Jessop, 1949) would have us considering the possibility that verbal estimates will be less precise than motor ones because they are phenomenologically less similar to the actually estimated medium—specifically, space—which Berkeley and others argued to be defined and perceived primarily through touch as a basic informant. Estimating a spatial property motorically means to estimate a property within its own dimension. In the tasks described previously, motor estimates had the same spatial scale as the estimated stimulus. For every degree along the estimated stimulus dimension, a participant's hand had to move a degree to make a correct estimate. Therefore, the response is highly related to the estimated stimulus dimension. Estimating the same stimulus verbally means to translate a stimulus property into a dimension and scale that is an abstract version of the original stimulus dimension. Although an accurate communication of a spatial property is an important interactive skill, achieving this accuracy may not be a matter of spatial memory per se. To create a stronger case for dual systems, future studies should at least compare action-related and abstract estimates with the same underlying dimension and scale.

Generally, bias is considered the result of top-down influences on coding. Consistent with this view, different bias patterns in verbal and motor responses to the same stimulus would justify proposing two different underlying memory systems (Bhalla & Proffitt, 1999). However, top-down processes might alternatively influence response production rather than spatial coding. The idea here is that performance differences in tasks involving the same stimulus type across modalities and situations could be caused by response-side factors acting on the same unitary memory representation. On initial consideration, this point may seem vague or trivial. Nevertheless, the study of spatial cognition has long been plagued by the implicit notion that there are as many different types of spatial memory as there are experimental tasks. This simply cannot be the case.

There may be merit in positing a single highly flexible memory system for spatial information that could support a vast variety of tasks. Conceptually, the distinction between this view and a poly-memory systems view can be portrayed as in Fig. 3.4. A single-system approach would predict that structured manipulations of stored spatial information should be detectable in results from all spatial tasks. A poly-memory system approach would predict that structured manipulations of the stored information in one store would not necessarily be detectable in responses based on spatial information from a different memory store.

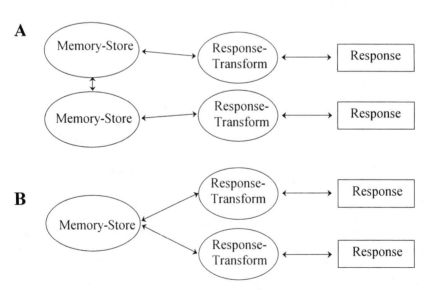

FIG. 3.4.   Dual versus single memory systems for generating verbal and motor estimates of spatial properties.

In a single-system view, working memory plays a major role, as information from a singular flexible record of experience is transformed into a representation necessary for specific task demands. According to this view, differences in bias patterns would be due to the task-specific representation that is created based on information that is stored in a single, perhaps unbiased spatial memory system. Accordingly, precision in spatial memory would result from situations in which the unitary mnemonic record of location is highly valid (because of salience and trace strength), and demands for precision are great. In contrast, proximity would result from situations in which either the mnemonic record of location is not so valid, but the demands for precision are high, or the mnemonic record of location is highly valid, but the demands for precision are low.

2 + 2 = 3. This odd bit of math reflects the possibility that the dual systems described for spatial memory actually include three different means of coding location, one that is sensorimotor in nature and two that are conceptual. As mentioned previously, the perception-action system described by Creem and Proffitt (1998) and the taxon systems described by O'Keefe and Nadel (1978) are compatible, although Creem and Proffitt (1998) were concerned with describing a mechanism for perception supporting immediate action, and O'Keefe and Nadel were concerned with describing mechanisms for associative learning. In some important ways, the input for this type of system is reminiscent of the proposed visual cache in visual-spatial working memory (Baddeley, 1986; Logie, 1995; see also Schumann-Hengsteler, Strobl, & Zoelch, chap. 5, this volume; Sholl & Fraone, chap. 4, this volume). Spatial information is maintained briefly in precise form to support action. Over time, the repeated pairing of specific visual experience with specific actions builds up habit strength that supports the behavioral precision characteristic of skilled performance.

Distinct conceptual processes are described in various two-system or two-process accounts of spatial memory. One of these involves categorical coding (Cream & Proffitt, 1998; Huttenlocher et al., 1991; Kosslyn, 1987), a robust means of remembering spatial information based on the gestalt of the environment encompassing the task. The range of factors influencing the apperception of this gestalt is considerable, but whether the result is a simple distinction between above and below or a more complicated division of surfaces or objects based on proximity or enclosure, the process typically includes a partitioning of space into bounded regions. Remembering spatial relations in this way is very economical in terms of the ratio between effort at encoding and relative accuracy during retrieval; however, it indeed gives rise to the telltale violations of metric and projective relations that are a source of fascination to researchers and nonresearchers alike. The other conceptual system involves coordinate coding (Huttenlocher et al., 1991; Kosslyn, 1987; O'Keefe & Nadel, 1978), which involves conceiving of objects or events existing in an abstract space consisting of an infinite number of points organized by a coordinate system. Remembering spatial relations in this way is relatively effortful, but it yields remarkable accuracy.

Thus, in this analysis we arrive at a three-part scheme consisting of a perception-action system, a categorical conceptual system, and a coordinate conceptual system. This should sound vaguely familiar. If we substitute the terms sensorimotor for perception-action, topological for categorical, and euclidean and projective for coordinate, we have the distinctions between different means for coding spatial relations posited by Piaget and Inhelder (1948/1967) a half century ago. In the current zeitgeist, Piagetian theory is considered passé or invalid by nativists and interactionists alike, with considerable disagreement about whether spatial concepts are better considered innate modules to be activated by relevant circumstances or mental constructs built up under relevant circumstances (see Landau, Spelke, & Gleitman, 1984; Newcombe & Huttenlocher, 2000; Newcombe & Sluzenski, chap. 2, this volume). Nonetheless, certain aspects of Piagetian theory are very useful to the general discussion of poly-systemic accounts of spatial memory. Among these are the ideas that (a) perception of spatial relations is supported by a complete elaboration of space, both projective and euclidean, at the sensorimotor level from infancy onward, which would allow for highly accurate motor-based estimates—or responses to—incline, azimuth, and so forth; (b) representation of spatial relations involves distinct topological and euclidean systems emerging at different times but coexisting and interacting from mid-childhood onward, which would allow for long-term memory for spatial relations being influenced by a combination of categorical and coordinate information; and (c) perception of spatial relations is influenced by the reflection or projection of representational systems back on to perception, which would account for slight categorical bias found in motor-based estimates of spatial relations (see Piaget & Inhelder, 1948/1967).

Summary

The study of spatial cognition has advanced significantly as a result of recent conceptual and empirical work. Essential to substantial progress has been attention to theory development, which has been a deficient aspect of this enterprise in the past. Contemporary theoretical work has provided a number of dual-system models to account for human spatial information processing in general and the distinction between proximity and precision in spatial cognition and behavior in particular. We are not yet convinced that any particular two-system account is sufficiently robust to account for the range of findings. Thus, we urge continued theory-based research aimed at distinguishing among one-, two-, and three-system accounts in the quest to achieve a theoretically sound, functionally robust account of spatial memory.

ACKNOWLEDGMENTS

We are grateful for the guidance and participation of Doug Wedell in the modeling work and for commentary by Eleanor Gibson, Jack Loomis, and Dennis Proffitt on the research discussed in this chapter.

REFERENCES

Acredolo, L. P., & Boulter, L. T. (1984). Effect of hierarchical organization on children's judgments of distance and direction. *Journal of Experimental Child Psychology, 37*, 409–425.

Allen, G. L. (1981). A developmental perspective on the effects of subdividing macrospatial experience. *Journal of Experimental Psychology: Human Learning and Memory, 7*, 120–132.

Anooshian, L. J., & Seibert, P. S. (1996). Diversity within spatial cognition: Memory processes underlying place recognition. *Applied Cognitive Psychology, 10*, 281–300.

Baddeley, A. (1986). *Working memory*. Oxford, England: Clarendon.

Bhalla, M., & Proffitt, D. R. (1999). Visual-motor recalibration in geographical slant perception. *Journal of Experimental Psychology: Human Perception and Performance, 25*, 1076–1096.

Bhalla, M., & Proffitt, D. R. (2000). Geographical slant perception: Dissociation and coordination between explicit awareness and visually guided actions. In Y. Rossetti & N. Revonsuo (Eds.), *Advances in consciousness research: Beyond dissociation: Interaction between dissociated implicit and explicit processing* (pp. 99–128). Amsterdam: Benjamins.

Bures, J. F., Kaminsky, Y., Rossier, J., Sacchetti, B., & Zinyuk L. (1999). Dissociation of exteroceptive and idiothetic orientation cures: Effect on hippocampal place cells and place navigation. In N. Burgess, K. Jeffery, & J. O'Keefe (Eds.), *The hippocampal and parietal foundations of spatial cognition* (pp. 167–185). Oxford, England: Oxford University Press.

Burgess, N., Jeffery, K. J., & O'Keefe, J. (Eds.). (1999). *The hippocampal and parietal foundations of spatial cognition*. New York: Oxford University Press.

Burgess, N., Maguire, E. A., & O'Keefe, J. (2002). The human hippocampus and spatial and episodic memory. *Neuron, 35*, 625–641.

Byrne, R. W. (1982). Geographical knowledge and orientation. In A. Ellis (Ed.), *Normality and pathology in cognitive functions* (pp. 239–264). London: Academic.

Chabris, C. F., & Kosslyn, S. M. (1998). How do the cerebral hemispheres contribute to encoding spatial relations? *Current Directions in Psychological Science, 7*, 8–14.

Creem, S. H., & Proffitt, D. R. (1998). Two memories for geographical slant: Separation and interdependence of action and awareness. *Psychonomic Bulletin and Review, 5*, 22–36.

Creem, S. H., & Proffitt, D. R. (2001a). Defining the cortical visual systems: "What," "where," and "how." *Acta Psychologica, 107*, 43–68.

Creem, S. H., & Proffitt, D. R. (2001b). Grasping objects by their handles: A necessary interaction between cognition and action. *Journal of Experimental Psychology: Human Perception and Performance, 27*, 218–228.

Easton, R. D., & Sholl, M. J. (1995). Object-array structure, frames of reference, and retrieval of spatial knowledge. *Journal of Experimental Psychology: Learning, Memory, and Cognition, 21*, 483–500.

Franklin, N., Henkel, L. A., & Zangas, T. (1995). Parsing surrounding space into regions. *Memory & Cognition, 23*, 397–407.

Goodale, M. A., & Milner, A. D. (1992). Separate visual pathways for perception and action. *Trends in Neurosciences, 15*, 20–25.

Hasher, L., & Zacks, R. (1979). Automatic versus effortful processes in memory. *Journal of Experimental Psychology: General, 105*, 356–388.

Hellige, J. B., & Michimata, C. (1989). Categorization versus distance: Hemispheric differences for processing spatial information: *Memory & Cognition, 17*, 770–776.

Huttenlocher, J., Hedges, L. V., & Duncan, S. (1991). Categories and particulars: Prototype effects in estimating spatial location. *Psychological Review, 98*, 352–376.

Huttenlocher J., Hedges L. V., & Vevea, J. L. (2000). Why do categories affect stimulus judgment? *Journal of Experimental Psychology: General, 129*, 220–241.

Kosslyn, S. M. (1987). Seeing and imagining in the cerebral hemispheres: A computational approach. *Psychological Review, 94*, 148–175.

Kosslyn, S. M. (1994). *Image and brain: The resolution of the imagery debate.* Cambridge, MA: MIT Press.

Kosslyn, S. M., Chabris, C. F., Marsolek, C. J., & Koenig, O. (1992). Categorical versus coordinate spatial relations: Computational analysis and computer simulations. *Journal of Experimental Psychology: Human Perception and Performance, 18*, 562–577.

Kosslyn, S. M., Koenig, O., Barrett, A., Cave, C. B., Tang, J., & Gabrieli, J. D. (1989). Evidence for two types of spatial representations: Hemispheric specialization for categorical and coordinate relations. *Journal of Experimental Psychology: Human Perception and Performance, 15*, 723–735.

Landau, B., Spelke, E., & Gleitman, H. (1984). Spatial knowledge in a young blind child. *Cognition, 16*, 225–260.

Logie, R. (1995). *Visuo-spatial working memory.* London: Lawrence Erlbaum Associates, Inc.

Luce, A. A., & Jessop, T. E. (Eds.). (1948). *The works of George Berkeley.* Volumes 1 and 2. London, England: Nelson.

Luce, R. D., Nosofsky, R. M., Green, D. M., & Smith, A. F. (1982). The bow and sequential effects in absolute identification. *Perception and Psychophysics, 32*, 397–408.

Maguire, E. A., Frith, C. D., Burgess, N., Donnett, J. G., & O'Keefe, J. (1998). Knowing where things are: Parahippocampal involvement in encoding object locations in virtual large-scale spaces. *Journal of Cognitive Neuroscience, 10*, 61–76.

Miller, G. A. (1956). The magical number seven, plus or minus two: Some limits on our capacity for processing information. *Psychological Review, 63*, 81–97.

Montello, D. R., Richardson, A. E., Hegarty, M., & Provenza, M. (1999). A comparison of methods for estimating directions in egocentric space. *Perception, 28*, 981–1000.

Newcombe, N. S., & Huttenlocher, J. (2000). *Making space: The development of spatial representation and reasoning.* Cambridge, MA: MIT Press.

O'Keefe, J., & Nadel, L. (1978). *The hippocampus as a cognitive map.* New York: Oxford University Press.

Piaget, J., & Inhelder, B. (1967). *The child's conception of space* (F. J. Langdon & J. L. Lunzer, Trans.). New York: Norton. (Original work published 1948)

Proffitt, D. R., Bhalla, M., Gossweiler, R., & Midgett, J. (1995). Perceiving geographical slant. *Psychonomic Bulletin and Review, 2*, 409–428.

Rieser, J. J. (1989). Access to knowledge of spatial structure at novel points of observation. *Journal of Experimental Psychology: Learning, Memory, and Cognition, 15*, 1157–1165.

Shemyakin, F. N. (1962). General problems or orientation in space and space representations. In B. Anan'vey et al. (Eds.), *Psychological science in the U.S.S.R.* (Vol. 1, pp. 186–255). Washington, DC: Office of Technical Services. (NTIS No. TT62–11083)

Siegel, A.W., & White, S. H. (1975). The development of spatial representations of large-scale environments. In H. Reese (Ed.), *Advances in child development and behavior* (Vol 10, pp. 9–55). New York: Academic.

Stevens, A., & Coupe, P. (1978). Distortions in judged spatial relations. *Cognitive Psychology, 10,* 422–437.

Ungerleider, L. G., & Mishkin, M. (1982). Two cortical visual systems. In D. Ingle, M. Goodale, & R. Mansfield (Eds.), *Analysis of visual behavior* (pp. 549–586). Cambridge, MA: MIT Press.

Wraga, M., Creem, S. H., & Proffitt, D. R. (2000). Perception-action dissociations of a walkable Mueller–Lyer configuration. *Psychological Science, 11,* 239–243.

II

The Task of Remembering "Where Is It?"

The four chapters in this section each have unique aspects but also share some important themes. In chapter 4 (this volume), Jeanne Sholl and Stephanie Fraone first provide a comprehensive review of the concept of spatial working memory and its application to small-scale space, that is, to the type of situation typically involving a stationary observer and a small, often two-dimensional figure, object, or object array. Then, they expand their consideration to the role of spatial working memory in large-scale space, that is, in the type of situation typically involving a mobile observer surrounded by large, stationary environmental objects. Thus, chapter 4 foreshadows the task of answering "Where am I?", which is the concern of the next section. In chapter 5, Ruth Schumann-Hengsteler, Martin Strobl, and Christof Zoelch present findings from a research program focused on the development of spatiotemporal memory in children. There is good conceptual continuity with the preceding chapter 4 in terms of invoking a working memory theme and good continuity with chapter 6 that follows in terms of examining memory for sequences versus memory for patterns of locations. In chapter 6, David Uttal and Cynthia Chiong are concerned with the multifaceted cognitive challenges and benefits of conceiving of patterns of locations, a phenomenon they refer to as "seeing space in more than one way." Again, the emphasis is on developmental analysis. In chapter 7, Albert Postma, Roy Kessels, and Marieke van Asselen examine the literature dealing with the neuropsychology of object-location memory and report extensive findings from their laboratory. The connections with other chapters in this section with respect to working memory mechanisms and spatiotemporal versus pattern memory are clear and compelling.

Visuospatial Working Memory for Different Scales of Space:
Weighing the Evidence

M. Jeanne Sholl and Stephanie K. Fraone
Boston College

It is commonly agreed that working memory (WM) entails the online maintenance and processing of information necessary for higher level cognitive functioning. Functional definitions of WM about which there is consensus include the "moment-to-moment monitoring, processing, and maintenance of information" in everyday cognition (Baddeley & Logie, 1999, p. 28) and the system underlying the maintenance of information in the service of complex cognition (Miyake & Shah, 1999). There is less consensus about the cognitive architecture that underlies WM. Baddeley's (e.g., Baddeley, 1986; Baddeley & Hitch, 1974) fractionation of short-term store (Atkinson & Shriffrin, 1971) into a multicomponent WM system with a domain-general central executive and two domain-specific subsidiary storage systems—verbal and visuospatial—has framed much of the theoretical debate and empirical research in this area. Although not all subscribe to this model of WM, the psychological reality of domain-specific verbal and visuospatial WM subcomponents is largely beyond dispute and is not reviewed here (see Shah & Miyake, 1996, for a brief review).

The primary objective of this chapter is to explore the construct of visuospatial WM and to raise the question of whether a single WM system operates across different levels of spatiotemporal extendedness or whether there is a different WM system for each behaviorally relevant scale of space.

We do not presume that we are able to answer this question here. Our more modest aim is to review the research on visuospatial WM at different spatial scales for the purpose of exploring underlying similarities and differences.

Montello (1993) identified three behaviorally relevant scales of space and has suggested that at each scale a different functional system may operate for processing visuospatial information. On a continuum of spatio-temporal extendedness, Montello differentiated between *figural space* (object-sized spaces), *vista space* (room-sized spaces), and *environmental space* (spaces that cannot be seen in their entirety from one vantage point). Montello made the case for functional differentiation outside the domain of WM, and in this chapter we apply his taxonomy to the construct of WM. To emphasize differences in scale, we restrict our review to figural and environmental scales of space, in the latter case focusing on regions of space small enough to be explored comfortably on foot. At both scales of space, we explore the construct of visuospatial WM from both a cognitive and a neuroscientific perspective. In some instances, the research we review on environmental space was actually conducted in room-sized space. However, in these instances vision was either obstructed or restricted so that the interobject relations defining the space were not simultaneously visible but instead were revealed over an extended trajectory, thus simulating, albeit at a reduced spatiotemporal scale, the properties of environmentally scaled space.

Perhaps because the construct of human WM developed from a chronometric analysis of cognitive functioning, the study of visuospatial WM has been largely limited to cognitive tasks using visuospatial displays small enough to fit onto a computer screen or a piece of paper. Others have provided comprehensive reviews of how WM operates at this figural scale of space (Logie, 1995; see also Schumann-Hengsteler, Strobl, & Zoelch, chap. 5, this volume), and we do not reiterate those efforts. Instead, we provide a limited review of some of the theoretical issues that have driven research on figural WM and from which evidence of its characteristic properties has emerged. We then explore the research on WM for larger scales of space.

Ideally, our review would include a comparison between the properties of figural WM and the properties of environmental WM. Such a comparison would allow a preliminary assessment of the extent to which the visuospatial WM system is unitary or divided because the greater the similarity in functional properties, the more likely there is to be a similar underlying architectural structure. However, although there has been extensive theoretically driven research on the properties of figural WM, there has been little research on the properties of environmental WM; therefore, a direct comparison of properties is not possible at this time.

Our review is organized into three sections. In the first section, we review WM for figural space from both a cognitive and neuroscientific perspective; in the second section, we do the same for environmental space; and in the last section, we explore the issue of their connectedness. Because the cognitive research on figural and environmental WM is at different stages of development, these sections are organized differently from one another. The cognitive review of WM for object-size spaces is organized around theoretical issues, whereas the cognitive review of WM for environment-size spaces is organized around tasks likely to require WM. The organizational structure mirrors the current state of cognitive research in each area, and the disparity in their organizational structure illuminates their current theoretical and empirical gaps. By laying out this disparity, our objective is to draw attention to some issues that may previously have been overlooked, to identify some of the gaps in our knowledge that would need to be filled before the question of spatiotemporal scale can be answered, and to suggest some possible lines of future inquiry.

THE VISUOSPATIAL WM SYSTEM(S) FOR A FIGURAL SCALE OF SPACE

In the first half of this section, we review some of the properties of WM for figural space and the theoretical issues that have driven cognitive research on these properties. Much of the research on visuospatial WM has been framed by Baddeley and Hitch's (1974) multicomponent model of WM. According to this model, a visuospatial store or "sketchpad" acts as a medium for the temporary storage of analogue cognitive representations, formed either as a result of the perceptual analysis of visual input or the retrieval of visuospatial knowledge from long-term memory (LTM). Analogue representations are "depictive representations" (Kosslyn, 1983, p. 33) that preserve the visuospatial properties of the physical stimulus. Visuospatial information is stored in the sketchpad when temporary retention is required to solve a spatial problem. Types of everyday WM problems thought to require figural visuospatial WM include anticipating the outcome of a spatial transformation ("Will the oversized chair fit through the narrow door opening if it is rotated this way?"), mental rearrangement of a group of objects ("Will the suitcase fit into the overhead compartment if the stuff already in it is rearranged?"), anticipating how the parts of a whole will fit together (a skill required to assemble anything that comes in pieces), and so on. The control processes recruited to operate on the stored visuospatial information draw processing resources from a domain-general central executive. This general framework has motivated a series of empirical questions that have helped to articulate further the properties of visuospatial WM. These questions include whether the visuospatial store can be further subdivided into separate visual and spatial stores, the extent to which the visuospatial store is separable from executive functioning, and the role of attention in visuospatial store.

In the second half of this section, we review some of the neuroscientific research on WM for figural space in both nonhuman primates and humans. In large part, the neuroscientific research on visuospatial WM has different scientific origins from the cognitive behavioral research, yet there are interesting parallels between the two domains of inquiry.

Visuospatial WM From a Cognitive Perspective

Visual Versus Spatial Temporary Store.   Interest in the fractionation of visuospatial store into separable visual and spatial subcomponents followed from empirical findings suggesting that its verbal counterpart, the phonological store, could be functionally subdivided into a phonological loop, which stores speech-based codes, and an articulatory mechanism, which refreshes the phonological codes to keep them activated. This led to the conjecture that analogous subdivisions may exist in the visuospatial store, with Logie (1995) having proposed a visual "cache" for the storage of visual information and an "inner scribe" that refreshes visual codes and is involved in the planning and control of movement. Logie equated space with movement; hence, he proposed a functional division between visual and spatial WM subcomponents.

Without subscribing to Logie's (1995) subdivision of visuospatial store and with the adoption of a more conventional, location-based definition of space, we review behavioral evidence related to the separability of visual and spatial storage systems. Arguably the most convincing behavioral evidence is the double dissociation observed in interference paradigms (Della Sala, Gray, Baddeley, Allamano, & Wilson, 1999; Logie & Marchetti, 1991; Tresch, Sinnamon, & Seamon, 1993). In this paradigm, two primary tasks are each paired with the same two secondary tasks. If one secondary task interferes only with one primary task and the other secondary task interferes only with the other primary task, then each pair of primary/secondary tasks is likely to rely on a common cognitive substrate that is different from the substrate common to the other pair. The properties of the shared cognitive substrate underlying performance on the primary and secondary tasks are inferred from an analysis of the tasks' commonalties.

The primary tasks used by Logie and Marchetti (1991) were short-term retention tasks in which participants held an inspection sequence in WM for 10 s prior to judging whether or not it matched a test sequence. In the visual primary task, the sequences consisted of four square patches in different shades (hues) of the same color, and in the spatial primary task, the sequences consisted of six square patches all of the same color shade but displayed at different locations. During a 10-s delay interval, participants performed a secondary task. They either engaged in a hand-movement task, which consisted of a nonsighted hand movement following a zigzag (ᴢ) trajectory, or they passively observed black and white line drawings of common objects and animals in an irrelevant-pictures task. The irrelevant-pictures task interfered with memory for hues but not locations, and the hand-movement task interfered with memory for location but not hues. These findings are consistent with a visual WM system that maintains information about color and shape over short delays and a spatial WM system that maintains information about spatial location in the service of action. Based on the latter finding, Logie and Marchetti argued that the primary function of a spatial WM system is to plan and execute spatially directed actions.

Using a similar experimental design but a very different set of primary and secondary tasks, Tresch et al. (1993) also found a double dissociation in visual and spatial short-term retention. Their spatial primary task tested retention of a single dot location for 10 s, and their visual primary task tested retention of a simple geometric form. Because of the simplicity of the primary tasks, stimulus duration was adjusted to produce an 80% to 90% accuracy rate. One secondary task was a movement-detection task—find the stationary character in a field of moving characters—and the other was color-discrimination task: judge whether a square is more blue than red or more red than blue. The movement-detection task interfered with the spatial but not the visual primary task, and the color-discrimination task interfered with the visual but not the spatial primary task.

Additional behavioral evidence for a functional dissociation between visual and spatial processing systems is provided by selective interference and developmental studies. In general selective interference paradigms show that spatial-motor secondary tasks, such as nonsighted movement of the hand/arm to track a swinging pendulum and nonsighted tapping of the four corners of a square grid, interfere with spatial but not visual temporary storage tasks (Baddeley & Lieberman, 1980). In contrast, visual secondary tasks, such as viewing flickering dot patterns or abstract paintings, interfere with visual but not spatial temporary storage tasks (Quinn & McConnell, 1996). Using tasks designed to test the capacity of WM and testing children between the ages of 5 and 12 years, one developmental study (Logie & Pearson, 1997) showed the capacity of a visual short-term storage system developed at a faster rate than the capacity of a spatial system. This finding was replicated by Pickering and colleagues (Pickering, Gathercole, Hall, & Lloyd, 2001) in experiments comparing children between the ages of 5 and 10. Interestingly, as measured by a spatial delayed response task, memory for spatial location continues to develop until age 20 (Zald & Iacono, 1998).

Although the interference paradigms provide convincing evidence for the separability of visual and spatial short-term retention systems, the developmental results are more difficult to interpret. In the developmental studies that measured WM span (Logie & Pearson, 1997; Pickering et al., 2001), the spatial span task differed from the visual span task on a temporal/dynamic dimension. In the visual task, participants had to recognize a static grid of filled and unfilled squares after a short retention interval, and span was measured by incrementally increasing the number of squares in the grid. The spatial task was similar, but instead of a simultaneous display of squares, filled squares were presented one at a time in different locations in the grid, and the participants remembered the locations in the order of their occurrence. Thus, spatial span has a strong temporal component, and it is unclear whether the delay in its development relative to visual span is due to difficulty remembering a set of locations or difficulty remembering the temporal order in which those locations occurred. Smyth and Scholey (1996) demonstrated that spatial span tasks show serial position effects similar to those shown by verbal span tasks, suggesting retention of temporal order may be subject to domain-general constraints.

Although visual and spatial components of WM can be dissociated in the laboratory, in natural cognition it is likely that the two are inextricably intertwined and work in concert with one another, unless damage to one system or the other disrupts their joint function. This conclusion is consistent with the extensive interconnectivity between the ventral and dorsal visual systems of the primate brain, which in turn indicates a high degree of cross talk and interactivity consistent with significant functional interdependence (e.g., DeYoe & Van Essen, 1988). We continue our review of visuospatial WM at a level of analysis that does not differentiate spatial from visual processing. This is largely because much of the research treats visuospatial WM as a unified system, but it is also based on the premise that the two subsystems normally work together as a single, highly integrated system. We only distinguish visual from spatial processing in subsequent sections when it is empirically or theoretically important to do so.

Separability of Storage and Executive Processes.   In the verbal domain, complex memory span tasks that test both storage capacity and central executive functioning, such as Daneman and Carpenter's (1980) reading span task, predict higher level verbal functions such as reading comprehension better than simple span tasks that test only storage capacity (Daneman & Merikle, 1996). The separability of on-line storage and executive functions in the verbal domain is illustrated by the differential predictive power of simple and complex span tasks, despite their high degree of correlation. Applying the terminology used by Miyake, Friedman, Rettinger, Shah, and Hegarty (2001), we call simple span tasks, which have only a storage requirement, *short-term memory (STM)-span* tasks and complex memory span tasks, which involve both storage and processing, *WM span* tasks.

Consistent with the premise that WM span is the better predictor of higher level cognitive functions, Engle, Tuholski, Laughlin, and Conway (1999) found that fluid intelligence is predicted better by verbal WM span than by verbal STM span. The separability of storage and processing in the verbal domain is illustrated by the Engle et al. finding that after controlling for the variance in fluid intelligence attributable to STM span, WM span still predicts fluid intelligence. In contrast, STM span does not predict fluid intelligence after controlling for the variance attributable to WM span. These findings can be interpreted as follows. WM and STM span tasks both involve the phonological store, but the WM span task also involves central-executive functioning, which is particularly important to fluid intelligence.[1]

Although WM span is a better predictor than STM span of higher level cognitive functioning in the verbal domain, the same pattern has not been observed in the spatial domain. Prior to reviewing the findings in the spatial domain, we describe a prototypical example of a STM span task and a WM span task. The Corsi blocks task (Corsi, 1973) is an example of a STM span task. The standard version of this task uses an irregular array of small wooden blocks affixed to a flat surface. The participant observes an experimenter tap a subset of the blocks one-by-one. The participant then must tap the same blocks in the same order as tapped by the experimenter. In the computerized version, the irregular array of squares appears on the computer screen and the tapping sequence is depicted by a brief change in the color of each square "tapped." The participant then uses a mouse and clicks on each square in the memorized order. The number of squares the participant can tap correctly is his or her STM span. The letter-rotation task (Shah & Miyake, 1996) is an example of a WM span task. On each trial, a single capital letter is presented in one of seven orientations on a computer screen. The participant makes a normal or mirror-image "handedness" judgment, which requires mental rotation, and concurrently stores the orientation of the letter. At the end of a sequence of trials, the participant's task is to recall each letter's orientation in the correct serial order. WM span is the number of orientations correctly recalled. Thus, in this example, WM span measures visuospatial storage capacity when storage requirements must be coordinated with the resource demands imposed by a competing mental-rotation task.

Contrary to findings in the verbal domain, Shah and Miyake (1996) found that visuospatial STM span predicts performance on psychometric tests of higher level spatial ability just as well as WM span. Following up on this finding, Miyake et al. (2001) used an individual-differences approach to investigate the extent to which the temporary storage of visuospatial information is separable from the executive functions that operate on the stored information. Latent variable analysis of a battery of tests, which included tests of visuospatial STM and WM span and tests of the efficacy of central-executive functioning (i.e., the Tower of Hanoi [Simon, 1975] and Random Number Generation [Evans & Graham, 1980])

---

[1]Engle et al. (1999) argued that controlled attention rather than executive functioning is the factor that differentiates WM span from STM span. They defined *controlled attention* as the capacity to activate LTM representations, to maintain activation in the face of interference or distraction, to inhibit the activation of competing representations, and to switch activation between representations in accordance with task demands. Here we use the more general construct of *executive functioning*, which includes controlled attention, but also goal-directed planning, regulation of the flow of information within the WM system, allocation of attentional resources to selected cognitive operations, and so on.

produced the following outcomes. STM and WM span tasks were highly intercorrelated, suggesting a unitary STM–WM system that includes storage capacity plus executive involvement. Consistent with strong executive involvement in the temporary storage of visuospatial information was the finding that both types of span tasks were equally and highly correlated with the central-executive tests. This pattern of correlation is consistent with a lack of functional separation between storage and executive processes in the visuospatial system. Of particular interest is the finding that individual differences on traditional psychometric tests of visuospatial ability, including spatial visualization, spatial relations, and perceptual speed, were largely accounted for by a weighted combination of executive functioning and STM–WM span. Path analysis indicated that perceptual speed was about equally accounted for by executive functioning and the STM–WM span variable, whereas spatial visualization and spatial relations were solely accounted for by executive functioning. That is not to say that spatial visualization and spatial relations do not require visuospatial storage because their first-order correlations with the STM–WM latent variable were .63 and .54, respectively, but that storage and executive functioning are largely inseparable. Thus, once executive functioning is held constant, the correlation of STM–WM span with spatial visualization and spatial relations falls to zero.

Interference studies provide converging evidence for major central-executive involvement in visuospatial storage. Smyth and Pelky (1992) reported a reduced spatial span at 15-s delays when a backward-counting task, which is a central-executive task, was performed during the delay interval of a subspan Corsi blocks task. A further reduction in STM span was found when participants engaged in backward counting during both the encoding and maintenance of a sequence of three block locations. This latter result suggests central executive involvement in both the encoding and the short-term storage of visuospatial information.

The Role of Attention in Visuospatial WM.   If maintaining active representations in visuospatial short-term storage requires attentional resources, it may in part account for the failure to find a functional distinction between STM and WM visuospatial span, given the assumption that the attentional resources recruited to maintain active representations in temporary store are drawn from the same pool as are the attentional resources used to perform cognitive operations on the temporarily active representations. Of interest in this regard is behavioral evidence reviewed by Awh and Jonides (2001) for an attention-based rehearsal mechanism in a subspan spatial STM task. In this task, participants had to retain the location of a single letter during a 5-s delay interval. During the delay interval, participants made a speeded response to a single letter-like probe that appeared at various locations on a computer screen. Responses to the probe were faster when the probe's location matched the memorized location of the letter than when it did not match. The faster responses to matching locations suggested that attentional resources were recruited to "mark" the place of the memorized location. Awh and Jonides tested a verbal subspan task identical to the spatial task with the exception that participants retained the name of the letter rather than its location. Because a similar advantage of matched over unmatched locations was not observed in a verbal version, resource allocation to a location appears to be specific to the retention of spatial information.

Awh and Jonides' (2001) findings are consistent with the selective attention literature showing that visual cues that occur within a narrow spotlight of focused visual attention are processed more efficiently than those cues that fall outside the spotlight (e.g., Posner, Snyder, & Davidson, 1980). However, as Awh and Jonides pointed out, evidence that selective attention marks a memorized location during a spatial STM task does not mean that selective attention functions as a rehearsal mechanism. Empirical support for its rehearsal function comes from studies that show a decrement in memory for spatial location when visual attention is diverted from the memorized location during the delay interval (e.g., Awh, Jonides, & Reuter-Lorenz, 1998).

In part because of the tight linkage between spatially directed attention and spatially directed action, it has been difficult to disentangle an attention-based from an implicit motor-based rehearsal process (i.e., a readiness to respond to an event at the memorized location). A motor-based mechanism implies that location is coded as the endpoint of a spatially directed eye or hand movement and that activation of an anticipatory motor program maintains the spatial code in STM, similar to the maintenance function performed by Logie's (1995) inner scribe. Much of the behavioral evidence for a motor-rehearsal mechanism comes from dual-task paradigms. In this paradigm, pairing a visuospatial span task, such as the Brooks matrix task[2] (a WM span task) or the Corsi blocks task (a STM span task), with a task requiring a planned, spatially directed arm or hand movement selectively disrupts performance on the visuospatial task (Baddeley & Lieberman, 1980; Brooks, 1968; Quinn, 1994; Quinn & Ralston, 1986; Salway & Logie, 1995; Smyth, Pearson, & Pendleton, 1988; Smyth & Pelky, 1992; Smyth & Pendleton, 1989; Smyth & Scholey, 1994).

Smyth and colleagues (Smyth et al., 1988; Smyth & Pendleton, 1989) have shown that interference is produced by concurrent movement that is spatially directed. Movements that are not spatially directed, such as repeated clenching or unclenching of the hand or repetitive body-directed

---

[2]The Brooks task (Brooks, 1967) qualifies as a WM span task because it involves both executive and storage processes: It requires the participant to read step-by-step instructions specifying how to create a pattern of filled cells in a mental grid. At each step the person reads an instruction telling him or her where the next filled cell is in relation to the prior filled cell and then mentally fills in the next cell while retaining the pattern completed up to that point.

hand movements, do not interfere with spatial span. However, attempts to establish whether interference is attributable to spatially directed attention or to spatially directed actions have produced mixed results (Smyth, 1996; Smyth & Scholey, 1994). If rehearsal is motor based, then prevention of eye movements during the delay interval of a spatial STM span task should reduce spatial span. However, fixation on a central target during the delay interval in a Corsi blocks type task did not reduce spatial STM span, suggesting that rehearsal is not dependent on overt eye movements but leaving open the possibility that it may depend on covert attentional shifts. If rehearsal is mediated by covert shifts of attention from one memorized location to the next, then an intervening task that directs attention to nonmemorized locations should interfere with spatial span. However, a secondary task using an auditory signal to direct attention automatically to either the right or the left did not interfere with STM span. Instead, interference was observed only when participants had to verbally categorize the location of the tone as either originating on the right or the left. However, in this case interference could have been caused by the difficulty associated with making a verbal right/left categorization rather than a shift of spatial attention to the right or the left.

Summary.   Existing behavioral evidence supports a spatial WM system that is separable from a visual WM system, although normally the two systems are likely to be highly integrated. In an integrated visuospatial WM system, executive processes are difficult to separate behaviorally from storage processes, perhaps because the temporary retention of visuospatial information requires attentional effort. The recruitment of attentional resources to mark a memorized location in a mental topographic map of the visual field, with covert shifts of visual attention to refresh the marked locations is one proposed rehearsal mechanism for the short-term visuospatial store. However, it has proved difficult to disentangle an attention-based from a motor-based rehearsal mechanism.

WM From a Neuroscientific Perspective

There is uniform agreement that the lateral prefrontal cortex plays an important role in human and nonhuman primate visuospatial WM (e.g., Goldman-Rakic, 1987; Petrides, 2000). There is also agreement that there may be important functional divisions between dorsolateral and ventrolateral regions of the prefrontal cortex. However, at present there are two major, alternative models for how WM maps onto the dorsolateral and ventrolateral areas. According to one model, which is called the *domain-specificity model*, the dorsolateral and ventrolateral prefrontal cortex are each part of different domain-specific WM circuits (Goldman-Rakic, 1987; Ungerleider, Courtney, & Haxby, 1998). The other model, called the *process-specific model*, proposes that these two areas are domain-general substrates for two levels of executive processing and that domain-specific STMs are stored in the posterior sensory association areas (Petrides, 2000). We consider each model in turn.

However, first it is important to clarify the boundaries of the dorsolateral and ventrolateral prefrontal cortex both in the monkey and human brain (see Fig. 4.1). In the monkey brain, the dorsolateral prefrontal cortex encompasses the principle sulcus and those areas dorsal to it, including Walker's Areas 46, 9, 8A, and 8B. The corresponding areas in the human brain (Broadman's Areas 46, 9, and 8) are contained in the middle and superior frontal gyri. In the monkey brain, the inferior convexity of the ventrolateral prefrontal cortex includes Walker's Area 47/12 and 45, with corresponding areas (Broadman's Areas 47, 45, and 44) contained in the inferior frontal gyrus of the human brain.

The Domain-Specificity Model of Prefrontal Function. Two major visual-processing channels have been identified in the primate brain: a dorsal

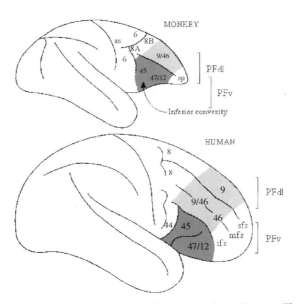

FIG. 4.1. Schematic of the monkey and human prefrontal cortex. The light grey area shows the mid-dorsolateral prefrontal cortex, and the dark grey area shows the ventrolateral prefrontal cortex. Pfdl = prefrontal dorsolateral; Pfv = prefrontal ventrolateral; sp = sulcus principalas; as = arcuate sulcus; sfs = superior frontal sulcus; mfs = medial frontal sulcus; ifs = inferior frontal sulcus. *Note.* From Comparative architectonic analysis of the human and the macaque frontal cortex, by M. Petrides and D. N. Pandya, 1994, in F. Boller & J. Gratman (Eds.), *Handbook of Neuropsychology,* Vol. 9, pp. 17–58. Amsterdam: Elsevier. Copyright © 1994 by Elsevier Science. Reprinted with permission.

stream that terminates in the posterior parietal cortex and is specialized for processing object location and a ventral stream that terminates in the inferior temporal cortex and is specialized for processing object identity (e.g., Goodale & Milner, 1992; Haxby et al., 1994; Ungerleider & Mishkin, 1982). According to the domain-specificity model, the divisions in visual processing originating in the posterior sensory and association areas extend to the lateral prefrontal cortex forming two parallel WM circuits (e.g., Goldman-Rakic, 1987; Ungerleider et al., 1998). In the monkey brain, the prefrontal substrate for spatial WM is located in the principle sulcus, which has bidirectional connections to the posterior parietal cortex. Similarly the prefrontal substrate for object WM is the inferior convexity, which has bidirectional connections to the inferior temporal cortex. Neurophysiological support for a prefrontal storage function comes from studies showing that external events initially registered in the posterior association areas are temporarily retained following stimulus offset by the sustained response of prefrontal neurons.

Single-cell recordings in the monkey lateral prefrontal cortex are consistent with a spatial WM system that is separable from an object WM system (Levy & Goldman-Rakic, 1999; Wilson, Seamas, Scalaidhe, & Goldman-Rakic, 1993). Cells in the principal sulcus and in the region anterior to the arcuate sulcus (Area 8A) respond selectively during the interval between stimulus offset and response execution in a spatial delayed-response task (Funahashi, Bruce, & Goldman-Rakic, 1989). Some of the cells in the principle sulcus have a preferred location. That is, the cell responds during the delay interval if the event occurs in its preferred location but not if the event occurred in some other location. Consistent with the single-cell data, dorsolateral prefrontal lesions produce deficits in spatial but not visual WM tasks (Levy & Goldman-Rakic, 1999). In contrast to the dorsolateral prefrontal region, single-cell recordings from the inferior convexity (Areas 12 and 45) show that most cells have sustained responses to visual patterns (with a small number responding to faces; Wilson et al., 1993).

In the human brain, neuroimaging studies and neuropsychological case studies are consistent with neuroanatomically separate dorsal and ventral visual subsystems in the posterior cortex for processing spatial location and object identity, respectively (e.g., Haxby et al., 1991; Levine, Warach, & Farah, 1985). However, regions of activation during spatial and object memory span tasks provide a more mixed picture of the extent to which the neuroanatomical subdivisions in posterior association areas are carried forward to the prefrontal cortex. In part, the picture has been clouded by a human language system that names objects, confounding the short-term retention of object shapes with the short-term retention of words. Unless otherwise indicated, the studies reviewed in this section avoided the problem of nameable objects by using unfamiliar geometric shapes, faces, or abstract visual patterns in their object memory span conditions.

Smith et al. (1995) conducted a functional magnetic resonance imaging study (fMRI) that compared regions of brain activity during tasks that required the short-term retention of either objects or locations. To rule out any differences in encoding processes, they used the same object displays in both their object and spatial STM subspan tasks. Each display contained two objects, and depending on the condition, participants retained either the objects' shapes or the objects' locations for a 3-s delay interval prior to judging whether or not a test object matched the shape or location of one of the memorized objects. The brain regions most activated during the spatial STM span task were distributed within the right hemisphere and included the ventrolateral prefrontal cortex (Area 47), premotor cortex (Area 6), occipital cortex (Area 19), and parietal cortex (Area 40). These findings replicate those reported by Jonides et al. (1993). In contrast, the left parietal cortex (Area 40) and the left inferotemporal cortex (Area 37) were the most active regions during the object STM task. Although this study provides support for a neuroanatomical division between object and spatial short-term storage systems, the observed divisions did not map onto the dorsolateral and ventrolateral prefrontal cortex as predicted by the domain-specific model.

In a similar study, Courtney, Petit, Maisog, Ungerleider, and Haxby (1998) compared regions of activation measured by fMRI during a face and a spatial STM subspan task. In their task, three faces, each in a different location on the computer screen, were sequentially presented, and after a 9-s delay interval, a test face was presented. Participants judged whether the test face matched the identity or the location of one of the memorized faces. Measuring regions of activation during the delay interval, Courtney et al. (1998) found that the superior frontal sulcus, just anterior to the frontal eye fields (Area 8), showed the greatest levels of sustained activity bilaterally during spatial delays and that the left inferior prefrontal region showed the most sustained activity during face delays. In an earlier positron emission tomography (PET) study conducted by Courtney, Ungerleider, Keil, and Haxby (1996) and reviewed by Ungerleider et al. (1998), the face STM subspan task produced greater activity than the location task in the ventral occipitotemporal area, as well as in the right ventrolateral (Areas 45/47) and right dorsolateral prefrontal cortex (Area 46/9). The location task produced greater activity than the face task in the dorsal occipitoparietal area that extended forward to a portion of the superior frontal sulcus just anterior to the frontal eye fields. Ungerleider et al. suggested that in the human cortex domain-specific spatial function may have been displaced posteriorly and superiorly from homologous areas in the monkey cortex.

The carefully controlled studies by Smith et al. (1995) and by Courtney and colleagues (Courtney et al., 1996, 1998) showed that different areas of the prefrontal cortex were activated by visual and spatial STM span tasks; however, there was little neuroanatomical consistency between the studies. This lack of consistency was borne out in a review of 24 neuroimaging studies (PET and fMRI) by D'Esposito et al. (1998). This review revealed that the prefrontal areas activated during spatial and nonspatial (including stimuli such as alphanumeric characters, familiar objects, faces, and abstract geometric figures) span tasks were fairly evenly distributed across the dorsolateral and ventrolateral regions of the prefrontal cortex. Thus, although some individual studies provide support for separate visual and spatial storage substrates, the neuroanatomical substrates are not consistent across studies. Although neuroanatomical results have been mixed, there is some psychopharmacological evidence for separate neurochemical systems for visual and spatial storage.

Luciana and Collins (1997) tested human performance on a spatial and visual delayed-response task under dopamine agonist and antagonist conditions. Psychopharmacological studies of monkeys had shown that dopamine agonists enhance and antagonists inhibit performance on spatial delayed-response tasks, findings that were consistent with the large concentrations of dopamine localized in the principle sulcus in the dorsolateral region of the monkey cortex. Luciana and Collins expected to find similar results in humans, who have dopamine concentrations similar to that of monkeys. However, because dopamine is also concentrated in the parietal, temporal, and ventrolateral prefrontal cortex, they expected modulation of dopamine activity to have domain-general effects on short-term storage. Therefore, it was also expected that the drug conditions would affect visual as well as spatial STM performance. In the visual task, participants judged after a delay interval whether a simple geometric test figure had been part of the more complex memorized figure. At 8-s delays in the spatial delayed-response task, the agonist condition increased accuracy by a small but significant 5.6%, whereas the antagonist condition decreased accuracy by 13.1%. Unexpectedly, the drug conditions had no effect on the visual STM task. In a follow-up study, Luciana, Collins, and Depue (1998) replicated the drug effects on spatial delayed response, but this time instead of using a dopamine antagonist, they used a serotonin agonist that because serotonin inhibits dopamine activity, was expected to and did act like a dopamine antagonist.

Although there were no clear neuroanatomical divisions between visual and spatial storage systems in the prefrontal cortex, the findings reviewed are consistent with functional subdivisions. Interestingly, cleaner neuroanatomical divisions appear to reemerge in the caudate nucleus, a subcortical structure located in the basal ganglia that receives widely distributed input from the cerebral cortex. Levy, Friedman, Davachi, and Goldman-Rakic (1997) reported enhanced metabolic activity in the dorsal and central parts of the caudate head of the monkey brain during a spatial WM task. This part of the caudate nucleus receives projections from the dorsolateral prefrontal cortex. In contrast, an object WM task was associated with enhanced activity in the posterior part of the caudate body, an area with inputs from the inferior temporal cortex. Human fMRI data showed greater activity in the head of the caudate (in 4 of 6 participants) when participants responded to a remembered spatial location than when they did not (Postle & D'Esposito, 1999). Moreover, the enhanced activity was observed only in the early part of the delay, suggesting a role in planning spatially directed motor responses. There was no caudate activity related to object WM, but this may have been attributable to lack of sufficient resolution in the fMRI images.

The Process-Specific Model of Prefrontal Function.   This model ascribes domain-general executive functions to dorsolateral and ventrolateral areas of the prefrontal cortex but attributes different levels of executive function to each area. According to the model, a high-level monitoring, planning, and manipulation function is instantiated in the dorsolateral prefrontal cortex, and a lower level of executive functioning that makes coarse temporal discriminations is instantiated in the ventrolateral prefrontal cortex. The domain-general executive functions operate on domain-specific input, which is relayed to the lateral prefrontal cortex from the posterior sensory association areas. Domain-specific information about external events is stored both temporarily and for the long term in the same posterior association areas where it is perceptually processed. Spatial information is forwarded from the posterior dorsal system to the executive system via the principle sulcus and the area surrounding the arcuate sulcus (Areas 8 & 6). Thus, this model attributes the spatial alternation and delayed-response deficits observed when the principle sulcus is lesioned to obstructing the flow of spatial information to the executive system. Object/face information is relayed from the posterior ventral system via the inferior prefrontal cortex to the executive systems.

The process-specific model was motivated by studies of nonhuman primates that produced findings consistent with domain-general functions for both the dorsolateral and ventrolateral frontal cortex (e.g., Petrides, 1994). Studies reviewed by Petrides (1994) can be summarized as follows. Lesions of the monkey mid-dorsolateral cortex (Areas 9 and 46) produce a severe impairment on self-ordered, externally ordered, and serially ordered object WM tasks but normal performance on delayed matching-to-sample tasks and delayed object-alternation tasks. All of these tasks involve temporary memory for one or more objects, but the latter two tasks can be solved with coarse primacy/recency judgments, whereas the former tasks require memory for the precise order of occurrence of a series of familiar objects. Lesions of the ventrolateral prefrontal cortex produce severe impairments in both spatial and object-alternation tasks, as well as on object and color delayed matching-to-sample tasks. On the basis of findings such as these, Petrides (1994) argued that the mid-dorsolateral prefrontal cortex makes fine-grained temporal discriminations to conduct higher level planning, monitoring, and manipulations involving multiple temporarily active mental representations. In contrast, the coarse primacy/recency judgments made by the ventrolateral prefrontal cortex are needed to execute processes such as the temporary retention of a stimulus in memory during response preparation and to initiate and control LTM retrieval processes.

Rao, Rainer, and Miller (1997) reported neurophysiological evidence consistent with the idea that the dorsolateral and ventrolateral parts of the prefrontal cortex are substrates for domain-general processes. They recorded from single cells during a two-phase "what" then "where" protocol with an object delay in the first half of each trial and a location delay in the second half. Over half the cells (52%) from which they recorded showed sustained responses during both the object and the spatial delays. Moreover, these cells were not indiscriminate in their responses but were tuned to particular objects and locations. A small proportion of cells (7%) retained specific object but not location information, and a larger proportion (41%) retained specific location but not object information. All three types of cells were distributed evenly over the dorsolateral (Areas 46 and 9) and ventro-lateral (Area 12) regions of the prefrontal cortex.

Human brain scanning studies provide varying degrees of support for a process-specific model. Mixed support is provided by the D'Esposito et al. (1998) review of 24 neuroimaging studies. They looked for evidence of do-main-specific segregation between the ventrolateral and dorsolateral prefrontal cortex but instead found evidence for functional segregation. In mapping function to structure, D'Esposito et al. divided WM tasks into two categories: those that required the maintenance of information during an unfilled delay period and those that required both the maintenance and the manipulation of information (analogous to the Miyake et al., 2000, distinc-tion between STM span and WM span). The domains of information sam-pled in these studies included objects, faces, locations, words, and alphanumerics. Maintenance-plus-manipulation tasks predominantly ac-tivated the dorsolateral prefrontal cortex irrespective of stimulus domain. Maintenance-only tasks were most likely to activate the ventrolateral prefrontal cortex, but the ventral area showed some evidence of domain specificity, with left-sided activation for nonspatial tasks and right-sided activation for spatial tasks. Objects have names, and because some studies included verbal stimuli, the observed lateralization may be attributable to the temporary activation of verbal labels rather than structural descriptions of objects or representations of faces. Relatedly, left hemisphere activation has been reported in verbal and object WM tasks and right hemisphere acti-vation in spatial WM tasks (Smith, Jonides, & Koeppe, 1996; Smith et al., 1995). Bearing in mind the limitations of generalizing across different neuorimaging studies, D'Esposito et al.'s review is consistent with the idea that the dorsolateral prefrontal cortex is the substrate for domain-general executive processes but suggests the possibility that the ventral areas of the prefrontal cortex may temporarily store domain-specific information.

A recent fMRI study by Owen et al. (1998) recorded brain activation dur-ing an n-back, WM task, which is a task that requires the kind of temporal monitoring that the process-specific model ascribes to the mid-dorsolateral prefrontal cortex. Owen et al. (1998) reported bilateral mid-dorsolateral prefrontal activation for both a spatial and a visual pattern n-back task accompanied by bilateral posterior parietal activation in the spatial task and anterior and inferior temporal activation in the visual-pattern task. In contrast, the ventrolateral prefrontal cortex was activated by maintenance-only tasks such as spatial (Owen, Evans, & Petrides, 1996) and visual (Lee, Manes, Bor, Robbins, & Owen, 2000) span tasks. However, the mapping of maintenance-only tasks onto the ventrolateral prefrontal cortex and of maintenance-plus-manipulation tasks onto the mid-dorsolateral prefrontal cortex is imperfect at best. Small changes in how the locations in a spatial span task are configured (either in two rows or randomly) can shift the region of activation from the ventrolateral to mid-dorsolateral prefrontal cortex (Bor, Duncan, & Owen, 2001). Moreover, a within-study comparison by Stern et al. (2000) of a memory span maintenance task to a maintenance-plus-monitoring task, both of which used abstract patterns as stimuli, showed that both tasks bilaterally activated mid-dorsolateral and ventrolateral portions of the prefrontal cortex. When activity produced by the maintenance-only task was subtracted from that produced by the maintenance-plus-monitoring task, there were few observable differences in signal intensity. One area that was more active in the maintenance-plus-monitoring task was the right mid-dorsolateral prefrontal cortex.

Overlap in WM and Selective Attention Neural Circuitry. In an earlier section we reviewed behavioral evidence consistent with the hypothesis that a selective-attention rehearsal mechanism refreshes spatial codes in STM span tasks. The rehearsal mechanism functions by shifting visual attention, either covertly or overtly, to each memorized location in turn. In support of a selective attention rehearsal process, Awh and Jonides (2001) pointed out that the brain regions activated by selective visual-attention tasks are the same brain regions activated during spatial STM span tasks: the occipital, dorsal-parietal, and superior-frontal regions of the right hemisphere. Awh and Jonides proposed that selective attention and spatial rehearsal both involve modulating activity levels in the early stages of visual analysis to mark the topographic coordinates of a visual event. In a traditional selective-attention task, a directional cue, which is presented at the center of the visual field, informs the observer on which side of the computer screen to expect a probe. Changes in activity levels in the occipital region contralateral to the to-be-attended hemifield are measurable within 100 ms of the onset of the directional probe.

To explore whether similar lateralized changes in occipital activity characterized a spatial STM span task, Awh and Jonides (2001) presented three unfamiliar, geometric characters at different locations unilaterally in either the left or the right visual field. At the end of a 6-s delay (the delay interval was filled with a flickering matrix that covered most of each hemifield), participants judged whether a probe occurred in one of the memorized locations. The fMRI recordings showed elevated activity in the occipital cortex (Areas 17, 18, and 19) contralateral to the hemifield in which the memorized locations had been presented. Appropriate controls indicated that the enhanced activity levels were largely attributable to retaining information about location and not to the encoding of unilaterally presented visual stimuli. Awh and Jonides described a carefully controlled follow-up to the fMRI study that directly compared visual responses evoked during a spatial STM span task to those evoked during a selective-attention task. They found a very similar time course and distribution of evoked responses for both types of tasks.

Summary. In neuroscientific studies of the role of the prefrontal monkey cortex in WM, one undisputed finding is that the principle sulcus is important for the short-term retention of information about spatial location. However, still unresolved is the function of the mid-dorsolateral region that lies above the principle sulcus and the ventrolateral region that lies below it. The current debate centers on whether the dorsal region is part of a domain-specific, spatial WM circuit or the substrate for domain-general executive functions. Similarly at issue is whether the ventral region is part of a domain-specific, visual WM circuit or the substrate for domain-general maintenance functions. Although some studies have shown that dorsolateral cells respond during a spatial delay and ventrolateral cells respond during a visual delay, a study that tested the same cells during both spatial and object delays (Rao et al., 1997) found that a significant number of them—evenly distributed across the dorsal and ventral regions—responded during both spatial and object delays. Human brain imaging and pharmacological studies suggest functionally separable visual and spatial WM systems, but the neural substrate for those systems within the prefrontal cortex is unclear, although there is some evidence suggesting that the prefrontal substrate for spatial WM is localized just anterior to the frontal eye fields and overlaps the neural circuitry mediating selective visual attention. There is also some support across human brain imaging studies for a dorsolateral executive function and a ventrolateral storage function; however, in a single, carefully controlled study (Stern et al., 2000), the evidence for processing specificity was weak.

THE VISUOSPATIAL WM SYSTEM
FOR AN ENVIRONMENTAL SCALE OF SPACE

WM From a Cognitive Perspective

To date, most of the cognitive research on WM for environmentally scaled space has been limited to whether or not WM has a role to play in spatial navigation. Keeping track of one's location relative to a known, environment-centered spatial framework; monitoring where one has been and where one is going; and maintaining in memory the location of immediate goals and the routes to reach them are examples of navigational tasks likely to recruit WM. The existing research has explored the role of WM in updating the body's location relative to the starting point of a trajectory, otherwise known as *path integration*, and updating relative to one or more external reference points, which may play a role in the acquisition of knowledge of interlandmark relations. We review this research in this section.

The experiments that have explored the role of WM in large-scale navigation have typically used a dual-task paradigm, pairing a navigational task with a concurrent resource-demanding task such as backward counting. According to prevailing logic, if the navigational task is disrupted by the backward-counting task, it is likely to rely on WM. Although backward counting requires the short-term retention and updating of numerical information, it also has a central-executive component, and as was seen from our review of figural WM, central-executive and storage operations are largely inseparable components at a figural scale of space.

A few developmental studies have used humanly scaled radial arm mazes or their equivalent to explore the development of WM, but because these studies use room-sized spaces, we only mention the results without elaboration. In essence, these studies show that 5- to 10-year-old children make minimal WM errors (revisiting the same location/arm more than once) and perform comparably to adults on both an 8-arm radial arm maze (Overman, Pate, Moore, & Peuster, 1996) and a "locomotor maze" that was equated for task difficulty across age groups (Lehnung et al., 1998). In contrast, children younger than 5 are more likely than older children to make WM errors on a 10-location search task (Foreman, Warry, & Murray, 1990). When the WM system is challenged by introducing a delay interval between arm visits in the radial maze task, 5- to 10-year-old children performed more poorly than adults but still well above chance (Overman et al., 1996).

Updating the Body in Relation to the Starting Point of a Trajectory. Path integration is a process that continuously updates the body's location relative to the starting point of a trajectory. It is a relatively primitive form of navigation, most notably characteristic of the desert ant who performs the remarkable feat of making a "beeline" to its nest, which is a featureless, pin-sized hole in the ground, at the conclusion of a long, convoluted trajectory across the desert floor in search of food (e.g., Gallistel, 1990). In principle, a path-integration problem can be solved by a single homing vector that codes and updates the straight-line distance and direction from the current location of the body to the origin of its current trajectory. Updating is a process of continuously adjusting the homing vector to compensate for the angular and linear displacements of the body with no computational requirement that a history of those displacements be retained. However, Loomis et al. (1993) demonstrated that a human path-integration process does indeed retain a representation of a path trajectory.

Human path integration relies heavily on the internal signals (i.e., proprioceptive, vestibular, motor-efferent signals) generated by the moving body. It differs from other forms of human navigation in that updating is not referenced to the external environment but is referenced instead to the point at which the body was last at rest. Despite its relatively primitive status, existing evidence suggests that humans are not particularly good at path integration (Loomis et al., 1993; Sholl, 1989; Sholl & Muehl, 2000). Typically, path integration has been tested by blindfolding participants, guiding them along a simple trajectory consisting of two or more linear segments connected by turning angles of varying magnitudes. At the end of the trajectory, participants either point to the start of the path or walk by the shortest route directly to the start point (in a two-segment trajectory, this is known as a *triangle completion task*). Human performance declines as paths are made more complex by adding more linear segments, by connecting the segments with angles that deviate from 90°, and by crossing one segment over another (Loomis et al., 1993; Sholl & Muehl, 2000).

Böök and Gärling (1980) tested whether path integration requires central processing resources by pairing a backward-counting task with a path-integration task. They found that counting backward while walking a two-segment path in a darkened room produced higher constant and variable errors in estimates of the distance and direction of the start point than did control conditions with no concurrent task. In a similar paradigm but using more complex trajectories through an underground culvert system, Lindberg and Gärling (1981) found that when participants were blindfolded during the trajectory, backward counting strongly affected accuracy, particularly for trajectories with greater numbers of path segments. Backward counting had much less of an effect in a sighted condition, and because the culverts were largely featureless, the primary difference between the sighted and nonsighted conditions was the availability of abstract optical flow in the former.[3] The apparently greater effect of backward counting in the nonsighted than the sighted condition suggests that computing angular and linear body displacements from internal motion signals is more resource demanding than computations based on internal signals plus optical flow. However, this conclusion may not be correct because even though the culverts were largely featureless, sighted walking may have revealed discrete visual cues in addition to abstract optical flow. If so, it raises

---

[3]Lindberg and Gärling (1981) reported no significant interaction between visual condition (blindfolded, sighted) and concurrent-task condition (no current task, concurrent task). However, inspection of their Figure 3 shows overlapping functions for the concurrent and no-concurrent task conditions in the sighted condition and a large separation between the concurrent and no-concurrent tasks in the blindfolded condition, suggesting that failure to find an interaction was likely due to lack of statistical power.

the possibility that a route-learning rather than a path-integration process was engaged in the sighted condition.

The interface between path integration and route learning has not been systematically studied in humans. By definition, they are completely separable processes. Path integration does not require vision, and the output of a path-integration process is knowledge of the shape of a route independent of the environmental context in which the route is embedded. Path integration enables navigators to retrace their route and to go directly from its endpoint to its start point. Route learning is highly dependent on vision, and the output of a route-learning process is a chain of stimulus-response associations specifying the correct response to make at key landmarks or choice points (e.g., turn right at the first traffic light). Thus, route knowledge is completely dependent on environmental context, and it permits limited wayfinding by describing a single trajectory through environmental space. Notably, in its most rudimentary form, route learning does not include knowledge of the shape of the trajectory connecting consecutive choice points; however, empirical evidence suggests that people do indeed acquire this knowledge and can use it to compute the euclidean relations connecting route landmarks (Thorndyke & Hayes-Roth, 1982). To summarize, it is difficult to distinguish behaviorally whether path integration, route learning, or both produce the memory traces formed during sighted walking. Failure to find effects of backward counting in a sighted condition could be because route learning requires little or no attentional resources or because path integration places less demand on attentional resources when both abstract optical flow and internal motion signals are available.

Updating the Body in Relation to an External Reference Frame. Navigation typically takes place in well-differentiated visual environments so that people can track their movement through space in relation to a rich array of visual cues. The process of monitoring one's movement in relation to a stationary framework of surrounding objects (or landmarks) is called *self-to-object updating*. There is an accumulating body of evidence suggesting that self-to-object updating is mediated by some form of visuospatial WM. One source of evidence comes from pairing self-to-object updating tasks with backward counting. When compared to people who traverse a path when not under a cognitive load, people who count backward by threes are less likely to update their location relative to remote landmarks (Smyth & Kennedy, 1982), and they are also less likely to code the euclidean relations (referring simply to "as-the-crow-flies" distance and direction connecting two landmarks) connecting landmarks on the path (Lindberg & Gärling, 1981).

In environmentally scaled space, one challenge faced by a cognitive mapping system is that the as-the-crow-flies distances and directions connecting landmarks are not perceptually specified unless landmarks co-occur in the same field of view. The greater the spatial and temporal separation between a pair of landmarks, the more complex the problem of connecting them becomes. Lindberg and Gärling (1981) hypothesized that a resource-demanding, self-to-object updating process computes the straight-line distances and directions separating landmarks. As a person moves along a trajectory, the body's location relative to a prior behaviorally relevant landmark is continuously updated by a mechanism that functions like a homing vector. When the person arrives at the next behaviorally relevant landmark on the trajectory, the homing vector specifies the straight-line distance and direction connecting the two landmarks. According to this account, building a cognitive map of a region of space is a process of building up a vector map from the output of a self-to-object updating process.

Research conducted by Lindberg and Gärling (1981) supports this account. The formation of a representation of euclidean interlandmark relations is inhibited if people count backward by threes while walking from one behaviorally relevant landmark to another along an interior route. In the Lindberg and Gärling (1981) task, participants counted backward as they walked from one landmark to the next, but at each landmark, they stopped counting and thought about where the current landmark was in relation to the other landmarks on the route. At the end of a learning phase, participants judged the euclidean distances and directions connecting all possible pairings of the route landmarks. When compared to a control group whose members did not engage in a concurrent activity, the backward-counting group showed evidence of route learning, whereas the control group showed evidence of survey learning. Route learning is behaviorally distinguished from survey learning by plotting the error in euclidean judgments as a function of the complexity of the route connecting two path landmarks. If error increases with complexity, it suggests that judgments are based on the route connecting the two landmarks, whereas if error is independent of route complexity, it suggests that judgments are based on direct knowledge of euclidean relations. A series of experiments by Sholl (1993) replicated this basic finding. In a follow-up study, Lindberg and Gärling (1983) showed that although survey learning was affected by manipulating demand on attentional resources, the mechanism(s) that produced survey knowledge appear to be engaged automatically and are not under volitional control. This conclusion was motivated by the finding that euclidean relations were judged just as accurately when learning was incidental as when it was intentional.

In a direct test of self-to-object updating, Smyth and Kennedy (1982) reported findings consistent with those reported by Lindberg and Gärling (1983) for survey-knowledge acquisition. In the Smyth and Kennedy study, participants walked from the entrance of a building along a path to an interior room in one of three conditions: an intentional condition in which participants were told that when they reached the test room, they would be asked to point in the direction of external landmarks (i.e., familiar campus landmarks outside the building); an incidental condition in which participants were simply told to walk with the experimenter to the test room; and a backward-counting condition in which participants counted backward by threes during the walk to the test room. When pointing to external landmarks, the intentional and incidental groups did not differ in the magnitude of their pointing error, which averaged about 19°. However, the backward-counting group made larger errors than the other two groups by a factor of 3 or 4, depending on the complexity of the path. Interestingly enough, all groups performed comparably when asked to describe or draw the path connecting the entrance to the test room. This latter finding is consistent with a path-integration or a route-learning process that retains a representation of the path's shape, operates independently of a self-to-object updating process, and uses few if any central processing resources during sighted walking.

A self-to-object updating process that operates outside of volitional control has also been demonstrated by Farrell and colleagues (Farrell & Robertson, 1998; Farrell & Thomson, 1998). In an ingenious variation on a perspective-taking task, participants first previewed a test space from an inspection site and were then blindfolded. In one study (Farrell & Thomson, 1998), after walking forward from the inspection site until told to stop, participants were then to ignore their linear displacement and to walk to a previewed target location as if they were still standing at the inspection location. In a second study (Farrell & Robertson, 1998), participants stood in place and rotated their body until told to stop. They were then to ignore the angular body displacement and to point to a target object as if they were still facing in the direction they had been facing during inspection. If participants were able to ignore the displacement and retrieve the location of the target from their memory of the test space as it appeared from the initial inspection site, their performance should have been as accurate as that of a control group whose location and facing direction at test was the same as at inspection. The results clearly showed that people were unable to ignore the displacement of the body, taking longer to respond and making greater errors than people in the control conditions. The inability to ignore a stimulus (in this case the internal self-motion signals produced by body movement) despite its being adventitious to do so is characteristic of a process that is automatically engaged.

Wang and Simons (1999; Simons & Wang, 1998) have tested whether people were as good at anticipating a change in self-to-object relations produced by object movement as they were at anticipating a change in self-to-object relations produced by body movement. In their change-detection task, participants previewed an array of objects on a round tabletop. The table was then obstructed from view during which time the experimenter moved a single object in the array, and the participant either moved 47° counterclockwise to a new viewing position or the table was rotated 47° clockwise. The table was then revealed, and the participant's task was to identify the object that the experimenter had moved.

In principle, movement of the body in a counterclockwise arc relative to a stationary table produces the same new view of the table as does the same amount of clockwise rotation of the table relative to the stationary body. If participants can anticipate changes in self-to-object relations, which in this context refers to the relation between each of the tabletop objects and the body, then an unanticipated change in object location (i.e., the change in object location produced by the experimenter) should be readily detectable. Change detection was better in the body rotation than the table rotation condition. In fact, body displacement produced change-detection accuracy that was similar to accuracy in the baseline condition in which both the body and the table remained stationary. Also, reminiscent of Farrell and colleagues (Farrell & Robertson, 1998; Farrell & Thomson, 1998) findings that body movement produces updating outside of volitional control, Wang and Simons (1999; Simons & Wang, 1998) have reported that when both the body and the table were displaced, the net effect of which was to produce a "new" viewpoint identical to the inspection viewpoint, change detection actually suffered. In this condition, the updating that accompanied body movement made it difficult for participants to recover what the array looked like prior to body movement.

Summary.   Behavioral evidence suggests that visuospatial WM plays a role in nonsighted path integration, the updating of self-to-object relations, and the formation of survey knowledge. It may have less of a role to play in sighted path integration or route learning, or both. Although self-to-object updating has WM requirements, it appears to be engaged automatically (i.e., outside volitional control) as the body moves through space. Moreover, the automatic monitoring of dynamic self-to-object relations is triggered by body movement and not object movement. It is notable that a nonspatial, central-executive task like backward counting disrupts visuospatial WM function, and this suggests a level of integration between executive functioning and visuospatial storage at an environmental scale similar to that observed at a figural scale of space.

WM From a Neuroscientific Perspective

The neuroscientific study of visuospatial WM for environmentally scaled space has been largely restricted to rodents. Visuospatial WM in rats was first systematically tested by Olton and colleagues (see Olton, 1977, for a review) with an eight-arm, radial-maze task. In this task, each arm of the maze is baited, and the optimal performance strategy is for the rat to visit each baited arm of the maze once so that all eight arms are visited in the first eight choices. To accomplish this, the rat must remember where it has been so that it can choose where to go next. Rats are very good at this; after a few days training, they make an average of 6.8 correct choices in their first eight choices. With each arm visited, the WM load increases and errors (i.e., revisiting an arm already visited) become more likely. Olton (1977) reported evidence suggesting that the increased likelihood of error after having made several successful choices is attributable to interference among the competing memory traces (for the locations visited) held in storage and not because of the decay of the traces over time. It is notable that the radial-arm task requires the storage of locations for longer temporal intervals than comparable tests of figural WM, consistent with a WM for environmental space that has a time scale extended to match its spatial scale.

Olton (1977) reported that lesions to any part of the hippocampal system disrupt visuospatial WM. More recently, studies have explored the role of the medial frontal cortex in visuospatial WM, which in the rat brain is the homologue of the dorsolateral prefrontal cortex in the primate brain (Kolb, 1990). Lesioning the medial prefrontal cortex produced a deficit in spatial WM tasks[4] and delayed nonmatching-to-sample (e.g., Dias & Aggleton, 2000; Granon, Vidal, Thinus-Blanc, Changeux, & Poucet, 1994; Shaw & Aggleton, 1993) and matching-to-sample tasks (e.g., Dias & Aggleton, 2000; Granon et al., 1994). In these tasks the "sample" is a single arm of a T maze that the rat visits on the sample trial. After a short delay, on the test trial the rat must either return to the sample arm (i.e., match-to-sample task) or visit the other arm (i.e., nonmatching-to-sample task). Medial prefrontal lesions also produced deficits in the online planning of spatial trajectories under challenging test conditions in a Morris Maze task (Morris, Garrud, Rawlins, & O'Keefe, 1982; Granon & Poucet, 1995). In contrast to the spatial WM deficits observed following medial prefrontal lesions, no deficits were observed in spatial reference memory referring to information constant across trials (e.g., Granon et al., 1994) or visual WM (Shaw & Aggleton, 1993).

To our knowledge, there has been little neuroscientific analysis of the neural substrates for environmental visuospatial WM in primates. Olton, Wible, and Markowska (1992) reported an experiment conducted on monkeys that tested the effects of fornix lesions on the performance of a delayed nonmatching-to-sample task conducted in a T maze scaled to size for monkeys. Lesioned monkeys showed a deficit on the task, but the deficit could be attributed to either a disruption of WM or a disruption in the encoding of place information.

Summary. Lesion studies of rats indicate that the hippocampus and the prefrontal cortex have a role to play in WM for locations in environmental space. Thus, the rat prefrontal cortex may play a role in visuospatial WM at

---

[4]The size of the prefrontal lesion may be an important determinant of the extent and duration of the deficit, although the evidence is mixed. Some have found deficits only when lesions are large enough to include both the dorsal anterior cingulate and the prelimbic area (Dias & Aggleton, 2000; Shaw & Aggleton, 1993), whereas others have reported deficits following lesions restricted to the prelimbic area (Granon & Poucet, 1995; Granon et al., 1994).

an environmental scale similar to the role that the primate prefrontal cortex plays in WM at a figural space. However, unlike the monkey prefrontal cortex, single-cell recordings in the rat prefrontal cortex during radial-arm maze tasks and delayed nonmatching-to-sample tasks have failed to reveal cells with "spatially dependent delay activity that might mediate WM for spatial locations" (Jung, Qin, McNaughton, & Barnes, 1998, p. 437). At this point, it is still too early to say whether the neural systems underlying visuospatial WM are organized similarly or differently in rodents and primates.

We have stressed the importance of scale when studying visuospatial WM within a single species; however, the issue is also important when making comparisons between species. Comparative studies of WM functions and structures are important for determining the viability of a single mammalian model of visuospatial WM (Olton et al., 1992). When comparing findings across species to test the validity of a single underlying organizational structure, it is important to take into account the fact that behavioral space is scaled relative to body size. Following Montello (1993), we have made the case that for a single body size, there are functionally distinct scales of space that vary in spatial-temporal extendedness. It goes without saying that average body size varies across species, as will the absolute size of the different functional scales of space for each species. At this time, the bulk of the research on monkeys has been done at a figural scale of space and the bulk of the research on rats has been done at an environmental scale of space, confounding species with functional spatial scale. Despite the technical difficulties, it is important that future comparative research use similar behavioral tests of visuospatial WM at similar functional scales of space.

THE RELATION BETWEEN VISUOSPATIAL WM
FOR FIGURAL AND ENVIRONMENTAL SPACE

We restrict our review in this section to research conducted with humans. As we pointed out earlier, it is not possible to compare directly the cognitive properties characteristic of a WM system for figural space to those characteristic of a WM system for environmental space because research on WM for environmental space is not sufficiently evolved at this time. Aside from the radial-arm maze developed to test spatial WM in rats (Olton, 1977) and adapted to test the development of spatial WM in children (e.g., Foremen et al., 1990; Lehnung et al., 1998; Overman et al., 1996), there are no environmentally scaled tests of visuospatial WM span. Tasks with environmental visuospatial WM requirements are likely to develop as cognitive models of environmentally scaled visuospatial WM are introduced. For now, we adopt the indirect approach of reviewing several correlational studies of the relation between psychometric tests of figural spatial ability and measures of large-scale spatial knowledge.

None of the studies we review below included WM span tasks in their test batteries. However in their latent variable analysis of visuospatial WM, Miyake et al. (2001) showed that the correlations (ranging from .60 to .71) between the spatial ability factors (spatial visualization, spatial relations, and perceptual speed) could be completely accounted for by their underlying correlations with the WM variables: a domain-free central executive and a WM–STM visuospatial storage system. This finding has an important implication in this context. If tasks measuring figural spatial ability and large-scale environmental knowledge are moderately to highly correlated with one another, it leaves open the possibility that the correlations are attributable to a shared cognitive substrate such as a common WM system. However, if the correlations between tests of figural spatial ability and large-scale environmental knowledge are weak, then a shared visuospatial WM substrate becomes less likely.

In factor analytic studies, tests of figural spatial ability and tests of large-scale environmental knowledge have been found consistently to load on separate factors (Allen, Kirasic, Dobson, Long, & Beck, 1996; Lorenz & Neisser, 1986; Pearson & Ialongo, 1986), with Pearson and Ialongo[5] having reported a .37 correlation between the two factors. Large-scale environmental knowledge is often measured by determining how accurately people can localize (point to) unseen landmarks from either an actual or imagined point of view. Reported first-order correlations between measures of pointing accuracy and psychometric tests of figural spatial ability have ranged from –.01 to –.37, reflecting lower pointing error associated with higher test performance (Allen et al., 1996; Bryant, 1982; Waller, 2000). Together, these studies suggest a fairly low correlation between figural and environmental cognitive tasks. Although not reporting the correlation between their spatial ability and environmental variables, Hegarty and colleagues (Hegarty, Richardson, Montello, Lovelace & Subbiah, 2002) found that self-reported sense of direction, which in their study measured people's self-attributions about a number of different environmental spatial skills, correlated with measures of environmental knowledge but not with tests of figural spatial ability.

In a path analytic study, Allen et al. (1996) reported that a variable they labeled *spatial-sequential memory* mediated the relation between a figural spatial ability variable and an environmental knowledge variable. Their environmental-knowledge variable measured route knowledge acquired from a guided walk through an unfamiliar urban environment, and the spatial-sequential variable measured people's ability to learn a complex path through a six-by-six unit matrix printed on paper over a series of

---

[5]For their environmental learning task, Pearson and Ialongo (1986) simulated a walk through an urban environment. We include their study here because like real environmental learning, their simulated walk required the integration of spatial knowledge across separate fields of view and extended temporal intervals.

study-test trials. Both the environmental-knowledge variable and the spa-tial-sequential variable measured people's ability to retain in LTM a tempo-rally ordered sequence of visuospatial elements but at different degrees of spatiotemporal extendedness. Whether or not a single visuospatial WM system is the cognitive substrate accounting for the mediating role played by spatial-sequential memory is a topic for future research. Interestingly, people's knowledge of the euclidean distances and directions connecting the landmarks experienced during the guided walk was not linked either directly or indirectly to the spatial-ability variable.

Summary.   At present, there is no research that explores directly the rela-tion between visuospatial WM for figural and environmental space. A re-view of correlational studies of figural and environmental spatial ability suggests at best a moderate relation between the two types of ability. The extent to which the relation is mediated by a single WM architecture is a topic for future research.

CONCLUSIONS

In part because different issues have motivated research on WM at figural and environmental scales of space, there is little intersection between the two research domains at either a cognitive or neuroscientific level of analy-sis. Figural visuospatial WM has been studied extensively, and as a conse-quence, a great deal is known about its cognitive properties and its neural substrate. Despite the evidence that environmental visuospatial WM is likely to have an important role to play both in the acquisition of survey knowledge and in spatial navigation, little is known about its properties. Even so, there are a few interesting parallels between WM functioning at figural and environmental scales of space.

One parallel has to do with the role of a domain-general, central-execu-tive system in visuospatial WM. Both psychometric (Miyake et al., 2001) and interference (Smyth & Pelky, 1992) approaches indicate that central-ex-ecutive processes and visuospatial storage capacity are highly integrated at a figural scale of space. It is therefore of interest that a secondary task that draws heavily on executive functioning—backward counting—disrupts spatial acquisition and orientation in environmental space, suggesting a similar degree of integration between domain-general executive function-ing and domain-specific storage at an environmental scale. That said, to better understand the domain-specific properties of short-term storage at an environmental scale, future research should test the extent to which the types of secondary tasks that disrupt WM function in figural space also dis-rupt WM function in environmental space. However, prior to conducting that kind of comparative study, it is important to develop an environmental STM–WM span task comparable to existing figural STM–WM span tasks. In this regard, it is interesting to note a certain irony. Several measures of

STM–WM span have been developed for figural space, and although there is considerable clarity about how the span tasks relate to cognitive measures of psychometric visuospatial ability, there is less clarity about the role of figural visuospatial STM–WM span in everyday cognition. In contrast, although there is some clarity about the role environmental WM plays in everyday cognition, there is less clarity about how to measure it.

Another parallel relates to the dissociation between object and spatial WM in figural space. Although to our knowledge no research has been done on this phenomenon at an environmental scale, personal experience suggests that such a dissociation exists. Consider the following and see if it doesn't ring true. You are at home or at work and you leave one room and walk to another to retrieve Object X, which you need to complete Task Y. You arrive at the place where Object X is located, but you suddenly cannot remember what it was that you needed. Or the complementary dissociation occurs. You are working with Object X to complete Task Y. You put Object X down and momentarily turn your attention to something else. Moments later you cannot remember where you put Object X. These anecdotal accounts are consistent with a dissociation between WM for objects and locations in environmentally scaled space and a selective failure in one system but not the other. The challenge, of course, is to bring the kinds of dissociations we recognize as occurring in everyday cognition under laboratory control.

In this chapter, we have provided a selective review of a vast literature on visuospatial WM at a figural scale of space and a more comprehensive review of a limited literature on WM at an environmental scale of space. We propose that a comprehensive account of visuospatial WM must take into account its cognitive and neural functioning at different degrees of visuospatial extendedness. Significant progress toward this objective will require cross-fertilization between the figural and environmental domains of inquiry.

REFERENCES

Allen, G., Kirasic, K. C., Dobson, S. H., Long, R. G., & Beck, S. (1996). Predicting environmental learning from spatial abilities: An indirect route. *Intelligence, 22,* 327–355.

Atkinson, R. C., & Shiffrin, R. M. (1971). The control of short-term memory. *Scientific American, 225,* 82–90.

Awh, E., & Jonides, J. (2001). Overlapping mechanisms of attention and spatial working memory. *Trends in Cognitive Sciences, 5,* 119–126.

Awh, E., Jonides, J., & Reuter-Lorenz, P. A. (1998). Rehearsal in spatial working memory. *Journal of Experimental Psychology: Human Perception and Performance, 24,* 780–790.

Baddeley, A. D. (1986). *Working memory.* Oxford, England: Clarendon.

Baddeley, A. D., & Hitch, G. J. (1974). Working memory. In G. Bower (Ed.), *The psychology of learning and motivation* (pp. 47–90). New York: Academic.

Baddeley, A. D., & Lieberman, K. (1980). Spatial working memory. In R. S. Nickerson (Ed.), *Attention and performance VIII* (pp. 521–539). Hillsdale, NJ: Lawrence Erlbaum Associates, Inc.

Baddeley, A. D., & Logie, R. H. (1999). Working memory: The multi-component model. In A. Miyake & P. Shah (Eds.), *Models of working memory: Mechanisms of active maintenance and executive control* (pp. 28–61). Cambridge, England: Cambridge University Press.

Böök, A., & Gärling, T. (1980). Processing of information about location during locomotion: Effects of a concurrent task and locomotion patterns. *Scandinavian Journal of Psychology, 21,* 185–192.

Bor, D., Duncan, J., & Owen, A. M. (2001). The role of spatial configuration in tests of working memory explored with functional neuroimaging. *Scandinavian Journal of Psychology, 42,* 217–224.

Brooks, L. R. (1967). The suppression of visualization by reading. *Quarterly Journal of Experimental Psychology, 19,* 289–299.

Brooks, L. R. (1968). Spatial and verbal components in the act of recall. *Canadian Journal of Psychology, 22,* 349–368.

Bryant, K. J. (1982). Personality correlates of sense of direction and geographical orientation. *Journal of Personality and Social Psychology, 43,* 1318–1324.

Corsi, P. M. (1973). Human memory and the medial temporal region of the brain. *Dissertation Abstracts International, 34,* 891.

Courtney, S. M., Petit, L., Maisog, J. M., Ungerleider, L. G., & Haxby, J. V. (1998, February 27). An area specialized for spatial working memory in human frontal cortex. *Science, 279,* 1347–1351.

Courtney, S. M., Ungerleider, L. G., Keil, K., & Haxby, J. V. (1996). Object and spatial visual working memory activate separate neural systems in human cortex. *Cerebral Cortex, 6,* 39–49.

Daneman, M., & Carpenter, P. A. (1980). Individual differences in working memory and reading. *Journal of Verbal Learning and Verbal Behavior, 19,* 450–466.

Daneman, M., & Merikle, P. M. (1996). Working memory and language comprehension: A meta-analysis. *Psychonomic Bulletin & Review, 3,* 422–433.

Della Sala, S., Gray, C., Baddeley, A. D., Allamano, N., & Wilson, L. (1999). Pattern span: A tool for unwelding visuo-spatial memory. *Neuropsychologia, 37,* 1189–1199.

D'Esposito, M., Aguirre, G. K., Zarahn, E., Ballard, D., Shin, R. K., & Lease, J. (1998). Functional MRI studies of spatial and nonspatial working memory. *Cognitive Brain Research, 7,* 1–13.

DeYoe, E. A. & Van Essen, D. C. (1988). Concurrent processing streams in monkey visual cortex. *Trends in Neuroscience, 11,* 219–226.

Dias, R., & Aggleton, J. P. (2000). Effects of excitotoxic prefrontal lesions on acquisition of nonmatching- and matching-to-place in the T-maze: Evidence for intact spatial working memory but differential involvement of the prelimbic-infralimbic and anterior cingulate cortices in providing behavioral flexibility. *European Journal of Neuroscience, 12,* 1–12.

Engle, R. W., Tuholski, S. W., Laughlin, J. E., & Conway, A. R. A. (1999). Working memory, short-term memory, and general fluid intelligence: A latent variable approach. *Journal of Experimental Psychology: General, 128,* 309–331.

Evans, F. J., & Graham, C. (1980). Subjective random number generation and attention deployment during acquisition and overlearning of a motor skill. *Bulletin of the Psychonomic Society, 15,* 391–394.

Farrell, M. J., & Robertson, I. H. (1998). Mental rotation and the automatic updating of body-centered spatial relationships. *Journal of Experimental Psychology: Learning, Memory, and Cognition, 24,* 227–233.

Farrell, M. J., & Thomson, J. A. (1998). Automatic spatial updating during locomotion without vision. *The Quarterly Journal of Experimental Psychology, 51A,* 637–654.

Foreman, N., Warry, R., & Murray, P. (1990). Development of reference and working spatial memory in preschool children. *The Journal of General Psychology, 117,* 267–276.

Funahashi, S., Bruce, C. J., & Goldman-Rakic, P. S. (1989). Mnemonic coding of visual space in the monkey's dorsolateral prefrontal cortex. *Journal of Neurophysiology, 61,* 331–349.

Gallistel, C. R. (1990). *The organization of learning.* Cambridge, MA, MIT Press.

Goldman-Rakic, P. S. (1987). Circuitry of primate prefrontal cortex and regulation of behavior by representational memory. In F. Plum & U. Mountcastle (Eds.), *Handbook of Physiology* (Vol. 5, pp. 373–417). Washington, DC: The American Physiological Society.

Goodale, M. A., & Milner, A. D. (1992). Separate visual pathways for perception and action. *Trends in Neuroscience, 15,* 20–25.

Granon, S., & Poucet, B. (1995). Medial prefrontal lesions in the rat and spatial navigation: Evidence for impaired planning. *Behavioral Neuroscience, 109,* 474–484.

Granon, S., Vidal, C., Thinus-Blanc, C., Changeux, J. P., & Poucet, B. (1994). Working memory, response selection, and effortful processing in rats with medial prefrontal lesions. *Behavioral Neuroscience, 108,* 883–891.

Haxby, J. V., Grady, C. L., Horwitz, B., Ungerleider, L. G., Mishkin, M., Carson, R. E., Herscovitch, P., Schapiro, M. B., & Rapoport, S. I. (1991, March 1). Dissociation of object and spatial visual processing pathways in human extrastriate cortex. *Proceedings of the National Academy of Science, USA, 88,* 1621–1625.

Haxby, J. V., Horwitz, B., Ungerleider, L. G., Maisog, J. M., Pietrini, P., & Grady, C. L. (1994). The functional organization of human extrastriate cortex: A PET-rCBF study of selective attention to faces and location. *Journal of Neuroscience, 14,* 6336–6353.

Hegarty, M., Richardson, A. E., Montello, D. R., Lovelace K., & Subbiah, I. (2002). Development of a self-report measure of environmental spatial ability. *Intelligence, 30,* 425–448.

Jonides, J., Smith, E. E., Koeppe, R. A., Awh, E., Minoshima, S., & Mintun, M. A. (1993, June 17). Spatial working memory in humans as revealed by PET. *Nature, 363,* 623–625.

Jung, M. W., Qin, Y., NcNaughton, B., & Barnes, C. A. (1998). Firing characteristics of deep layer neurons in prefrontal cortex in rats performing spatial working memory tasks. *Cerebral Cortex, 8,* 437–450.

Kolb, B. (1990). Prefrontal cortex. In B. Kolb & R. C. Tees (Eds.), *The cerebral cortex of the rat* (pp. 437–458). Cambridge, MA: MIT Press.

Kosslyn, S. M. (1983). *Ghosts in the mind's machine.* New York: Norton.

Lee, A. C. H., Manes, F. F., Bor, D., Robbins, T. W., & Owen, A. M. (2000). Dissociating planning and working memory processes within the human lateral frontal cortex. *Society for Neuroscience Abstracts, 749,* 6.

Lehnung, M., Leplow, B., Friege, L., Herzog, A., Ferstl, R., & Mehdorn, M. (1998). Development of spatial memory and spatial orientation in preschoolers and primary school children. *British Journal of Psychology, 89,* 463–480.

Levine, D. N., Warach, J., & Farah, M. (1985). Two visual systems in mental imagery: Dissociation of "what" and "where" in imagery disorders due to bilateral posterior cerebral lesions. *Neurology, 35,* 1010–1019.

Levy, R., Friedman, H. R., Davachi, L., & Goldman-Rakic, P. S. (1997). Differential activation of the caudate nucleus in primates performing spatial and nonspatial working memory task. *The Journal of Neuroscience, 17,* 3870–3882.

Levy, R., & Goldman-Rakic, P. S. (1999). Association of storage and processing functions in the dorsolateral prefrontal cortex of the nonhuman primate. *Journal of Neuroscience, 19,* 5149–5158.

Lindberg, E., & Gärling, T. (1981). Acquisition of locational information about reference points during blindfolded and sighted locomotion: Effects of a concurrent task and locomotion paths. *Scandinavian Journal of Psychology, 22,* 101–108.

Lindberg, E., & Gärling, T. (1983). Acquisition of different types of locational information in cognitive maps: Automatic or effortful processing? *Psychological Research, 45,* 19–38.

Logie, R. H. (1995). *Visuo-spatial working memory.* Hillsdale, NJ: Lawrence Erlbaum Associates, Inc.

Logie, R. H., & Marchetti, C. (1991). Visuo-spatial working memory: Visual, spatial or central executive? In R. H. Logie & M. Denis (Eds.), *Mental images in human cognition* (pp. 105–115). Amsterdam: Elsevier.

Logie, R. H., & Pearson, D. G. (1997). The inner eye and the inner scribe of visuo-spatial working memory: Evidence from developmental fractionation. *European Journal of Cognitive Psychology, 9,* 241–257.

Loomis, J. M., Klatzky, R. L., Gollege, R. G., Cincinelli, J. G., Pellegrino, J. W., & Fry, P. A. (1993). Nonvisual navigation by blind and sighted: Assessment of path integration ability. *Journal of Experimental Psychology: General, 122,* 73–91.

Lorenz, C. A., & Neisser, U. (1986). *Ecological and psychometric dimensions of spatial ability* (Emory Cognition Project Rpt. No. 10). Atlanta, GA: Emory University, Department of Psychology.

Luciana, M., & Collins, P. F. (1997). Dopaminergic modulation of working memory for spatial but not object cues in normal humans. *Journal of Cognitive Neuroscience, 9,* 330–347.

Luciana, M., Collins, P. F., & Depue, R. A. (1998). Opposing roles for dopamine and serotonin in the modulation of human spatial working memory functions. *Cerebral Cortex, 8,* 218–226.

Miyake, A., Friedman, N. P., Rettinger, D. A., Shah, P., & Hegarty, M. (2001). How are visuospatial working memory, executive functioning, and spatial abilities related? A latent-variable analysis. *Journal of Experimental Psychology: General, 130,* 621–640.

Miyake, A., & Shah, P. (Eds.). (1999). *Models of working memory: Mechanisms of active maintenance and executive control.* Cambridge, England: Cambridge University Press.

Montello, D. R. (1993). Scale and multiple psychologies of space. In A. U. Frank & I. Campari (Eds.), *Spatial information theory: A theoretical basis for GIS* (pp. 312–321). Berlin, Germany: Springer-Verlag Lecture Notes in Computer Science 716.

Morris, R. G., Garrud, P., Rawlins, J. N., & O'Keefe, J. (1982). Place navigation impaired in rats with hippocampal lesions. *Nature, 297,* 681–683.

Olton, D. S. (1977, June). Spatial memory. *Scientific American, 236,* 82–98.

Olton, D. S., Wible, C. G., & Markowska, A. L. (1992). A comparative analysis of the role of the hippocampal system in memory. In R. G. Lister & H. J. Weingartner (Eds.), *Perspectives on cognitive neuroscience* (pp. 186–196). New York: Oxford University Press.

Overman, W. H., Pate, B. J., Moore, K., & Peuster, A. (1996). Ontogeny of place learning in children as measured in the radial arm maze, Morris search task, and open field task. *Behavioral Neuroscience, 110,* 1205–1228.

Owen, A. M., Evans, A. C., & Petrides, M. (1996). Evidence for a two-stage model of spatial working memory processing within the lateral frontal cortex: A positron emission tomography study. *Cerebral Cortex, 6,* 31–38.

Owen, A. M., Stern, C. E., Look, R. B., Tracey, I., Rosen, B. R., & Petrides, M. (1998, June 23). Functional organization of spatial and nonspatial working memory processing within the human lateral frontal cortex. *Proceedings of the National Academy of Science, USA, 95,* 7721–7726.

Pearson, J. L., & Ialongo, N. S. (1986). The relationship between spatial ability and environmental knowledge. *Journal of Environmental Psychology, 6,* 299–304.

Petrides, M. (1994). Frontal lobes and working memory: Evidence from investigations of the effects of cortical excisions in nonhuman primates. In F. Boller & J. Grafman (Eds.), *Handbook of neuropsychology* (Vol. 9, pp. 59–82). Amsterdam: Elsevier.

Petrides, M. (2000). The role of the mid-dorsolateral prefrontal cortex in working memory. *Experimental Brain Research, 133,* 44–54.

Petrides, M., & Pandya, D. N. (1994). Comparative architectonic analysis of the human and the macaque frontal cortex. In F. Boller & J. Grafman (Eds.), *Handbook of neuropsychology* (Vol. 9, pp. 17–58). Amsterdam: Elsevier.

Pickering, S. J., Gathercole, S. E., Hall, M., & Lloyd, S. A. (2001). Development of memory for pattern and path: Further evidence for the fractionation of visuo-spatial memory. *The Quarterly Journal of Experimental Psychology, 54A,* 397–420.

Posner, M. I., Snyder, C. R. R., & Davidson, B. J. (1980). Attention and the detection of signals. *Journal of Experimental Psychology: General, 109,* 160–174.

Postle, B. R., & D'Esposito, M. (1999). "What"-Then-"Where" in visual working memory: An event-related fMRI study. *Journal of Cognitive Neuroscience, 11,* 585–597.

Quinn, J. G. (1994). Towards a clarification of spatial processing. *The Quarterly Journal of Experimental Psychology, 47A,* 465–480.

Quinn, J. G., & McConnell, J. (1996). Irrelevant pictures in visual working memory. *Quarterly Journal of Experimental Psychology: Human Experimental Psychology. Special Issue: Working Memory, 49A,* 200–215.

Quinn, J. G., & Ralston, G. E. (1986). Movement and attention in visual working memory. *The Quarterly Journal of Experimental Psychology, 38A,* 689–703.

Rao, S. C., Rainer, G., & Miller, E. K. (1997, May). Integration of what and where in the primate prefrontal cortex. *Science, 276,* 821–824.

Salway, A. F. S., & Logie, R. H. (1995). Visuo-spatial working memory, movement control and executive demands. *British Journal of Psychology, 86,* 253–269.

Shah, P., & Miyake, A. (1996). The separability of working memory resources for spatial thinking and language processing: An individual differences approach. *Journal of Experimental Psychology: General, 125,* 4–27.

Shaw, C., & Aggleton, J. P. (1993). The effects of fornix and medial prefrontal lesions on delayed non-matching-to-sample by rats. *Behavioural Brain Research, 54,* 91–102.

Sholl, M. J. (1989). The relation between horizontality, rod-and-frame, and vestibular navigational performance. *Journal of Experimental Psychology: Learning, Memory & Cognition, 15,* 110–125.

Sholl, M. J. (1993, November). *The effect of restricting vision to the central field on spatial knowledge acquisition.* Paper presented at the Annual Meeting of the Psychonomic Society, Washington, DC.

Sholl, M. J., & Muehl, K. (2000, November). *The contribution of idiothetic and visual information to sense of direction.* Paper presented at the Annual Meeting of the Psychonomic Society, New Orleans, LA.

Simon, H. A. (1975). The functional equivalence of problem solving skills. *Cognitive Psychology, 7,* 268–288.

Simons, D. J., & Wang, R. F. (1998). Perceiving real-world viewpoint changes. *Psychological Science, 9,* 315–320.

Smith, E. E., Jonides J., & Koeppe, R. A. (1996). Dissociating verbal and spatial working memory using PET. *Cerebral Cortex, 6,* 11–20.

Smith, E. E., Jonides, J., Koeppe, R. A., Awh, E., Schumacher, E. H., & Minoshima, S. (1995). Spatial versus object working memory: PET investigations. *Journal of Cognitive Neuroscience, 7,* 337–356.

Smyth, M. M. (1996). Interference with rehearsal in spatial working memory in the absence of eye movements. *The Quarterly Journal of Experimental Psychology, 49A,* 940–949.

Smyth, M. M., & Kennedy, J. E. (1982). Orientation and spatial representation within multiple frames of reference. *Bristish Journal of Psychology, 73,* 527–535.

Smyth, M. M., Pearson, N. A., & Pendleton, L. R. (1988). Movement and working memory: Patterns and positions in space. *The Quarterly Journal of Experimental Psychology, 40A,* 497–514.

Smyth, M. M., & Pelky, P. L. (1992). Short-term retention of spatial information. *British Journal of Psychology, 83,* 359–374.

Smyth, M. M., & Pendleton, L. R. (1989). Working memory for movements. *The Quarterly Journal of Experimental Psychology, 41A,* 235–250.

Smyth, M. M., & Scholey, K. A. (1994). Characteristics of spatial memory span: Is there an analogy to the word length effect, based on movement time? *The Quarterly Journal of Experimental Psychology, 47A,* 91–117.

Smyth, M. M., & Scholey, K. A.. (1996). Serial order in spatial immediate memory. *The Quarterly Journal of Experimental Psychology, 49A,* 159–177.

Stern, C. E., Owen, A. M., Tracey, I., Look, R. B., Rosen, B. R., & Petrides, M. (2000). Activity in ventrolateral and mid-dorsolateral prefrontal cortex during nonspatial visual working memory processing: Evidence from functional magnetic resonance imaging. *NeuroImage, 11,* 329–399.

Thorndyke, P. W., & Hayes-Roth, B. (1982). Differences in spatial knowledge acquired from maps and navigation. *Cognitive Psychology, 14,* 560–589.

Tresch, M. C., Sinnamon, H. R., & Seamon, J. G. (1993). Double dissociations of spatial and object visual memory: Evidence from selective interference in intact human subjects. *Neuropsychologia, 31,* 211–219.

Ungerleider, L. G., Courtney, S. M., & Haxby, J. V. (1998, February 3). A neural system for human visual working memory. *Proceedings of the National Academy of Science, USA, 95,* 883–890.

Ungerleider, L. G., & Mishkin, M. (1982). Two cortical visual systems. In D. J. Ingle, M. A. Goodale, & R. J. W. Mansfield (Eds.), *Analysis of visual behaviour* (pp. 549–586). Cambridge, MA: MIT Press.

Waller, D. (2000). Individual differences in spatial learning from computer-simulated environments. *Journal of Experimental Psychology: Applied, 6,* 307–321.

Wang, R. F., & Simons, D. J. (1999). Active and passive scene recognition across views. *Cognition, 70,* 191–210.

Wilson, A. W., Seamas, P. O., Scalaidhe, O., & Goldman-Rakic, P. S. (1993, June). Dissociation of object and spatial processing domains in primate prefrontal cortex. *Science, 260,* 1955–1958.

Zald, D. H., & Iacono, W. G. (1998). The development of spatial working memory abilities. *Developmental Neuropsychology, 14,* 563–578.

Temporal Memory for Locations:

On the Coding of Spatiotemporal Information in Children and Adults

Ruth Schumann-Hengsteler, Martin Strobl, and Christof Zoelch
Katholische Universität Eichstätt

Our work is focused on the development of a specific type of temporary spatial memory, specifically, children's memory for locations in a small-scale environment. Using the working memory model of Baddeley and Hitch (1974; Baddeley, 1986) as our theoretical base, we have addressed the following general questions: What role do different types of mental representations play in children's memory for location at different ages, and at what age do nonverbal strategies emerge for maintaining location information for a short period of time? In particular, we are concerned with when and how relations among several individual locations are combined into a pattern. On one hand, this combination might be configurational, connoting a static representation. From this point of view, the critical issue is the extent to which observers are capable of proceeding "beyond the information given" to connect successively perceived spatial information and integrate it into a stable constellation through the use of mental imagery. On the other hand, the combination just mentioned might be sequential, connoting a dynamic representation. From this perspective, the critical issue is an observer's ability to link individual locations step-by-step into an imagined path that could be mentally scanned repeatedly by means of a rehearsal-like process.

In this chapter, we first describe evidence concerning the distinction between coding locations alone versus coding associations between items and their locations. Then, we present results showing that even younger children are able to combine information concerning individual locations into static mental configurations (Gestalten). Finally, we discuss data from a series of studies with the Corsi block task (Corsi, 1972) showing the gradual emergence of children's strategic use of spatiotemporal information when coding a series of positions. On the whole, our general experimental strategy is not directed toward a demonstration of age differences per se, but we want to examine age-specific performance patterns that will allow inferences about the use of specific strategies or modes of processing.

CODING SINGLE LOCATIONS IN TEMPORARY MEMORY: THEORETICAL CONSIDERATIONS

The coding and internal representation of the locations of objects is a central aspect of visuospatial working memory. As Logie (1995) stated, "One way in which to think of the term spatial is as a reference to the location of items in space and the geometric relationships between those items. Visual information might then refer to properties of those items such as their shape, color, and brightness (pp. 77–78)."

When we consider the matter of coding spatial location, our focus is on temporary memory. Thus, we are not concerned with issues such as whether spatial representations are coded or formatted in long-term memory as propositions or images (Anderson, 1978; Kosslyn, 1980; Pylyshyn, 1981; Zimmer, 1992). Rather, our attention is focused on the information necessary to maintain memory for one or more object locations for a short time. Information-processing accounts typically involve one of three general assumptions—sometimes explicit, often implicit—about such memory: (a) spatial information specifies location as an absolute property of individual objects; (b) spatial information specifies a connection between two objects, that is, a relation; or (c) spatial information specifies a pattern created by a set of individual locations.

Kahneman, Treisman, and Gibbs' (1992) approach, for example, incorporates the first assumption. They posited representational object files in which spatial location is coded as one of several characteristics of an object. A different but very influential model was offered by Kosslyn, Van Kleeck, and Kirby (1990), who proposed two different means of coding location. For one system, they conceptualized a visual buffer, analogous to a computer screen, as a representational surface medium wherein relevant locations are coded in a coordinate framework. As a separate system, Kosslyn et al. (1990) postulated a less exact alternative involving categorical coding of a location in relation to a reference frame. This way of coding location suggests relational concepts such as the topological representation of space described by Piaget and Inhelder (1948/1975; for a critical review, see Huttenlocher & Newcombe, 1984) or the categorical coding of single locations in relation to so-called anchors introduced in Newcombe and Huttenlocher's (2000; Huttenlocher, Newcombe, & Sandberg, 1994) hierarchical coding model.

In addition, spatial information can be represented as a constellation of locations and accordingly can be "chunked", that is, individual positions can be linked to form a pattern and that pattern can be processed as a whole. However, such a pattern need not be represented only as a static constellation; it can also be represented as a dynamic spatiotemporal sequence. This fact brings to mind the application of different strategies for memorizing visuospatial information. In particular, it suggests a form of visuospatial rehearsal parallel to the phonologically based rehearsal of speech-related information. Using visuospatial rehearsal, an observer could memorize multiple locations as a dynamic sequence of visual scanning movements with a path-like character (see, e.g., Logie, 1989; Quinn, 1991).

Our approach to studying temporary spatiotemporal memory, and especially this distinction between static and dynamic spatial patterns, leads directly to consideration of a model of working memory as proposed by Baddeley and Hitch (1974; Baddeley, 1986) and further specified with respect to visual-spatial processing by Logie (1995). According to this model, the working memory system consists of a central executive (CE) and at least two additional subsystems, specifically the "phonological loop" (PL) and the "visuo-spatial sketchpad" (VSSP). The central executive is responsible for controlling ongoing processing (Baddeley, 1996); the phonological loop maintains acoustically based information temporarily (Gathercole & Baddeley, 1993; Gathercole & Hitch, 1993); and the visuo-spatial sketchpad (VSSP) maintains visual and spatial information, either directly perceived or internally generated by mental imagery, for a brief period of time. In his specification of the VSSP, Logie (1995) differentiated two further subcomponents, the "visual cache" for static visual information about the appearance of objects and the "inner scribe" for representing dynamic spatial information. Furthermore, the inner scribe might work as a tool for maintaining visuospatial information during additional processing, just as the PL functions to maintain sound-based information in the service of more complex cognitive activity.

This approach to working memory is not designed specifically to reflect or explain age-related changes in cognitive performance, and indeed R. Logie (personal communication, June 1999) himself mentioned that his model is not to be considered a developmental one. Nevertheless, we argue that the conceptual distinction between static and dynamic aspects of spatial information processing is of interest from a developmental point of view, particularly because of its implications for the development of strategic behavior.

THE DISTINCTION BETWEEN OBJECT-LOCATION
ASSOCIATIONS AND PURE LOCATION INFORMATION

First of all, we point to an empirically (and too often also theoretically) neglected consideration with regard to memory for locations. Particularly in developmental studies, locations are often investigated as features of objects. Hence, it is not locations themselves that have to be maintained in memory but the positions of specific objects in a matrix. The memory game "Concentration" serves as an example. In this game, children select pairs of locations from a matrix to reveal matching pairs of objects. Thus, the memory requirement is not the locations themselves but the association between objects and their positions (Schumann-Hengsteler, 1996a, 1996b). However, these are quite different task demands compared to the maintenance of spatial information per se.

Schumann-Hengsteler (1992) used a picture reconstruction task with children to distinguish empirically object-location memory from location memory per se. A similar distinction was more recently made by Postma and De Haan (1996) in experimental work with adults (see also Postma, Kessels, & van Asselen, chap. 7, this volume). The picture reconstruction task (Schumann-Hengsteler, 1992) consists of a picture-like arrangement of several line-drawn items (e.g., house, child, car, tree). The amount of information varies dependent on the number of items per picture (in her studies four to seven items). Presentation time corresponds to the amount of information. After removing the display, the child was asked to reconstruct the previously seen picture on an empty sheet of paper of the same size as the original display. Children had to first select the appropriate objects out of 21 alternatives and second place them in such a way as to make the same picture again. In short, the task involves a brief simultaneous presentation of a scene portrayed in line drawings followed by a reconstruction task. In a study (Schumann-Hengsteler, 1992) with 5-, 8-, and 10-year-olds, there was a clear age-dependent increase of performance with respect to memory for the object-location associations. The older the children, the more correct placement of objects. However, if one took into account the number of locations remembered correctly whether or not the correct objects were matched with them, then the age effect disappeared. If one considers only the number of correct locations selected, 5-, 8-, and 10-year-old children did not differ. Although younger children tended to place more objects in incorrect locations compared to older children, they did not select more incorrect locations. In a second study (Schumann-Hengsteler, 1992), the same age trend emerged for 4-year-olds in contrast to 6-year-olds.

We interpret this result as indicating a relatively weak coding of object-location associations in younger children. At the same time, these children seem to use a kind of brief, fuzzy representation of filled and unfilled space to retain information concerning locations per se in the picture reconstruction task. Additionally, we take these results as strong evidence in favor of distinguishing between the development of object-location memory (i.e., the ability to match a set of objects with a set of locations) and the development of memory for pure location (i.e., the ability to remember a set of locations).

Another line of results points toward the same conclusions, but it sheds more light on the type of encoding children of different ages use for positional information. In these studies, a more schematic version of the picture reconstruction task was used consisting again of four to seven familiar, uniform, line-drawn objects (Schumann-Hengsteler, 1995). However, in this instance, the objects were not arranged into a scene. If the robust memory for locations in younger children is based on a rather fuzzy internal representation of the static whole-frame pattern of filled and unfilled space, then they should benefit from the simultaneous presentation of the whole stimulus array. In contrast, a very general representation of the frame as a whole would be more difficult to form if the array were experienced piecemeal. Thus, younger children's memory for locations should be impaired with serial presentation of the same stimulus.

Contrary to this expectation, results from a study involving 6-, 8-, and 10-year-old children (Schumann-Hengsteler, 1995) failed to show impaired performance with serial in comparison to simultaneous presentation (Fig. 5.1), despite the fact that simultaneous presentation allowed the direct perception of relational information between objects (i.e., the entire constellation). The lack of benefit for younger children contradicted the preference for analogue internal representations that was hypothesized for children at this age (Schumann-Hengsteler, 1995). This unexpected result was replicated in an additional study comparing 6-year-olds, 8-year-olds, and adults (Schumann-Hengsteler, Demmel, & Seitz, 1995). Children showed better performance with serial presentation compared to simultaneous presentation of the items in the picture reconstruction task. However, in this study, the adults showed no effect of presentation mode (Schumann-Hengsteler et al., 1995).

It occurred to us that object information in the picture reconstruction task could be influencing the results in comparing simultaneous to serial presentation mode. Thus, the next step was to reduce object information by presenting arrangements consisting of several, identical line drawings (Schumann-Hengsteler, 1995). By this it was intended to remove differentiating objects as cues for target locations. Considerations such as "Where was the tree?" were no longer helpful in the reconstruction process. It was hypothesized that as a result, children would focus more on the idea that "something was around here and here ...," and so forth. As Fig. 5.1 illustrates, the results showed a pattern opposite of that found in the previous studies involving different pictures. With identical pictures, simulta-

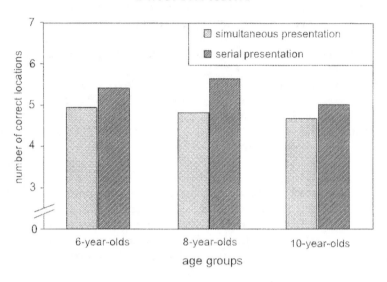

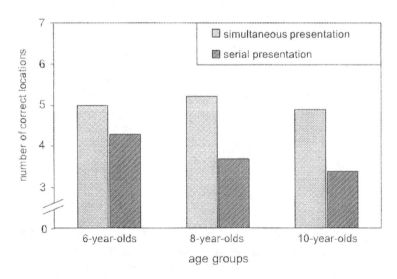

FIG. 5.1. Location memory for serial presentation versus simultaneous presentation of (a) different items and (b) identical items in picture reconstruction tasks.

neous presentation led to superior performance for all age groups (Schumann-Hengsteler, 1995).

TEMPORAL MEMORY FOR MULTIPLE SPATIAL LOCATIONS: CONFIGURATIONAL ASPECTS

As can be seen in Fig. 5.1, performance clearly dropped when a pattern or configuration of locations containing identical items was presented serially rather than all at once. This was true for all the age groups. This finding is consistent with the idea that distinct items presented serially provide associative cues that can be used in the reconstruction process. However, evidence of this kind raises additional questions. How might children of different ages encode spatial information about a set of target locations when there is neither a perceivable configurational pattern as in simultaneous presentation nor object identities serving as additional cues? We believe that under these circumstances, mental imagery might be involved.

Consideration of the role of mental imagery plays in spatiotemporal working memory tasks leads to studies of Brandimonte and colleagues (Brandimonte & Gerbino, 1996; Brandimonte, Hitch, & Bishop, 1992a, 1992b) concerning the fusion and subtraction of parts of pictures in imagination. Brandimonte et al. (1992b) showed that even young children are able to carry out visuospatial mental transformations as evidenced by their ability to connect or disconnect visuospatial information internally, thus implicating an active role for mental imagery in a VSSP. In light of these results, we were led to investigate whether children of various ages and adults spontaneously construct complete patterns or constellations from successively presented individual location. If so, we predicted that patterns forming a meaningful or nameable constellation would be reconstructed more correctly than would meaningless patterns. In this case, *meaning* was defined operationally in terms of semantic familiarity, specifically, participants' ability to label spontaneously a set of simultaneously presented locations (see Fig. 5.2 for an illustration).

More precisely, we asked whether isolated individual locations were gradually combined in a temporary visual-spatial processing system to form a complete pattern, which finally is recoded semantically. If this occurs, meaningful patterns should always be easier to reconstruct than meaningless patterns irrespective of the order in which component locations are presented. In sum, the central issue is the extent to which children and adults are capable, in the sense of going beyond the information given, of connecting serially experienced spatial information and integrating it internally to form an entire constellation. In this context, internal connotes a visual buffer sensu Kosslyn (1980; Kosslyn et al., 1990) or a VSSP sensu Baddeley (1990; Logie & Baddeley, 1990).

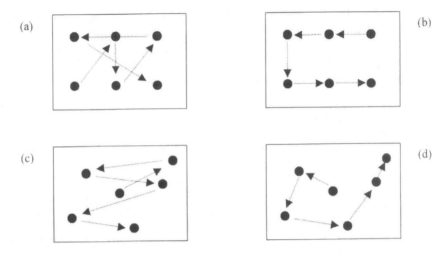

FIG. 5.2.   The manipulation of configurational (meaningful vs. meaningless patterns) and sequential (ordered vs. disordered sequences) information in the pattern reconstruction task.

The Pattern Reconstruction Task

To investigate this issue, we used the pattern reconstruction task, a modification of the picture reconstruction task described previously. In the pattern reconstruction task, several black dots were arranged on a roughly 45 × 30 cm pad. All patterns were presented serially, with each dot exposed on the pad for 1.5 s. Thus, only one target location was visible at a time, and the entire constellation was never seen directly. Immediately after the final presentation, participants had to reconstruct these locations by placing the original number of dots.

We manipulated two factors. First, because we were interested in the role of meaningfulness of the constellation, we selected two groups of stimulus patterns. Half of the patterns depicted familiar, easily named figures (triangle, circle, square, semicircle), and the other half were meaningless dot constellations that could not be named spontaneously or consistently (see Fig. 5.2a and 5.2b vs. 5.2c and 5.2d, respectively).

Second, because we were interested in examining possible age-related effects of temporal order on spatial processing, we additionally manipulated the sequence in which location information was presented. We reasoned that a sequence presenting contiguous locations in the constellation, referred to as an *ordered sequence*, would allow for an economic visuospatial rehearsal process that would facilitate the tasks of memorizing locations and then perceiving relations among them. In contrast, integrating information from sequences involving noncontiguous locations in the constellation, referred to as a *disordered sequence*, was expected to involve a more effortful (and therefore more developmentally sensitive) dynamic sequential coding process. Of course, order of presentation would not be expected to influence coding target locations as unrelated coordinates. To test these predictions, we developed and administered the two types of presentation orders mentioned previously, that is, ordered sequences in which the presentation followed the path of shortest distances between contiguous locations without any crisscrossing of the path connecting them (see Fig. 5.2b and 5.2d), and disordered sequences in which the presentation revealed noncontiguous locations and always consisted of an overlapping path (see Fig. 5.2a and 5.2c).

Results from an initial study with adult participants (Schumann-Hengsteler, Strobl, & Brandimonte, 1998) showed a general advantage of meaningful constellations over their meaningless counterparts. Furthermore, there was an interaction between order of presentation and meaningfulness of configuration. Meaningful constellations presented in an ordered sequence led to most accurate reconstructions. However, the beneficial effect of an ordered presentation was lost when the constellation of locations was meaningless. Hence, a general advantage of meaningful constellations over their meaningless counterparts did not exist. In addition, the advantage of ordered sequences over disordered ones was clearly limited to meaningful constellations.

Do these findings provide the basis for conclusions regarding the conditions under which individual spatial locations are connected via imagery to form overall patterns? At least there is initial evidence supporting the view that for adults, the semantics of configurational shape support processes in a visuospatial working memory. Easily identifiable geometric patterns facilitate memory-based pattern reconstruction. In addition, there is evidence that presentation order impacts adults' performance in the sense that reconstruction of meaningful patterns is facilitated when spatially contiguous locations are shown in succession, suggesting an economical visual scan pattern that contains no interference-producing crisscrossing. Such ordered presentation with a meaningful pattern allows for successful additional semantic recoding of the spatiotemporal information.

These findings are particularly significant in the context of imagery processes in visuospatial working memory. Factors assisting the creation of images should have a positive effect on encoding location-relevant information. In line with this argument, a constellation's meaningfulness as well as the orderliness of the presentation facilitate the process of mentally connecting individual locations to form an overall spatial constellation. Furthermore, the effect of presentation order may be taken as a first indication of a functional aspect of visuospatial working memory, that is, the strategic role of the inner scribe (Logie, 1995). We assume that a number of locations may be related by a dynamic process of visual scanning, referred to as *visuospatial rehearsal*. Visuospatial rehearsal is likely to be thwarted by a disordered presentation sequence because crisscrossing scan paths provides ample opportunities for interference within the VSSP. In contrast, an ordered presentation excludes crisscrossing scan paths as a source of interference, thus allowing undisturbed rehearsal of individual locations and aiding the final creation of the constellation as a whole. These considerations raise a number of developmental issues that can be addressed by a study of these same manipulations of meaningfulness and presentation order in the pattern reconstruction task administered to children.

A Developmental Study With the Pattern Reconstruction Task

This study involved 29 kindergarten children, 30 fourth graders, and 30 university students. For the pattern reconstruction task, we used the same experimental manipulations as in the adult study described previously (Fig. 5.2). However, for the youngest age group we had to reduce the six-dots patterns to four-dots patterns, as preliminary trials showed six dots to lay beyond the performance capacities of these children. The experimental procedure did not differ for the age groups. Again, we integrated a short practice section into the introductory phase to enable adults and children to get acquainted with the task. All experiments consisted of eight different test patterns. Dependant variables were (a) the accuracy of reconstruction indicating spatial working memory performance, and (b) the similarity between presentation order and the participants' reconstruction order. The latter variable is assumed to indicate the extent to which a given spatiotemporal order might be used to maintain the locations by means of visuospatial rehearsal. In particular, deviations of reconstruction order from presentation order are incompatible with the idea of straightforward repetition of the scanning path between successive locations as visuospatial rehearsal.

Figure 5.3 shows the results with respect to accuracy of reconstruction for the three age groups. Again, adults showed the greatest accuracy when reconstructing meaningful constellations that had been presented in an ordered sequence. Accuracy of reconstruction was relatively lower for the other three experimental conditions. Hence, the advantage of meaningful constellations was clearly limited to ordered presentation sequences (Fig. 5.3). Comparable results were found for the 10-year-old fourth graders. They, too, showed the significant advantage of meaningful constellations with an ordered presentation, and no differences in reconstruction accuracy could be discerned for the other three conditions (Fig. 5.3). However, results looked quite different for the youngest age group. For 6-year-old kindergartners, only the meaningfulness of the constellation had a significant influence on reconstruction, with meaningful

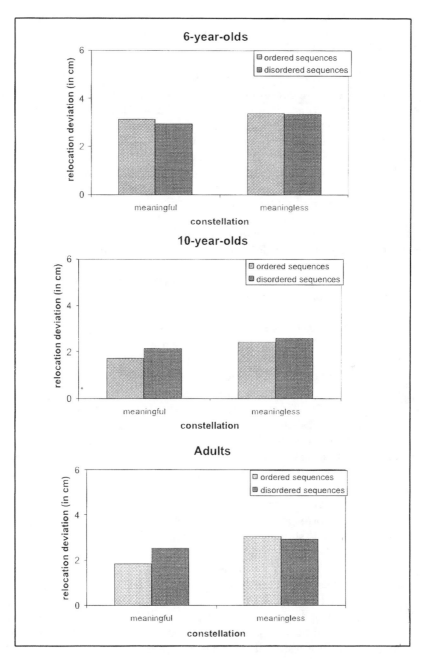

FIG. 5.3. Effects of the manipulation of configurational and sequential information in pattern reconstruction tasks for 6-year-olds, 10-year-olds, and adults.

patterns leading to more accurate reconstruction than their meaningless counterparts. No effect of presentation order was found, neither for meaningful nor for meaningless constellations.

Order of Reconstruction.   As argued previously, deviations of reconstruction order from presentation order are not compatible with the assumption of reconstruction based on straightforward visuospatial rehearsal. Our data showed a general age trend toward preserving the presentation sequence in the reconstruction process. The youngest age group rarely reproduced the presentation sequence, but such behavior was relatively common for the older children and adults. The 10-year-olds reproduced presentation order in about 50% of the trials with ordered presentations. Adults extended this tendency to the point of reproducing the sequence even in 40% of the disordered presentations, although in doing so they made a meaningful constellation more difficult to apprehend. Altogether, these results indicate a clearly increasing dominance of sequential information with age.

Hence, we can sum up our results concerning children's and adults' temporary memory for a pattern of spatial locations by three main arguments:

1. *Adults are sequential strategists*—and not always to their advantage. The adults in our studies showed little tendency toward or success in internally reorganizing individually experienced spatial locations into a meaningful pattern. Thus, our data do not indicate mental reorganization of spatial information in a VSSP, at least in this type of task. Rather, our results show a strong dependency on the given spatiotemporal sequence. In summary, nothing we found supports the position that spatial locations are stored in a VSSP as individually specified coordinates that can be combined and recombined at will. Instead, our findings from adults support the notion of reliance on a visuospatial rehearsal strategy in the sense of mental scanning of an imaginary path connecting successively presented locations.

2. *Even 10-year-olds use visuospatial rehearsal strategies*—but only if the given sequence corresponds to the shape of the constellation. In contrast to adults, 10-year-olds show signs of successful visuospatial rehearsal only if the presentation sequence is not complex, that is, it involves neither long distances between successive locations nor crisscrossing of the scan path.

3. *Six-year-olds do not show signs of visuospatial rehearsal.* They could hardly have used the given sequence as scanning path for memorizing the locations in view of the fact that they reproduced the presentation sequence in less than 20% of the trials. Instead, younger children relied more exclusively on the configurational information available in the task.

This argument is strengthened by additional analyses of accuracy in the reconstruction task. The data clearly show the performance of older children to be superior to that of younger children with respect to the average metric deviation between presented and reconstructed positions. Yet, younger children in particular seem to be able to preserve the configurational information despite large overall average deviation. In discussing this phenomenon in a methodological paper, Newcombe (1998) demonstrated that there could be complete preservation of the entire configuration (e.g., a triangle) without having a single location scored as correct on the basis of the absolute deviation. Uttal (1994, 1996) has proposed several algorithms for dealing with this problem in large-scale environments. We developed specific configurational analysis parameters based on mathematical similarity transformations for small-scale situations like the pattern reconstruction task. Reanalyzing data with these tools made obvious that the youngest of our participants were quite good in preserving static configurational information, despite showing large absolute deviations in their pattern reconstruction (Strobl, 2001; Strobl, Wirsching, & Schumann-Hengsteler, 1999).

TEMPORAL MEMORY FOR SPATIOTEMPORAL INFORMATION: SEQUENTIAL ASPECTS

Our findings with the pattern reconstruction experiments provided evidence for a developmental trend in the emergence of spontaneous visuospatial rehearsal as a strategy for the temporary maintenance of location information. To investigate the emergence of the visuospatial rehearsal in more detail, we decided to reduce task demands as far as possible to concentrate solely on the spatiotemporal aspect of location memory. This consideration led us to adopt as an experimental task the Corsi blocks, a well known clinical span procedure (Corsi, 1972; Milner, 1971). In contrast to the picture and pattern reconstruction task, the Corsi blocks demand memory for a sequence of defined locations only, that is, associations between spatial positions and temporal positions. It is not necessary to encode the exact position itself by coordinates because the relevant positions remain visible during the solution process. Neither is any verbal recoding necessary. Hence, the Corsi blocks explicitly demand the encoding of sequential spatial information and therefore suit perfectly well for an investigation of children's emerging ability to use a spatiotemporal rehearsal strategy.

We do not know very much about children's performance in the Corsi blocks task. Usually this task is said to measure the dynamic component of a visuospatial working memory (Logie & Pearson, 1997; Pickering, Gathercole, Hall, & Lloyd, 2001). However, the processes involved in task performance for children of different ages are not yet clearly specified. The few developmental studies conducted thus far have reported a linear increase in performance from a span of about 2.5 Corsi blocks in 5-year-olds up to 5.5 Corsi blocks in 15-year-olds (Isaacs & Vargha-Khadem, 1989; Kail, 1997; Orsini, 1994; Orsini, Schiappi, & Grossi, 1980; Schumann-Hengsteler

& Pohl, 1996). The absolute values vary partly as a result of methodological factors, in particular the emphasis given to path information by different procedures (e.g., the way target blocks are marked by hand movements).

Visuospatial rehearsal is conceptualized as an analog to verbal rehearsal. Hence, we assume that visuospatial rehearsal is used to encode and maintain spatiotemporal information by means of repeated activation of the imagined path connecting successive locations using eye movements. If this is the case, the nature of this imagined scanning path should have an effect on performance levels. Previously, the only established criterion for difficulty on the Corsi block task was the number of blocks that constitute a span (Berch, Krikorian, & Huha, 1998). Based on our conception of visuospatial rehearsal, we proposed that complexity of the imagined scanning path should be another factor affecting task performance.

In a first study, we used the original Corsi board consisting of nine blocks that are arranged in an unsystematic way on a rectangle frame. We manipulated the complexity of the block sequences independent of the number of blocks defining the span. This was done by contrasting so-called simple sequences, which connected target blocks by the shortest possible path avoiding any crisscrossings, with complex sequences, which were substantially longer and contained crisscrossings of the path. Figure 5.4 illustrates the manipulation by contrasting a simple and a complex sequence using the same seven blocks.

The results were quite clear. Besides the expected age effect, we found an effect of complexity for 5- to 10-year-olds as well as for adults (Schumann-Hengsteler & Pohl, 1996).

In a further study with a computerized version of the Corsi blocks, we intended to define complexity more exactly. Based on a detailed analysis of adults' Corsi block processing behavior (Zoelch & Schumann-Hengsteler,

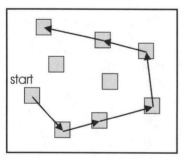
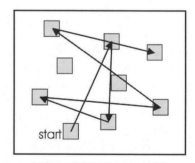

low sequence complexity   high sequence complexity

FIG. 5.4.   The manipulation of sequence complexity in the Corsi blocks.

2002), we identified and manipulated three aspects of complexity in a developmental study. These three aspects were as follows: first, the length of the scanning path irrespectively of the number of blocks that have to be maintained; second, the crisscrossings of path segments; and third, the presence of barriers across the scanning path, referring to cases in which the imagined path goes across blocks that are not part of the sequence (see the middle block in Fig. 5.4). We posited that effects of the absolute length of the imagined scanning path reflect temporal processing parameters. Thus, in analogy to the phonological working memory subsystem, the path length effect in the Corsi blocks might correspond to the well-established word length effect in verbal span tasks. We further proposed that the effects of crisscrossings and barriers are the result of interference, analogous to the phonological similarity effects in verbal span tasks.

For adults, there were independent effects of the sequence length on one hand and crisscrossings and barriers on the other hand. The same pattern of results was found for 10-year-old children. In contrast, the performance of 6-year-olds was not influenced by these variables. Neither sequence length nor the presence of crisscrossings in the imagined scanning path had a significant impact on performance.

At this point, we concluded that the processing of spatiotemporal information seems to be rather similar for older children and adults; both of these groups showed sequence complexity effects in a Corsi task when complexity was defined, not in terms of the number of blocks in the pattern but via the processing demands of the task in terms of path length and crisscrossings of the scanning path connecting target blocks. We interpret these effects as a path length effect and a visuospatial interference effect. Neither of these effects appeared for younger children. Hence, we take this as at least indirect evidence for the absence of a spontaneously applied mental scannning strategy for 6-year-olds in this task.

The Processing of Path Information:
A Developmental Study With the Corsi Blocks

Theories in the field of verbal strategy development have identified different types of deficits affecting successful strategic behavior in younger children. A mediation deficiency would prevent the child's application of a strategy even if one were provided for his or her use. A production deficiency alone, however, would mean that the child did not spontaneously generate a strategy but would benefit from a strategy if he or she were made aware of one (Bjorklund & Harnishfeger, 1990; Schneider & Bjorklund, 1998). A production deficit implies that it is possible to evoke a strategy in a child if the task conditions are to either lower the cognitive costs or strengthen the salience for applying a strategy. If a production deficit underlies the lack of visual rehearsal in 6-year-olds documented in the experiment described previously, one could try to evoke visuospatial rehearsal by facilitating the access to explicit path information. This was the aim of an experiment we conducted with forty-three 6-year-olds, forty-six 10-year-olds, and 26 adults. Two different computer versions of the Corsi blocks were applied, one with and one without explicit path information. Explicit path information (high path salience) was realized by a "Smiley" symbol wandering from block to block. The condition without explicit path information (low path salience) consisted of a flashing Smiley that did not move along the block sequence (Fig. 5.5). As in our previous studies, simple and complex sequences were used, but span was not manipulated. To control the quantitative effect of the normal span procedure (increasing number of blocks), the number of blocks was kept constant according to the upper span level of each age group. Hence, the fixed number of blocks per sequence was four for the preschoolers, six for the elementary school children, and seven for the adult participants.

We hypothesized that making the path explicit by the movement of the Smiley would induce the use of a spatiotemporal rehearsal strategy in those children who did not generate a mental path spontaneously. This hypothesis was supported by the data (Fig. 5.6). For all the age groups, there was an effect of complexity. However, the effect of the salience of path information varied clearly with age. Only the performance of the youngest age group was improved by the explicit path information when solving simple Corsi block tasks. Ten-year-olds' performance was improved with complex sequences but not with simple ones. For adults, the manipulation of path salience in the Corsi blocks did not have any effect.

The contrast between the effects in younger and older children is compatible with a combination of strategy emergence assumptions and capacity assumptions. In our view, the youngest children did not spontaneously use a visuospatial rehearsal strategy for encoding and maintaining the spatiotemporal information. However, this must be interpreted as a pro-

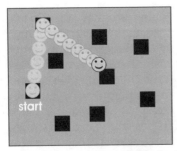

high path salience (moving smiley)   low path salience (flashing smiley)

FIG. 5.5.   The manipulation of path salience in the Corsi blocks.

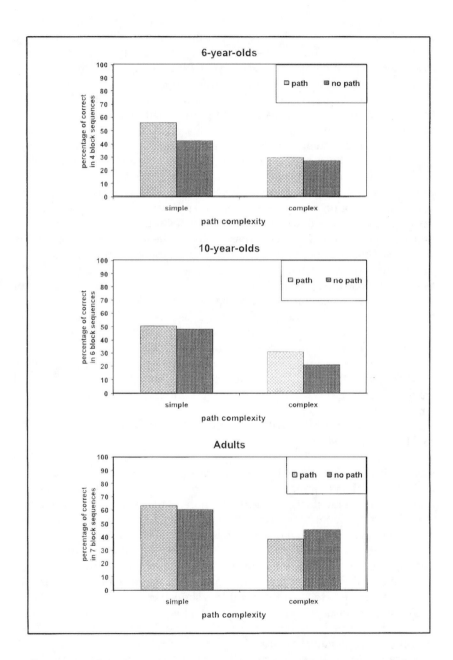

FIG. 5.6. Effects of path complexity (simple vs. complex) and path salience (path vs. no path) in the Corsi blocks for 6-year-olds, 10-year-olds,
and adults.

duction deficit in view of the fact that making path information more salient evoked the use of this sequential information at least with simple paths, that is, those that were short and contained no interfering elements. With greater path complexity, visuospatial interference becomes an issue, and the performance of younger children drops dramatically irrespective of the salience of the path information. A different story was told by the data from 10-year-old children who did not perform differentially with explicit path information in simple sequences. Thus, we conclude that they spontaneously produced such a strategy. Yet, as the Corsi task becomes more complex, which really makes a difference in six-block items as used for the 10-year-olds, making the path information explicit improved their performance. Given that the central executive of Baddeley's (1996) working memory model is not only responsible for the application of strategies but also provides capacity for the inhibition of irrelevant information, as in our study the crisscrossing path or crossed blocks, the following interpretation of our findings seems plausible. When processing demands are relatively low, such as for the simple sequences in our experiment, the application of a visuospatial strategy is facilitated. However, when the processing of visuospatial information is more demanding per se, there is not enough capacity left for using a strategy. That is the case for our complex sequences, which require the inhibition of irrelevant information (crisscrossing path, crossed blocks) in addition to defending coded location against decay. One might take this as an indication of a strategy utilization deficit in the 10-year-olds with those Corsi sequences, which have a higher task demand with respect to time characteristics and potential interference.

CONCLUSIONS AND IMPLICATIONS FOR MEASURING WORKING MEMORY

Concerning the encoding and processing of spatiotemporal information in children, the data obtained with the pattern reconstruction task on the one hand and the Corsi blocks on the other hand point toward the same conclusions. We proposed that one basic strategy acting in a VSSP sensu Baddeley and Logie is visuospatial rehearsal. Visuospatial rehearsal can be a rather basic, straightforward strategy involving the repetition of a mental scanning path to maintain visuospatial information for a brief period of time. Our data indicate that this strategy gradually emerges in children between 6 and 10 years of age. The 5- to 6-year-old children show a general production deficit with respect to visuospatial rehearsal in that they do not engage in it spontaneously. However, if the strategy is evoked by salient task conditions and if the processing demands of the task are not too high, even these younger children are able to use a mental scanning path to facilitate memory for locations.

Our evidence is consistent with the view that older children use visuospatial rehearsal spontaneously, but benefits depend on task demands. In simpler tasks, these older children behave as if they generated and applied the strategy. However, if the processing demands of the scanning paths are too high, as when the paths are subject to spatial interference, the performance of these children does not suggest success in the spontaneous application of this strategy. It is under high processing demands that facilitating visuospatial rehearsal by experimental manipulation helps the older children. One might take this as indicating a utilization deficit pertaining to difficult sequences for children between about 8 and 10 years of age.

In analogy to cumulative verbal rehearsal, visuospatial rehearsal can be conceptualized as a maintenance strategy for retaining location information that would otherwise decay during a retention interval. This aspect is not addressed in the studies reported previously. However, other experimental results from our laboratory showed that short delays of about 5 s in the Corsi block task brought about a dramatic decrease in 5-year-olds' performance. Apparently, they did not use any strategic tools for holding on to location information during this time interval. In contrast, the performance of 10-year-olds and adults did not show a negative effect of this delay. This outcome is clearly compatible with the position that the strategic use of visual rehearsal for maintaining location information is not typical of younger children.

Overall, there are strong parallels between the emergence of visuospatial rehearsal and verbal rehearsal. One might speculate about a possible reason for this parallel: Both strategies are directed toward holding sequential information. In both the verbal and visualspatial case, keeping an arbitrary order of information is the central demand. We believe that the ability to process and maintain sequence information is largely independent of modality and is not fully developed until the end of elementary school age.

The emphasis on the sequential character of spatial memory leads directly toward the distinction between static and dynamic spatial information made in Logie's (1995) theoretical extension of the VSSP. Logie and Pearson (1997) developed their position by obtaining developmental evidence of a so-called developmental fractionation. Developmental fractionation in this instance means that the processing of static visuospatial information does not show the same age trends compared to the processing of dynamic visuospatial information. Logie and Pearson (1997) as well as Pickering et al. (2001) have demonstrated this differentiation by comparing developmental trends for a static matrix span with a dynamic Corsi block span. In a way, our data on the effects of configurational versus sequential manipulations of the pattern reconstruction task point in the same direction. There are clear age effects with respect to processing sequential spatial information but no comparable age trends with respect to the ability to process configurational information. Uttal, Gregg, and Chamberlin (2001) demonstrated that even younger children can benefit from additional meaningful pattern information when remembering single specific locations in a large-scale setting. We conclude that younger children rely more heavily on static configurational spatial information than do older children and adults who are competent with dynamic spatiotemporal information processing. This position is even more plausible in view of the fact that visuospatial rehearsal, thought to be one basic mechanism of the inner scribe, does not emerge until school age. Hence, data on the development of visuospatial rehearsal could be taken as additional evidence for the distinction between working memory components for static versus dynamic visuospatial information.

Experimentally obtained results like those reported previously concerning a specification of different components of visuospatial working memory have to be taken into account when trying to establish measurement tools. As we outlined at the beginning, there are clearly different developmental trends in memory for locations per se compared to memory for item-location associations. This differentiation can be related to different *where* versus *what* processing systems (Farah, 1988; Logie & Marchetti, 1991; Postma & De Haan, 1996). In a recent overview, Turnbull, Denis, Mellet, Ghaëm, and Carey (2001) discussed the arguments for and against this distinction from an experimental point of view. However, firm empirical evidence or theoretical implementation in developmental psychology is rather sparse.

In addition, the distinction between static and dynamic visuospatial information-processing mechanisms has relevance for theoretical accounts of cognitive development. However, too often attempts to measure visuospatial working memory in children do not take into account these important distinctions. Global span procedures in the neo-Piagetian tradition of Pascual-Leone (1970) and Case (1985), such as the Mr. Peanut task (see de Ribaupierre & Bailleux, 1994; Kemps, De Rammelaere, & Desmet, 2000) are often used to obtain a general measure of spatial working memory capacity with little consideration of the specific processing demands of different span tasks. Based on our growing knowledge of specific working memory processes, it might be advantageous in the future to be more mindful of relations between the information-processing demands of specific visuospatial span tasks and performance of complex, real-world cognitive tasks. This is especially relevant when investigators seek to relate working memory components to specific learning disabilities (such as dyslexia or dyscalculia) or to neurodevelopmental disorders.

At the second conference on "Practical Aspects of Memory," Baddeley (1988) emphasized the importance of relating basic processing mechanisms to everyday cognition in the following memorable statement: "But in the meantime can I once again suggest that when we next see a temptingly elegant experimental phenomenon, we should pause, and ask ourselves the question, 'But what the hell is it for?'" (p. 15). Transposed to temporal memory for locations, the question arises as to what role visuospatial working memory plays in spatial cognition in naturalistic environments. This matter is hardly addressed thus far. Very few developmental studies are directed toward the investigation of particular spatial processing phenomena such as visuospatial rehearsal or capacity limitations that might be influential in children's navigation behavior or map-reading behavior, to name only two characteristic aspects of everyday spatial cognition. A first approach was made by Allen and colleagues (Allen, Kirasic, Dobson, Long, & Beck, 1996; Allen & Ondracek, 1995) when they related spatial working memory to spatial knowledge and environmental learning. However, this work often relies on the derivation of a general measure of spatial working memory as criticized previously rather than on a differentiation of processes within working memory.

Based on the increasing knowledge about the development of basic visuospatial processing mechanisms, developmental researchers should take the challenge deriving plausible hypotheses about which specific processing components might be dominant in complex spatial cognition tasks. We should work toward the goal of becoming more and more able to define working memory capacities and mechanisms as preconditions for successful spatial behavior in everyday situations.

ACKNOWLEDGMENT

Part of the research was supported by a grant of the German Research Foundation to the first author (Schu 840/5-1, 5-2)

REFERENCES

Allen, G., Kirasic, K., Dobson, S., Long, R., & Beck, S. (1996). Predicting environmental learning from spatial abilities: An indirect route. *Intelligence, 28,* 327–355.

Allen, G., & Ondracek, P. (1995). Age-sensitive cognitive abilities related to children's acquisition of spatial knowledge. *Developmental Psychology, 31,* 934–945.

Anderson, J. R. (1978). Arguments concerning representations for mental imagery. *Psychological Review, 85,* 249–277.

Baddeley, A. D. (1986). *Working memory.* Oxford, England: Clarendon.

Baddeley, A. D. (1988). But what the hell is it for? In M. M. Gruneberg, P. E. Morris, & R. N. Sykes (Eds.), *Practical aspects of memory: Current research and issues* (pp. 3–18). New York: Wiley.

Baddeley, A. D. (1990). *Human memory.* London: Erlbaum.

Baddeley, A. (1996). Exploring the central executive. *Quarterly Journal of Experimental Psychology, 49,* 5–28.

Baddeley, A. D., & Hitch, G. (1974). Working memory. In G. Bower (Eds.), *The psychology of learning and motivation* (pp. 47–89). New York: Academic.

Berch, D., Krikorian, R., & Huha, E. (1998). The Corsi block-tapping task: Methodological and theoretical considerations. *Brain and Cognition, 38,* 317–338.

Bjorklund, D., & Harnishfeger, K. (1990). Children's strategies: Their definition and origins. In D. Bjorklund (Ed.), *Children's strategies: Contemporary views of cognitive development* (pp. 303–323). Hillsdale, NJ: Lawrence Erlbaum Associates, Inc.

Brandimonte, M. A., & Gerbino, W. (1996). When imagery fails: Effects of verbal recoding on accessibility of visual memories. In C. Cornoldi, R. Logie, M. Brandimonte, G. Kaufman, & D. Reisberg (Eds.), *Stretching the imagination* (pp. 31–76). New York: Oxford University Press.

Brandimonte, M. A., Hitch, G. J., & Bishop, D. V. M. (1992a). Influence of short-term memory codes on visual image processing: Evidence from image transformation tasks. *Journal of Experimental Psychology: Learning, Memory, and Cognition, 18,* 157–165.

Brandimonte, M. A., Hitch, G. J., & Bishop, D. V. M. (1992b). Manipulation of visual mental images in children and adults. *Journal of Experimental Child Psychology, 53,* 300–312.

Case, R. (1985). *Intellectual development.* New York: Academic.

Corsi, P. M. (1972). *Human memory and the medial temporal region of the brain.* Unpublished doctoral dissertation, McGill-University, Montreal, Quebec, Canada.

de Ribaupierre, A., & Bailleux, C. (1994). Developmental changes in a spatial task of attentional capacity: An essay toward an integration of two working memory models. *International Journal of Behavioral Development, 17,* 5–35.

Farah, M. J. (1988). Is visual imagery really visual? Overlooked evidence from neuropsychology. *Psychological Review, 95,* 307–317.

Gathercole, S. E., & Baddeley, A. D. (1993). *Working memory and language.* London: Erlbaum.

Gathercole, S. E., & Hitch, G. J. (1993). Developmental changes in short-term memory: A revised working memory perspective. In A. Collins, S. Gathercole, M. Conway, & P. Morris (Eds.), *Theories of memory* (Vol. 1, pp. 189–209). Hove, England: Lawrence Erlbaum Associates, Inc.

Huttenlocher, J., & Newcombe, N. (1984). The child's representation of information about location. In C. Sophian (Ed.), *The origin of cognitive skills* (pp. 81–111). Hillsdale, NJ: Lawrence Erlbaum Associates, Inc.

Huttenlocher, J., Newcombe, N., & Sandberg, E. (1994). The coding of spatial location in young children. *Cognitive Psychology, 27,* 115–147.

Isaacs, E. B., & Vargha-Khadem, F. (1989). Differential course of development of spatial and verbal memory span: A normative study. *British Journal of Developmental Psychology, 7,* 377–380.

Kahneman, D., Treisman, A., & Gibbs, B. (1992). The reviewing of object files: Object-specific integration of information. *Cognitive Psychology, 24,* 175–219.

Kail, R. (1997). Processing time, imagery, and spatial memory. *Journal of Experimental Child Psychology, 64,* 67–78.

Kemps, E., De Rammelaere, S., & Desmet, T. (2000). The development of working memory: Exploring the complementarity of two models. *Journal of Experimental Child Psychology, 77,* 89–109.

Kosslyn, S. M. (1980). *Image and mind.* Cambridge, MA: Harvard University Press.

Kosslyn, S. M., Van Kleeck, M. H., & Kirby, K. N. (1990). A neurologically plausible model of individual differences in visual mental imagery. In P. J. Hampson, D. F. Marks, & J. T. E. Richardson (Eds.), *Imagery* (pp. 39–77). London: Routledge.

Logie, R. (1989). Characteristics of visual short-term memory. *European Journal of Cognitive Psychology, 1,* 275–284.

Logie, R. (1995). *Visuo-spatial working memory.* Hove, England: Lawrence Erlbaum Associates, Inc.

Logie, R., & Baddeley, A. (1990). Imagery and working memory. In P. J. Hampson, D. F. Marks, & T. E. Richardson (Eds.), *Imagery* (pp. 103–128). London: Routledge.

Logie, R., & Marchetti, C. (1991). Visuo-spatial working memory: Visual, spatial or central executive? In R. H. Logie & M. Denis (Eds.), *Mental images in human cognition* (pp. 105–115). Amsterdam: North-Holland.

Logie, R., & Pearson, D. (1997). The inner eye and the inner scribe of visuo-spatial working memory: Evidence from developmental fractionation. *European Journal of Cognitive Psychology, 9*, 241–257.

Milner, B. (1971). Interhemispheric differences in the localization of psychological processes in man. *British Medical Bulletin, 27*, 272–277.

Newcombe, N. (1998). New perspectives on spatial representation: What different tasks tell us about how people remember location. In N. Foreman & R. Gillett (Eds.), *Handbook of spatial research paradigms and methodologies* (Vol. 1, pp. 85–102). Hove, England: Psychology Press.

Newcombe, N., & Huttenlocher, J. (2000). *Making space.* Cambridge, MA: MIT Press.

Orsini, A. (1994). Corsi's block tapping test: Standardization and concurrent validity with WISC–R for children aged 11 to 16. *Perceptual and Motor Skills, 79*, 1547–1554.

Orsini, A., Schiappi, O., & Grossi, D. (1980). Sex and cultural differences in children's spatial and verbal memory span. *Perceptual and Motor Skills, 53*, 39–42.

Pascual-Leone, J (1970). A mathematical model for the transition rule in Piaget's developmental stages. *Acta Psychologica, 32*, 301–345.

Piaget, J., & Inhelder, B. (1975). *Die Entwicklung des räumlichen Denkens beim Kinde* [The development of spatial thinking in children]. Stuttgart, Germany: Klett. (Original work published 1948)

Pickering, S., Gathercole, S., Hall, M. & Lloyd, S. (2001). Development of memory for pattern and path: Further evidence for the fractionation of visuo-spatial memory. *Quarterly Journal of Experimental Psychology: Human Experimental Psychology, 54*, 397–420.

Postma, A., & De Haan, E. (1996). What was where? Memory for object locations. *The Quarterly Journal of Experimental Psychology, 49A*, 178–199.

Pylyshyn, Z. W. (1981). The imagery debate: Analogue media versus tacit knowledge. *Psychological Review, 88*, 16–45.

Quinn, G. (1991). Encoding and maintenance of information in visual working memory. In R. H. Logie & M. Denis (Eds.), *Mental images in human cognition* (pp. 95–104). Amsterdam: North-Holland.

Schneider, W., & Bjorklund, D. (1998). Memory. In D. Kuhn & R. Siegler (Eds.), *Handbook of child psychology* (5th ed., Vol.2, pp. 467–521). New York: Wiley.

Schumann-Hengsteler, R. (1992). The development of visuo-spatial memory: How to remember location. *International Journal of Behavioral Development, 15*, 455–471.

Schumann-Hengsteler, R. (1995). *Die Entwicklung des visuell-räumlichen Gedächtnisses* [The development of visuospatial memory]. Göttingen, Germany: Hogrefe.

Schumann-Hengsteler, R. (1996a). Children's and adults' visuo-spatial memory: The Concentration game. *Journal of Genetic Psychology, 157*, 77–92.

Schumann-Hengsteler, R. (1996b). Visuo-spatial memory in children: Which memory codes are used in the Concentration game? *Psychologische Beiträge, 38*, 368–382.

Schumann-Hengsteler, R., Demmel, U., & Seitz, K. (1995). Effekte des Darbietungsmodus auf die visuell-räumliche Arbeitsgedächtnisleistung bei Kindern und Erwachsenen [Effects of presentation mode on visuospatial memory in children and adults]. *Zeitschrift für Experimentelle Psychologie, 42*, 594–616.

Schumann-Hengsteler, R., & Pohl, S. (1996, July). *Children's temporary memory for spatial sequences in the Corsi blocks.* Paper presented at the International Conference on Memory, Padua, Italy.

Schumann-Hengsteler, R., Strobl, M., & Brandimonte, M. (1998). *Untersuchungen zum Enkodieren von Positionsinformation bei Kindern und Erwachsenen: Effekte der spatiotemporalen und konfiguralen Information* [Studies on the encoding of location information in children and adults: Effects of spatiotemporal and configurational information]. Eichstaetter Berichte zur Entwicklungs- und Pädagogischen Psychologie, No.11. University of Eichstaett, Germany.

Strobl, M. (2001). *Das Gedächtnis für Positionen: Zum Problem der Erfassung eines Konfigurationserhalts bei visuell-räumlichen Aufgaben* [Memory for locations: How to evaluate configurations in visuospatial memory tasks]. Hamburg, Germany: Kovac.

Strobl, M., Wirsching, G., & Schumann-Hengsteler, R. (1999). *Zur Analyse des Konfigurationserhalts mit Hilfe von Ähnlichkeitstransformationen* [A Method to analyze configurations by using similarity transformations]. Eichstaetter Berichte zur Entwicklungs- und Pädagogischen Psychologie, No.18. University of Eichstaett.

Turnbull, O., Denis, M., Mellet, E., Ghaëm, O., & Carey, D. (2001). The processing of visuo-spatial information: Neuropsychological and neuroimaging investigations. In M. Denis, R. Logie, C. Cornoldi, M. de Vega, & J. Engelkamp (Eds.), *Imagery, language, and visuo-spatial thinking* (pp. 81–108). Hove, England: Psychology Press.

Uttal, D. (1994). Preschooler's and adults' scale translation and reconstruction of spatial information acquired from maps. *British Journal of Developmental Psychology, 12,* 259–275.

Uttal, D. (1996). Angles and distances: Children's and adults' reconstruction and scaling of spatial configurations. *Child Development, 67,* 2763–2779.

Uttal, D., Gregg, V., & Chamberlin, M. (2001). Connecting the dots: Children's use of meaningful pattern to facilitate mapping and search. *Developmental Psychology, 37,* 338–350.

Zimmer, H. D. (1992). Von Repräsentationen, Modalitäten und Modulen [About representations, modalities, and modules]. *Sprache und Kognition, 11,* 65–74.

Zoelch, C., & Schumann-Hengsteler, R. (2002). *Aspects of complexity in the Corsi task.* Manuscript submitted for publication.

6

Seeing Space in More Than One Way:
Children's Use of Higher Order Patterns in Spatial Memory and Cognition

David H. Uttal and Cynthia Chiong
Northwestern University

The movie *James and the Giant Peach* (Selick, Burton, & DiNovi, 1996) opens with James and his parents relaxing at the shoreline. Lying on their backs, they look at the sky and begin to see patterns in the clouds. With a little effort, James begins to see various shapes, including a camel, a train, and a rotated version of the world's tallest building (at that time, the Empire State Building). James is delighted because he has found a new joy in something as simple as looking at clouds. He has realized that he can use information about familiar shapes to reinterpret other, more amorphous forms such as the shapes of clouds.

Our focus in this chapter is on the development of children's ability to see spatial patterns in the way that James saw the shapes of clouds. We are interested in the consequences and the development of the ability to think about spatial locations in more than one way—to find structures and patterns in distributions of locations that are not given by the properties of the locations themselves. We suggest that thinking about spatial locations or configurations in this way can facilitate spatial cognition and its development substantially. We demonstrate that finding structure in otherwise unstructured forms or locations can facilitate spatial memory, mapping, and communication.

As an example of how these structures might facilitate spatial cognition and its development, consider a child who is learning about U.S. geography. The child will hear, for example, about the panhandle of Texas or Florida, about the thumb of Michigan, or that Italy is a boot. Learning these names and what they mean will facilitate the student's knowledge substantially. For example, if the student is told that Tallahassee is in the panhandle of Florida, then the range of the state of Florida that he or she must search on a map is constrained substantially; most of the state is eliminated from the search. Moreover, the information will now be much easier to communicate to another person, as the range of locations that must be described will be reduced substantially.

People's tendency to think about spatial location in terms of familiar patterns or structures has an important history in psychological research. Indeed, since the time of the Gestaltists, psychologists and geographers have stressed that the perception and cognition of spatial locations involves more than remembering individual locations. Instead, people attempt to structure locations either in terms of contiguities or patterns within the locations. For example, ancient navigators imposed constellations on patterns of stars; doing so made the locations of specific stars easier to remember and easier to communicate to others. However, this tendency to impose structure on otherwise amorphous or random structures is not limited solely to constellations. It shows up also when a person labels geographic structures in terms of well-known objects or figures as well as when a person uses the constellations to locate or communicate information about stars.

Despite the historical importance of this work, relatively little research has focused on the development of children's ability to think about spatial information in terms of well-known figures or pattern. In addition, the majority of the work that has been conducted has focused primarily on perceptual development; relatively little research has examined how these issues may apply to tasks that are typically considered to be within the realm of spatial cognition, such as searching for hidden objects or communicating location. In this chapter, we make the case that learning to think about space in terms of familiar patterns may contribute substantially to the development of spatial cognition.

This chapter is organized as follows. First, we consider the advantages of thinking about spatial locations in terms of higher order patterns. Next, we consider the potential role of higher order spatial patterns in the development of spatial cognition. We argue that the ability to think about spatial relations in this way is an important but relatively unexplored aspect of the development of spatial cognition. Coming to think of locations in terms of patterns is an important accomplishment in the development of spatial cognition. We then present research that has addressed this capability, the results of which highlight the challenges and advantages that children can gain by thinking in this manner.

Before beginning this discussion, it is important to define what we mean by the term *higher order pattern*. We are referring to relatively knowledge-driven, or "top-down," processes that involve an active construal of locations. The defining feature is an application of prior knowledge of a structure to a new set of locations or bits of information. Perceiving or thinking about spatial locations in terms of higher order patterns requires that an individual go substantially beyond the characteristics of the information that is presented; it requires instead that the person recruit knowledge of a pattern and apply (or map) this pattern onto a set of locations or individual elements within a distribution of locations. For example, a constellation is not defined solely by the properties of the objects in which it is embedded; there really is not a dipper or a pair of twins in the sky. Our knowledge of these figures must be transferred, at least in part, to the pattern of the relevant stars to perceive the relevant structure (constellation) in the sky.

Because our interest is in cognitive-mediated patterns, we focus less on the role of other mechanisms of perceptual organization. For example, we do not discuss children's use of gestalt principles in spatial organization, in part because these issues have been discussed at length elsewhere (e.g., Stiles & Tada, 1996; Vurpillot, 1976). Our principle focus here is on what could not be given by gestalt principles per se, which is a construal of a set of locations based on properties of those locations that are not given by the locations themselves. For example, gestalt principles could explain why we perceive a set of locations as forming a line, but they could not explain why we see these locations as a camel or a skyscraper. Obviously, gestalt principles are not unimportant in that they contribute to the higher order organization of spatial patterns. For example, a precondition of construing a location in terms of a camel or a dipper might be that a certain number of locations must be arranged closely enough so that gestalt principles would dictate that these locations would be seen as forming a line. This line then could become part of the higher order pattern, perhaps as a leg of a camel or a handle of the dipper.

SPATIAL ADVANTAGES OF HIGHER ORDER CONSTRUALS

Although it may be entertaining to see camels in the patterns of clouds, does doing so actually facilitate spatial thinking or communication? If seeing locations in terms of higher order patterns does facilitate communication, how does the facilitative effect occur? To address these questions, we consider in this section three characteristics or effects of higher order patterns that can facilitate performance in spatial tasks

Redundancy of Form

The first and most general facilitative effect of higher order patterns is that they give a person more than one way to think about a location or set of locations. Consequently, the structured pattern provides redundancy that can be useful at both encoding and retrieval. For example, one could encode the location of a city in Italy both in terms of cardinal directions as well as in terms of a particular part of a boot. Likewise, one can remember the location of a star both in terms of its position relative to other stars as well as in terms of its position within a constellation. These multiple forms of encoding provide redundancies that increase the probability that relevant cues can be generated or used at recall. If a person forgets, for example, a specific location, then he or she can think of the general part of the figure in which the target was located. This information then could help to refresh the memory of the specific location.

The redundancy of form also can contribute substantially to spatial communication. One of the most important challenges of spatial communication is establishing a common perspective or reference frame. Communicators must search for "common ground," and it is well known that young children have difficulty establishing a common perspective or taking the perspective of another in a spatial communication task (Shantz, 1993). More recent evidence suggests that even adults are at least initially "egocentric" (referring to reliance on their own perspective) and that they work on finding common ground only when it becomes clear that the interlocutor does not understand the descriptions or instructions (Keysar, Barr, Balin, & Brauner, 2000; Keysar, Barr, Balin, & Paek, 1998; see also Schwartz, 1995).

The problems of egocentrism and finding common ground can be reduced somewhat if the locations can be construed in terms of a higher order pattern. For example, once both interlocutors agree that a set of locations can be construed as a pattern, then the parts of the pattern provide a clear common ground. For example, if people perceive that a set of stars forms the outline of a crab, then both interlocutors will often agree on what constitutes a part of the tail or a part of a claw. Put another way, well-known figures typically have a canonical orientation and a clear set of parts (Olson & Bialystok, 1983). Both of these characteristics can serve the function of orienting and establishing common ground.

Limiting the Search Space

As we mentioned earlier, higher order patterns can also limit substantially the potential search space that must be considered when searching for a location. People can eliminate many possible locations if they know the general region of the pattern in which a hidden object is located. This reduction in search space in turn can increase dramatically the probability of identifying the target location. A person may not know, for example, the precise location of an east African nation, but if they can remember that it is in the horn of Africa, then they can eliminate most of the continent as a possible location. A similar advantage accrues when one is attempting to communicate a location. For example, when a person hears that a star is located on one side of Orion's belt, then the number of possible stars that must be considered in finding the target is greatly reduced.

Limiting the possible search space can also have important advantages when a person is attempting to use a chart or map. One of the central challenges of using maps or other spatial representations is to establish correspondences (mappings) between information on the map or chart and the corresponding locations in the represented space. This is not always a trivial task; even adults can find it difficult to establish correspondences, particularly when the amount of detail is high, and young children often have great difficulty establishing correspondences between spatial relations on maps and in the world (Liben, 1999, 2000; Uttal, Gregg, Tan, Chamberlin, & Sines, 2001)

Systematicity

Redundancy and limits on search space are important characteristics, but they do not capture all of the advantages of thinking about spatial locations in terms of higher order patterns. An important and unique advantage is that construing locations in terms of the higher order pattern helps to convey a degree of systematicity to what might otherwise be random relations (Clement & Gentner, 1991; Gentner & Markman, 1997; Uttal et al., 2001). As used here, the term *systematicity* means a predictable, hierarchically organized set of relations among locations. Systematicity implies that knowing about one part of the figure also gives a person knowledge about other parts. For example, if people know that a to-be-remembered location is in the tail of a constellation figure, then they know something about the relation of the locations that constitute the tail to the locations that constitute the remainder the body. Thus, higher order patterns allow us as humans to borrow from our knowledge of real-world figures, knowledge not only of the parts of the figure but also the relation among the parts of the figure. Having established the whole, one can then use relations between the whole and its constituent parts to describe relations.

The role of systematicity in higher order patterns helps to explain why so many of the constellations are based on animate figures, including both variations of the human form (sisters, hunters, etc.) as well as various animals. Animate figures are both well known and well organized in terms of part–whole relations (Tverksy & Hemenway, 1984). Animate figures thus are often inherently systematic, and mapping these to a set of locations can convey to the locations some of the same organizational advantages that are given in the original figure.

The effects of systematicity can be particularly helpful in tasks that involve spatial communication. Spatial relations are often very difficult to describe verbally because each relation must be described in a serial fashion (Linde & Labov, 1975; Ondracek & Allen, 2000; Taylor & Tversky, 1992a, 1992b, 1996). For example, people may have to say, "It's one over from the left, two up from bottom, and three over from the far right." Each of these spatial relations must be stored in short-term memory, and processing limits may constrain the amount of information that can be recalled or integrated into a survey-like representation (Ondracek & Allen, 2000). However, the systematicity of a higher order pattern makes it possible to describe these locations on the basis of relations between parts and wholes.

DEVELOPMENT OF CHILDREN'S USE OF HIGHER ORDER PATTERNS

Up to this point, we have described several ways in which thinking about a set of locations in terms of a higher order pattern can facilitate spatial memory, mapping, and communication. Do these advantages also apply to young children? Children might gain a substantial advantage from thinking about locations in terms of higher order patterns. For example, as noted previously, children often have difficulty using maps when the correspondence between the map and the represented locations must be established on the basis of spatial relations rather than on the correspondences between individual locations (Blades & Cooke, 1994; Bluestein & Acredolo, 1979; Liben, 1999, 2001; Liben & Downs, 1992; Loewenstein & Gentner, 2001; Uttal et al., 2001). Construing locations in terms of a higher order pattern could be of considerable assistance on these kinds of tasks. Higher order patterns make spatial relations more systematic and hence more tractable; it is easier to think about how a set of locations relates to a well-known figure than it is to think about (and map) them in terms of complex and perhaps arbitrary spatial relations.

Likewise, it is well known that children under 5 or 6 years of age often have difficulty describing a single location among many alternatives (Flavell, 1968; Glucksberg & Krauss, 1967; Plumert, Ewert, & Spear, 1995). In particular, children have difficulty communicating spatial information when they must take into account the relations among multiple locations. When adults are faced with such a task, they often impose a well-known structure on a set of locations. Descriptions then can be based on the structure of and relations within the pattern rather than on an arbitrary set of spatial relations (Gentner & Rattermann, 1991; Uttal et al., 2001). Learning to think about and use patterns may, therefore, contribute to the development of spatial communication.

The possible advantages for young children of construing a set of locations in terms of higher order patterns motivates a research program that we have pursued for the past few years. Uttal et al. (2001) studied the development of young children's ability to impose a higher order pattern on a set of locations. The research examined specifically (a) the development of the ability to think of a set of locations in two different ways and (b) to exploit these higher older construals to facilitate memory, mapping, and search. We have studied both how a higher order pattern could facilitate mapping and search and how it could facilitate spatial communication. In the next sections, we present summaries of these lines of research. The results reveal that a higher order pattern can indeed facilitate children's spatial behavior. However, there are important developmental prerequisites that children must achieve before they can take advantage of what higher order patterns can offer.

Using a Higher Order Pattern to Facilitate Mapping and Search: Conceptual Issues

This research focused on whether young children could benefit from construing a set of locations in terms of a higher order pattern and whether they could use this construal to facilitate mapping and search. Uttal et al. (2001) asked young children to use a map to find objects that were hidden in a room. In this regard, our studies resembled those of classic studies of the development of map-reading skills; the children were asked to use a simple map to find a hidden object (Blades & Spencer, 1987; Bluestein & Acredolo, 1979; Marzolf & DeLoache, 1994; Presson, 1982). Whether they succeeded provides an index of their ability to understand and to exploit a correspondence between a map and a space that it represents (see Blades, Spencer, Plester, & Desmond, chap. 12, this volume).

However, in a different sense, our studies are quite different from previous research on the development of map-reading skills. Our (Uttal, Chiong, & Wilson, 2002; Uttal et al., 2001) research asked whether children could interpret a set of locations in a new way—whether they could impose a structured pattern on a set of locations. Specifically, the set of locations that served as hiding locations (and that were represented on the map) could be interpreted as forming the outline of a familiar figure, a dog. We investigated when the children could interpret the locations as a dog and the cognitive consequences of doing so. We hypothesized that if children could think of the locations in this higher order way, then they might gain a substantial advantage, both in terms of memory and in terms of the process of establishing a mapping between the map and the space.

Facilitating Mapping and Search (Uttal et al., 2001)

The participants for this study were 3-year-olds, 4-year-olds, and 5-year-olds, approximately equally divided between the two sexes. The children were recruited through direct mail to their parents. The majority of the children were White and middle class to upper middle class. Approximately 25 % were minorities. All of the children came from the north side of Chicago and the northern suburbs. The children were randomly assigned to one of two groups. The no-lines group saw a simple map that represented the locations that were shown on the map. The lines group showed the same circles but with one addition; these locations were connected with lines to indicate the overall shape of the dog pattern. Figure 6.1 shows the two maps.

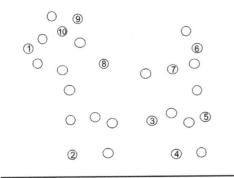

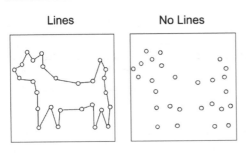

Lines   No Lines

FIG. 6.1. The top panel shows the locations. The numbers represent the locations at which the sticker was hidden on different trials. The bottom panel shows the lines and no-lines configurations. *Note*. From "Connecting the Dots: Children's Use of a Systematic Figure to Facilitate Mapping and Search," by D. H. Uttal, V. H. Gregg, L. S. Tan, M. H. Chamberlin, and A. Sines, 2001, *Developmental Psychology, 37,* 338–350. Copyright © 2001 by the American Psychological Association. Reprinted with permission.

The search space was a 10 ft × 10 ft yellow piece of felt. The felt was placed within a larger room. There were windows at one end of the room. However, although these windows were not shown on the map and because successful searches could only be accomplished by using the map (or by very lucky guessing), it seems unlikely that the windows could have served as landmarks or otherwise influenced children's performance. The hiding locations were paper coasters that were distributed across the felt.

The experiment began with a brief introduction to the task. The experimenter showed the children the felt carpet with the coasters scattered across it. He or she told the child that a second experimenter would hide a sticker under one of the coasters and that the child would be asked to find the sticker. The experimenter then showed the child the map for the condition to which the child was assigned. To help children understand the map, the experimenter pointed out correspondences between two circles on the map and the corresponding circles in the space. The experimenter did not tell the child that the locations formed the pattern of a dog, regardless of the condition to which the child was assigned.

The experimenter then took the child behind a room divider so that he or she could not see the search space. The second experimenter then hid a sticker under one of the 27 coasters in the search space. The second experimenter walked across the entire length of the felt carpet on each trial to reduce the possibility that sound cues could communicate the location at which the sticker was hidden. While the second experimenter hid the sticker, the first experimenter indicated the corresponding location on the map. The child was asked to point to the location three times to ensure that he or she could remember the location. The experimenter then said, "Now it's time to go look for the sticker." The child was not allowed to take the map with him or her during the search. The child was allowed to turn over up to three coasters while searching for the toy. If the child still had not found the sticker after three attempts, the experimenter pointed out the correct location.

This basic procedure was repeated across the 10 trials. On each trial, the sticker was hidden under a different coaster. Figure 6.1 (top panel) shows the locations under which the sticker was hidden. There were four different hiding orders; children were assigned randomly to one of the orders.

The results were clear: Seeing the lines maps (and hence becoming aware of the dog pattern) improved the performance of the 5-year-olds substantially. The 5-year-olds in the lines group averaged 71% correct searches (SD = 16%), whereas those in the no-lines condition averaged 54% correct searches (SD = 13%). The performance of the 3- and 4-year-olds were not affected by seeing the lines map. However, different factors accounted for the lack of an effect in the two younger age groups. The 3-year-olds overall had substantial difficulty with the task, averaging less than 25% correct searches. These children may simply not have understood that the map was relevant to finding the sticker. The 4-year-olds performed better, averaging approximately 36% correct searches, but the lines and no-lines 4-year-olds performed nearly identically. Thus, the 4-year-olds clearly could use the map to guide their searches in the room, but they did not benefit from seeing the dog pattern.

These results raise two important questions: How did seeing the dog pattern facilitate children's performance, and why was the effect limited to the 5-year-olds? We consider several possible answers in the next section.

Is the Effect Due Solely to Facilitating Memory? One possible explanation for the results is that seeing the dog pattern facilitated children's memory for the correct location. As mentioned previously, one of the primary reasons that people interpret locations in terms of higher order patterns is that doing so facilitates memory for individual locations. Could this explanation account for the results in this case?

It is certainly true that seeing the dog pattern on the map could have facilitated children's memory for the locations. However, this alone would not be enough to help the children find the sticker in the room. Recall that the lines that defined the dog pattern were not present in the room. All children saw the same space when they were asked to find the hidden sticker; this space consisted of a room within which we distributed the 27 coasters.

The lines that one half of the children saw on the map were never present in the space. Therefore, to realize the advantage that they gained from seeing the dog pattern on the map, the children had to reinterpret the locations in the room in terms of this pattern. The better memory for the locations on the map could only help if the children mapped the structure of the dog pattern in the space to the unlined locations in the room. This mapping process is not one only of memory. It requires that the children construe locations in the room in terms of the pattern that they had seen on the map; they had to carry over the higher order pattern from the map and then reapply it to the locations in the room. Put simply, the memory advantages of using the dog pattern derived from children's ability to first map the dog pattern to the locations in the room.

Could the Results Have Stemmed Solely From Lower Order Effects of Adding Lines to the Map?   One potential limitation of Experiment 1 in Uttal et al. (2001) concerns how the higher order pattern was instantiated; the locations were connected with lines. Pilot testing had revealed that this method was the most effective way of communicating the higher order construal of the locations. In addition, adding lines to the location was most consistent with the way that higher order patterns are communicated in the real world; astronomical charts often show constellations by connecting stars with lines. However, that the locations were connected with lines does raise the possibility that the effect was due more to the lines per se rather than to what the lines formed. The sheer presence of the lines themselves may have affected children's performance, regardless of the pattern that the lines formed. For example, the lines might have helped to parse the locations into sets of unrelated parts on the basis of perceptual characteristics such as local minima of lines. Parts can be defined on the basis not only of relations to a whole figure but also on the geometric properties of the region themselves (Hoffman & Richards, 1984; Hoffman & Singh, 1997). Because their claim is that children imposed a higher order pattern on the locations in the room, Uttal et al. felt it was important to pursue in greater detail whether the sheer presence of lines per se on the map could facilitate children's performance on these tasks.

To address this question, Uttal et al. (2001) used a second figure, shown in Fig. 6.2, which we called the "scrambled dog." This figure has the same number of parts as the original dog figure, but they are arranged in a different ordering. This created a pattern, but it was not, by our definition, a higher order pattern; there was no clear mapping between a well-known figure and the new, scrambled dog. Uttal et al. predicted that adding lines to the scrambled dog would convey no advantage specifically because the lines do not convey a higher order pattern.

The study was similar in all other aspects to the original study; the children saw the map (either with lines or without lines), pointed to the location, and then were asked to find the hidden sticker in the room. The lines

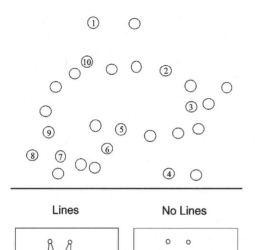

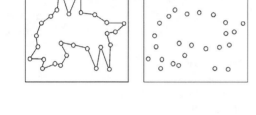

FIG. 6.2.   The top panel shows the scrambled dog configuration. The bottom panel shows and the lines and no-lines configurations. *Note.* From "Connecting the Dots: Children's Use of a Systematic Figure to Facilitate Mapping and Search," by D. H. Uttal, V. H. Gregg, L. S. Tan, M. H. Chamberlin, and A. Sines, 2001, *Developmental Psychology, 37,* 338–350. Copyright © 2001 by the American Psychological Association. Reprinted with permission.

and no-lines groups performed almost identically, averaging 42% ($SD =$ 21%) and 45% ($SD = 21\%$) correct searches, respectively. Of importance, the average level of performance in this study did not differ significantly from that of the no-lines group in the original study. Across the two studies, all groups of 5-year-olds performed comparably except those who saw the dog pattern highlighted with lines.

However, Tan and Uttal (2001) demonstrated in another follow-up study that 5-year-olds could gain advantages from seeing the lines on the scrambled dog pattern but only if they had first used the dog pattern. In this study, Tan and Uttal gave 5-year-olds experience with the dog pattern; the children completed 5 searches using the map with lines that showed the regular dog pattern. Then the children were shown the scrambled dog pattern and completed 10 searches in this space. Thus, the children completed a total of 15 searches. Their performance was compared to a control group that used the scrambled dog pattern for all 15 trials. The performance of the prior experience group was substantially and significantly greater than that of the control group.

Tan and Uttal's (2001) results suggest that children transferred their knowledge of the higher order dog pattern to the scrambled dog. In essence, when they saw the scrambled dog pattern, they saw only a disconnected set of parts, and this did not convey an advantage in the search task. In contrast, when they first saw the dog pattern, the children may have gained insight into the idea that these locations formed a familiar pattern. They then gained the advantage of mapping and relational thinking that the dog pattern conveyed initially.

Taken together, the results of these follow-up studies strongly suggest that the effect of adding the lines in the original study was to convey a higher order pattern. Children only benefited from seeing the lines if those lines formed a meaningful pattern or if the relation to a meaningful pattern was instantiated through prior experience.

We suggest that seeing the dog pattern facilitated performance because the pattern makes it easier for the children to think about and use spatial relations. The dog pattern not only facilitated memory; it also helped children to establish connections between spatial relations on the map and corresponding relations in the room. The task required that children map spatial relation because very few of the locations could be thought of as distinct or unique; the locations could only be mapped and discriminated from one another on the basis of spatial relations. This is a task that young children often find difficult. The dog pattern facilitated performance because its systematicity made the spatial relations more tractable and more memorable. In essence, the dog pattern provided a scaffold for thinking about and mapping spatial relations, and hence, it allowed the children to succeed at a task that is normally quite difficult for them.

Using Higher Order Patterns to Facilitate Spatial Communication: Conceptual Issues

We turn now to a brief summary of an ongoing series of studies on the use of higher order patterns to facilitate spatial communication. Although the task is different, the results converge with those of the mapping and search task presented earlier. Thus far, our focus has been on the ability to use structured patterns to facilitate memory and search. However, as we posited earlier, the advantages of using higher order patterns are not limited to these tasks. Indeed, one of the most common uses of higher order patterns is to facilitate spatial communication. We now consider an ongoing series of studies that is investigating the development of children's use of a higher order pattern to aid spatial communication.

Chiong, Wilson, and Uttal (2001) investigated whether, and when, children can benefit from using a higher order pattern in a referential communication task. The task was in some ways similar to the previously described search task; the children saw the same configuration that we used in the prior studies (see Fig. 6.1). However, rather than search for a hidden object, the children instead communicated locations to a listener. The results revealed important developmental differences in the ability to recruit the higher order construal and to use this to facilitate referential communication.

Facilitating Communication: An Illustrative Study

The children for the Uttal et al. (2002) study were ages 4 through 6. We also included a group of university students to provide a standard to compare with the children's performance. The participants were recruited from the same sources as in the prior studies.

As in the earlier experiments, the participants were assigned randomly to see either the lines or the no-lines configuration. The participant sat on one side of an opaque screen, and another person (the listener) sat on the other side. We told the participants that we would place a small piece of clay on one of the to-be-described locations and that their job was to tell the listener where the clay was located. We had children describe 10 locations, 1 at a time. On each trial, we placed the clay on a new location and asked the children to describe it. If the child's description of a given circle did not provide enough information to specify the precise location, then the experimenter requested additional information. These requests were tailored to the children's first description. For example, if a child said, "It's in the tail," the listener would say, "Can you tell me where in the tail?"

One challenge in this research involves coding and scoring children's descriptions. In contrast to the prior search studies, we could not simply score performance in terms of correct searches. Instead, we had to code children's descriptions in two different ways to capture different aspects of their performance. One coding addressed what characteristics of the configuration the children mentioned in their descriptions. Some of the most common strategies for descriptions included references to parts of the dog, counting (e.g.," it's one over from the top"), and use of spatial references and prepositions (*left, over, above,* etc.). The second coding addressed the accuracy or specificity of the descriptions. We based this coding on the approximate number of locations that a given description eliminated. A perfect description would eliminate all locations except the target. A poor description would eliminate no possible descriptions. For example, saying, "It's on the dog," tells the listener no useful information, because every location was part of the dog. We also coded intermediate descriptions such as "It's in the dog's head," or "It's near the top." These descriptions eliminate some, but not all, of the locations.

The results in terms of the specificity of the descriptions were for the most part straightforward. In general, children who saw the dog pattern (as instantiated with the lines) performed better than those who did not see the dog pattern. This effect diminished with age, as the older participants (particularly the adults) performed well regardless of whether they saw the lines. However, seeing the dog pattern did not benefit the 4-year-olds and many of the 5-year-olds.

The codings of the content of children's descriptions revealed two major findings. First, the younger children (most of the 4-year-olds and many of the 5-year-olds) rarely mentioned the dog pattern unless the locations were connected with lines. Second, the younger children in the lines group tended to describe the locations only in terms of the dog; they would mention a part of the dog and little else. Thus, the children tended to describe the locations either in terms of the dog (and only the dog) or in terms of spatial characteristics of the locations but not both. In the minds of many of the younger children, they thought about (and communicated) either a dog or a set of locations but not both. The two construals of the locations (as a set of a circles and as a dog) seemed not to coexist in the minds of the younger children. Consequently, the younger children's descriptions were less specific than the older children's were, even when they used the dog figure to describe the locations.

CONCLUSIONS CONCERNING SEEING SPACE IN MORE THAN ONE WAY

Taken together, the results of the research discussed converge on the same conclusions. First, they provide evidence that higher order patterns can indeed facilitate children's performance in spatial tasks. In both studies, it was the relational nature of the dog pattern that facilitated children's performance. Seeing the dog pattern helped children to remember, map, and communicate locations. Many of the challenges that young children typically face in thinking about and remembering spatial locations were ameliorated when the children could rely on the relations inherent in a familiar pattern rather than on arbitrary and complex relations among unrelated spatial locations.

Second, the studies indicate that age 5 may represent an important developmental transition in children's ability to exploit higher order patterns. In both series of studies, children less than 5 did not benefit from seeing the dog pattern. Moreover, the results (particularly) with 4-year-olds cannot be attributed to children failing to pay attention to the task or to the task simply being too difficult for them. For example, in the mapping and search tasks, the 4-year-year-olds performed much better than would have been expected by chance, which indicates that they understood and paid attention to the task. Nevertheless, they did not benefit from seeing the dog pattern.

In this final section, we consider a possible source of the developmental difference that we observed. Why did the 5-year-olds benefit from the pattern, and why did the 4-year-olds not benefit? The answer may lie in the development of the ability to perceive one stimulus in two different ways. A critical prerequisite for benefiting from a higher order pattern is being able to perceive the locations in two different ways: as a set of possible hiding places and as parts of a structured pattern. The 3- and 4-year-olds in these studies did not benefit from the dog pattern because they could not see the locations in both of these ways.

Before explaining in detail how this could account for the developmental results that we observed, we first review a series of studies that may be highly relevant to understanding the challenges of using a higher order pattern. For example, Elkind and colleagues (Elkind, 1964; Elkind, Koelger, & Go, 1964; Elkind & Scott, 1962) have demonstrated that young children seem incapable of thinking simultaneously about a whole figure and its constituent parts. In these studies, Elkind and colleagues created figures in which the whole and its parts could be interpreted in different ways. For example, one of the figures was a face that was composed of drawings of individual pieces of fruit. Young children tended to see either the fruit or the face; very few children simultaneously mentioned both the fruit and the face. Despite several attempts, Elkind and colleagues could not convince the children that the figure could represent both individual pieces of fruit and in composite an entire face.

More recently, Gopnik and Rosati (2001) have reached similar conclusions using a somewhat different task. They investigated whether children could conceive of both interpretations of an ambiguous figure such as the "Rabbit Duck" or the "Rat Man" figures that appear in many introductory psychology textbooks (See Fig. 6.3). The results were clear: Children less than 5 did not appear capable of seeing (or entertaining the possibility of) two interpretations of the same figure. For example, children saw the figure as either a Rabbit or Duck, and the experimenter could not convince them that the figure could be seen in alternate ways. Even after the experimenter showed how the figure could be disambiguated (by moving the eye in the case of the rabbit duck figure), the children still insisted that their initial in-

FIG. 6.3.   Examples of ambiguous figures. The figure in the top panel can be seen as either a duck or a rabbit. The figure in the bottom panel can be seen as either a rat or a man. *Note.* From "Duck or Rabbit? Reversing Ambiguous Figures and Understanding Ambiguous Representations," by A. Gopnik and A. Rosati, 2001, *Developmental Science, 4*, pp. 175–183. Copyright © 2001 by Blackwell Publishing. Reprinted with permission.

terpretation was the only one possible. Despite several attempts, the children did not conceive of the figure as reversible.

These and similar results (e.g., Vurpillot, 1976) suggest that children younger than about 5 years of age cannot perceive spatial figures in more than one way. How might these results relate to children's use of higher order patterns and to the developmental results that we observed? We suggest that successfully using a higher order pattern in a spatial task requires that people think simultaneously about the pattern and about the locations that are embedded within the pattern. It would do little good, for example, to think of the locations as forming a dog if one did not also keep in mind precisely how the locations related to the dog pattern. Both of our tasks (search and communication) required that children think about not only the pattern but also about the relation between the individual locations and that pattern. We suggest that the 3- and 4-year-olds in our task did not do this; they thought either about a set of locations or about a dog but not both.

This limitation could have affected the younger children in the work reviewed here. In the mapping and search task (Uttal et al., 2001), the younger children would have had difficulty relating the lined pattern on the map to the unlined pattern of the coasters in the room. They knew about the dog when they saw it on the map, but when they entered the room, all they saw was the coasters.

The results of the spatial communication task strongly support our interpretation of the developmental differences. The 4-year-olds did sometimes use the dog pattern in their descriptions, but when they did so, this was all the information they provided. When the dog pattern was obvious (because we connected the locations with lines), the younger children lost sight of the more local information about the circles that formed the dog. (Navon, 1977). Consequently, they provided descriptions almost solely in terms of the dog. Their descriptions either mentioned the dog or spatial properties of the individual circles but not both characteristics.

In summary, we conclude that what the younger children lacked was the ability to think simultaneously about the dog pattern and about the locations that constituted the dog pattern. The research presented here therefore demonstrates that children can benefit from higher order patterns in ways that are analogous to how adults can benefit. Much like ancient navigators, the children in our studies benefited substantially by reinterpreting a set of locations in terms of what is essentially a constellation. Once the children could think of the locations as a dog, many of the problems that they typically encounter in remembering or communicating spatial information were ameliorated. At the same time, our results highlight the importance of what is perhaps a fundamental transition in cognitive development: acquiring the ability to see, and to think about, one thing in two different ways. Spatial cognition can be facilitated greatly by being able to think about locations in more than one way.

ACKNOWLEDGMENTS

Portions of the work that is reviewed in this chapter were presented at the April 2001 meetings of the Society for Research in Child Development, Albuquerque, New Mexico The work was supported by National Science Foundation Grant 0087516 and National Institute of Health Grant R29HD34929. We thank Maeve Hennerty, Carolyn Freedman, Catherine Fried, and Catherine Learned for their help.

REFERENCES

Blades, M., & Cooke, Z. (1994). Young children's ability to understand a model as a spatial representation. *Journal of Genetic Psychology, 155,* 201–218.

Blades, M., & Spencer, C. (1987). The use of maps by 4-6-yr-old children in a large-scale maze. *British Journal of Developmental Psychology, 5,* 19–24.

Bluestein, M., & Acredolo, L. (1979). Developmental changes in map reading skills. *Child Development, 50,* 691–697.

Chiong, C., Wilson, C., & Uttal, D. H. (2001, April). *Thinking and talking about space: Systematic patterns facilitate referential communication of locations.* Paper presented at the biennial meetings of the Society for Research in Child Development, Minneapolis, MN.

Clement, C., & Gentner, D. (1991). Systematicity as a selection constraint in analogical mapping. *Cognitive Science, 15,* 89–132.

Elkind, D. (1964). Ambiguous pictures for the study of perceptual development and learning. *Child Development, 35,* 1391–1396.

Elkind, D., Koegler, R. R., & Go, E. (1964). Studies in perceptual development: II. Part-whole recognition. *Child Development, 35,* 755–756.

Elkind, D., & Scott, L. (1962). Studies in perceptual development: The decentering of perception. *Child Development, 33,* 619–630.

Flavell, J. H. (1968). *The development of role-taking and communication skills in children.* New York: Wiley.

Gentner, D., & Markman, A. B. (1997). Structure mapping in analogy and similarity. *American Psychologist, 52,* 45–56.

Gentner, D., & Rattermann, M. J. (1991). Language and the career of similarity. In S. A. Gelman & J. P. Byrnes (Eds.), *Perspectives on language and thought: Interrelations in development* (pp. 225–277). New York: Cambridge University Press.

Glucksberg, S., & Krauss, R. M. (1967). What do people say after they have learned how to talk? Studies of the development of referential communication. *Merrill-Palmer Quarterly, 13,* 309–316.

Gopnik, A., & Rosati, A. (2001). Duck or rabbit? Reversing ambiguous figures and understanding ambiguous representations. *Developmental Science, 4,* 175–183.

Hoffman, D. D., & Richards, W. A. (1984). Parts of recognition. *Cognition, 18,* 65–96.

Hoffman, D. D., & Singh, M. (1997). Salience of visual parts. *Cognition, 63,* 29–78.

Keysar, B., Barr, D. J., Balin, J. A., & Brauner, J. S. (2000). Taking perspective in conversation: The role of mutual knowledge in comprehension. *Psychological Science, 11,* 32–38.

Keysar, B., Barr, D. J., Balin, J. A., & Paek, T. S. (1998). Definite reference and mutual knowledge: Process models of common ground in comprehension. *Journal of Memory & Language, 39,* 1–20.

Liben, L. S. (1999). Developing an understanding of external spatial representations. In I. E. Sigel (Ed.), *Development of mental representation: Theories and applications* (pp. 297–321). Mahwah, NJ: Lawrence Erlbaum Associates, Inc.

Liben, L. S. (2000). Map use and the development of spatial cognition: Seeing the bigger picture. *Developmental Science, 3,* 270–274.

Liben, L. S. (2001). Thinking through maps. In M. Gattis (Ed.), *Spatial schemas and abstract thought* (pp. 45–77). Cambridge, MA: MIT Press.

Liben, L. S., & Downs, R. M. (1992). Developing an understanding of graphic representations in children and adults: The case of GEO-graphics. *Cognitive Development, 7,* 331–349.

Linde, C., & Labov, W. (1975). Spatial networks as a site for the study of language and thought. *Language, 51,* 924–939.

Loewenstein, J., & Gentner, D. (2001). Spatial mapping in preschoolers: Close comparisons facilitate far mappings. *Journal of Cognition & Development, 2,* 189–219.

Marzolf, D., & DeLoache, J. S. (1994). Transfer in young children's understanding of spatial representations. *Child Development, 65,* 1–15.

Navon, D. (1977). Forest before trees: The precedence of global features in visual perception. *Cognitive Psychology, 9,* 353–383.

Olson, D. R., & Bialystock, E. (1983). *Spatial cognition.* Hillsdale, NJ: Lawrence Erlbaum Associates, Inc.

Ondracek, P. J., & Allen, G. L. (2000). Children's acquisition of spatial knowledge from verbal descriptions. *Spatial Cognition & Computation, 2,* 1–30.

Plumert, J. M., Ewert, K., & Spear, S. J. (1995). The early development of children's communication about nested spatial relations. *Child Development, 66,* 959–969.

Presson, C. C. (1982). The development of map-reading skills. *Child Development, 53,* 196–199.

Schwartz, D. L. (1995). The emergence of abstract representations in dyad problem solving. *Journal of the Learning Sciences, 4,* 321–354.

Selick, H. (Producer), Burton, T., & DiNovi, D. (Directors). (1996). *James and the giant peach* (film). Disney Studios, San Francisco.

Shantz, C. U. (1993). Children's conflicts: Representations and lessons learned. In R. R. Cocking & A. K. Renninger (Eds.), *The development and meaning of psychological distance* (pp. 185–202). Hillsdale, NJ: Lawrence Erlbaum Associates, Inc.

Stiles, J., & Tada, W. L. (1996). Developmental change in children's analysis of spatial patterns. *Developmental Psychology, 32,* 951–970.

Tan, L., & Uttal, D. (2001, April). *Mechanisms of transfer: Analogical transfer with maps.* Poster session presented at the annual meeting of the Society for Research in Child Development, Minneapolis, MN.

Taylor, H. A., & Tversky, B. (1992a). Descriptions and depictions of environments. *Memory & Cognition, 20,* 483–496.

Taylor, H. A., & Tversky, B. (1992b). Spatial mental models derived from survey and route descriptions. *Journal of Memory & Language, 31,* 261–292.

Taylor, H. A., & Tversky, B. (1996). Perspective in spatial descriptions. *Journal of Memory & Language, 35,* 371–391.

Tversky, B., & Hemenway, K. (1984). Objects, parts, and categories. *Journal of Experimental Psychology: General, 113,* 169–193.

Uttal, D. H., Gregg, V. H., Tan, L. S., Chamberlin, M. H., & Sines, A. (2001). Connecting the dots: Children's use of a systematic figure to facilitate mapping and search. *Developmental Psychology, 37,* 338–350.

Vurpillot, E. (1976). *The visual world of the child* (W. E. C. Gillham, Trans.). New York: International Universities Press.

The Neuropsychology
of Object-Location Memory

Albert Postma, Roy P. C. Kessels,
and Marieke van Asselen
Utrecht University

Spatial memory involves information about location, orientation, and direction. It supports a multitude of cognitive and behavioral activities ranging from basic "spatiomotor" actions and locomotion to navigation and recognizing complex figures. In this chapter, we focus on the neuropsychology of memory for object locations. Object-location memory includes several specific functional characteristics, some of which may set it apart from other types of spatial memory. First, and most important, unlike navigation, remembering object locations typically does not involve storing a sequence of spatial decisions or temporally ordered spatial information (cf. Schumann-Hengsteler, Strobl, & Zoelch, chap. 5, this volume). Instead, it is a representation or description of where things are in space, independent from how and in which order the observer wants to attend to these locations. Second, object-location memory can apply to small-scale space (e.g., "Where is your manuscript, on your desktop or computer screen?") as well as to space in a larger scale (e.g., "Where are your running shoes within your house?"). In both cases, the essential coding processes are supposed to be viewer independent. Small-scale displays, however, usually include an alignment of test and presentation displays (see also Goldstein, Canavan, & Polkey, 1989). Thus, items are perceived from the same perspective, and performance might essentially rely on viewer-centered coding. Third, object-location memory primarily represents abstract knowledge about a person's environment without directly prescribing motor actions. In other words, people may know where an object is, but it is another question how they should act on this object. The latter requires navigational knowledge (how to reach the object) and memory-guided spatiomotor actions

143

(how to pick up the item). Fourth, object-location memory reflects on the multiattribute nature of the visual world. Visual scenes contain various distinct features that somehow have to be grouped together in coherent units. One of the most important features is location. People not only need to know which locations are relevant but often also have to remember which other features—for example, shape, color, object identity—correspond to those locations. Knowing "what is where" essentially concerns the question of how features are bound together in memory to form complex memory traces (Chalfonte, Verfaellie, Johnson, & Reiss, 1996).

Various neurological pathologies affect the ability to remember where things are. M. L. Smith and Milner (1981, 1984, 1989) were among the first to describe impaired spatial memory after focal lesions to the right hippocampal formation. The last decade has shown that functional impairments can also arise after more widespread neurological damage. Impairments in remembering spatial information, in particular object-to-location associations, appear to be at the core of Korsakoff's disease (Kessels, Postma, Wester, & De Haan, 2000; Mayes, Meudell, & Pickering, 1991; Shoqeirat & Mayes, 1991). Moreover, deficits in object-location memory have been reported in patients with Parkinson's disease (Pillon et al., 1996, 1997, 1998). Similarly, others have found a decline in spatial memory performance in patients suffering from Alzheimer's disease (Adelstein, Kesner, & Strassberg, 1992; Bucks & Willison, 1997; Sahakian et al., 1988). In fact, forgetting where things are—most likely "mobile" objects such as keys or glasses—is one of the first clinical symptoms of dementia, illustrating the ecological significance of object-location memory research (Bucks & Willison, 1997).

The goal of the present chapter is to present an overview of the neuropsychology of object-location memory. First, we discuss the functional architecture of object-location memory. Part of the evidence regarding the various processing components has a neurocognitive character, that is, linking functional mechanisms to neuroanatomical structures. Second, we elaborate on this latter notion by formulating some tentative conclusions with respect to localization of the alleged functional components in the human brain.

A FUNCTIONAL ANALYSIS OF OBJECT-LOCATION MEMORY

Remembering where things are requires a number of functional steps. Figure 7.1 presents a face-value analysis of object-location memory assuming three distinct processing components: object processing, spatial-location processing, and the binding of objects to locations. These components feature in both memory and perception. Although our emphasis is on memory, we switch flexibly to the perceptual counterparts.

First, the various items contained in the to-be-remembered display need to be processed. It has been well documented that there is a specialized route in the visual system originating at the primary visual cortex and projecting to

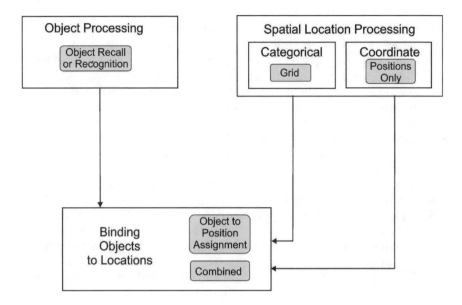

FIG. 7.1.   A functional analysis of object-location memory. Rectangular shapes depict processing components. Grey ellipses show the tasks presumed to assess these components.

the posterior inferior temporal cortex (i.e., the ventral stream), which is crucial for object recognition. Evidence for this so-called what pathway comes from several neurophysiological studies in primates and from lesion studies in humans (Milner & Goodale, 1995; Ungerleider & Mishkin, 1982). The inability to recognize visually presented items consciously typically occurs after damage to temporal areas in the ventral stream.

Second, a component might be distinguished that is relevant for processing the necessary location information. Originally, it was thought that the dorsal stream, encompassing occipitoparietal projections, would form the exclusive circuitry of the "where" stream. More recently, Milner and Goodale (1995) and others have argued convincingly that certain forms of spatial information processing are also performed by the ventral areas. As such, both parietal and temporal areas might contribute to spatial-location processing, engaging both an egocentric and an allocentric frame of reference, respectively. Both types of references contribute to object-location memory, although there is an emphasis on the allocentric frame. In addition, there is a further distinction involving the grain of position codes. Figure 7.1 suggests that there may be two levels of detail in coding position (Hellige & Michimata, 1989; Jager & Postma, 2003;

Kosslyn, 1994; Kosslyn, Koenig, Barrett, & Cave, 1989; Laeng, 1994; see also Lansdale, 1998). Categorical locations correspond to a relative, topological sense of position: Object A is in the left corner of the room. Coordinate location coding gives a fine-grained, metric sense of position. Interestingly, whereas the left hemisphere is thought to be specialized for categorical spatial relations, the right hemisphere is supposed to be superior in processing coordinate information.

Finally, common to all visual processing and central in object-location memory, the object-identity information and the spatial information need to be combined. In Fig. 7.1, it is suggested that objects can be bound either to categorical or to coordinate locations. An important question that has dominated spatial-memory research for some decades is whether spatial memory in general and binding in particular occurs with or without attentional effort. Hasher and Zacks (1979) reasoned that spatial memory would work automatically. That is, even when attention is inhibited and learning is incidental, participants will perform adequately in recalling and recognizing event locations. However, several others have contended that spatial memory does depend on attentional resources (cf. Naveh-Benjamin, 1987, 1988; see also Caldwell & Masson, 2001, for an excellent overview). In other words, attention would be necessary to bring objects and events together with their locations.[1] Caldwell and Masson (2001) convincingly argued that spatial memory performance typically reflects the combined results from both automatic and effortful processing. As such, one could expect certain aspects or forms of spatial memory to rest more on the automatic components than others. Creem-Regehr (chap. 8, this volume) argues that position processing might be mostly automatic, whereas identity processing ("what") requires central effort.

Because spatial memory often includes both knowing where and knowing what is where, it typically engages automatic as well as effortful components. Speculatively, positions per se can be presumed to be coded automatically. Object-to-position links, that is, the binding component, in turn might be formed with more conscious effort. Attention thus seems to play two roles. First, at a relatively early stage, it is necessary for binding different perceptual features to form coherent percepts (Baylis, Gore, Rodriguez, & Shisler, 2001). Second, at a later stage, it works to consolidate the the same multidimensional perceptual events to memory and even further to integrate single perceptual events into more complex memory episodes.

---

[1]Note that this controversy reminisces the discussion on the role of attention in perception. The so-called feature-integration theory held that in short-lived representations of visual information, attention is necessary to integrate different features in space (Treisman & Gelade, 1980). Illusory conjunctions may occur when attention is distracted. In other words, attention forms the glue to link shapes, colors, and complete objects to locations. Elsewhere, however, it has been pointed out that features can be preattentively bound to locations (Cohen & Ivry, 1989).

Regarding this linkage process, Baddeley (2000) recently proposed an episodic buffer in working memory that acts as an extension of central-executive control in integrating information from a number of different sources into coherent episodes. In addition, this buffer would form an important stage in long-term episodic learning.

TASKS PROCEDURES: OPERATIONALIZING COMPONENTS OF OBJECT-LOCATION MEMORY

Given the foregoing simplified analysis of the mental components that constitute object-location memory, the obvious next step is to determine how these components can be measured. We mainly elaborate here on an experimental paradigm developed some years ago (Postma & De Haan, 1996) and later extended (Kessels, Postma, & De Haan, 1999a). The basic procedure employed in this paradigm, as well as in many other studies, consists of showing participants for some period of time a number of objects within a frame on a computer screen. Next, either with or without a delay in between, participants have to perform several memory tasks. First, it is assessed how well the participant remembers which items have been shown. This can be measured either by object name recall or by object recognition (Nunn, Graydon, Polkey, & Morris, 1999; Postma, Jager, Kessels, Koppeschaar, & van Honk, 2003; M. L. Smith & Milner, 1981). The former not only taps visual memory but also includes verbal labeling efficiency and verbal memory. This could also apply to the recognition measure, although to a lower extent (one might still visually recognize an item as old, even when one can not name it). The latter method was used by Kessels and colleagues (Kessels, Postma, Kappelle, & De Haan, 2000; Kessels, Postma, Wester et al., 2000), as shown in Fig. 7.2.

A second test to be conducted should bear on the spatial location processing component. Postma and De Haan (1996) designed the following

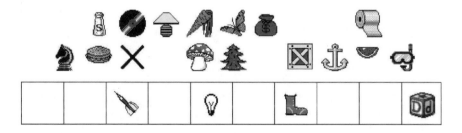

FIG. 7.2.   Object recognition memory test: Choose the 10 previously shown items out of a 20-item set. The participants are told that the spatial location is irrelevant here and that items can be placed in any of the 10 positions.

procedure (see Fig. 7.3). Here, a number of completely identical objects are shown within the frame for some time. Next, the same set of objects is shown again above the empty frame and has to be relocated to their original positions. We labeled this the *positions-only* or *positional-memory* condition. It can be seen as a measure of precise, coordinate-level position memory without the need to distinguish between different objects. Third, the binding process should be tested. One way to do this consists of the object-to-position-assignment condition in which multiple different objects are presented, but during relocation, the exact locations are marked by dots. Hence, the binding of objects to (categorical) locations is important, without the need for retaining the precise positional layout. In addition, there is what we have called the *combined* or *integration* condition. Now participants are shown multiple different objects that have to be relocated to their precise positions (without marks). Arguably, this condition requires both knowledge of the precise positions that have been presented and knowledge of which object belongs to which location. Hence, it samples binding of objects to coordinate position information.

In this way, we have covered most of the presumed components of object-location memory. Object processing is measured by using either object-recall or recognition scores. The positions-only condition reflects the ability to process coordinate location information into memory. The binding aspect can be assessed by both the object-to-position-assignment procedure

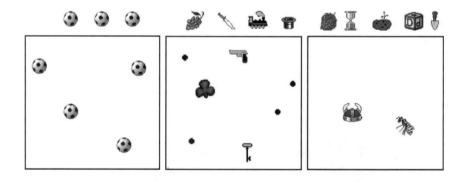

FIG. 7.3. Object-location memory conditions: (a) positions only, (b) object-to-position-assignment, and (c) combined. Different error measures are used in each condition. In the combined condition, the distance between an item's original and its relocated position is computed. For the positions-only condition, the best positional fit is computed for the stimulus as a whole. Note that a similar best fit measure can be derived in the combined condition as well by ignoring object identities. In the object-to-position-assignment condition, the percentage of mislocated objects is used.

(i.e., linking items to categorical locations) and by the combined condition (i.e., linking objects to coordinate positions; see Kessels, De Haan, Kappelle, & Postma, 2002). The only component not thoroughly examined in object-location memory tasks is the categorical-position condition. One possibility is to fill a number of cells in a grid (cf. Kosslyn, Maljkovic, Hamilton, Horwitz, & Thompson, 1995); this would not involve precise metric positional memory. However, when the number of cells increases, the distinction between categorical and coordinate location processing becomes less clear (Postma, 1996). Another possibility is to decompose the aggregate performance in the positional memory condition into a precise, metric component and a biased, categorical component, reflecting the tendency to reconstruct positions in the direction of protopical category values (Huttenlocher, Hedges, & Duncan, 1991; Allen & Haun, chap. 3, this volume).

NEUROPSYCHOLOGICAL DISSOCIATIONS BETWEEN OBJECT-LOCATION MEMORY COMPONENTS

To further distinguish between the proposed components of object-location memory as well as to delineate their precise characteristics, we take a look at some of the available empirical evidence. Our main interest here is studies of patients with cerebral lesions.

Object Processing Versus Spatial-Location Processing

As we have already argued, there is abundant evidence supporting a distinction between knowing what and knowing where, that is, between object processing and spatial-location processing. Object recognition comprises both viewer-centered and object-centered representations that have parallel access to stored descriptions of the structures of known objects and to subsequent semantic properties (Ellis & Young, 1996). Impairments to these representations can lead to particular deficits in visual object recognition (i.e., visual agnosia). On one hand, the role of the right hemisphere has been emphasized in object recognition, in particular its contribution to processing noncanonical views (Layman & Greene, 1988; McAuliffe & Knowlton, 2001; Warrington & James, 1986; Warrington & Taylor, 1973, 1978). On the other hand, Marsolek (1999) and Burgund and Marsolek (2000) have argued that a viewpoint-abstract, category-tuned object-recognition system would be operating in the left hemisphere, whereas a viewpoint-dependent, exemplar system would be situated in the right hemisphere. Moreover, transcranial magnetic stimulation (TMS) at the left posterior inferior temporal cortex caused a picture identification deficit (Stewart, Meyer, Frith, & Rothwell, 2001), whereas right-sided TMS did not. Laeng, Shah, and Kosslyn (1999) argued that the left hemisphere performs superiorly for encoding objects in novel, contorted poses, whereas the right hemisphere is better in encoding familiar, conventional poses of objects.

The role of object processing has not been fully examined yet within the context of object-location memory. M. L. Smith and Milner (1981, 1984) demonstrated normal immediate object-name recall both in patients with left-hemisphere lesions and in patients with right-hemisphere lesions, with disordered object-location recall in the right temporal lobe patients only. Delayed object recall was impaired in all patients, most strongly in those with left-hemisphere lesions (M. L. Smith & Milner, 1981; see also Nunn et al., 1999). It should be mentioned that their object-location recall measures primarily taxed binding components and thus to some extent "knowing what" was also important. Kessels, Postma, Kappelle, and De Haan (2002) found that right-hemisphere stroke patients were most affected on an object-recognition task as well as on a purely positional memory task. We do not know to what extent the fact that in this study the objects were always shown from the same viewpoint might have engaged the right hemisphere more. Abrahams, Pickering, Polkey, and Morris (1997) did not find any object-memory deficit at all in left and right hippocampal patients.

Partly different working-memory paradigms have revealed further dissociations between object and location processing. In a brain-imaging study, E. E. Smith et al. (1995) contrasted object working memory with spatial working memory and found that the former activated left-parietal and temporal areas, whereas the latter activated right-sided occipitoparietal and prefrontal areas. In addition, Hecker and Mapperson (1997) and Kessels, Postma, and De Haan (1999b) have had normal controls perform a task in which five items were shown serially for 500 ms in a 3 × 3 grid. Subsequently, participants had to choose from nine items the five original targets and place them in their correct locations again. It was found that concurrent chromatic flicker affected item identity recognition, whereas contrast flicker interfered selectively with positional recognition. The two types of flicker were associated with saturation of the parvocellular and magnocellular channel, respectively. Apparently, shape and location recognition clearly dissociate within hemispheric circuits.

In short, we may identify a distinct object-processing component, presumably in the ventral stream. As yet, it is unclear whether its role in object-location memory is mainly confined to the left hemisphere (Nunn et al., 1999) or also recruits right-hemisphere resources (Kessels, De Haan, et al., 2002).

Left Versus Right Brain: Dissociating Binding from Positional Memory Per Se

In previous studies with healthy control participants, we already found certain differences between the aforementioned object-location memory conditions bearing on the distinction between the binding components and task procedures measuring positional memory per se. In particular,

Postma and De Haan (1996) observed that the former were clearly affected by performing a verbal dual task, whereas the latter were not or to a much smaller extent. In turn, sex differences favoring males pertain mostly to the tasks requiring retention of precise positional information (Postma, Izendoorn, & De Haan, 1998; Postma, Winkel, Tuiten, & Van Honk, 1999). In line with this, in two recent studies on individual cases testing tumor and stroke patients (Kessels, Postma, Kappelle, et al., 2000, 2002), selective impairments of the binding and positional components of object-location memory were observed. Four patients showed specific difficulty in positional memory, with normal performance on the other conditions. In contrast, six other patients had problems restricted to binding objects with locations, two of whom had a problem only in the object-to-position-assignment condition but not in the combined condition. Accordingly, we clearly can say that there are multiple components in object-location memory, which may be selectively impaired. Figure 7.4 shows the performance of the individual stroke cases.

Regarding the critical neuroanatomical sites of these lesions, a recent group study of cortical stroke patients is important (Kessels, Postma, et al.,

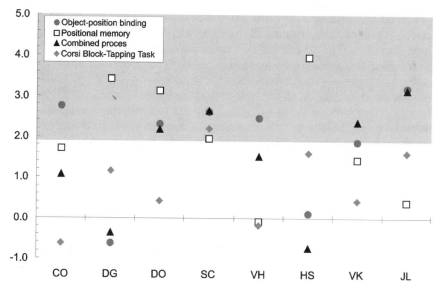

FIG. 7.4. Standardized scores for eight stroke patients on object-location memory conditions and spatial working memory (Corsi Block-Tapping Task). Five patients had parietal lesions; one suffered hippocampal ischaemia; one patient had subcortical infarcts; and one had multiple frontal, temporal, and parietal infarcts (Adapted from Kessels, Postma, Kappelle, & De Haan, 2001).

2002). Patients were tested at least 5 months after the onset of the stroke. Lesions were most frequent in the temporo-occipitoparietal area. Most interesting, Kessels, Postma, et al. (2002) observed that left-hemisphere patients had problems in the binding conditions—specifically the object-to-position-assignment condition—whereas the right-hemisphere patients performed poorly in the positions-only condition. Two conjectures can be made with respect to this result. First, it might be that in the former conditions either the object processing component[2] itself or the binding mechanism in someway depends on verbal processing. Note that Postma and De Haan (1996) also found a verbal interference effect in this condition. Similarly, Goldstein et al. (1989) subscribed spatial-memory problems in left temporal-lobe patients to co-occurring naming difficulties. M. L. Smith, Leonard, Crane, and Milner (1995) observed comparable disorders in left and right temporal-lobe patients when multiple object-location recall trials were given. The impaired performance of the left-hemisphere group was also presumed to derive from difficulties in verbal processing. Second, this result might reflect the differential lateralization, which is thought to apply to categorical and coordinate location processing. Kosslyn (1994; Kosslyn et al., 1989) has argued that the left posterior parietal cortex would be specialized in processing categorical spatial relations, whereas the right hemisphere is superior in coordinate spatial relations. Accordingly, Laeng (1994) observed left-hemisphere stroke patients do worse for categorical decisions. In contrast, right-hemisphere patients performed poorly on coordinate decisions. The positions-only condition bears directly on coordinate processing and the object-to-position-assignment condition indirectly on categorical coding (cf. Postma & De Haan, 1996).

One complication with the foregoing reasoning is that it clearly seems to conflict with the contention offered by many previous studies that object-location memory problems solely or most prominently occur after right hemispheric damage, namely, to the hippocampal formation (Bohbot et al., 1998; Goldstein et al., 1989; Nunn et al., 1999; M. L. Smith and Milner, 1981, 1984, 1989). Several factors might be responsible. First, and most important, the types of patients were different. Whereas other studies included patients with damage to the medial temporal lobe and hippocampal formation, Kessels and colleagues (Kessels, Postma, et al., 2002) tested patients with cortical, primarily parietotemporal lesions. Potentially, this may lead to both lateralization differences and encoding versus retention differences. Second, the stimuli tended to keep the same alignments with respect to the body of the observer. Hence, egocentric coding factors may be important, which are less dependent on right (hippocampal) integrity (Goldstein et al., 1989; Holdstock et al., 2000;

---

[2]Note, however, that the left-hemisphere group did not have problems in object recognition. Rather, the right-hemisphere group scored significantly lower than the controls.

Morris, Pickering, Abrahams, & Feigenbaum, 1996; O'Keefe & Nadel, 1978). Third, as far as we know, the binding factor in the object-to-position-assignment condition has not been assessed previously.

A second complication is that the components of object-location memory do not form simple additive mental processes. As can be seen in Fig. 7.4, patient DG is severely impaired on positional memory, that is, he has severe difficulty in reconstructing the positions of a set of identical objects but performs even slightly above average in the combined condition: He nevertheless can perfectly well place multiple different objects back, not only in their relative location (as in the object-to-position-assignment condition) but also in their fine-grained position (as in the combined condition). How can this patient normally reconstruct the coordinate positions of multiple different objects when he cannot make a correct positional map to start with? One solution is that performance in the combined condition depends more on binding ability than on precise positional memory. Clearly, larger errors arise when objects are interchanged (a binding error) than when they are displaced (a positional-memory failure). Indeed, as expected, correlations between object-to-position-assignment and the combined condition tend to be much higher than between the positions-only and combined condition (Kessels, Postma, et al., 2002). Intriguingly, patients CO and VH perform significantly worse on the object-to-position-assignment condition while achieving normally in the combined condition. This can suggest that in the combined condition—sampling aggregated object-location memory scores—depending on the particular circumstances partial compensation is possible. That is, when one cannot remember where something was globally, one might profit from concentrating more on the precise locations shown (or vice versa). Alternatively, the binding process itself might encompass separate categorical and coordinate binding subcomponents.

Anterior Versus Posterior Cortex: Dissociating Spatial Working Memory From Object-Location Memory

As will be clear from the foregoing, the neural circuitry underlying spatial memory in general and object-location memory in particular is widespread. Both hippocampal and posterior cortical areas play a critical role. In addition, the (right) prefrontal cortex seems important. There is substantial evidence that the prefrontal cortex is relevant for binding features in working memory (Baddeley, 2000; Mitchell, Johnson, Raye, & D'Esposito, 2000), specifically including spatial features (Fletcher, Shallice, & Dolan, 1998; Fletcher, Shallice, Frith, Frackowiak, & Dolan, 1998; Kessels, Postma, Wijnalda, & De Haan, 2000). Nevertheless, the involvement of the prefrontal cortex in object-location memory is less clear. M. L. Smith and Milner (1989) observed right frontal lobe patients to have normal object recall. Only when multiple subsequent trials were given, frontal patients started to get worse, possibly because of accumulating proactive interference (Smith et al., 1995). One factor that might be critical to frontal lobe functioning is time. Frontal lobes might serve as a temporary visuospatial working memory and binding device and might not be involved in retaining information over longer periods of time. As object-location memory tasks typically present stimuli for periods of time that allow transfer into more sustained memory format, the role of the frontal lobes is minimized. At the same time, when recall of object-location is fast enough, posterior lobe patients may perform fairly well, benefiting from remaining working memory traces (Miotto, Bullock, Polkey, & Morris, 1996; M. L. Smith & Milner, 1989).

A second relevant factor concerns the extent to which active spatial search and processing is involved in the task. Being linked to executive functioning in general (Robbins, 1996), the prefrontal cortex typically plays a role in tasks engaging planning and keeping track of search through space. A classical example is the executive golf task (Miotto et al., 1996), which requires participants to find a target hole within a number of golf holes presented on a computer screen. The ability to plan an efficient search path is disordered in frontal lobe patients (Miotto et al., 1996). Perhaps the deficit in strategy formation is further aggravated by the need for active spatial processing in this task. In recent patient studies, most of the lesions were in the posterior cortex (Kessels et al., 2000, 2001, 2002a & b). Notably, although there were clear impairments in both immediate and delayed object-location memory, performance on the Corsi Block-Tapping Task (Kessels, Van Zandvoort, Postma, & De Haan, 2000) was impaired only in one of the patients (see Fig. 7.4). The Corsi Block-Tapping Task requires reproduction of an active spatial pattern. That is, a sequence of identical blocks has to be tapped in the same order as presented (see Schumann-Hengsteler et al., chap. 5, this volume). Frontal lobe patients, however, tend to achieve poorly on this task (Ferreira, Verin, Pillon, Levy, & Dubois, & Agid, 1998). In short, the prefrontal cortex might be relevant for object-location memory only when time periods for encoding and recall are in the working memory range or when there is a dynamic, temporal aspect involved in the spatial task (cf. Pickering, 2001).

Long-Term Retention and Binding: The Hippocampal Formation

In their seminal work *The Hippocampus as a Cognitive Map*, O'Keefe and Nadel (1978) most explicitly formulated the proposal that the hippocampus serves as the neural substrate for allocentric cognitive mapping of a person's environment. That is, it would contain viewer-independent representations of either topological or fine-grained locations and of the objects that occupy these locations, as well as of the connections or routes between them. As such, and in line with the foregoing overview, the hippocampus is crucial for object-location memory. Regarding the characteristics of this hippocampal involvement, one issue has already been dealt with previously: time. M. L. Smith and Milner (1989) showed that hippocampal patients had normal object-location memory recall when tested immediately after exposure to the object array. However, if recall was delayed for more than 4 min, performance deteriorated. Notice that this delay effect has not been examined much and needs further corroboration. Nevertheless, in light of the generally alleged hippocampal functions, it seems reasonable to assume that the hippocampus particularly serves to retain and consolidate information after encoding (Burgess, Jeffery, & O'Keefe, 1999). The cortical (prefrontal and posterior) areas discussed previously might serve either encoding or retrieval processes. Furthermore, Rosenbaum et al. (2000) demonstrated that spatial memory for well-consolidated, remote (i.e., moment of learning is distant from the testing moment) information may shift from the hippocampus to the cortex.

If we follow the foregoing suggestion, the next question is what are the characteristics of the object-location memory traces stored in the hippocampus? Neurophysiological studies in animals have indicated the presence of "place and view-independent" cells in the hippocampus (Burgess et al., 1999). Accordingly, an allocentric sense of location is supposed. Underlying and extending this allocentric position system could be the fact that the hippocampus is an area where highly processed and multimodal cortical as well as subcortical projections come together. The hippocampal formation thus might be critical to (long-term) binding of these different pieces of information. Interestingly, patients with amnesia are often reported to have distinctive problems in spatial memory even when their recall of general item information was controlled for (cf. Shoqeirat & Mayes, 1991). In line with the context deficit hypothesis of amnesia, it has been claimed that episodic memory disorders arise from failure to place events (or objects) in the proper context (e.g., Where did it happen?; Where did the items reside?). Cave and Squire (1991), however, showed that patients with amnesia with hippocampal lesions do not necessarily suffer disproportional spatial-memory deficits.

The foregoing considerations raise the question whether the hippocampus is relevant only for the binding conditions or whether it is also engaged in positional memory. In support of the former, Owen, Milner, Petrides, and Evans (1996) found in a positron emission tomography study more activation in the enthorinal cortex[3] when subtracting a location-retrieval condition from an object-location retrieval condition. In a functional MRI working-memory study, Mitchell et al. (2000) showed greater hippocampal activation in a binding condition than in individual feature conditions. Similarly, Chalfonte et al. (1996) argued that the hippocampal-diencephal circuitry is

---

[3]We simplify here by not differentiating between the various components of the hippocampal formation, such as the enthorinal cortex, the parahippocampal gyrus, and the hippocampus proper. There are several indications that these structures might serve different roles in visual and spatial memory (Bohbot et al., 1998).

central to integrating different features, specifically with respect to associating location to other features. In contrast, in a recent meta-analysis on human lesion studies, Kessels, De Haan, Kappelle, and Postma (2001) concluded that both object-location binding and positional memory suffer from hippocampal damage, especially from right-sided impairments. Although the number of positional memory studies was limited (only three), effects were quite large. Clearly, this is a topic needing further examination. The notion that the hippocampus serves both knowing where and knowing what was where is in general concordance with the cognitive map hypothesis.

CONCLUSIONS

Reaching the end of our overview of the neurocognitive basis of object-location memory, it has become clear that the picture is still fragmentary with many gaps to be filled in. We have seen that certain cortical areas, in particular posterior parietal and temporal regions, are critically involved in object-location memory. We speculate that their contribution bears predominantly on object recognition and spatial encoding factors. Parietal lobes are relevant in computing fine-grained and categorical spatial coordinates, lateralized to the right and the left hemisphere, respectively. It should be mentioned that the parietal lobes also are part of a distributed frontoparietal network underlying working memory. We have speculated that the frontal component could process active spatial working memory, whereas the parietal circuit might be more specialized in static visuospatial displays. Bringing all this information together and, moreover, retaining it in a more durable format seems the function of the hippocampal formation. Not only is it involved in binding objects to locations, it also serves to construct an absolute, allocentric positional map (independent from what is where). For the latter, it might use categorical and coordinate spatial computations in the parietal lobes, which essentially could be egocentric, and transform them into allocentric location codes. There seems abundant evidence that these hippocampal functions are lateralized, but the extent of lateralization may depend on whether the specific assessment task allows for effective verbal recoding of task components.

What does our functional analysis of object-location memory tell us about possible everyday life failures in relevant behaviors of patients and other specific subject populations (e.g., elderly)? Specifically, these behaviors would comprise searching for and finding tools, documents, keys, and so forth in the home environment. We speculate here on the consequences of disorders in prosposed functional components. Several hypothetical patient types can be considered. A patient with a deficit in object processing might feel the inclination to look for certain things but does not have a clear memory of which things precisely. In turn, damage to the positional coding system could cause forgetting of important locations where things generally are stored (e.g., cupboards). Finally, damage to the binding system might cause aberrant remembering of particular objects, either within rooms (the metric binding) or between rooms (categorical binding).

ACKNOWLEDGMENTS

This study was supported by a grant from the Dutch Organization for Fundamental Research (NWO No. 440–20–000). We thank Professor L. J. Kappelle, Department of Neurology, University Medical Center Utrecht, for his help in the patient studies.

REFERENCES

Abrahams, S., Pickering, A., Polkey, C. E., & Morris, R. G. (1997). Spatial memory deficits in patients with unilateral damage to the right hippocampal formation. *Neuropsychologia, 35*, 11–24.

Adelstein, T. B., Kesner, R. P., & Strassberg, D. S. (1992). Spatial recognition and spatial order memory in patients with dementia of the Alzheimer type. *Neuropsychologia, 30*, 59–67.

Baddeley, A. (2000). The episodic buffer: A new component of working memory. *Trends in Cognitive Sciences, 4*, 417–423.

Baylis, G. C., Gore, C. L., Rodriguez, P. D., & Shisler, R. J. (2001). Visual extinction and awareness: The importance of binding dorsal and ventral pathways. *Visual Cognition, 8*, 359–379.

Bohbot, V. D., Kalina, M., Stepankova, K., Spackova, N., Petrides, M., & Nadel, L. (1998). Spatial memory deficits in patients with lesions to the right hippocampus and to the right parahippocampal cortex. *Neuropsychologia, 36*, 1217–1238.

Bucks, R. S., & Willison, J. R. (1997). Development and validation of the Location Learning Test (LLT): A test of visuospatial leaning designed for use with older adults and in dementia. *Clinical Neuropsychologist, 11*, 273–286.

Burgess, N., Jeffery, K. J., & O'Keefe, J. (1999). Integrating hippocampal and parietal functions: A spatial point of view. In N. Burgess, K. J. Jeffery & J. O'Keefe (Eds.), *The hippocampal and parietal foundations of spatial cognition.* New York: Oxford University Press.

Burgund, E. D., & Marsolek, C. J. (2000). Viewpoint-invariant and viewpoint-dependent object recognition in dissociable neural subsystems. *Psychonomic Bulletin and Review, 7*, 480–489.

Caldwell, J. L., & Masson, M. E. J. (2001). Conscious and unconscious influences of memory for object location. *Memory & Cognition, 29*, 285–295.

Cave, C. B., & Squire, L. R. (1991). Equivalent impairment of spatial and nonspatial memory following damage to the human hippocampus. *Hippocampus, 1*, 329–340.

Chalfonte, B. L., Verfaellie, M., Johnson, M. K., & Reiss, L. (1996). Spatial location memory in amnesia: Binding item and location information under incidental and intentional encoding conditions. *Memory, 4*, 591–614.

Cohen, A., & Ivry, R. (1989). Illusory conjunctions inside and outside the focus of attention. *Journal of Experimental Psychology: Human Perception and Performance, 15*, 650–663.

Ellis, A. W., & Young, A. W. (1996). *Human cognitive neuropsychology.* Hove, England: Psychology Press.

Ferreira, C. T., Verin, M., Pillon, B., Levy, R., Dubois, B., & Agid, Y. (1998). Spatio-temporal working memory and frontal lesions in man. *Cortex, 34,* 83–98.

Fletcher, P. C., Shallice, T., & Dolan, R. J. (1998). The functional roles of prefrontal cortex in episodic memory: I. Encoding. *Brain, 121,* 1239–1248.

Fletcher, P. C., Shallice, T., Frith, C. D., Frackowiak, R. S. J., & Dolan, R. J. (1998). The functional roles of prefrontal cortex in episodic memory: II. Retrieval. *Brain, 121,* 1249–1256.

Goldstein, L. H., Canavan, A. G., & Polkey, C. E. (1989). Cognitive mapping after unilateral temporal lobectomy. *Neuropsychologia, 27,* 167–177.

Hasher, L., & Zacks, R. T. (1979). Automatic and effortful processes in memory. *Journal of Experimental Psychology: General, 108,* 356–388.

Hecker, R., & Mapperson, B. (1997). Dissociation of visual and spatial processing in working memory. *Neuropsychologia, 35,* 599–603.

Hellige, J. B., & Michimata, C. (1989). Categorization versus distance: Hemisferic differences for processing spatial information. *Memory & Cognition, 17,* 770–776.

Holdstock, J. S., Mayes, A. R., Cezayirli, E., Isaac, C. L., Aggleton, J. P., & Roberts, N. (2000). A comparison of egocentric and allocentric spatial memory in a patient with selective hippocampal damage. *Neuropsychologia. 38,* 410–425.

Huttenlocher, J., Hedges, L., & Duncan, S. (1991). Categories and particulars: Prototype effects in estimating spatial location. *Psychological Review, 98,* 352–376.

Jager, G., & Postma, A. (2003). On the hemispheric specialization for categorical and coordinate spatial relations: A review of the current evidence. *Neuropsychologia, 41,* 504–515.

Kessels, R. P. C., De Haan, E. H. F., Kappelle, L. J., & Postma, A. (2001). Varieties of human spatial memory: A meta-analysis on the effects of hippocampal lesions. *Brain Research Reviews, 35,* 295–303.

Kessels, R. P. C., De Haan, E. H. F., & Kappelle, L. J., & Postma, A. (2002). Lateralization of spatial-memory processes in humans: Evidence on spatial span, maze learning, and memory for object locations. *Neuropsychologia, 40,* 1465–1473.

Kessels, R. P. C., Postma, A., & De Haan, E. H. F. (1999a). Object Relocation: A program for setting up, running, and analyzing experiments on memory for object locations. *Behavior Research Methods, Instruments, & Computers, 31,* 423–428.

Kessels, R. P. C., Postma, A., & De Haan, E. H. F. (1999b). P and M channel-specific interference in the what and where pathway. *Neuroreport, 10,* 3765–3767.

Kessels, R. P. C., Postma, A., Kappelle, L. J., & De Haan, E. H. F. (2000). Spatial memory impairment in patients after tumor resection: Evidence for a double dissociation. *Journal of Neurology, Neurosurgery, and Psychiatry, 69,* 389–391.

Kessels, R. P. C., De Haan, E. H. F., Kappelle, L. J., & Postma, A. (2002). Selective impairments in object-location binding, metric encoding and their integration after ischaemic stroke. *Journal of Clinical and Experimental Neuropsychology, 24,* 115–129.

Kessels, R. P. C., Postma, A., Wester, A. J., & De Haan, E. H. F. (2000). Memory for object locations in Korsakoff's amnesia. *Cortex, 36,* 47–57.

Kessels, R. P. C., Postma, A., Wijnalda, E. M., & De Haan, E. H. F. (2000). Frontal-lobe involvement in spatial memory: Evidence from PET, fMRI, and lesion studies. *Neuropsychology Review, 10,* 101–113.

Kessels, R. P. C., Van Zandvoort, M. J. E., Postma, A., & De Haan, E. H. F. (2000). The Corsi block-tapping task: Standardisation and normative data. *Applied Neuropsychology, 7,* 252–258.

Kosslyn, S. M. (1994). *Image and Brain.* Cambridge, MA: MIT Press.

Kosslyn, S. M., Koenig, O., Barrett, A., & Cave, C. B. (1989). Evidence for two types of spatial representations: Hemispheric specialization for categorical and coordinate relations. *Journal of Experimental Psychology: Human Perception and Performance, 15,* 723–735.

Kosslyn, S. M., Maljkovic, V., Hamilton, S. E., Horwitz, G., & Thompson, W. L. (1995). Two types of image generation: Evidence for left and right hemisphere processes. *Neuropsychologia, 33,* 1485–1510.

Laeng, B. (1994). Lateralization of categorical and coordinate spatial functions: A study of unilateral stroke patients. *Journal of Cognitive Neuroscience, 6,* 189–203.

Laeng, B., Shah, J., & Kosslyn, S. (1999). Identifying objects in conventional and contorted poses: Contributions of hemisphere-specific mechanisms. *Cognition, 70,* 53–85.

Lansdale, M. W. (1998). Modeling memory for absolute location. *Psychological Review, 105,* 351–378.

Layman, S., & Greene, E. (1988). The effect of stroke on object recognition. *Brain and Cognition, 7,* 87–114.

Marsolek, C. J. (1999). Dissociable neural subsytems underlie abstract and specific object recognition. *Psychological Science, 10,* 111–118.

Mayes, A. R., Meudell, P. R. & Pickering, A. (1991). Disproportionate intentional spatial-memory impairments in amnesia. *Neuropsychologia, 29,* 771–784.

McAuliffe, S. P., & Knowlton, B. J. (2001). Hemispheric differences in object identification. *Brain and Cognition, 45,* 119–128.

Milner, A. D., & Goodale, M. A. (1995). *The visual brain in action.* Oxford, England: Oxford University Press.

Miotto, E. C., Bullock, P., Polkey, C. E., & Morris, R. G. (1996). Spatial working memory and strategy formation in patients with frontal lobe excisions. *Cortex, 32,* 613–630.

Mitchell, K. J., Johnson, M. K., Raye, C. L., & D'Esposito, M. (2000). fMRI evidence of age-related hippocampal dysfunction in feature binding in working memory. *Cognitive Brain Research, 10,* 197–206.

Morris, R. G., Pickering, A., Abrahams, S., & Feigenbaum, J. D. (1996). Space and the hippocampal formation in humans. *Brain Research Bulletin, 40,* 487–490.

Naveh-Benjamin, M. (1987). Coding of spatial location information: An automatic process? *Memory & Cognition, 4,* 595–605.

Naveh-Benjamin, M. (1988). Recognition memory of spatial location information: Another failure to support automaticity. *Memory & Cognition, 16,* 437–445.

Nunn, J. A., Graydon, F. J., Polkey, C. E., & Morris, R. G. (1999). Differential spatial memory impairment after right temporal lobectomy demonstrated using temporal titration. *Brain, 122,* 47–59.

O'Keefe, J., & Nadel, L. (1978). *The hippocampus as a cognitive map.* Oxford, England: Oxford University Press.

Owen, A. M., Milner B., Petrides, M., & Evans, A. C. (1996). A specific role for the right parahippocampal gyrus in the retrieval of object-location: A positron emission tomography study. *Journal of Cognitive Neuroscience, 8,* 588–602.

Pickering, S. J. (2001). Cognitive approaches to the fractionation of visuo-spatial working memory. *Cortex, 37,* 457–473.

Pillon, B., Deweer, B., Vidailhet, M., Bonnet, A., Hahn-Barma, V., & Dubois, B. (1998). Is impaired memory for spatial location in Parkinson's disease domain specific or dependent on 'strategic' processes? *Neuropsychologia, 36,* 1–9.

Pillon, B., Ertle, S., Deweer, B., Bonnet, A., Vidailhet, M., & Dubois, B. (1997). Memory for spatial location in 'de novo' Parkinsonian patients. *Neuropsychologia, 35,* 221–228.

Pillon, B., Ertle, S., Deweer, B., Sarazin, M., Agid, Y., & Dubois, B. (1996). Memory for spatial location is affected in Parkinson's disease. *Neuropsychologia, 34,* 77–85.

Postma, A. (1996). Reconstructing object locations in a 7 × 7 matrix. *Psychologische Beiträge, 38*, 383–392.

Postma, A., & De Haan, E. H. F. (1996). What was where? Memory for object locations. *Quarterly Journal of Experimental Psychology, 49A*, 178–199.

Postma, A., Izendoorn, R., & De Haan E. H. F. (1998). Sex differences and object location memory. *Brain and Cognition, 36*, 334–345.

Postma, A., Jager, G., Kessels, R. P. C., Koppeschaar, H. P. F., & Van Honk, J. (2000). *Selective sex differences for various forms of spatial memory.* Manuscript submitted for publication.

Postma, A., Winkel, J., Tuiten, A., & Van Honk, J. (1999). Sex differences and menstrual cycle effects in human spatial memory. *Psychoneuroendocrinology, 24*, 175–192.

Robbins, T. W. (1996). Dissociating executive functions of the prefrontal cortex. *Philosophical Transactions of the Royal Society of London, 351B*, 1463–1470.

Rosenbaum, R. S., Priselac, S., Köhler, S., Black, S. E., Gao, F., Nadel, L., & Moscovitch, M. (2000). Remote spatial memory in an amnesic person with extensive bilateral hippocampal lesions. *Nature Neuroscience, 10*, 1044–1048.

Sahakian, B. J., Morris, R. G., Evenden, J. L., Heald, A., Levy, R., Philpot, M. P., & Robbins, T. W. (1988). A comparative study of visuospatial memory and learning in Alzheimer-type dementia and Parkinson's disease. *Brain, 111*, 695–718.

Shoqeirat, M. A., & Mayes, A. R. (1991). Disproportionate incidental spatial-memory and recall deficits in amnesia. *Neuropsychologia, 29*, 749–769.

Smith, E. E., Jonides, J., Koeppe, R. A., Awh, E., Schumacher, E. H., & Minoshima, S. (1995). Spatial versus object working memory: PET investigations. *Journal of Cognitive Neuroscience, 7*, 337–356.

Smith, M. L., Leonard, G., Crane, J., & Milner, B. (1995). The effects of frontal- or temporal-lobe lesions on susceptibility to interference in spatial memory. *Neuropsychologia, 33*, 275–285.

Smith, M. L., & Milner, B. (1981). The role of the right hippocampus in the recall of spatial location. *Neuropsychologia, 19*, 781–793.

Smith, M. L., & Milner, B. (1984). Differential effects of frontal-lobe lesions on cognitive estimation and spatial memory. *Neuropsychologia, 22*, 697–705.

Smith, M. L., & Milner, B. (1989). Right hippocampal impairment in the recall of spatial location: encoding deficit or rapid forgetting? *Neuropsychologia, 27*, 71–81.

Stewart, L., Meyer, B., Frith, U., & Rothwell, J. (2001). Left posterior BA37 is involved in object recognition: A TMS study. *Neuropsychologia, 39*, 1–6.

Treisman, A., & Gelade, G. (1980). A feature-integration theory of attention. *Cognitive Psychology, 12*, 97–136.

Ungerleider, L. G., & Mishkin, M. (1982). Two cortical visual systems. In D. J. Ingle, M. A. Goodale & R. J. W. Mansfield (Eds.), *Analysis of visual behavior* (pp. 549–586). Cambridge, MA: MIT Press.

Warrington, E. K., & James, M. (1986). Visual object recognition in patients with right-hemisphere lesions: Axes or features. *Perception, 15*, 355–366.

Warrington, E. K., & Taylor, A. M. (1973). The contribution of the right parietal lobe to object recognition. *Cortex, 9*, 152–164.

Warrington, E. K., & Taylor, A. M. (1978). Two categorical stages of object recognition. *Perception, 7*, 695–705.

III

The Task of Remembering "Where Am I?"

Picking up the issue of large-scale space raised by Jeanne Sholl and Stephanie Fraone in chapter 4 (this volume), this group of chapters is concerned with spatial memory as a basis for spatial orientation and wayfinding. In chapter 8 (this volume), Sarah Creem-Regehr analyzes the literature on spatial updating, that is, the process of keeping track of the change in a person's spatial relations to environmental objects after movement. She focuses on differences between physical and imagined transformations, viewer and object transformations, and the relation between spatial transformations and responding. Chapter 9 (this volume) provides "good continuation," as Ed Cornell and Don Heth continue their productive, long-term, scientific partnership by proposing an integrated view of two major wayfinding mechanisms, dead reckoning and orienting by cognitive map. The proposal points to a highly informative research agenda. In chapter 10 (this volume), Robin Morris and David Parslow provide insight into the neurocognitive bases of spatial memory in large-scale environments, with consideration of path integration and cognitive mapping processes that maps directly onto the previous chapters in this section.

8

Remembering Spatial Locations:
The Role of Physical Movement in Egocentric Updating

Sarah H. Creem-Regehr
University of Utah

Knowing "where things are" even when objects go out of sight is a skill that comes easily to humans. A number of different paradigms have studied the process of *egocentric spatial updating,* or the mechanisms involved in locating positions in space relative to oneself after a given spatial transformation. As active observers, we as humans experience a moving world as a result of our own motion or the motion of objects in the environment. Gibson's (1979) perspective that a primary goal of perception is action (see also Milner & Goodale, 1995) can influence the way one conceptualizes spatial representation. Although Gibson did not consider mental representation a component of perception, a focus on motion of objects and actions of the body can provide a useful link between perception and memory of locations in space. In this chapter, I consider the influence of physical movement on two interactive components of spatial updating: self-transformations and object transformations and the response of the observer.

Within the domain of human spatial representation, researchers have examined the influence of self-movement in several different ways. One focus has been on the ability to carry out nonvisual locomotion to previously seen targets (Loomis, Da Silva, Fujita, & Fukusima, 1992; Loomis, Klatzky, Golledge, & Philbeck, 1999; Philbeck & Loomis, 1997; Rieser, Guth, & Hill, 1986). A second focus has been on updating tasks involving real versus imagined self-transformations. Some studies have involved comparing translational and rotational movement (Easton & Sholl, 1995; Farrell & Robertson, 1998; Presson & Montello, 1994; Rieser, 1989). Others have required participants to perform a real rotation or translation but to ignore it (Farrell & Robertson, 1998; Farrell & Thomson, 1998; May & Klatzky, 2000). Still others have compared rotation and translation of one's body in a virtual environment to transformations of the environment itself (Chance, Gaunet, Beall, & Loomis, 1998; Creem & Proffitt, 2000; Klatzky, Loomis, Beall, Chance, & Golledge, 1998; Pausch, Proffitt, & Williams, 1997; Wraga, Creem-Regehr, & Proffitt, in press). Together, these studies suggest that automatic updating of spatial locations occurs when participants are able to physically move their bodies, leading to more efficient, superior performance on updating tasks.

The influence of object movement on spatial representation has also been examined within different contexts. In updating tasks requiring imagination without real movement, object transformations have been shown to be difficult (Amorim & Stucchi, 1997; Creem, Wraga, & Proffitt, 2001; Presson, 1982; Wraga, Creem, & Proffitt, 2000b). The addition of haptic feedback during nonvisual object rotation (Wraga et al., 2000b) or visual object movement during an imagined transformation (Creem-Regehr, 2003) has been shown to facilitate updating, but similar results have not been found for scene recognition (Wang & Simons, 1999). Related studies have investigated the influence of motor representations in the facilitation of mental rotation tasks (Wexler, Kosslyn, & Berthoz, 1998; Wohlschlager & Wohlschlager, 1998), with evidence showing that physical motor rotation of an object influences mental rotation performance. Spatial updating studies using virtual environments comparing movement of the body to movement of the environment have suggested that information gained from body rotation is more helpful in spatial localization than that gained from the visual information of world movement alone (Chance et al., 1998; Wraga et al., in press). However, Creem and Proffitt (2000) suggested that the efficiency and accuracy of updating may rely on the compatibility between a given response measure and the type of rotation.

Recently, researchers have begun to pay attention to the influence of response measure on spatial updating performance (Creem & Proffitt, 2000; de Vega & Rodrigo, 2001; Wang, 2001; Wraga, in press). This focus introduces ideas that have been promoted by vision researchers (Bridgeman, Lewis, Heit, & Nagle, 1979; Creem & Proffitt, 2001; Milner & Goodale, 1995) about the processing of visual information by separable visual systems for distinct goals. Two separable but interactive cortical visual systems projecting from the primary visual cortex have been defined to subserve different goals, conscious perception, and visually guided action. One stream projects ventrally to the inferotemporal cortex mediating conscious perception, whereas the other stream projects dorsally to the posterior parietal cortex mediating visually guided action. This view suggests that the traditional dichotomy between "what" and "where" (Ungerleider & Mishkin,

1982) may be better described as "what" and "how" (Milner & Goodale, 1995). This revised description of the two visual systems places an emphasis on the goal of the task and on the frames of reference that are used to carry it out. Rather than placing the distinction on broadly defined object and spatial tasks, it is important to consider how information might be used differently by different response systems. The aim of this chapter is to examine the importance of movement of the self and of objects with respect to different spatial transformations and response requirements involved in spatial updating tasks.

BODY MOVEMENT AND UPDATING: ROTATIONS AND TRANSLATIONS

Nonvisual Locomotion

One example of the human ability of spatial updating can be seen in the accuracy of visually directed walking. Numerous studies have shown that when given the task to view a target and walk to it without vision, the average person will stop very close to the target for a large range of distances up to about 20 m (Loomis et al., 1992; Loomis et al., 1999; Philbeck & Loomis, 1997; Rieser et al., 1986; Thomson, 1983). It is generally agreed on that observers update the representation of the target's location as they are locomoting. Loomis, Da Silva, Philbeck, and Fukusima (1996) demonstrated this point by the evidence that indirect measures of visually directed behavior that could not involve preplanning produce accurate performance similar to direct walking. For example, in *triangulation by pointing,* an observer attempts to point continuously in the direction of a previously viewed target while walking; in *triangulation by walking,* the observer walks on an oblique path and at a signal turns to walk in the direction of the target. Updating in this context relies on the mechanism of *path integration* in which one's own location is updated through sensory signals of self-velocity or self-acceleration (Mittelstaedt & Mittelstaedt, 1982). Information can come from various signals: proprioceptive cues from the muscles and joints, vestibular cues of linear acceleration and rotation from the otolith organs and semicircular canals, and efferent feedback from the motor system. These cues form the idiothetic system as described in animal navigation. Loomis et al. (1999) defined a more broad meaning of path integration encompassing navigation processes in which discrete or continuous rotations and translations "are integrated to provide an estimate of position or orientation within a larger spatial framework" (p. 129).

The ease and accuracy of walking without vision to targets may occur because updating of space happens automatically with self-movement. Automatic, in this sense, means a process without intention, not necessarily one that requires little attentional or cognitive resources (Farrell & Robertson, 1998). Several studies have investigated the automaticity of updating with movement by using paradigms that require participants to ignore a given movement during the updating task. In one visually directed walking task involving translation and then rotation, Farrell and Thomson (1998) instructed participants to walk without vision to a target but to ignore their locomotion and imagine that they had not moved from their initial position. Participants performed in three conditions: updating, ignoring, and control. In the updating task, they viewed four targets in a layout, closed their eyes, and walked to the far side of the layout. Then they turned 180° so that they were facing back to the targets. A target was identified and the participant walked directly toward it without delay. In the ignoring task, participants followed the same procedure, but they were instructed to walk to the named target as if they had not performed the initial walking or rotation. In the control task, participants walked directly to a named target without vision from the starting point. The results indicated that accuracy was greater in the updating and the control task compared to the ignoring task, suggesting that updating occurred automatically with the initial locomotion. In a second experiment, Farrell and Thomson reasoned that given enough time for additional cognitive processing, participants might be able to overcome the automatic updating and perform as accurately on the ignore condition as on the updating and control conditions. They replicated the first experiment but introduced additional time before walking to the target. With a delay, the participants were able to compensate for the automatic updating and showed no decrement in performance in the ignore versus the other conditions.

Farrell and Robertson (1998) conducted a similar study involving only rotation to demonstrate the importance of having one's egocentric frame of reference aligned with the environment. The task was to view seven targets spaced evenly around a circle, rotate to face a given direction, and then point to the actual position of a named target. As in Farrell and Thomson (1998), in one condition, participants were asked to ignore their physical rotation and imagine they were still facing in their original direction. They also performed in an updating, imagination, and control condition. The results indicated that participants were less accurate and slower to respond in the ignoring and imagination conditions than the control condition. Participants found it easier to update their positions than to imagine that they had not moved. In both the imagine and ignore conditions, reaction time increased as a function of the angular distance from one's actual heading. (Note that *heading* refers to one's facing direction of orientation relative to a reference direction [Loomis et al., 1999].) In the imagine condition, participants required additional time to imagine a new heading. In the ignore condition, participants may have updated their orientation automatically as they rotated (even when instructed to ignore) and then needed additional time to reimagine themselves in their original position. The updating condition did not show any increase in reaction time with angle of rotation, suggesting that participants updated the spatial locations of the targets during the movement itself.

May and Klatzky (2000) recently expanded on the ignore paradigm by comparing both motor and nonmotor ignore tasks. They used a return-to-origin task in which participants walked along a path and then tried to return to their original starting position. In their first experiment, participants walked a simple one-legged path without vision and attempted to return to their starting position. During the outbound walking, they were interrupted at a random point and asked to perform a distractor task involving verbalization, counting backward, moving rightward, or moving backward. Only the moving-backward distractor had an effect on accuracy of returning to the origin. In subsequent experiments, May and Klatzky used a two-legged path in which participants had to return to their starting position after walking two legs of an isosceles triangle. They were interrupted to perform the distractor task along the first or second leg. Introducing rightward movement during the second leg led to increased error in turning and distance estimation, suggesting that participants found it more difficult to ignore the change of bearing produced by the movement distractor. (Note that *bearing* refers to the direction from the observer to an object or location with respect to a reference direction [Loomis et al., 1999].) May and Klatzky's fourth experiment used a virtual environment to assess whether movement specified by vision without corresponding vestibular and proprioceptive input would lead to the automatic updating seen in the previous experiments that provided vestibular and proprioceptive information without vision. Using a similar one-legged path as in the first experiment, the effect established in the first experiment was replicated, suggesting that ignoring positional changes (even without corresponding vestibular/proprioceptive information) that occur during real movement is difficult, requires additional cognitive computation, and produces systematic errors.

The ignore studies (Farrell & Robertson, 1998; May & Klatzky, 2000) suggest that physical body movement is tightly coupled to spatial updating, noticeably for transformations involving rotation beyond translation. Consistent with this claim are a number of earlier studies directly comparing the influence of physical self-movement during rotation and translation. For example, Rieser (1989) tested observers' abilities to access spatial positions from memory after imagined versus real rotation and translation. Observers studied an array of objects, and without vision, they attempted to point to a given object after facing another object using a pointer mounted on a protractor. During real-movement trials, the observer was guided to rotate to a new direction. During the imagined movement, the observer remained stationary and imagined facing a new direction. Rieser (1989) found that additional time was needed to respond to the imagined trials and that the reaction time increased as a function of the amount of rotation required. Rieser's second experiment used similar methodology but required separate trials of imagined translation and rotation. In the translation task, participants were asked to point at a given object as if standing at another object compared to facing in the rotation task. In contrast to the rotation task, performance after imagined translation to a new object did not differ from the baseline of no change in point of observation. Real movement was not included in this experiment. Rieser (1989) explained the distinction in performance between translation and rotation as a result of the frames of reference involved in updating of spatial representations. He proposed that without movement, observers access object-to-object relations rather than self-to-object relations, which do not change as a result of translation of observation point but do change with rotation.

Presson & Montello (1994) replicated Rieser's (1989) general findings providing a direct comparison between real and imagined translation and rotation and equating the changes of direction for the two types of movement. Updating was superior when comparing real versus imagined movement for rotation but not translation. Presson and Montello suggested that the difficulty in imagined rotations can be partially explained by a conflict between primary and secondary frames of reference. The primary egocentric frame of reference is one's front–back, left–right, and up–down axes relative to the immediate environment. Imagining a rotation requires the construction of a secondary egocentric frame of reference (a new front, back, left, and right) that conflicts with the primary frame of reference. Real rotation eliminates this conflict by aligning the two frames of reference. With imagined translation, the axes of one's primary frame of reference remain parallel to the secondary frame of reference, allowing for ease of pointing to an object from a new observation point. It is important to note, however, that all of the studies described so far have used similar action-based response measures—pointing or walking. In later sections, I discuss the importance of considering that different ways of responding may rely on different spatial information. An active response coming from one's own body might rely more on one's primary frame of reference grounded in physical body position, and measures that rely on representations that are not tied to body position (e.g., language or nonegocentric frameworks) might produce different results. Some evidence in support of this claim (Creem & Proffitt, 2000; de Vega & Rodrigo, 2001; Wraga, in press) is discussed later.

Visual Locomotion

Similar to studies involving nonvisual updating, the differential influence of physical movement on rotation and translation is apparent in tasks that provide visual information. Studies have used virtual environments to examine the relative contribution of vestibular, proprioceptive, and efferent motor information on updating (Chance et al., 1998; Creem & Proffitt, 2000; Klatzky et al., 1998; Wraga et al., in press). The research of Klatzky et al. (1998) provides a good link between the research presented previously on imagined and real movements in the real world and movement in virtual environments because it involved both visual and nonvisual real and imagined tasks. Klatzky et al. used a task in which an observer was asked to imagine/move on one leg of a path, turn, then imagine/move the second leg and then face their origin. Observers participated in one of five conditions, two of which involved a virtual environment. In the real-world conditions, participants heard a description of and imagined walking the path (describe), viewed the experimenter walk the path (watch), or walked the path blindfolded with a guide (walk). In the virtual conditions, optical flow patterns were presented that would be produced by translating along the first leg. In one condition (real turn), an experimenter turned the participant, and then the visual flow for leg two was presented. In a second condition (visual turn), optic flow patterns were presented for both translation and rotation components. Klatzky et al. found that in the conditions that did not allow a physical turn (describe, watch, and visual turn), participants made large systematic errors in updating their heading. The visual information without vestibular and proprioceptive information provided in the visual-turn virtual condition was not effective for accurate updating.

A similar finding of the importance of physical rotation was demonstrated by Chance et al. (1998) when they tested updating performance of participants using a virtual maze after three different locomotion modes that involved varying amounts of coupling between vestibular, proprioceptive, and visual information. In a real-walking condition, vestibular and proprioceptive information from real movement was coupled with the visual information for translation and rotation in a virtual environment. In a real-rotation condition, translation was specified visually only (by moving a joystick), but rotations were performed physically. In a visual-rotation condition, both translations and rotations were signaled by visual information alone. Chance et al. found that participants were significantly better at updating locations after real walking compared to transporting themselves entirely with a joystick (visual rotation). Performance accuracy with real rotation alone fell in between real walking and visual rotation.

In a study involving only rotation, Wraga et al. (in press) compared observers' ability to update the locations of unseen alcoves in a rectangular or circular room after rotation of themselves to a new perspective (viewer task) or after rotation of the room itself (display task). Participants were asked to search for a target by rotating. After finding the target, they indicated the location of an unseen location. In addition to varying the correspondence between visual and vestibular/proprioceptive information, Wraga et al. (in press) also manipulated whether the viewer rotation was performed actively or passively by having the participant rotated in a swivel chair. They found superior updating performance in the viewer task, which provided the additional body- movement information corresponding to the optic flow, compared to the display task, which decoupled body and visual information. They found little effect of the active–passive manipulation, however, suggesting that proprioceptive and efference information may have played a smaller role in updating than vestibular cues.

The visual and nonvisual locomotion studies imply differences in the cues necessary for updating with rotations versus translations. With respect to translation, May and Klatzky (2000) found that observers could not ignore the backward translation specified by optic flow in their virtual environment experiment. Chance et al. (1998) found that observers performed relatively well with visually specified translation as long as physical body-rotation information was present. Based on these results together, one might expect that a condition that required ignoring visual rotation in a virtual environment might not interfere with updating because of the apparent importance of physical self-rotation in updating heading. Updating during translation may be carried out easily without visual information if self-movement is allowed (visually directed walking) and without movement if vision is allowed (virtual environments). However, updating during rotation is greatly facilitated by at least some of the information provided by physical self-movement. Whether or not the facilitation relies differentially on efference copy, proprioceptive, or vestibular system information is a question that needs to be addressed further.

Other memory domains support distinctions with respect to rotational and translational movement and may help to elucidate fundamental differences in processing with respect to the two types of transformations. Price and Gilden (2000) tested memory for direction of motion comparing isolated visual presentation of rotations, translations, and looming motions. In a study phase, participants were shown objects that were either translating across a screen or rotating around their centers. In testing, the previously studied displays were presented along with new animations, and the participant determined whether the presented stimulus was "old" (the one they had seen before) or "new." Using the same procedure, a second study introduced looming motions in which objects appeared to be either expanding or contracting. The results indicated accurate direction memory for translations and looming motions but no accurate direction memory for rotations. Despite the lack of memory for rotation direction, observers remembered the objects themselves and the class of motion (translation or rotation). Price and Gilden suggested that people consciously remember motions that involve displacements of locations in space. Directions of translations left or right or forward or backward (expansion and contraction) have consequences for where things are. Direction of rotation does not necessarily predict where an object will be located because any displacement could be achieved by clockwise or counterclockwise motion. This reasoning could explain the human ability to use visual information specifying translation without corresponding vestibular/motor information better than the ability to use visual rotation information alone, as seen in Chance et al. (1998) and Klatzky et al. (1998).

OBJECT/WORLD MOVEMENT AND UPDATING: ROTATIONS AND TRANSLATIONS

As humans are active organisms, intuitively movement might be more influential relative to self-transformations in spatial updating compared to object transformations. However, movement associated with objects or the environment has been shown to facilitate spatial representations and spatial updating in several contexts. The cognitive task of imagining what an array of objects in the world would look like after an observer or the array has rotated has been examined extensively in recent studies (Amorim & Stucchi, 1997; Creem, Wraga, et al., 2001; Huttenlocher & Presson, 1979; Presson, 1980, 1982; Wraga et al., 2000b). Updating after imagined object relative or environmental transformations has been shown to be difficult compared to imagined self-transformations. Initial studies by Presson and colleagues (Huttenlocher & Presson, 1979; Presson, 1980, 1982) have compared imagined viewer and object rotations in adults and children finding varying results depending on the type of information given. Overall, when an array of objects had to be rotated holistically, performance was poor. More recently, Amorim and Stucchi (1997) found a viewer advantage in a study comparing imagined object rotation and self-rotation. They asked participants to imagine that they were standing outside of a huge clock that was lying on the horizontal ground plane. Instead of hour and minute hands, the participants were to imagine that an upright three-dimensional uppercase letter "F" was in the center the clock. In the viewer task, they imagined moving to a given location around the periphery of the clock and updated the position of the letter from their new perspective. In the object task, they imagined that the letter was pointing to a new position around the clock and updated their own position on the clock with respect to the new letter position. Performance on the viewer task was faster and more accurate.

Wraga et al. (2000b) conducted six variations on a task initially conducted by Presson (1982) in which participants were asked to spatially update the positions of objects or parts of objects during imagined self-rotations or object rotations. In three of the experiments, participants stood facing four objects in a diamond-shaped array placed on pedestals on the floor. They first memorized the position of the objects with respect to top, bottom, left, and right. In testing, they were given a degree of rotation and a position in the array, and they were asked to verbally name the object that corresponded to the given position after either imagined self-rotation or array rotation without vision (e.g., "Rotate 90°, what's on the right?"). Wraga et al. (2000b) found that when the question was phrased in this way, the viewer task was faster and more accurate. Wraga et al. (2000b) proposed that the consistent viewer advantage resulted from the human cognitive ability to transform the egocentric frame of reference cohesively and efficiently. In contrast, the array-rotation task involved transformation of the object-relative frame, which may be represented and transformed with less internal cohesion. Three additional experiments demonstrated this claim. In one experiment, the four-object array was replaced with a single wooden rectangular block with four differently colored sides. Participants memorized the colors of the sides of the block as they had memorized the objects in the array. Performance replicated the advantage found in the four-object array studies for updating after viewer versus object rotation. In a second experiment, the colored square was replaced with a toy car with four familiar sides (driver-side, passenger-side, hood, and trunk). Using a familiar configuration improved imagined array-rotation performance, but not to the level of the viewer task. Finally, in a third experiment, the wooden block was physically rotated in the participant's hand while the imagined rotation question was asked. Although participants were blindfolded, they gained haptic information about the turning of the block. Reaction time and errors for this condition decreased to the level of viewer rotation performance. Wraga et al. (2000b) suggested that the block-turning manipulation enabled participants to transform the object's frame of reference in a more cohesive manner, thus facilitating updating.

The difficulty of imagined object rotations and the distinctions seen previously between imagined self-rotation and self-translation introduces the question of whether imagined object translations might be easier to perform than imagined object rotations in the context of spatial updating tasks. Price and Gilden (2000) showed that memory for translation direction is better than for rotation direction. Thus, if humans have a better ability to remember translations of objects, they could have a better ability to imagine the translation of objects. Following this reasoning, one might not expect to see a difference between imagined viewer and object translation as seen in the rotation tasks (Amorim & Stucchi, 1997; Presson, 1982; Wraga et al., 2000b).

To test this question, Creem-Regehr (2003) recently compared imagined viewer and object translation using a paradigm similar to Wraga et al. (2000b) and then introduced a physical movement manipulation. In the imagined-transformation studies, participants were presented with a row of seven colored wooden squares on a large board. In one experiment, they stood with the array to their left with three objects extending in front and behind them in the sagittal plane. In a second experiment, the array was placed in front of the observer with objects extending to the right and left in the fronto-parallel plane (see Fig. 8.1).

Participants memorized the positions of the colored blocks with respect to steps (zero, one, two or three) in front or behind (or left and right). Without vision, they were given a number of steps to imagine translating and a position in the array relative to themselves (e.g., "Two forward, what's in front?"). They performed a set of trials of imagined self-translation and a second set of trials requiring imagined array translation. The order of task condition was counterbalanced between participants. They were instructed to respond verbally with the name of the colored block and response time (RT) and accuracy were recorded. Similar to the imagined

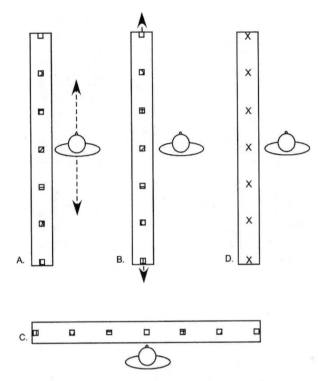

FIG. 8.1. Schematic representation of viewer and array for forward–backward movement (A, B, D) and left–right movement (C). A: In imagined viewer translation, the observer imagined moving forward or backward without vision. B: In imagined array translation, the observer imagined the array moving forward or backward without vision. C: Configuration of viewer relative to the array in the left–right imagined movement task. D: In the real versus imagined tasks, the blocks were removed showing placement markers, and the observer moved his or her body or watched the experimenter move the board. Adapted from Creem-Regehr (2003).

rotation studies, there was a large difference between performance between the self-tasks and array tasks for both RT and accuracy. Participants were faster and more accurate at updating with self-translation compared to object translation. In the self-translation task, RT did not increase with number of steps. In the object-translation task, RT increased with increasing steps of translation above zero. There was no significant effect of direction of movement or front versus back position in either task. Figure 8.2 presents the RT and accuracy data for the forward–backward and right–left imagined-movement conditions. In contrast to what might have been predicted based on distinctions between translation and rotation, these results

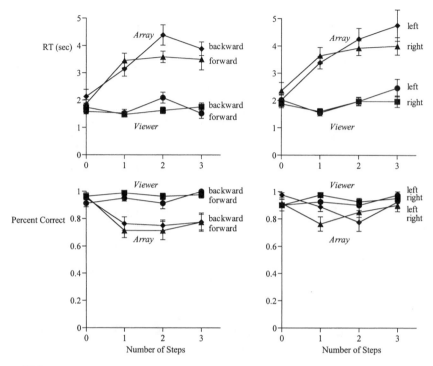

FIG. 8.2.   Reaction time (RT) and percent correct (+/− 1 *SE*) as a function of number of steps for the viewer and array imagined translation tasks forward–backward and left–right. Adapted from Creem-Regehr (2003).

indicated that the relative difficulty of imagined object and viewer translations was similar to that seen with imagined rotations.

In the next set of experiments, Creem-Regehr (2003) examined the influence of physical movement on an updating task with both object and viewer translations. Using the same layout as the forward–backward task in the previous experiment, one experiment directly compared updating after imagined versus real viewer translation. A second experiment directly compared updating after imagined versus real array translation. After the positions of the objects were memorized, the experimenter removed the blocks from the board on which they were placed, and the participant remained with eyes open during the entire experiment. This allowed for visual experience of the movement of the board in the real translation condition. Unlike the previous experiments, a 2-s delay was introduced after the transformation was specified to allow time to physically move either oneself or the array. For example, participants heard, "two forward [2-s de-lay], front?." During the delay, they either imagined moving two steps or physically moved forward two steps in the viewer task; in the array task, the participant imagined the array moving two steps or the experimenter physically moved the array two steps. Overall, there was no difference be-tween the real and imagined viewer translation task as would be expected from previous self-translation studies (e.g., Presson & Montello, 1994). Par-ticipants were as efficient and accurate in the imagined task as in the physi-cal self-movement task. More important, real movement of the array facilitated updating with array translation to the level of the viewer task (see Fig. 8.3). In addition, an effect of order (real first, imagined second vs. imagined first, real second) was seen in the array task. Performance on the imagined translation task improved when it was performed after the real translation condition.

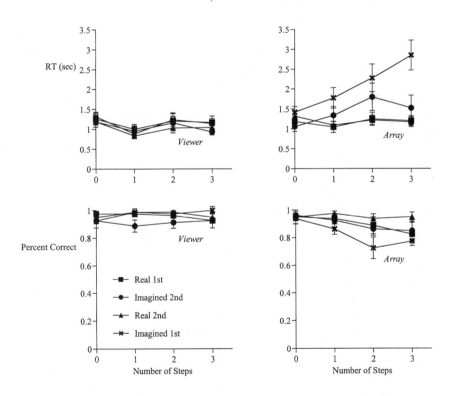

FIG. 8.3.   Reaction time (RT) and percent correct (+/–1 SE) as a function of number of steps for the real versus imagined viewer (left) and array (right) tasks. Adapted from Creem-Regehr (2003).

These results indicate that physical movement of an array that was specified visually without physical contact with the observer led to facilitation of updating similar to the facilitation seen in self-rotation studies as a function of physical self-movement. These findings lend support to the notion that the ease with which frames of reference may be transformed influences the speed and accuracy of spatial updating. When information about an array's moving frame of reference was provided, participants were able to update the locations of the objects automatically, leading to a flat RT function. Furthermore, additional information about the array's moving frame of reference appeared to transfer to the imagined translation task when the real translation was experienced first. More studies are needed to assess the generalizability of visual motion information for facilitating updating. The translation results are consistent with the suggestion that visual optic flow presented in virtual environments may lead to a similar updating experience as physical locomotion (May & Klatzky, 2000, Experiment 4). However, it remains to be seen whether visual rotation of display without haptic feedback will lead to facilitation in the context of spatially updating the positions of objects.

In a related domain, the influence of physical movement on imagined object rotation can be seen in cognitive paradigms that have used dual-task paradigms involving both mental rotation of an image and manual rotation of a dial or joystick (Wexler et al., 1998; Wohlschlager & Wohlschlager, 1998). Both series of experiments used stimuli based on the cube figures used originally by Shepard and Metzler (1971) and required participants to decide whether a rotated stimulus matched another stimulus. Wohlschlager and Wohlschlager (1998) found that motor rotation of a dial in a direction concordant with mental rotation facilitated performance, whereas motor rotation in a discordant direction inhibited performance. Wexler et al. (1998) demonstrated that a change in the speed of motor rotation of a joystick correspondingly affected the speed of mental rotation. Although these tasks involved object-based decisions about the orientation, they suggest both the close connection between real and imagined movements as well as a facilitation of spatial decisions when additional movement information is provided.

It is worthwhile to note that neuroimaging methods have provided a means to assess the recruitment of neural areas associated with motor processing in imagined spatial transformations (Cohen et al., 1996; Creem, Downs, et al., 2001; Kosslyn, DiGirolamo, Thompson, & Alpert, 1998; Kosslyn, Thompson, Wraga, & Alpert, 2001; Parsons et al., 1995). These studies have suggested shared neural substrates for imagined and real actions, although differences have been found in the extent of motor areas based on the type of transformation, the frame of reference, or explicit strategies.

THE RESPONSE MATTERS: DIRECT ACTION
VERSUS REPRESENTATION

It is clear from the research outlined previously that physical movement during transformation has an influential effect on spatial updating with respect to both self-transformations and object transformations. It is equally important, however, to consider how movement is related to the goal of the task. Specifically, a question remains as to the extent to which a given response measure may influence the processes involved in spatial updating. Theories of the modularity of visual processing suggest the importance of considering the goal of the task in understanding how visual information is transformed and used. The studies reviewed in the previous sections have involved physical and imagined transformations and pointing and verbal responses. Often, general mechanisms are proposed that are not defined with respect to a given response measure. In vision, the same visual information may be processed in different ways by different neural networks for specific goals. Similarly, spatial updating may rely on different mechanisms depending on the information provided and the response required.

In visual processing, broad distinctions have been made between object and spatial processing, or "where" versus "what" functions (Held, 1968; Schneider, 1969; Trevarthen, 1968; Ungerleider & Mishkin, 1982). More recently, theories have incorporated actions into the goals of vision (Bridgeman, Peery, & Anand, 1997; Goodale & Milner, 1992; Jeannerod, 1997). Milner and Goodale's (1995) theory maintains that a single general-purpose representation of objects or space does not exist. Instead, the visual system is defined by the requirements of the output that each stream subserves. Thus, separate systems are defined for conscious visual experience, perception or what, and visuomotor transformation, action or how. This perspective is based largely on defining systems for the use of different frames of reference. Both streams use the same object and spatial information but transform it differently for different purposes. The ventral what stream represents the visual world in both egocentric and viewer-invariant frameworks that promote an awareness of the world's persistent structure. In contrast, the dorsal how stream transforms the information about the location and orientation of objects in predominantly egocentric coordinates for action. The functions of the two streams can be differentiated on the basis of time as well as reference frame. If the goal is to represent an object over time, visually or spatially, then it is a function of the ventral stream. If the goal is to act on the object immediately, then the function is performed by the dorsal stream.

A number of studies support the dissociation between phenomenal awareness and visually guided actions. Many of these studies suggest that whereas conscious judgments appear to elicit biased responses, visually guided actions made directly toward a stimulus (such as grasping or pointing) are usually quite accurate. These results indicate a dissociation between two systems because although the same visual information is used, two different responses may be elicited. In a series of studies, Bridgeman and his colleagues (Bridgeman, Kirch, & Sperling, 1981; Bridgeman et al., 1979) asked participants to judge verbally, to point, or to make saccadic eye movements to where a target was displaced. In several experiments, participants were able to make saccades and point accurately to a displaced target, even though they did not verbally report that they detected the displacement. More recently, visual illusions have been used as stimuli to test perception-action dissociations. For example, Haffenden and Goodale (1998) presented participants with the Ebbinghaus illusion in which two same-size discs appear to be different sizes depending on the size of the surrounding circles. Participants gave a perceptual estimation through a manual task of matching the distance between their thumb and index finger to the diameter of the target disk. They also responded with a visuomotor task in which they grasped the disk without the view of their hand. Participants' maximum grip aperture corresponded to the actual size of the disk, regardless of the appearance of the disk. In contrast, the manual perceptual estimations of disk size were influenced by the illusion.

Subsequent studies have both supported (Aglioti, DeSouza, & Goodale, 1995; Brenner & Smeets, 1996; Bridgeman et al., 1997; Daprati & Gentilucci, 1997; Gentilucci, Chieffi, Daprati, Saetti, & Toni, 1996; Haffenden & Goodale, 2000; Jackson & Shaw, 2000; Proffitt, Bhalla, Gossweiler, & Midgett, 1995; Wraga, Creem, & Proffitt, 2000a) and countered (Franz, Gegenfurtner, Bulthoff, & Fahle, 2000; Pavani, Boscagli, Benvenuti, Rabuffetti, & Farne, 1999; Vishton, Rea, Cutting, & Nunez, 1999) the claim that visual illusions elicit perception-action dissociations. Most importantly, these studies have shown that careful attention should be placed on stimulus presentation and task demands when considering perception-action dissociations.

Incorporating this view into a spatial updating task, Creem and Proffitt (2000) concluded that updating performance may depend on the compatibility between the mode of spatial encoding and the mode of response. Creem and Proffitt manipulated whether or not the participant physically performed a rotation to encode a scene as well as the type of response involved—direct action or manipulating a pointing icon. Participants searched a virtual display by rotating their bodies or by controlling a device that rotated the virtual display about them. Then they pointed to a location in the display either using a visible compass controlled by a trackball or pointing directly with their arm. An interaction was found between mode of rotation and response measure. When participants rotated their bodies, their ability to point to an unseen target was best when they pointed directly with their bodies. In contrast, when people moved the external environment, their ability to point to an unseen target was best when they pointed with an external device. These findings suggest the importance of encoding-response compatibility in spatial updating performance.

Creem and Proffitt's (2000) intent was to assess the effects of compatibility between the mode of spatial encoding during rotation and the mode of the spatial updating pointing response. In two experiments, participants stood within a virtual circular room and memorized the positions of six colored alcoves, unevenly spaced insets into the walls of the virtual room. Their task was to search for an object by rotating in the room and then, without turning further, to point to a given alcove using two different response measures—pointing directly with their arm (ARM), or setting the pointer on a compass with a trackball (COMPASS). In Experiment 1, participants rotated their perspective by turning their body and head. Participants responded faster and more accurately when using their arm to point compared to using the trackball to control the compass. As Fig. 8.4 shows, the response time functions were flat for both response tasks, indicating that participants were able to automatically update locations of the alcoves as they rotated. This is consistent with other updating studies involving physical rotation (Farrell & Robertson, 1998; Wraga et al., in press).

Although Creem and Proffitt (2000) found a difference in mean error and reaction time between the two response tasks in the viewer-rotation updat-

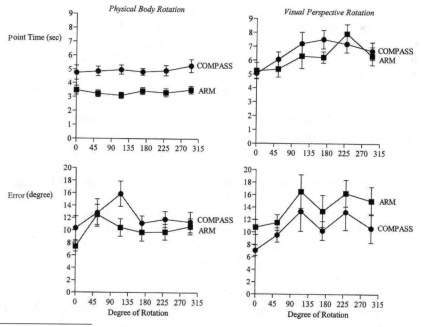

FIG. 8.4. Pointing time and error (+/– 1 *SE*) as a function of degree of rotation for ARM and COMPASS measures in the body (Experiment 1) and perspective (Experiment 2) rotation tasks of Creem & Proffitt (2000).

ing task, they questioned whether the advantage for pointing would generalize to other spatial transformations. It could be that a direct pointing measure would lead to superior updating performance under any circumstances, even without coupled vestibular and visual information available. Creem and Proffitt predicted, however, that the pointing advantage was tied to internal knowledge of body position that resulted from physical movement of one's body. If participants experienced rotation of the external world, Creem and Proffitt predicted that they would not show an advantage for direct pointing. Experiment 2 attempted to answer this question by comparing the same two response tasks in a rotation task that provided uncoupled visual and vestibular information. Participants rotated their perspective by revolving the virtual room around themselves using a trackball. The results indicated no advantage of the ARM response task compared to the COMPASS when participants rotated their perspective without body movement. The advantage actually reversed in the measure of accuracy. Participants were more accurate when pointing with the compass compared to directly pointing with an arm. For pointing time, there was no difference between the two tasks. However, there was a between-subject difference between Experiments 1 and 2 with regard to response times in the ARM task. As Fig. 8.4 shows, ARM responses in Experiment 2 were slower than those in the first study to the point of equaling times for COMPASS responses. The overall increase in response time with degree of rotation suggests that unlike Experiment 1, participants were not able to automatically update the positions of the alcoves during rotation. Instead, participants needed additional time to update the positions of the alcoves after rotation. This finding is consistent with other updating studies involving only visual change (Wraga et al., in press) or imagined rotation (Farrell & Robertson, 1998; Reiser, 1989).

The loss of an advantage for direct pointing can be explained by the nature of encoding and rotation induced by the perspective rotation. With visual rotation only, a conflict results between the observer's physical position in the room of the laboratory and their new perspective in the virtual scene (a distinction between one's primary and secondary frame of reference similar to Presson and Montello's, 1994, imagined rotation studies). Because pointing with an arm is necessarily tied to one's real body position, participants must ignore that position and compute the transformation needed to point accurately from the new viewpoint. The compass, as a conceptual representation, may provide an alternate strategy of pointing that is based on an environmental representation that is detached from the viewer. Participants may have encoded the spatial relations of the alcoves relative to other alcoves or relative to the framework of the circular room. Together, these studies indicate that updating tasks, like other spatial tasks, may reveal differential performance as a function of the response measure itself. Furthermore, the performance with a particular mode of response was influenced by the type of information provided in the rotation component of the task.

Overall, these findings tie together previous work on spatial updating after transformations and perception-action dissociations. In spatial updating, Creem and Proffitt (2000) replicated the distinction between updating with and without body movement seen in previous studies involving both real and imagined transformations (Chance et al., 1998; Klatzky et al., 1998; Presson & Montello, 1994; Rieser, 1989; Wraga et al., in press). Participants were faster at updating the locations of alcoves after body rotation compared to perspective rotation alone. Across both response measures, the pointing times as a function degree of rotation clearly differed between the two types of rotation. When observers were allowed to physically rotate their bodies, time to point did not vary as a function of degree of rotation. These findings suggest that people can automatically update locations in space as they are moving. When observers rotated their perspective alone, they demonstrated an increase in updating time for rotations above 0°. This pattern indicates that the updating did not occur automatically and that additional processing was needed.

With regard to the distinction between perception and action, Creem and Proffitt (2000) differentiated between a conceptual pointing measure and a direct action measure. For accuracy, a double dissociation was found. Participants showed an advantage for direct pointing compared to compass pointing in the body-rotation task. In contrast, they showed an advantage for compass pointing compared to direct pointing in the perspective-rotation task. For reaction time, the advantage seen for direct pointing in Experiment 1 was lost in Experiment 2, leading to equal performance between the two response conditions. Because the type of rotation (body or perspective) was a between-subject manipulation, it remains a possibility that the differential performance effects could be attributed to individual differences between groups of participants. Future research is needed to replicate the dissociation. However, the idea that different spatial measures of updating in the same space may elicit distinctions in performance is consistent with much recent research supporting a dissociation of the two visual systems.

Research with neuropsychological patients and normal adults has suggested that one main consideration involved in defining a dissociation between visual systems may be whether the response is framed in a direct action (Bridgeman et al., 1997; Goodale & Haffenden, 1998; Haffenden & Goodale, 1998; Proffitt et al., 1995). The visuomotor system may be characterized as operating independently from the perceptual/cognitive system when probed with a one-to-one relation between target position and motor response. When this isomorphism is eliminated, a conceptual object or spatial representation is required, and the visuomotor system no long works independently. Research indicates a difference between two types of spatial tasks: acting directly in space (such as pointing, walking, or picking something up) and making a cognitive decision about space (communicating a spatial location through an alternative verbal or visual response). The arm versus compass results point out that one type of response is not necessarily "better" or more accurate than another. Rather, the distinctions between perception and action should be placed on understanding the relation between the information provided and the response task required. The results of Creem and Proffitt show first that an advantage for direct action is tied to information about one's own body position, and second, that when this information is not provided, people may rely on other means of encoding their environment that may be better served by a mode of response that corresponds to that encoding mode. The visual information used in the perspective-rotation task was better served by a conceptual pointing response that did not rely on the observer's actual body position.

Comparing response measures that may differentially rely on the visuomotor system introduces the question of the memory of the motor system itself. Within the framework of the two visual systems, research has shown that the independence of the how system is limited by time. A number of studies with normal (Bridgeman et al., 1997; Creem & Proffitt, 1998; Gentilucci et al., 1996) and patient populations (Goodale, Jakobson, & Keillor, 1994; Rossetti, 1998) suggest that different representations for conscious perception and visually guided action exist only in the short term. When delays are introduced between perceiving and acting, then actions are influenced by a conscious representation. For example, Bridgeman and colleagues (Bridgeman & Huemer, 1998; Bridgeman et al., 1997) used the Roelofs effect to elicit both separation and interaction between systems for conscious perception and visually guided action. In this effect, people tend to misperceive the location of a target in a rectangular frame when the frame is presented to the left or right of the center of the visual field. Despite this bias in perception that is revealed through an object-relative perceptual estimation communicated through a keyboard, a point or jab directly at the target showed accurate spatial localization. When a 4-s delay was added between the presentation of the target and the response, the frame biased the motor response as well.

This framework can be used to define differential performance seen in spatial updating tasks. Direct visually guided actions rely on an egocentric representation based on the immediate spatial relation of an object to an observer. With physical rotation of the observer, this egocentric representation is constantly updated and should be available to directly inform action. Without physical rotation (visual perspective change alone or imagined rotation), the motor system no longer has a direct one-to-one relation with the environment. Thus, it must rely on information from a stored spatial representation. The spatial representation may inform egocentric action with cognitive effort, or in some cases, it may inform a different response involving nonegocentric frames of reference (such as the environment-centered compass representation) more easily than the direct action.

De Vega and Rodrigo (2001) recently examined the relation between body position and measures of spatial localization. They compared pointing and verbal responses after real or imagined rotation to examine how language may constrain spatial conceptualization. Participants were given a verbal description of the landmarks in an environment. In their first study, participants pointed in the direction of a given landmark after real or imagined rotation. Their pointing method involved pressing one of four arrow keys on a computer keyboard. Participants were more accurate in the physical compared to the imagined-rotation condition. In their second experiment, participants performed the same experiment but were asked to respond with the verbal labels "left," "right," "front," or "back." Using verbal labels, participants performed with similar accuracy under both physical and imagined rotation. De Vega and Rodrigo suggested that pointing is highly connected to one's current body position, but labeling (a mental framework) is independent of body position.

De Vega and Rodrigo's (2001) study provides a similar comparison between a pointing and conceptual response in updating as in Creem and Proffitt (2000), finding a similar result of an advantage for pointing after physical body movement. However, De Vega and Rodrigo's response measures were defined differently. The "pointing" of de Vega and Rodrigo was not a direct action but rather a button press of an arrow that symbolically related a direction. This pointing measure seems more analogous to the compass pointing in Creem and Proffitt. However, both studies found an advantage with the pointing measures for physical rotation. It may be that the arrow response resembles the direct arm pointing more than the compass because it does not provide any additional conflicting frame of reference. A unique quality of the compass in the Creem and Proffitt study was the circular room frame of reference that it provided visually. Observers were instructed to imagine that they were standing inside of the circular compass and to move the pointer relative to themselves. It may be that this second-order egocentric frame of reference (detached from one's physical body position) contributed to the decrement in performance seen in pointing after body rotation. The environmental frame of reference of the compass itself would help, however, if participants did not physically move and were relying on object-to-object and object-to-environment relations to remember the spatial locations.

Wraga (in press) has examined the influence of spatial reference frames on spatial updating in a series of studies comparing imagined and physical self-rotation and multiple response measures. As in other studies (de Vega & Rodrigo, 2001; Presson & Montello, 1994; Rieser, 1989), updating during physical self-rotation was superior to imagined self-rotation when the response measure involved pointing. However, Wraga found that updating during imagined rotation was superior to physical rotation when participants used a verbal response or a keyboard response in which directional arrows were offset from the viewer's reference frame. She suggested that imagined rotation is inferior with direct pointing because the pointing response attaches the viewer's reference frame to their body, leading to greater spatial conflict between physical and imagined egocentric reference frames. In contrast, updating performance during imagined rotation is facilitated with responses that are less connected to the body (e.g., verbal or keyboard responses), reducing the reference-frame conflict.

CONCLUSIONS

Keeping track of locations in space as we move or as objects move is a skill that allows humans to maintain the representation of a stable world. For example, when walking along a city street, pedestrians understand that as they pass a building, it is now behind them, and as they turn to the right, the sign that was in front of them is now on their left. This skill extends to an ability to imagine transformations or to use visual information without coupled vestibular and proprioceptive information to specify movement. If the pedestrians stop to give directions to another person on the street, they might imagine the viewpoint of the other person to specify the locations from the other person's perspective instead of their own. Certain tasks suggest no difference between transformations that involve physical movement and those that do not. Other tasks show distinct differences, with physical movement facilitating the updating process. In this chapter, I focused on research that has examined differences between physical and imagined transformations, viewer and object transformations, and the relation between spatial transformations and responding. Broadly, research suggests a relative advantage in memory tasks involving translations versus rotations and viewer versus object transformations. Humans use multiple frames of reference to encode, represent, and act in space. Examining how physical movement influences different transformations with respect to the spatial representations formed and the goal of the response task can help us as humans to understand the mechanisms underlying our knowledge and memory of spatial relations.

With respect to self-transformations, updating during rotation is generally facilitated when information from physical body movement is available. This is apparent in nonvisual imagined tasks and nonmotor visual locomotion tasks in virtual environments. Much of the work using ignore paradigms and action responses suggests that locations are automatically updated with respect to the observer when physical movement is made. This movement helps in rotation tasks because the viewer's frame of reference is automatically reoriented to a new heading. Translations of the self are easier to perform. Humans appear to have the ability to imagine and update changes resulting from their own translations in a manner equivalent to physical translation in space. Physical body motion also contributes largely to translational updating, as seen through visually directed walking studies that do not involve vision, but a few studies with virtual environments suggest that translational space may be updated nearly as well with visual information alone. One difference between self-translations and ro-tations is that translations do not involve the change in heading of the ob-server as seen in rotation. Another explanation for superior performance for visual translations versus rotations may be an adaptive one based on the importance in judging an object's distance from oneself, as suggested by Price and Gilden (2000). Translations of objects in a given direction specify displacements of locations in space (i.e., an object moves closer or farther away); visual direction of rotation does not provide information about the resulting object distance from the observer.

Updating tasks involving imagined object transformations are more dif-ficult than those involving imagined self-transformations for both rotation and translation. The addition of physical movement aids updating for rota-tion when haptic feedback is provided and for translation with the presen-tation of a visual moving frame of reference. Studies of imagined object translation suggest that updating a frame of reference external to oneself is difficult to imagine regardless of whether the transformation involves an orientation change. A question remains as to whether visual motion infor-mation specifying rotation of an external frame of reference will facilitate object rotation in imagined tasks and interfere with updating in visual loco-motion tasks, as seen in the translation studies presented in this chapter.

Consideration of movement is important not only to understanding the processes underlying spatial transformations but also to defining the rela-tion updating and responding as specific transformations. Accounts of the processes underlying updating should consider the goal of the task as speci-fied by a given response measure. I have shown that the compatibility be-tween method of transformation and the response measure may influence updating performance. Just as different frames of reference may be accessed in different transformation tasks, reference frames also vary in the response that is required. Physical transformations of the body appear to be most use-ful to a body-centered motor response. Visual transformations of perspective alone may correspond more logically to a response that relies on an object- or environment-centered representation. Future research may more clearly de-fine the influence of self-motion and object motion on multiple stages in spa-tial updating in the context of the type of response required.

REFERENCES

Aglioti, S., DeSouza, J. F. X., & Goodale, M. (1995). Size-contrast illusions deceive the eye but not the hand. *Current Biology, 5,* 679–685.

Amorim, M., & Stucchi, N. (1997). Viewer- and object-centered mental explorations of an imagined environment are not equivalent. *Cognitive Brain Research, 5,* 229–239.

Brenner, E., & Smeets, J. B. J. (1996). Size illusion influences how we lift but not how we grasp and object. *Experimental Brain Research, 111,* 473–476.

Bridgeman, B., & Huemer, V. (1998). A spatially oriented decision does not induce consciousness in a motor task. *Consciousness & Cognition: An International Journal, 7,* 454–464.

Bridgeman, B., Kirch, M., & Sperling, A. (1981). Segregation of cognitive and motor aspects of visual function using induced motion. *Perception and Psychophysics, 29,* 336–342.

Bridgeman, B., Lewis, S., Heit, G., & Nagle, M. (1979). Relation between cognitive and motor-oriented systems of visual position perception. *Journal of Experimental Psychology: Human Perception & Performance, 5,* 692–700.

Bridgeman, B., Peery, S., & Anand, S. (1997). Interaction of cognitive and sensorimotor maps of visual space. *Perception & Psychophysics, 59,* 456–469.

Chance, S., Gaunet, F., Beall, A., & Loomis, J. (1998). Locomotion mode affects the updating of objects encountered during travel: the contribution of vestibular and proprioceptive inputs to path integration. *Presence, 7,* 168–178.

Cohen, M. S., Kosslyn, S. M., Breiter, H. C., DiGirolamo, G. J., Thompson, W. L., Anderson, A. K., Bookheimer, S. Y., Rosen, B. R., & Belliveau, J. W. (1996). Changes in cortical activity during mental rotation. A mapping study using functional MRI. *Brain, 119,* 89–100.

Creem, S. H., Downs, T. H., Wraga, M., Harrington, G. S., Proffitt, D. R., & Downs, I. J. H. (2001). An fMRI study of imagined self-rotation. *Cognitive, Affective, and Behavioral Neuroscience, 1,* 239–249.

Creem, S. H., & Proffitt, D. R. (1998). Two memories for geographical slant: Separation and interdependence of action and awareness. *Psychonomic Bulletin and Review, 5,* 22–36.

Creem, S. H., & Proffitt, D. R. (2000, November). *Egocentric measures of spatial updating: Is there an advantage for action?* Poster session presented at the 41st annual meeting of the Psychonomic Society, New Orleans, LA.

Creem, S. H., & Proffitt, D. R. (2001). Defining the cortical visual systems: "What," "Where," and "How." *Acta Psychologica, 107,* 43–68.

Creem, S. H., Wraga, M., & Proffitt, D. R. (2001). Imagining physically impossible transformations: Geometry is more important than gravity. *Cognition, 81,* 41–61.

Creem-Regehr, S. H. (2003). Updating space during imagined self- and array-translations. *Memory & Cognition, 31,* 941–982.

Daprati, E., & Gentilucci, M. (1997). Grasping an illusion. *Neuropsychologia, 35,* 1577–1582.

de Vega, M., & Rodrigo, M. J. (2001). Updating spatial layouts mediated by pointing and labeling under physical and imaginary rotation. *Journal of European Cognitive Psychology, 13,* 369–393.

Easton, R. D., & Sholl, M. J. (1995). Object-array structure, frames of reference and retrieval of spatial knowledge. *Journal of Experimental Psychology: Learning, Memory, and Cognition, 21,* 438–500.

Farrell, M. J., & Robertson, I. H. (1998). Mental rotation and the automatic updating of body-centered spatial relationships. *Journal of Experimental Psychology: Learning, Memory, and Cognition, 24,* 227–233.

Farrell, M. J., & Thomson, J. A. (1998). Automatic spatial updating during locomotion without vision. *The Quarterly Journal of Experimental Psychology, 51A,* 637–654.

Franz, V. H., Gegenfurtner, K. R., Bulthoff, H. H., & Fahle, M. (2000). Grasping visual illusions: No evidence for a dissociation between perception and action. *Psychological Science, 11,* 20–25.

Gentilucci, M., Chieffi, S., Daprati, E., Saetti, M. C., & Toni, I. (1996). Visual illusion and action. *Neuropsychologia, 34,* 369–376.

Gibson, J. J. (1979). *The ecological approach to visual perception.* Boston: Houghton Mifflin.

Goodale, M. A., & Haffenden, A. (1998). Frames of reference for perception and action in the human visual system. *Neuroscience & Biobehavioral Reviews, 22,* 161–172.

Goodale, M. A., Jakobson, L. S., & Keillor, J. M. (1994). Differences in the visual control of pantomimed and natural grasping movements. *Neuropsychologia, 32,* 1159–1178.

Goodale, M., & Milner, A. D. (1992). Separate visual pathways for perception and action. *Trends in Neuroscience, 15,* 20–25.

Haffenden, A. M., & Goodale, M. A. (1998). The effect of pictorial illusion on prehension and perception. *Journal of Cognitive Neuroscience, 10,* 122–136.

Haffenden, A., & Goodale, M. A. (2000). Independent effects of pictorial displays on perception and action. *Vision Research, 40,* 1597–1607.

Held, R. (1968). Dissociation of visual functions by deprivation and rearrangement. *Psychologische Forschung, 31,* 338–348.

Huttenlocher, J., & Presson, C. C. (1979). The coding and transformation of spatial information. *Cognitive Psychology, 11,* 375–394.

Jackson, S. R., & Shaw, A. (2000). The ponzo illusion affects grip force but not grip aperture scaling during prehension movements. *Journal of Experimental Psychology: Human Perception & Performance, 26,* 1–6.

Jeannerod, M. (1997). *The cognitive neuroscience of action.* Oxford, England: Blackwell.

Klatzky, R. L., Loomis, J., Beall, A., Chance, S., & Golledge, R. G. (1998). Updating an egocentric spatial representation during real, imagined, and virtual locomotion. *Psychological Science, 9,* 293–298.

Kosslyn, S. M., DiGirolamo, G. J., Thompson, W. L., & Alpert, N. M. (1998). Mental rotation of objects versus hands: Neural mechanisms revealed by positron emission tomography. *Psychophysiology, 35,* 151–161.

Kosslyn, S. M., Thompson, W. L., Wraga, M., & Alpert, N. M. (2001). Imagining rotation by endogenous versus exogenous forces: Distinct neural mechanisms. *Neuroreport, 12,* 2519–2525.

Loomis, J. M., Da Silva, J. A., Fujita, N., & Fukusima, S. S. (1992). Visual space perception and visually directed action. *Journal of Experimental Psychology, 18,* 906–921.

Loomis, J. M., Da Silva, J. A., Philbeck, J. W., & Fukusima, S. S. (1996). Visual perception of location and distance. *Current Directions in Psychological Science, 5,* 72–77.

Loomis, J. M., Klatzky, R. L., Golledge, R. G., & Philbeck, J. W. (1999). Human navigation by path integration. In R. G. Golledge (Ed.), *Wayfinding behavior: Cognitive mapping and other spatial processes* (pp. 125–151). Baltimore: Johns Hopkins University Press.

May, M., & Klatzky, R. L. (2000). Path integration while ignoring irrelevant movement. *Journal of Experimental Psychology: Learning, Memory, and Cognition, 26,* 169–186.

Milner, A. D., & Goodale, M. A. (1995). *The visual brain in action.* Oxford, England: Oxford University Press.

Mittelstaedt, H., & Mittelstaedt, M. L. (1982). Homing by path integration. In F. P. H. G. Wallraff (Ed.), *Avian navigation* (pp. 290–297). Berlin: Springer.

Parsons, L. M., Fox, P. T., Downs, J. H., Glass, T., Hirsch, T. B., Martin, C. G., Jerabek, P. A., & Lancaster, J. L. (1995). Use of implicit motor imagery for visual shape discrimination as revealed by PET. *Nature, 375,* 54–58.

Pausch, R., Proffitt, D. R., & Williams, G. (1997). Quantifying immersion in virtual reality. In *Proceedings of the 24th annual conference on computer graphics and interactive techniques (SIGGRAPH),* 13–18.

Pavani, F., Boscagli, I., Benvenuti, F., Rabuffetti, M., & Farne, A. (1999). Are perception and action affected differently by the Titchner circles illusion? *Experimental Brain Research, 127,* 95–101.

Philbeck, J. W., & Loomis, J. M. (1997). Comparison of two indicators of perceived egocentric distance under full-cue and reduced-cue conditions. *Journal of Experimental Psychology, 23,* 72–85.

Presson, C. C. (1980). Spatial egocentrism and the effect of an alternate frame of reference. *Journal of Experimental Child Psychology, 29,* 391–402.

Presson, C. C. (1982). Strategies in spatial reasoning. *Journal of Experimental Psychology: Learning, Memory, and Cognition, 8,* 243–251.

Presson, C. C., & Montello, D. R. (1994). Updating after rotational and translational body movements: Coordinate structure of perspective space. *Perception, 23,* 1447–1455.

Price, C. M., & Gilden, D. L. (2000). Representations of motion and direction. *Journal of Experimental Psychology: Human Perception & Performance, 26,* 18–30.

Proffitt, D. R., Bhalla, M., Gossweiler, R., & Midgett, J. (1995). Perceiving geographical slant. *Psychonomic Bulletin & Review, 2,* 409–428.

Rieser, J. J. (1989). Access to knowledge of spatial structure at novel points of observation. *Journal of Experimental Psychology: Learning, Memory, and Cognition, 15,* 1157–1165.

Rieser, J. J., Guth, D. A., & Hill, E. W. (1986). Sensitivity to perspective structure while walking without vision. *Perception, 15,* 173–188.

Rossetti, I. (1998). Implicit short-lived motor representation of space in brain-damaged and healthy subjects. *Consciousness and Cognition, 7,* 520–558.

Schneider, G. E. (1969, February 28). Two visual systems: Brain mechanisms for localization and discrimination are dissociated by tectal and cortical lesions. *Science, 163,* 895–902.

Shepard, R. N., & Metzler, J. (1971, February 19). Mental rotation of three-dimensional objects. *Science, 171,* 701–703.

Thomson, J. A. (1983). Is continuous visual monitoring necessary in visually guided locomotion? *Journal of Experimental Psychology: Human Perception & Performance, 9,* 427–443.

Trevarthen, C. B. (1968). Two mechanisms of vision in primates. *Psychologische Forschung, 31,* 299–337.

Ungerleider, L. G., & Mishkin, M. (1982). Two cortical visual systems. In D. J. Ingle, M. A. Goodale, & R. J. W. Mansfield (Eds.), *Analysis of visual behavior* (pp. 549–586). Cambridge, MA: MIT Press.

Vishton, P. M., Rea, J. G., Cutting, J. E., & Nunez, L. N. (1999). Comparing effects of the horizontal-vertical illusion on grip scaling and judgment: Relative versus absolute, not perception versus action. *Journal of Experimental Psychology: Human Perception and Performance, 25,* 1659–1672.

Wang, R. F. (2001, November). *Beyond imagination: On perspective change problems.* Poster session presented at the 42nd annual meeting of the Psychonomic Society, Orlando, FL.

Wang, R. F., & Simons, D. J. (1999). Active and passive scene recognition across views. *Cognition, 70,* 191–210.

Wexler, M., Kosslyn, S. M., & Berthoz, A. (1998). Motor processes in mental rotation. *Cognition, 68,* 77–94.

Wohlschlager, A., & Wohlschlager, A. (1998). Mental and manual rotation. *Journal of Experimental Psychology: Human Perception and Performance, 24,* 397–412.

Wraga, M. (in press). Thinking outside the body: An advantage for spatial updating during imagined versus physical self-rotation. *Journal of Experimental Psychology: Learning, Memory and Cognition.*

Wraga, M., Creem, S. H., & Proffitt, D. R. (2000a). Perception-action dissociations of a walkable Muller–Lyer configuration. *Psychological Science, 11,* 239–243.

Wraga, M., Creem, S. H., & Proffitt, D. R. (2000b). Updating displays after imagined object and viewer rotations. *Journal of Experimental Psychology: Learning, Memory, and Cognition, 26,* 151–168.

Wraga, M., Creem-Regehr, S. H., & Proffitt, D. R. (in press). Spatial updating of virtual displays during self- and display rotation. *Memory & Cognition.*

Memories of Travel: Dead Reckoning Within the Cognitive Map

Edward H. Cornell and C. Donald Heth
University of Alberta, Canada

When Herman Melville (1851) revealed the dark obsessions of Captain Ahab's soul, he did so by having Ahab destroy the ship's quadrant and revert to a more elemental form of navigation:

> "Curse thee, thou quadrant!" dashing it to the deck, "no longer will I guide my earthly way by thee; the level ship's compass, and the level dead-reckoning, by log and by line; *these* shall conduct me, and show me my place on the sea.."
>
> Melville, 1851/1967, p. 412

Whatever the allegorical content, the practical consequences of abandoning celestial navigation were immediately apparent to Ahab's doomed crew, who were later to rue his folly and, in the person of Starbuck, ask, "gropes he not by mere dead reckoning of the error-abounding log?" (Melville, 1851/1967, p. 422).

Navigation without fixed references and landmarks has been especially intriguing to comparative and cognitive psychologists. The former have tended, like Ahab, to emphasize its simple sufficiency, whereas the latter, as Starbuck did, have worried about its proneness to error. Humans' everyday experience would seem to favor the active processing of landmarks and reference points. Certainly, our visual facility with objects in spatial frames contrasts sharply with the unease that we feel when we try to traverse a room in the dark. Yet there are compelling examples of species who have somehow managed to beat the odds of the "error-abounding log" and who

191

rely on navigation systems that apparently mirror the computational steps of the mariner's dead reckoning. It is apparent that there exist many different systems for navigation both within and across species that may be related to the geometry and ecology of the animal's navigational requirements (Dyer, 1998). In this chapter, we examine the relevance of these systems for human way finding and their implications for the processing of memories of travel.

DEFINITION OF THE PROBLEM

There are many types of tasks and problems that require spatial information processing, such as the recall of spatial locations, route planning, and rotation of frames of reference. Our particular concerns in this chapter are those modes of spatial processing that allow an organism to move from a current location to a target or goal. Dyer (1998) suggested that navigational systems in species are tightly bound to the geometry of the goal. There are, for example, some animals for which the goal may be a shoreline, as in the case of sea turtles that hatch on land but must reach the ocean before they are captured by predators. Navigation in this case is directed toward a linear feature extended across a two-dimensional surface. There are other cases of navigation in which the space within which navigation occurs is likewise two-dimensional, but the goal is punctate. This latter case differs from the first in that the system must be sufficiently robust to error that the navigator can get within the immediate vicinity of the goal. The cone of headings that will accomplish this task is often quite narrow. For the linear feature geometry, the amount of error that can be tolerated is much larger because any bearing that is half-plane bounded by the feature will work.

Our emphasis is on navigational systems that allow an organism to move to or predict the location of a point on a two-dimensional surface. Defined in this way, navigation tasks differ in the way spatial information is made available to the organism. There are generally two elements common to most navigation tasks. First, the organism must perceive a fixed environmental feature. This may be its current location (e.g., when a configuration of landmarks is recognized) or it may be the goal itself (e.g., when a distant food source produces an odor plume). Establishing the location of a fixed referent point calibrates the organism's representation of its current position; it may also establish the nodes of an organism's cognitive map (Biegler, 2000). That is, for some animals, distinct neural systems represent episodic memories of places within a spatial framework (O'Keefe & Nadel, 1978). Second, the organism is moved to the current location, either under its own power or otherwise, and thereby received information relevant to computing its current displacement. This second process is dynamic and requires that the organism update its current representation of position. There is an analogy with the way shipboard navigators update positional references on a chart on occasions when movement information is logged. However, the mariner's plotting is intermittent and the last estimate of position is represented as the endpoint of a configuration of paths. In contrast, some animals use feedback from motion to calculate position continuously; the history of movements may not be preserved when position is always up-to-date.

In some navigation tasks, plotting and calibration are tightly coupled in a process known as "piloting" (Gallistel, 1990). *Piloting* describes the way mariners use sightings of landmarks with known coordinates as they traverse coastal waters (Hutchins, 1995). Piloting provides immediate feedback of movements on calibrated positions through a series of positional fixes. It requires a map with many known reference points or with frequent positional fixes to interpolate between reference points.

Although piloting might appear to be the predominant type of navigation used by humans, we suggest that it must often be supplemented by other forms. People commonly venture into novel territory, and their frequent shifts of attention might disrupt the cycle of positional fixes that underlie piloting. A good example is children who are expanding their home range (Cornell, Hadley, Sterling, Chan, & Boechler, 2001). As they explore new places, they encounter large gaps in their knowledge of landmarks, sometimes under conditions in which other factors (e.g., city traffic) place strong demands on their attention. In such cases, knowledge of position must be estimated through other forms of navigation. Two such methods are known as *dead reckoning* and *path integration*. In each of these modes, sensations of movements may be monitored for long periods without calibration against known landmarks. Because they stand in contradistinction to piloting, dead reckoning and path integration have usually been treated as synonymous. However, we feel that it is useful to consider them as different forms of nonpiloting navigation.

DEAD RECKONING AND PATH INTEGRATION

Melville may have delighted in the use of "dead" reckoning as a metaphor for Ahab's decision, but, as many authors have pointed out, the term may derive from *deduced reckoning*—the steps by which a navigator can calculate direction and distance from experiences and observations along the route. Although now superceded by modern modes of navigation, it is a skill still useful to mariners and aircraft pilots. Burch (1986) provided a modern and readable account of the techniques that dead reckoning comprises. At heart, the navigator must be able to calculate speed, time, and direction of travel and, Burch stressed, be able to estimate the error associated with each of these. The latter is especially important because navigation by dead reckoning is inherently error prone and must be appropriately recalibrated. Estimates of positional error guide the navigator in determining when other means are necessary to fix a location or when other heuristics for finding the goal must be used.

For example, a mariner using dead reckoning will need to estimate distance. On the open sea, the mariner cannot directly measure the distance from a location in the morning to a location at day's end. Consequently, estimates of distance are normally performed by sampling speed. Traditionally, a line is knotted at regular intervals, attached to a chip of wood, and cast overboard. As the line plays out, the mariner counts the number of knots passing into the water during a specified period of time. These observations are combined to obtain speed. At the end of the day, the navigator must decide how this estimate characterizes the vessel's speed during the day. If, for example, wind and current are judged to have yielded steady progress for a 12-hr period, the obtained speed is multiplied by 12 hr to provide an estimate of distance during that interval.

Notice in this example that daily distance is derived from two estimates, each of which can contain error. There is the risk that the measurement operation was performed during unique circumstances of travel, resulting in sampling error of daily speed. In addition, the speed obtained during the sampled period may itself reflect two sources of measurement error: The knots along the line might not have the right spacing or the interval of time during which they are counted might be wrong. The astute navigator will sample speed regularly in uneven seas and factor variability into the final estimate. Error in the final estimate of speed is equal to the square root of the sum of the sampled estimates squared. The art of dead reckoning, therefore, consists not only of procedural expertise but also of judgment concerning relative contributions to error.

Closely related to the procedure of dead reckoning is path integration. In principle, it is possible to compute a location by integrating directed velocity over time (Mittelstaedt & Mittelstaedt, 1982). A navigator may sense velocity by the flow of visual patterns, the feel of the wind, the fading of sounds, or other means, especially vestibular sensations of acceleration; the resulting changes in position cumulate in a process similar to the mathematical operation of integration. When the information for path integration comes from internal sensations of movement (proprioception), the process is called *inertial path integration*. When the information comes from the changes in flow of external events such as textures, the process is called *noninertial path integration*.

The result of path integration is conceptualized to be a probabilistic variable that encodes both distance and direction to some reference point. A good example of this approach is the model proposed by Fujita, Loomis, Klatzky, and Golledge (1990) in which movements by an organism produce changes to a vector in a history-free manner. Specifically, location along a path is represented by the instantaneous value of this vector without reference to its previous values. Direction and distance from the last point of calibration are given by direct readout of the vector. Trowbridge (1913) described a similar idea in describing how an animal, having no knowledge of the points of the compass or of the extent of the world, could find its way home:

> In the case of insects, birds, mammals, etc., which orient themselves domicentrically, it is as if the living creature were attached to its home by one very strong elastic thread of definite length. Hence, in this case, all changes of position of the creatures can be referred at any moment, to definite distances and angles, forming a simple trigonometric figure which gives the direction to home. (p. 890).

A key feature of path integration is that calibration in reference to external landmarks does not occur continuously as in the case of piloting. Instead, calibration typically occurs after significant events along a path. For example, Collett and Collett (2000) trained desert ants of the species *Cataglyphis fortis* to walk along a channel to a feeder, after which they were shifted to a new location such that the return bearing was clockwise of the outward path. Ants were later tested by being displaced from the feeder to a novel location. Their attempted return path was still shifted clockwise of the outward bearing; more tellingly, the return path was generally a straight line. Collett and Collett's interpretation of these data is that the ant's representation of where it was located was calibrated only at the feeder and not during travel back to the nest.

Dead reckoning is likewise a navigation process in which calibration usually occurs at significant path nodes. However, the etymology of the term suggests a useful distinction from path integration. In contrast to the latter, dead reckoning is retrospective, implying processes that depend on representations of previous segments of the path. In humans, this might be apparent in deductive inferences about location based on remembered configurations of the path. According to this taxonomy, path integration would refer to those models for which information about velocity and acceleration is processed continuously and ahistorically and represented by state variables of low dimension (e.g., a two-dimensional vector; Loomis et al., 1993). Dead reckoning, however, would refer to models of navigation in which velocity and time estimates are used retrospectively and at punctate occasions to alter a multidimensional representation of a route or journey (but cf. Loomis, Klatzky, Golledge, & Philbeck, 1999, p. 129). An important part of the representation might be the error associated with specific segments of the route.

The navigation system of *C. fortis* would appear to be one in which path integration is an appropriate description. When *C. fortis* foragers are displaced from an outbound path, they are able to establish a return bearing. The accuracy of this bearing does not seem to be affected by where in the outbound journey the displacement occurs (Collett & Collett, 2000). This would imply a history-free updating characteristic of path integration. In contrast, human navigation seems to fit with models of dead reckoning because people produce organized memories of their travel.

COGNITIVE MAPPING OF SPATIAL MEMORIES

Kitchin and Freundschuh (2000) presented a good historical review of the uses of the terms *cognitive map* and *cognitive mapping*. Our use is based on revival of the terms by behavioral geographers:

> Cognitive mapping is a process composed of a series of psychological transformations by which an individual acquires, stores, recalls, and decodes information about the relative locations and attributes of the phenomena in his everyday spatial environment. (Downs & Stea, 1973, p. 9)

> Information extracted from large-scale external environments and stored in human memory exists in some type of psychological space whose metricity may be unknown. (Golledge, 1999, p. 7)

The first statement suggests that cognitive mapping is not an unusual method of processing memories into and out of a knowledge base, but the information processed is spatial. The second statement reflects that knowledge of the environment may not be uniform; a metric representation of space satisfies certain mathematical axioms, for example, that the quantitative distance between two locations does not depend on the direction of measurement between the two locations. In contrast, people's sketch maps, distance estimates, proximity rankings, and directional judgments indicate an incomplete, distorted, torn, or folded geometry of space, although some well-known areas may be locally Euclidean (Montello, 1989).

The core issues concerning the form and function of cognitive maps have been recently reviewed by Kitchin and Blades (2002). Researchers now know that cognitive maps represent global and local environmental features in a network structure with hierarchical properties. Places may be represented as schemas such as what comes to mind when told that the village of Rosarita is a beach resort. Spatial information may be encoded as image-like units, conceptual propositions, or both, depending on task demands and individual differences. The survey representations that characterize cartography are a special product of this knowledge base. Survey maps preserve the angle of bearings and the scale of distances between environmental features; the arrangement of symbols for the environmental features is as seen from the overhead perspective.

To summarize, the term *cognitive map* is theoretically akin to other terms describing the structure of memories such as *semantic network*, *mental lexicon*, or *number fact retrieval table*. There are some properties that are particular to the information in the cognitive map, for instance spatial primitives such as distance relations between events (Golledge, 1995). Nevertheless, because it is the product of normal memorial processes, researchers assume that the cognitive map is derived from associative, sequential, or configural memories. All of these forms of representation may be useful during way finding.

COULD WE MAKE IT BACK HOME?

On Trowbridge's (1913) account, pulled by its elastic thread, the homeward-bound animal would eventually encounter a familiar region containing "minor reference points," or objects that give a "definite reaction" to the home (p. 890). It is easy to see the prescience of this two-process description. The elastic thread is the line given by path integration, and the definite reaction is calibration of its location vector based on landmarks whose positions are known relative to home.

Of course, the story is more developed now. Some animals may not navigate in the territory close to home by knowing a configuration of several landmarks. There can be recognition of an environment feature that emanates from a unitary site. For example, home may be distinguished by a particular odor. The dispersion of the odorant follows the topography near its source and the prevailing wind. Sensing the concentration of the odorant thus allows for beacon homing, with minimal need to represent the location of objects in the neighborhood (Gallistel, 1990).

The foremost path integrator, C. fortis, shows limited knowledge of the features around its nest (Burkhalter, 1972). If an ant is trapped immediately after emerging from its nest and placed on the terrain a short distance away, it searches for home in all directions and wanders for an extraordinary amount of time. Yet, the ants return directly from much farther distances when they themselves have traveled away from the nest (Wehner & Srinivasan, 1981).

When researchers move foraging ants after they have traveled to a distant feeding station, the ants return as if they are heading for home from their last self-determined location. Their return is linear up to a distance where they should have encountered their nest, then their path changes to a loopy search. Wehner and Srinivasan (1981) showed that the onset and pattern for the search for home are the result of the ant's mechanisms for computing its displacement. There is little evidence that the ant recognizes its neighborhood, but presumably it recognizes its doorstep.

Given the remarkable path integration by the desert ant, could humans do as well? Blindfolded, ears covered, nose clothespinned and led on a distant foraging expedition, could we return to our doorstep via the most direct possible route? Although our intuitions say no, we consider that people may use different cognitive processes to find their way when normal environmental input is restricted. We believe most human solutions are best described as dead reckoning. As we noted previously, the term suggests that problems in orientation and navigation can be solved by a variety of methods. Some heuristics for dead reckoning may not involve computation of metric information, whereas path integration is associated with the sensing and continuous mathematical integration of linear and rotary velocities or the double integration of accelerations.

In humans, the proprioceptive system provides a variety of information that could be integrated to provide a record of translation and rotation relative to the start of a path. The proprioceptive system can be considered to include the vestibular and kinesthetic sense systems as well as representations of efferent commands (Geldard, 1972; Klatzky et al., 1990). The vestibular sense system includes mechanisms for registering acceleration and position relative to gravity. The kinesthetic sense system includes mechanisms for registering the movements of joints, muscle, and skin. Efferent commands are represented as intentions or preparation of the motor system preceding movement.

Path integration and dead reckoning both operate on feedback from proprioception, although processes of dead reckoning allow for occasional rather than continuous sampling of feedback. Hence, memories of movement and patterns of movement are often important for humans to deduce their bearings. To resolve questions about the representation of self-movement and the accuracy of human dead reckoning, we consider what constitutes systematic performance.

INDICATIONS OF NONRANDOM SPATIAL PERFORMANCE

Etienne, Berlie, Georgakopoulos, and Maurer (1998) summarized evidence that arthropods and mammals show an intriguing systematic bias when returning from an L-shaped outbound journey. In the examples they illustrate (see Fig. 9.1), all species made an inbound error by overcompensating the rotation on the outbound path. Etienne et al. suggested that the systematic bias is owing to the way path integration is computed. Specifically, they favored an iterative mathematical algorithm that describes homing behavior by ants (Müller & Wehner, 1994). The algorithm serves to scale down successive angular deviations between the ant's steps as a function of the distance that the ant has moved away from its nest. Because the computation of mean direction of travel is differentially weighted by the distance traveled, the algorithm is an approximation of path integration by trigonometry. However, there is evidence that human performance may be more variable (Kearns, Warren, Duchon, & Tarr, 2002; Loomis et al., 1993; Riecke, van Veen, & Bültoff, 2002; Sholl, 1989).

Although the algorithm describes the systematic biases illustrated in Fig. 9.1, there may be a variety of mechanisms that produce the same behavior. Notice that overcompensation, or more turning inbound than was done on the outbound travel, results in an inbound path that intercepts the earlier portion of the outbound path. The bias returns the animal to territory

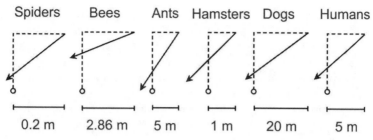

FIG. 9.1. Triangle completion performance by arthropods and mammals (redrawn from Etienne, Berlie, Georgakopoulos, & Maurer, 1998). The animal's point of departure is illustrated as an open circle, and the two legs of its outbound path are illustrated as dashed lines. The animals returned in the direction illustrated by the darker arrowed line. *Note.* From *Spatial Representation in Animals*, p. 56, by S. Healy (Ed.), 1998, New York: Oxford University Press. Copyright 1998 by Oxford University Press. Reprinted with permission.

that it may be familiar with. For example, children are known to remember the beginning better than the middle portions of new outdoor routes (primacy effects; Cornell, Heth, Kneubuhler, & Sehgal, 1996). If children encounter portions of a route after taking a shortcut, they are likely to recognize landmarks or paths that are associated with returning along the route (Cornell, Heth, & Alberts, 1994). They would be in unfamiliar territory if they miss the outbound route by undershooting their turn at the onset of their shortcut. Animals who rely on their own scent trails would also benefit from the bias illustrated in Fig. 9.1. If animals are wandering or searching for familiar ground, they present more opportunities for predation, meteorological buffeting, or exhaustion. Hence, we would expect that evolutionary factors would act so as to select any mechanism that allows the returning animal to intersect familiar territory.

INNATE REPRESENTATION OF SPACE

Systematic performance in dead reckoning is philosophically interesting. Many modern nativists believe that humans have innately specified, domain-specific representations. They have used findings from developmental psychology or neuropsychology and arguments from evolutionary psychology to assert that the human brain is not only innately prespecified for perceptual processes such as registering haptic-kinesthetic flow during movement but also for higher level spatial representations such as Euclidean mental maps (Landau, Spelke, & Gleitman, 1984; see Karmiloff-Smith, 2000, for a critique). For example, the study of object localization by a blind girl has led to the interpretation that humans' spatial knowledge system is structured early in life and is independent of the modality of experience of space

(Landau & Spelke, 1985). Her spatial knowledge system was inferred to be a geometric mental map because after being led along specific paths between objects in a small room, the 34-month-old girl could generate new paths among those same objects. The researchers reported that the girl's movements during these new paths were imperfect; 3 of her 12 test paths ended when she lost her bearings and 3 of her remaining 9 test paths curved toward the wrong object and then curved back toward the correct target. Despite these missteps, the researchers considered her localization to be better than chance because on most test paths, her initial orientation was in the correct direction and the end of her path fell within a 40° range subtending the target object. However, these criteria for reaching targets 1 to 2 m away seem liberal. Moreover, the girl's failure to walk direct lines suggests that path integration was not controlling locomotion. Liben (1988) questioned whether the methods allow the strong conclusion that the young blind girl knew the angular and distance relations between the objects in the room.

VEERING

There may be an important distinction between turning accurately toward an invisible target and walking a straight-line path to that target. People generally veer when they walk, and direct paths may be seen as a performance requirement that leads researchers to underestimate human competence in path integration tasks. The asymmetries of veering and the extent of veering were early issues in the study of geographical orientation, but the study of veer did not reveal much about the role of kinesthetic and vestibular mechanisms in registering movement (Howard & Templeton, 1966). Extrapolations from a recent careful study (Klatzky et al., 1990) indicated that blindfolded adults on average veer about 22° when attempting to walk a straight line for 30 m at normal speed. Individuals tended to veer in the same direction over successive walks, but veering to right and left occurred equally often over all individuals. Hence, performance deficits owing to veer suggest that humans cannot solely use inertial cues to maintain straight paths across distances they typically travel outdoors (see Fig. 9.2; see also Guth & LaDuke, 1994, 1995).

There are a variety of prospective strategies for correcting error owing to veer. If several travelers are aligned one behind the other, the person at the back of the group can judge the linearity of the column and call forward to the leader to correct to the right or left. The strategy is traditionally used in featureless expanses, as when mushers on snowfields check their line of dogs or camel drivers on deserts shout to the head of the train. Another strategy comes from the sport of orienteering in which runners seek to maintain the most direct line between outdoor check stations. To prevent veer in territory where landmarks can not be identified, runners will alternate the direction taken when encountering barriers so that if they circumvent a first large boulder by going left, they will circumvent the next large

Congenitally Blind	Adventitiously Blind	Blindfolded Sighted

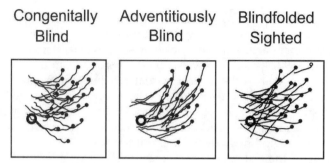

FIG. 9.2.   Tracings of return paths by three individuals in triangle-completion tasks conducted in a 12 m × 12 m room (redrawn from Loomis et al., 1993). The person's point of departure for 27 two-legged outbound routes is illustrated as an open circle. The closed circles indicate the ends of the outbound routes, and the squiggly lines indicate paths walked during attempted returns to the point of departure. The panels represent performance by the fifth participants within three groups who were deprived of vision. *Note.* From "Nonvisual Navigation and Sighted: Assessment of Path Integration Ability," by J. M. Loomis et al., 1993, *Journal of Experimental Psychology: General, 122,* pp. 80–81. Copyright 1993 by American Psychological Association. Reprinted with permission.

boulder by going right. Perhaps the most mentalistic strategy occurs when experienced hikers imagine a straight-line bearing to their destination at the start of their journey (Jonsson, 2002). Even when distant cues are hidden, the hikers may "steer a course" or make adjustments to return to the imagined bearing after deviations through travel corridors. Despite these strategies for correcting veer, navigators and way finders seize opportunities to update their position by reference to geography and landmarks. These observations affirm that people are aware of error and the need to calibrate their movement-based representations.

TASKS IN ROOMS

Most tasks used to assess path integration abilities are conducted in rooms. Researchers assume that the mechanisms used are the same as those used in larger scale spaces, although a view of a room prior to blindfolding can suggest a geometric shape or regularized framework to situate movement (Werner, 2002). Results indicate that small rooms may be restrictive. A "wall effect" limits the range of errors of some participants (Liben, 1988); they may stop because they are apprehensive of collisions or researchers may interrupt their paths before they encounter a wall. In addition, test rooms are clear of furniture; floor, walls, and ceiling typically provide large, flat surfaces. These are good conditions for echolocation and tactile sensing of reflected ventilation. Researchers have prevented use of auditory cues by fitting participants with occluding headphones. However, studies of visually deprived individuals indicate that participants may also be sensitive to olfactory and tactile cues (James, 1890/1950); these may divert attention from the internal proprioceptive cues that are the basis of inertial path integration. Finally, performance on path integration tasks in rooms is often extrapolated without actually testing whether the obtained error is cumulative over greater distances or determining the conditions that precipitate self-correcting mechanisms while way finding in the greater outdoors.

The scale of the test space is important when considering interpretations of path integration abilities. Typically, adults are asked to reproduce a sequence of path segments they have walked with guidance, or they are asked to directly walk from the end of their last path segment to the beginning of their walk. Although researchers have devised a variety of revealing path configurations (Klatzky et al., 1990; May & Klatzky, 2000), triangle completion tasks are common. After walking a path segment (leg), turning, then walking a second leg and stopping, a direct return to the origin of the walk is presumed to indicate a form of survey representation of the relations between the legs. Assuming certain criteria for accuracy, performance in the triangle completion task is taken as evidence for a Euclidean representation of metric values of distance and bearing relations. Hence, the length of path segments may determine accuracy of performance and inferences about mechanisms of path integration and the nature of mental representation of space.

For example, the encoding-error model of pathway completion without vision (Fujita, Klatzky, Loomis, & Golledge, 1993) assumes that uncertainty about the distances of a paths is resolved with a working solution. The distance of a path segment is encoded as a compromise between an uncertain actual value and the mean of presented values. The encoding results in people overestimating small distances and underestimating large ones, an error of regression to the mean (Stevens & Greenbaum, 1966). Notice that calculation of the mean of experienced values requires that people have memories of the distances of path segments they have completed at the time they encode the distance of the most recent path segment. In rooms, people may easily retrieve and summarize path memories after being led through a short series of segments of 2, 4, or 6 m in length. However, paths in large-scale natural environments typically take more time to traverse and do not include systematic variation in lengths. Estimation may be biased toward memories of early path segments (Anderson, 1981). Under natural conditions, people may use a variety of heuristics to estimate distances that do not rely on a mean value (Hirtle & Mascolo, 1991).

As we show, studies with path segments of 2 to 18 m in length indicate that humans can be systematic in processing feedback from locomotion to solve pathway completion tasks. However, these studies indicate a mechanism different than homing based on continuous metric calculations.

HOMING

Homing is travel that follows a vector to the point of origin of travel. Homing can be accomplished by piloting or nonpiloting navigation. After finding a morsel, the desert ant provides evidence of a homing vector when it turns and attempts a straight-line return to its nest. Several analyses suggest that the homing vector can be the result of automatic processing of locomotor feedback. Self-velocity and turning can provide input for trigonometric calculation of the distance and bearing of the point of origin (Biegler, 2000; Fujita et al., 1993; Mittelstaedt & Mittelstaedt, 1982). Bearing within this framework is the angular deviation between the traveler's current heading, or forward direction of travel, and the location of the start of the path. One of the most interesting features of navigation by many animals is that they maintain a vector representation of their way home at all points along their outbound path of travel yet may be unable to retrace the paths they have taken from home (Gallistel, 1990; Healy, 1998). Because the homing vector is evident at any place along the animal's outbound path, the process for calculating it must be continuous or at least occur at distances as short as a footstep. A homing vector is considered by some to be a minimal form of survey representation of space (Loomis et al., 1993), although it is not clear that a homing animal has knowledge of the geometric configuration of its paths as seen from an overhead perspective. Because the animal may show no evidence of memories of its outbound path or landmarks in the neighborhood of its home, the representation of the homing vector in these cases is history free.

There is accumulating evidence that humans do not accomplish path integration by continuous calculation of a homing vector. We first note that sighted people who are blindfolded are not very accurate at returning to the origin of even very simple paths. For example, Klatzky et al. (1990) tested the path completion abilities of blindfolded people after a walk contained within a 10-m diameter circle. Their mean absolute error turning toward the origin of the walk increased from 22° to 35° as the number of outbound path segments increased from one to three. Mean absolute distance between the endpoint of the participant's return and the origin of the walk also increased as the number of path segments increased from one to three. Klatzky et al. suggested that the increase in errors with path complexity indicated that each segment increased the processing load. This was an interesting interpretation because there were only preliminary indications that accuracy was related to the representation of segments. Error could accumulate within a history-free mechanism, such as an inexact computational algorithm that discards feedback from locomotion as the homing vector is updated (e.g., Müller & Wehner, 1994).

The cumulative effect of error when sighted humans navigate a large-scale environment without vision was indicated in a recent study by Greidanus (2003). University students were led along a sequence of five connected paths in an unfamiliar suburban neighborhood. The paths ranged between 380 and 580 m in length and included two or three turns. At the end of a path, students were stopped and asked to point to the origin of that path. Students who had walked the paths with total restriction of their vision (occluding goggles) pointed with a mean absolute error of 52° deviation from the actual origin. Students who had walked the paths with normal sight pointed with a mean absolute error of 29°. Students who had walked the paths with their vision restricted to 1 m around their feet pointed with a mean absolute error of 41°. The performance of the latter group is interesting because they could not see landmarks off the path during their walks. They could see the flow of texture of sidewalks and curbs.

There are now several indications that humans without vision use memories of the outbound path to estimate distance and direction to the origin. Loomis et al. (1993) found that the latency to initiate a return to the origin of a two- or three-segment path increased with the complexity of the path. If a homing vector had been continuously updated during the outbound travel, calculation of the vector at the point of return should have required the same time regardless of the path taken to reach that point. The fact that more path complexity increases latency suggests that participants are estimating from memories of their travel. The memories may preserve some spatial relations or may be primitives for constructing a representation of the configuration of path segments and turns (Golledge, 1995). The memories are readily available, because Loomis et al. found that human participants could retrace their outbound path on demand, even when the task might have called for a shortcut back to the origin. However, the memories of positional and directional change are not accurate and as we discuss later, are probably encoded with bias toward categorical divisions of space.

HUMAN TRAVEL IS A SEGMENTED HISTORY

People can easily recall aspects of their movements along paths. Proprioception provides humans memories of velocity, acceleration, and rotation and our physiology provides us concomitant memories of effort and duration. Several internal events are caused by external events so, for example, walking from a straight to a curved path results in an asymmetry in the efforts of the separate legs and causes a bending of the cupula within the semicircular canals of the inner ear. The perceived changes in the stream of these internal phenomena allow humans to segment a sequence of movement, which may be *encoded* verbally, for example, as "a few forward steps followed by a hard right." Whether translated into a verbal code or not, the segmented memories can be the basis of an estimation of the origin of travel (Péruch et al., 1999; Potegal, 1982; von der Heyde, Riecke, Cunningham, & Bültoff, 2000).

An important experimental approach to understanding the processes humans use for path integration involves psychophysics and computational modeling (Fujita et al., 1993) Psychophysical methods are first used to determine human performance when estimating and reproducing distances and turns (Klatzky et al., 1990). For example, guided by sliding a hand along a rope, blindfolded participants walked a straight line for 4, 6, 8, 10, or 12 m. They then estimated the length of the path according to a 2-m standard and reproduced it by walking what they felt to be an equivalent distance from a new starting point. To suppress counting of footsteps, the participant was required to repeat a phrase out loud while following the path. Signed errors indicate underestimation or overestimation and were calculated by the participant's estimate minus the actual distance. Absolute errors were the magnitude value of the signed error. A hand-held guide was also used to assess turn estimation and reproduction. The participants stood, then rotated while sliding their hands along a ring of aluminum with an outside diameter of 94 cm. Clamps were placed on the ring to stop rotation at 60° to 300° on different trials. The participant estimated the amount of turning in terms of a clock face. The researcher then removed the end clamp, and the participant attempted to reproduce the rotation. Signed and absolute errors were analyzed.

Performance in these tasks and similar observations by Loomis et al. (1993) served as data to evaluate a model. The model accounts for errors by people deprived of vision who are attempting triangle-completion tasks (Fujita et al., 1993). The model assumes that people in these circumstances have an internal representation of their outbound path that satisfies Euclidean axioms; for example, the length of the legs walked determines the scale of a triangle that is completed by walking the third leg. In this model, systematic error arises from poor encoding of components of the outbound path rather than an inaccurate computation of a homeward trajectory by use of the axioms. Hence, the success of the model relies on accurate representation of how people encode their movements during travel.

As a start, the model is based on evidence that people make a regression error when they reproduce some turns or distances. That is, the model assumes that people represent the range of turning and distances experienced within some window of recent pathways. When people are asked to reproduce some of the larger turns or walk some of the longer distances, they produce lesser values by ending their movement prematurely. Conversely, when people are asked to reproduce smaller turns and shorter distances, they tend to overshoot. Given the assumption that people encode values of their movements with regression to the mean of recent experiences, the model nicely accounts for data from triangle-completion tasks (Fujita et al., 1993). The model has also been used to infer how people may represent more complex pathways (May & Klatzky, 2000).

PHENOMENOLOGY OF MOVEMENT

The success of this model suggests that it is important to know more about how people perceive and encode movements. For example, both Klatzky et al. (1990) and Loomis et al. (1993) had blindfolded people estimate and reproduce distances after they had walked them while repeating a nonsense phrase. Although the repeated vocalization was intended to suppress counting of footsteps, it could have also interfered with other processes that are normally used to register the duration or effort of walking. The requirement to vocalize repeatedly ensures that participants do not update deliberately during travel and can only estimate when they stop at the end of a path. An estimate at a juncture that considers the path as a whole may be different than a cumulative estimate from subjectively determined episodes of processing.

Certainly, subjective categories are known to be important when people are remembering turns. People are more accurate reproducing turns of 90°, 180°, and 270° than turns of 60°, 120°, and 300° (Klatzky et al., 1990; Loomis et al., 1993; Sadalla & Montello, 1989). Following the analysis by Howard and Templeton (1966), Sadalla and Montello pointed out that orthogonal reference axes (e.g., 90°, 180°) are inherent to egocentric orientation. Humans, like many animals with bilateral symmetry, have a front and rear, as determined by the position of systems for sensing events in the path of motion, and arms and legs that can be extended at right angles to the direction of forward motion. Hence, a history of movement may be encoded with reference to the orthogonal planes and axes of the human body.

This encoding is likely to be a process of categorization. Categorization or segmentation is evident when values along a continuous metric dimension, such as the values between 0° and 360° of rotation, are not perceived, remembered, or spoken about as if they only differed in magnitude. Instead, some values along the dimension are special. They are prototypes that serve to organize and represent a category of events. If information about a spatial event is inexactly encoded or only vaguely remembered, estimates of its value along a physical dimension may be weighted toward a prototypical value (Huttenlocher, Hedges, & Duncan, 1991). For example, using a circular measuring device, people tended to estimate their own angles of rotation as more like 90° than they actually were; turns between 0° and 90° were overestimated, and turns between 90° and 180° were underestimated (Sadalla & Montello, 1989). These results suggest that process models of how people reproduce and complete pathways might benefit from an assumption that encoding errors involve regression to prototypes.

In general, researchers will need to know more about the phenomenology of turning and distance traversal to provide an account of dead reckoning by humans. For example, psychophysical studies of turning have been limited. Early methods sought to isolate how a rotation is perceived and produced from a standstill, but errors in reproducing turns are different when people experience those turns while walking (Loomis et al., 1993). In addition, researchers know little of how turns of different radii are estimated or reproduced. The presence of veering suggests that some gradual turns (large radii) are not even perceived as turns. It is possible that when errors and categories of representation of movement are known, the components of human path experience will not be useful for trigonometric calculations. People might use other heuristics to solve the problem of how to head home:

> Successful computation might be achieved by an internal scanning process, performed on a spatial image, that derives the direction and distance of the origin. Alternatively, the computation might be a more abstract process that takes as its input nonspatial, even symbolic values of segment lengths and turn extents (Fujita et al., 1993, p. 311).

CONFIGURAL REPRESENTATION OF PATHS

Memories of human locomotion may be organized to represent both the order of actions and the direction and extent of actions. Since the demonstrations of cognitive maps in animals (Tolman, 1948), psychologists have been particularly intrigued with the notion that the representation of humans' movements while on the ground is organized to reflect a survey of the territory as if seen from above. However, when people cannot see the environment while walking, they may be preoccupied representing what their internal sensations of movements mean with reference to the horizon. As we show, the imagined flow of events along the horizon can provide a dynamic frame of reference for making inferences such as a bearing to a landmark or a shortcut home (Rieser, 1999).

An overhead view of the course of travel is a unique perspective. At the least, such a survey of the course of travel would be a configuration, a line figure consisting of path segments and their relations to one another. If the line figure is closed, as it would be when all of the segments are represented in a triangle-completion task, there are geometric properties associated with its shape. Hence, trigonometric computations of a bearing may be based on the episodic memories of two path segments and one turn. The analysis may only have to occur once when memories are retrieved at the end of the second segment rather than occurring as a step-by-step or continuous updating during travel. Even without metric computations, shortcuts and detours could be estimated when path segments are remembered and organized as a configuration. A survey representation allows the viewer to imagine lines directly connecting to points along the figure (Kosslyn, 1980).

One of the first indications that configural properties of paths are important for dead-reckoning performance is illustrated in Fig. 9.3 (Klatzky et al., 1990). The middle and right panels illustrate a survey view of 2 of 12 pathway completion problems conducted within a circular area within a 12 m × 12 m room. The illustrated problems contained three path segments of approximately equal total length at the same point of termination. However, the paths in the middle panel crossed over, forming a closed shape, whereas the paths in the right panel did not. When attempting to return to the origin of the three paths, some blindfolded participants in the problem depicted in

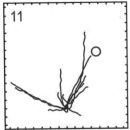 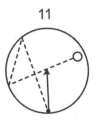 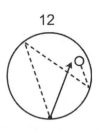

FIG. 9.3.   The left panel depicts tracings of return walks by 12 individuals in a path completion problem conducted in a 12 m × 12 m room. (redrawn from Klatzky et al., 1990). The middle panel summarizes the problem. The point of departure is illustrated as an open circle, and the three legs of the outbound path are illustrated as dashed lines. The closed circle indicates the end of the outbound path, and the arrowed solid line is the vector representing the average return heading and distance of all 12 participants. The left panel indicates the variability around the average vector in this problem. The right panel illustrates a problem that does not involve a crossing over of outbound paths, although the number of legs, total distance walked, and point of return are similar to those in the middle panel. *Note.* From "Acquisition of Route and Survey Knowledge in the Absence of Vision," by R. L. Klatzky et al., 1990, *Journal of Motor Behavior, 22*, pp. 34, 38. Copyright 1990 by Heldref Publications, 1319 18th Street, NW, Washington, DC, 20036-1802. www.heldref.org Reprinted with permission of the Helen Dwight Reid Educational Foundation.

the middle panel apparently did not register that they had crossed over the earlier path. As detailed by the tracings in the left panel, they turned at various angles then walked only short distances. The difficulties on the problem would not be predicted by abstract computational or homing-vector models (Klatzky et al., 1990). Participant's difficulties could reflect a bias not to represent their path memories as a crossover because none of the other path completion problems included such a topology. This interpretation presumes that participants were monitoring the types of configurations formed by path segments.

People may use heuristics for combining memories of separate turns and distances to estimate a heading. For example, a cumulative record could be that the first turn was almost a complete turnaround to the right, and the second turn was almost a complete turnaround to the left. Hikers know this pattern of movement as a switchback and sailors know this pattern as tacking. The opposing turns allow gradual progress forward in the face of resistance. If a participant were familiar with such a sequence, they may know that the origin of their travel is always somewhat behind them as they progress. It is not established that an overhead view of paths of movement is necessary to have this realization.

However, certain tasks may provide evidence that is consistent with spatial inference from a survey representation. For example, it would be interesting to determine the conditions that allow people to draw or recognize a bird's-eye view of paths they have walked while deprived of vision. In one study, after leading blindfolded university students along paths in an unfamiliar suburban neighborhood, Greidanus (2003) periodically removed the blindfolds and asked the students to choose a line drawing that best represented an overhead view of their paths. Figure 9.4 illustrates the configuration of one actual path and five foils. Patterns of avoidance of foils could indicate that the path had been encoded as a sequence of left–right turns or as having a segment with a gradual curve to the left or right.

Blindfolded students chose the configuration representing the actual paths reliably (29% correct). Sighted students did even better (45% correct). None of the students immediately recognized the configuration representing the bird's-eye view but typically spent minutes eliminating foils on the basis of memories of particular path segments and turns. Interestingly, students whose vision was restricted to views of the path within 1 m of their feet performed as if completely sighted (43% correct). Because during travel these students could not see landmarks that would be useful at the point where they had to identify the configuration of their paths, the results indicate the importance of optic flow for accurate encoding of movements.

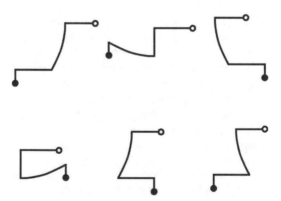

FIG. 9.4.   Line drawings representing a possible overhead view of a 458 m walk through an unfamiliar suburban neighborhood (redrawn from Greidanus, 2003). The dark circles indicate the start of the walk where vision was restricted for some adults. The open circles indicate the end location where all participants were sighted and asked to select one of these line drawings as a bird's-eye view of their route. The correct configuration is in the upper right. Adapted with permission.

DEAD RECKONING ON THE BASIS OF OPTIC FLOW

Normally, people monitor their position, heading, and movements in relation to their environmental surround. They can perceive their travel in terms of changes in the perspective of scenes or the position and faces of objects. There is a natural correlation between the perceived rates and directions of self-movement and the perceived changes in environmental perspectives (Gibson, 1979). Moreover, the correlation holds true as textures of surfaces are seen to flow around and to the sides of the traveler; environmental feedback does not require the presence of discrete landmarks. Sensitivity to changes in optic flow seems particularly useful in situations in which only the textures near paths can be seen. For example, a way finder can maintain a straight heading in tall, dense forest by monitoring both the internal sensations of turning and the relative rate of movement of environmental textures on the left and right. There are indications that access to optic flow makes it easier for travelers to structure movements in large-scale space than if they were limited to proprioceptive feedback and memories of efferent motor commands (Greidanus, 2003; Riecke, van Veen, & Bültoff, 2002).

Extending these observations, Rieser (1999) suggested that people register their movements while blindfolded in light of their experience with optic flow under normal viewing conditions. When people are walking without vision, they typically describe their paths in terms of external referents that they remember such as "parallel to the line of spruce trees." Evidently, proprioceptive cues associated with self-movement allow blindfolded travelers to imagine how the visual surround would be changing. People are even capable of imagining that they are in remote territory and then correctly judging their orientation to landmarks in that imagined territory while walking without vision in the laboratory (Rieser, Garing, & Young, 1994). These observations suggest that blindfolded people may solve path completion tasks by situating their actual walking within an imagined familiar environment. They recall memories of scenes. They could, for example, infer a shortcut to the origin of their walk from the bearings of landmarks imagined at the point of return. This inference is of course evidence of Euclidean knowledge of space but may be principally derived from imagined flow of visual events along the horizon rather than from a representation of path configuration from overhead.

PLURALITY OF HUMAN DEAD RECKONING

Intuitively, human navigation seems based on piloting. The conventional model of human way finding views the way finder as constantly updating positional representations by coordinating external views of landmarks against a cognitive map. This may indeed be the modal method by which people find their way. However, there are many cases in which the cognitive map contains important gaps or is absent altogether. Nonpiloting methods, for example, may be particularly important during childhood, when expansion of the individual's home range is dramatic and rapid.

Our review suggests that people do not accomplish nonpiloting navigation by the continuous metric computations that characterize models of animal path integration. People have random and systematic bias in their memories of self-movement. Although these errors may be accommodated within models that assume mathematical formalisms (Fujita et al., 1993), we suggest that people deprived of vision may use some other procedures for making inferences from memories.

For example, some people may update a record of turning by occasionally adding estimates of rotations from their initial heading. Updates could occur at sites where changes in heading occur in the manner of "My first turn was a bit to the right of my direction of walking from the start and this turn is an extreme left, so I am progressing moderately left of my initial heading." Updating at the immediate turn would reduce memory load for turning and provide an anchor point for monitoring the relative amount of travel along the new bearing.

We suspect that heuristics operate on route-based phenomenology because people typically describe the environments they walk through as a sequence of events rather than as a configuration (Levelt, 1982; Linde & Labov, 1975). There is no obvious reason why language should lead to descriptions such as, "Walk forward about 10 meters, take a hard right, then walk forward a few less steps and stop" rather than descriptions such as, "It is an L-shaped route." As illustrated in the former description, verbal directions and notes indicate that spaces people move within are represented with both metric and categorical information (Taylor, 2000).

Sighted people invariably describe a variety of methods when asked how they solve orienting and way-finding tasks in large-scale environments (Cornell & Heth, 2000; Cornell, Sorenson, & Mio, 2003; Hill, 1997). The descriptions involve several levels of analysis of features of landscape, often with clever discernment of details and patterns that are unique to particular environmental events. People often report more than one strategy to devise a response to pointing and way-finding tasks and report different methods for responding at different sites or as tasks progress. Verbal protocols are consistent with models of executive selection of processes to use readily interpretable information, to monitor progress, and to react to anomalous outcomes. These descriptions suggest that normal orienting and way finding, such as reading, writing, and many other complex human performances, involve several interactive and compensatory cognitive processes. We suggest that human solutions to dead reckoning without visual input will be found to be similar.

If this is true, group performance on dead reckoning tasks may be an amalgamation of different individual strategies. Averaged data would make it difficult to interpret the processing of memories of segments and turns and discover how people choose certain heuristics to make inferences from these memories (Siegler, 1987). Protocol analyses and task analyses could help to unravel how information is used during dead reckoning (Ericsson & Simon, 1996).

When environmental cues are obscure, one solution seems particularly suited to human cognition. It relies on humans' ability to recall spatial events to provide a context for travel (Werner & Schmidt, 1999). With our eyes closed, we can imagine that we are in a familiar place, or we can reconstruct the immediate environment as it surrounded us before vision was restricted. We slowly begin to walk, and our memories of the patterns of visual flow that accompany self-movement allow us to envision how the view of landmarks would change. In this solution, we are dead reckoning within the cognitive map.

ACKNOWLEDGMENTS

Our research is supported by grants from the Natural Sciences and Engineering Research Council and the National Search and Rescue Secretariat of Canada. We thank Michael Snyder and Jack Loomis for their helpful comments.

REFERENCES

Anderson, N. H. (1981). *Foundations of information integration theory.* New York: Academic.

Biegler, R. (2000). Possible uses of path integration in animal navigation. *Animal Learning & Behavior, 28,* 257–277.

Burch, D. (1986). *Emergency navigation.* Camden, ME: International Marine.

Burkhalter, A. (1972). Distance measuring as influenced by terrestrial clues in *Cataglyphis bicolor (Formicidae,* Hymenoptera). In R. Wehner (Ed.), *Information processing in the visual system of arthropods* (pp. 303–308). Berlin: Springer-Verlag.

Collett, T., & Collett, M. (2000). Path integration in insects. *Current Opinion in Neurobiology, 10,* 757–762.

Cornell, E. H., Hadley, D. C., Sterling, T. M., Chan, M. A., & Boechler, P. (2001). Adventure as a stimulus for cognitive development. *Journal of Environmental Psychology, 21,* 219–231.

Cornell, E. H., & Heth, C. D. (2000). Route learning and wayfinding. In R. Kitchin & S. Freundschuh (Eds.), *Cognitive mapping: Past, present, and future* (pp. 66–83). London: Routledge.

Cornell, E. H., Heth, C. D., & Alberts, D. M. (1994). Place recognition and way finding by children and adults. *Memory and Cognition, 22,* 633–643.

Cornell, E. H., Heth, C. D., Kneubuhler, Y., & Sehgal, S. (1996). Serial position effects in children's route reversal errors: Implications for police search operations. *Applied Cognitive Psychology, 10,* 301–326.

Cornell, E. H., Sorenson, A., & Mio, T. (2003) Human sense of direction and way finding performance. *Annals of the American Association of Geographers, 93,* 402–428.

Downs, R. M., & Stea, D. (1973). Cognitive maps and spatial behavior: Process and products. In R. Downs & D. Stea (Eds.), *Image and environment: Cognitive mapping and spatial behavior* (pp. 8–26). Chicago: Aldine.

Dyer, F. C. (1998). Cognitive ecology of navigation. In R. Dukas (Ed.), *Cognitive ecology* (pp. 201–260). Chicago: University of Chicago Press.

Ericsson, K. A., & Simon, H. A. (1996). *Protocol analysis: Verbal reports as data.* Cambridge, MA: MIT Press.

Etienne, A. S., Berlie, J., Georgakopoulos, J., & Maurer, R. (1998). Role of dead reckoning in navigation. In S. Healy (Ed.), *Spatial representation in animals* (pp. 54–68). New York: Oxford University Press.

Fujita, N., Klatzky, R. L., Loomis, J. M., & Golledge, R. G. (1993). The encoding-error model of pathway completion without vision. *Geographical Analysis, 25,* 295–314.

Fujita, N., Loomis, J. M., Klatzky, R. L., & Golledge, R. G. (1990). A minimal representation for dead-reckoning navigation: Updating the homing vector. *Geographical Analysis, 22,* 326–335.

Gallistel, C. R. (1990). *The organization of learning.* Cambridge, MA: MIT Press.

Geldard, F. A. (1972). *The human senses* (2nd ed.). New York: Wiley.

Gibson, J. J. (1979). *The ecological approach to visual perception.* Boston: Houghton Mifflin.

Golledge, R. G. (1995). Primitives of spatial knowledge. In T. Nyerges, D. Mark, R. Laurini, & M. Egenhofer (Eds.), *Cognitive aspects of human-computer interaction for geographic information systems* (pp. 29–44). Dordrecht, The Netherlands: Kluwer Academic.

Golledge, R. G. (1999). Human wayfinding and cognitive maps. In R. Golledge (Ed.), *Wayfinding behavior: Cognitive mapping and other spatial processes* (pp. 5–45). Baltimore: Johns Hopkins University Press.

Greidanus, E. (2002). *The representation of dead reckoning during a suburban walk.* Unpublished manuscript, University of Alberta, Edmonton, Alberta, Canada.

Guth, D., & LaDuke, R. (1994). The veering tendency of blind pedestrians: An analysis of the problem and literature review. *Journal of Visual Impairment & Blindness, 88,* 391–400.

Guth, D., & LaDuke, R. (1995). Veering by blind pedestrians: Individual differences and their implications for instruction. *Journal of Visual Impairment & Blindness, 89,* 28–37.

Healy, S. (Ed.). (1998). *Spatial representation in animals.* New York: Oxford University Press.

Hill, K. (Ed.). (1997). *Managing the lost person incident.* Chantilly, VA: National Association for Search and Rescue.

Hirtle, S. C., & Mascolo, M. F. (1991). The heuristics of spatial cognition. In K. Hammond & D. Gentner (Eds.), *Proceedings of the thirteenth annual conference of the Cognitive Science Society* (pp. 629–634). Hillsdale, NJ: Lawrence Erlbaum Associates, Inc.

Howard, I. P., & Templeton, W. B. (1966). *Human spatial orientation.* New York: Wiley.

Hutchins, E. (1995). *Cognition in the wild.* Cambridge, MA: MIT Press.

Huttenlocher, J., Hedges, L. V., & Duncan, S. (1991). Categories and particulars: Prototype effects in estimating spatial location. *Psychological Review, 98,* 352–376.

James, W. (1890/1950). *The principles of psychology* (Vol. 1). New York: Dover.

Jonsson, E. (2002). *Inner navigation: Why we get lost and how we find our way.* New York: Scribner's.

Karmiloff-Smith, A. (2000). Why babies' brains are not Swiss army knives. In H. Rose & S. Rose (Eds.), *Alas, poor Darwin: Arguments against evolutionary psychology* (pp. 144–156). London: Jonathon Cape.

Kearns, M. J., Warren, W. H., Duchon, A. P., & Tarr, M. J. (2002). Path integration from optic flow and body senses in a homing task. *Perception, 31,* 349–374.

Kitchin, R., & Blades, M. (2002). *The cognition of geographic space.* London: Tauris.
Kitchin, R., & Freundschuh, S. (2000). Cognitive mapping. In R. Kitchin & S. Freundschuh (Eds.), *Cognitive mapping: Past, present and future* (pp. 1–8). London: Routledge.
Klatzky, R. L., Loomis, J. M., Golledge, R. G., Cicinelli, J. G., Doherty, S., & Pellegrino, J. W. (1990). Acquisition of route and survey knowledge in the absence of vision. *Journal of Motor Behavior, 22,* 19–43.
Kosslyn, S. M. (1980). *Image and mind.* Cambridge, MA: Harvard University Press.
Landau, B., & Spelke, E. (1985). Spatial knowledge and its manifestations. In H. Wellman (Ed.), *Children's searching: The development of search skill and spatial representation* (pp. 27–52). Hillsdale, NJ: Lawrence Erlbaum Associates, Inc.
Landau, B., Spelke, E., & Gleitman, L. (1984). Spatial knowledge in a young blind child. *Cognition, 16,* 225–260.
Levelt, W. J. M. (1982). Linearization in describing spatial networks. In S. Peters & E. Saarinen (Eds.), *Processes, beliefs, and questions* (pp. 199–220). Dordrecht, The Netherlands: Reidel.
Liben, L. S. (1988). Conceptual issues in the development of spatial cognition. In J. Stiles-Davis, M. Kritchevsky, & U. Bellugi (Eds.), *Spatial cognition: Brain bases and development* (pp. 167–194). Hillsdale, NJ: Lawrence Erlbaum Associates, Inc.
Linde, C., & Labov, W. (1975). Spatial networks as a site for the study of language and thought. *Language, 51,* 924–940.
Loomis, J. M., Klatzky, R. L., Golledge, R. G., Cicinelli, J. G., Pellegrino, J. W., & Fry, P. A. (1993). Nonvisual navigation by blind and sighted: Assessment of path integration ability. *Journal of Experimental Psychology: General, 122,* 73–91.
Loomis, J. M., Klatzky, R. L., Golledge, R. G., & Philbeck, J. W. (1999). Human navigation by path integration. In R. Golledge (Ed.), *Wayfinding behavior: Cognitive mapping and other spatial processes* (pp. 125–151). Baltimore: Johns Hopkins University Press.
May, M., & Klatzky, R. L. (2000). Path integration while ignoring irrelevant movement. *Journal of Experimental Psychology: Learning, Memory and Cognition, 26,* 169–186.
Montello, D. R. (1989). The geometry of environmental knowledge. In A. Frank, I Campari, & V. Formentini (Eds.), *Theories and methods of spatio-temporal reasoning in geographic space* (pp. 136–152) [Lecture Notes in Computer Science No. 639]. Berlin: Springer-Verlag.
Mittelstaedt, H., & Mittelstaedt, M. L. (1982). Homing by path integration. In F. Papi & H. Wallraff (Eds.), *Avian navigation* (pp. 290–297). Berlin: Springer.
Melville, H. (1851/1967). *Moby Dick; or The Whale.* H. Hayford & H. Parker (Eds.). New York: Norton.
Müller, M., & Wehner, R. (1994). The hidden spiral: Systematic search and path integration in desert ants, *Cataglyphis fortis. Journal of Comparative Physiology A, 175,* 525–530.
O'Keefe, J., & Nadel, L. (1978). *The hippocampus as a cognitive map.* New York: Oxford University Press.
Péruch, P., Borel, L., Gaunet, F., Thinus-Blanc, C., Magnan, J., & Lacour, M. (1999). Spatial performance of unilateral vestibular defective patients in nonvisual versus visual navigation. *Journal of Vestibular Research, 9,* 37–47.
Potegal, M. (1982). Vestibular and neostriatal contributions to spatial orientation. In M. Potegal (Ed.), *Spatial abilities: Developmental and physiological foundations* (pp. 361–387). New York: Academic.
Riecke, B. E., van Veen, A. H. C., & Bültoff, H. H. (2002). Visual homing is possible without landmarks: A path integration study in virtual reality. *Presence: Teleoperators and Virtual Environments, 11,* 443–473.

Rieser, J. J. (1999). Dynamic spatial orientation and the coupling of representation and action. In R. Golledge (Ed.), *Wayfinding behavior: Cognitive mapping and other spatial processes* (pp. 168–190). Baltimore: Johns Hopkins University Press.

Rieser, J. J., Garing, A. E., & Young, M. F. (1994). Imagery, action, and young children's spatial orientation: It's not being there that counts, it's what one has in mind. *Child Development, 65,* 1262–1278.

Sadalla, E. K., & Montello, D. R. (1989). Remembering changes in direction. *Environment and Behavior, 21,* 346–363.

Sholl, M. J. (1989). The relation between horizontality and rod-and-frame and vestibular navigational performance. *Journal of Experimental Psychology: Learning, Memory & Cognition, 15,* 110–125.

Siegler, R. S. (1987). The perils of averaging data over strategies: An example from children's addition. *Journal of Experimental Psychology: General, 116,* 250–264.

Stevens, S. S., & Greenbaum, H. B. (1966). Regression effect in psychophysical judgment. *Perception & Psychophysics, 1,* 439–446.

Taylor, H. A. (2000). A view of space through language. In R. Kitchin & S. Freundschuh (Eds.), *Cognitive mapping: Past, present and future* (pp. 179–196). London: Routledge.

Tolman, E. C. (1948). Cognitive maps in rats and men. *Psychological Review, 55,* 189–208.

Trowbridge, C. C. (1913, December 19). On fundamental methods of orientation and "imaginary maps." *Science, 38,* 888–897.

von der Heyde, M., Riecke, B. E., Cunningham, D. W., & Bültoff, H. H. (2000). Humans can extract distance and velocity from vestibular perceived acceleration [Abstract]. *Journal of Cognitive Neuroscience, 63C,* 77.

Wehner, R., & Srinivasan, M. V. (1981). Searching behavior of desert ants, genus *Cataglyphis* (*Formicidae,* Hymenoptera). *Journal of Comparative Physiology, 142,* 315–338.

Werner, S. (2002, August). *Integration of spatial reference systems for wayfinding in natural and built environments.* Presented at the meetings of the Cognitive Science Association for Interdisciplinary Learning, Hood River, Oregon.

Werner, S., & Schmidt, K. (1999). Environmental reference systems for large-scale spaces. *Spatial Cognition and Computation, 1,* 447–473.

Neurocognitive Components of Spatial Memory

Robin G. Morris and David M. Parslow
King's College London

Spatial orientation is an essential capability of almost all animals; hence, the extensive research in this area, including investigations of its neurobiological basis. In humans, two main methods have been applied in this neurobiological analysis: investigating patients with focal brain lesions and studying the pattern of brain activation associated with types of spatial orientation activity (Burgess, Jeffery, & O'Keefe, 1999). The aim of this chapter is to review progress in both these methods with specific reference to recent studies conducted by Morris and coworkers (e.g., Abrahams, Pickering, Jarosz, Cox, & Morris, 1999; Abrahams, Pickering, Polkey, & Morris, 1997; Feigenbaum, Polkey, & Morris, 1996; Nunn, Graydon, Polkey, & Morris, 1999; Nunn, Polkey, & Morris, 1998; Worsley et al., 2001). Such studies distinguish between different types of memory representations and their relation to the network of neuronal structures that support spatial orientation.

In this field, cross-species comparison may provide important insights into how the human brain supports memory function. These point toward the involvement of certain key structures, in particular the hippocampal formation. In rodents, for example, there is the evidence that bilateral lesions of the hippocampus produce spatial memory impairment on different types of tasks (Morris, Garrud, Rawlins, & O'Keefe, 1982; Olton, Walker, & Gage, 1978); neurophysiological recording has identified place cells in the hippocampus that fire when the rodent is in a particular location (O'Keefe, 1976; Wilson & McNaughton, 1993). In nonhuman primates, bilateral hippocampal lesions again produce spatial memory impairment (Angeli, Murray, & Mishkin, 1993). However, differences have emerged with respect to neurophysiological recording, and single unit recordings have identified different cell types. These include cells that respond to a combination of object location and specific objects as well as view cells, which respond to where the animal is looking, irrespective of its position (Rolls, 1999; Rolls & O'Mara, 1995).

In humans, there is also evidence linking spatial orientation to the hippocampal formation, as we outline in the following sections. Here again, the nature of the representations supporting navigation ability are again likely to be complex, with the addition of language or symbolic facilities that can interact with spatial encoding (Frank, Campari, & Formentini, 1992). Early research in this area involved studying patients with neurosurgical temporal lobe lesions, which are used for the treatment of intractable epilepsy, and more specifically, the unilateral temporal lobectomy (TL), which includes removal of anterior hippocampus. Surgery of this type in the language- dominant hemisphere was found to cause verbal memory impairment, whereas similar surgery in the right side was found to produce nonverbal impairment (Smith, 1989). Further study of such patients has demonstrated dissociations relating to spatial orientation ability and, in combination with evidence from structural imaging, helped to specify the specific structures involved. Research on spatial memory in humans has also benefited greatly from contemporary functional neuroimaging techniques, tools that have allowed researchers to complement findings from brain lesion studies and explore features of a more widespread neuronal network (Aguirre, Detre, Alsop, & D'Esposito, 1996; Burgess, Maguire, Spiers, & O'Keefe, 2001; Maguire et al., 1998a; Maguire, Frith, Burgess, Donnett, & O'Keefe, 1998).

TYPES OF MEMORY AND FUNCTIONAL DISTINCTIONS

For the purposes of this chapter, spatial memory processes are split into three main types of activities (see Fig. 10.1), reflecting the neuropsychological investigations described:

1. *Cue guidance:* Spatial navigation frequently depends on the use of landmarks or prominent features in the landscape. Where vision is used, landmarks are remembered because of their dominant form, the peculiarity of their structure, or their meaning or connotations (Appleyard, 1970). A simple form of navigation is to approach a landmark directly, referred to as *cue guidance.* In cognitive terms, such processing depends on visual recognition memory or recall and is not dependent on memory for location. Thus, cue-based navigation typically invokes pattern or object perception, with memory of previous encounters guiding the response.

2. *Cognitive mapping:* This term was coined by Tolman (1948) and captures the notion that spatial information is internally represented in the form of vectors between different locations or landmarks. It enables, for ex-

A. Cue Guidance: Approaching directly a visual cue

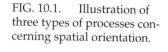

FIG. 10.1. Illustration of three types of processes concerning spatial orientation.

B. Cognitive Mapping: Encoding the relative direction and distances between landmarks

C. Path Integration: integration outward bound vectors to provide a homing vector

ample, wayfinding ability in which a person can navigate to a distal location not perceived directly. It also structures various landmarks into a configural whole based on perception. Another feature is that it can generate knowledge of relative direction of landmarks independent of participant viewpoint, hence incorporating the notion of allocentric or viewer-independent memory.

3. *Path integration:* This is the facility to update relative position based on perception of movement (Loomis, Klatzky, Golledge, & Philbeck, 1999). For example, where visual cues are not directly available, a person can use kinesthetic, vestibular, and other motion cues to update his or her position relative to a known starting place. To some extent, path integration is strongly linked with sense of direction and may be involved in the initial formation of cognitive maps (McNaughton et al., 1996).

The studies outlined following indicate how it may be possible to dissociate these three types of processes in humans through neuropsychological investigation and to differentiate the brain structures underlying the representations resulting from these processes.

Patient Studies and Brain Lesions

As previously indicated, the principal patient brain lesions type to be investigated in relation to spatial memory is the unilateral TL. This operation involves more extensive neurosurgical removal than just the anterior hippo campus and includes the temporal pole, the amygdala, and cortical areas surrounding the hippocampus, such as the entorhinal cortex and parahippocampal gyrus. The exact procedure varies within and between centers. For example, in the Montreal Neurological Institute (MNI) where much of the surgery was pioneered, there are "small" hippocampal removal operations in which the hippocampus is spared entirely and large ones in which the main body of the hippocampus is removed along with the overlapping parahippocampal gyrus. Additionally, various centers have used more selective operations sparing the temporal pole and removing the hippocampus and amygdala, the so-called amygdala-hippocampectomy (Goldstein & Polkey, 1993). Various studies have explored the extent of hippocampal removal and visuospatial memory impairment. Results have shown that the "large" TL produces more impairment on, for example, recall of spatial location, maze learning, and design recall (Jones-Gotman, 1986; Smith & Milner, 1981, 1989). Additionally, it has been shown that the amygdala-hippocampectomy tends to produce the same degree of spatial memory impairment as that resulting from larger lesions (Goldstein & Polkey, 1993).

In our own center, the King's Neurosciences Centre, the en bloc resection is used, which is closer to the large TL used in the MNI, with removal of about 5.5 to 6.5 cm of temporal lobe and the anterior two thirds of the hippocampus (Polkey, 1987). The extent of tissue removal is illustrated in a series of studies (Graydon, Nunn, & Morris, 2001; Nunn et al., 1999, 1998) using structural magnetic resonance imaging (MRI) and correlating measurements of removal against spatial memory function (see also following section). Contiguous coronal images were taken, with slice thickness of 1.5 mm. A lesion analysis has been applied to the MRI images (see Fig. 10.2) in which the temporal lobe is segmented into four regions using a radial division technique,

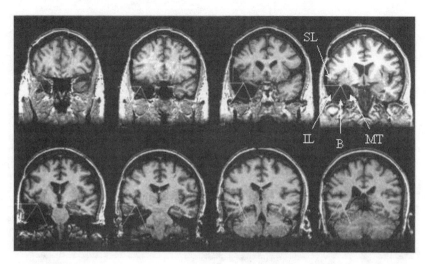

FIG. 10.2. Structural magnetic resonance imaging coronal sections showing the en bloc unilateral temporal lobectomy operation. Representative coronal slices are shown covering the temporal lobes from the temporal pole to the posterior hippocampus. The lesion analysis technique is also shown with the temporal lobe divided into superiorlateral (SL), inferolateral (IL), basil (B), and mesiotemporal (MT) regions.

namely Superiorlateral (SL), Inferolateral (IL), Basal (B), and Mesiotemporal (MT). The latter was also split into the parahippocampal and hippocampal regions. Visual ratings of each separate coronal slice covering the length of the hippocampus were conducted using a 4-point scale ranging from *no resection* (1) to *complete resection* (4). By summing the ratings for each slice, a total resection score for each region was obtained and correlated against neuropsychological performance. In the study by Graydon et al. (2001), this analysis revealed an inverse relation between extent of right hippocampal removal and performance on two tasks that involved drawing spatially complex figures from memory. This technique has also been exploited by Nunn et al. (1999, 1998) in further explorations of spatial memory (see section on cue guidance vs. spatial memory).

The relatively large lesions associated with unilateral TL may make it more difficult to tease apart the critical temporal lobe structures, although the lesion analysis as outlined previously can help do this. An alternative is to study patients with more focal hippocampal lesions. A group that fits this criterion includes the same patient type as those individuals who undergo the TL operation but in the preoperative phase. In a subsample of these patients, there are those who have mesiotemporal lobe sclerosis (MTS; see Fig. 10.3) with atrophy and neuronal loss mainly restricted to ei-

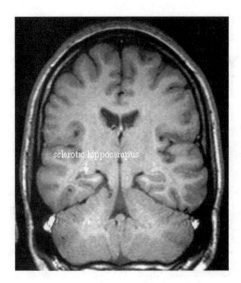

FIG. 10.3. Structural magnetic resonance imaging coronal section showing hippocampal sclerosis restricted to the right hemisphere (left and right reversed in this radiological image).

ther the left or right hippocampus (Bruton, 1988). Histological studies suggest that the most prominent areas of MTS tend to be in CA1, CA3, and CA4 fields of the hippocampus, the subiculum-prosubiculum, and fascia dentate (Babb & Brown, 1987; Margerison & Corsellis, 1966). This pattern is identifiable using structural MRI, which in turn can be used to select patients suitable for such studies. An example is the study by Abrahams et al. (1999), as described in the section below on cognitive mapping.

In summary, neurosurgery for epilepsy involving the temporal lobe points toward the right temporal lobe being involved in visuospatial memory, with the hippocampus implicated by the relation between performance deficit and amount of tissue removed. This relation suggests a key to cross-species comparisons. Specifically, the posterior hippocampus in humans corresponds topographically to the dorsal hippocampus in rodents. Lesions to this portion of the hippocampus and not the ventral region are associated with spatial memory impairment (Moser, Moser, & Andersen, 1993).

Spatial Memory and Everyday Life

To what extent do these deficits translate into problems with spatial memory in everyday life? Anecdotal evidence combined with clinical histories suggests that spatial memory impairment results in difficulties with navigation, particularly in unfamiliar surroundings. This is complicated by the fact that in many situations navigation can be supplemented by verbal encoding of directions. For example, when finding a new house, it is possible to navigate purely by following a series of verbally encoded street directions culminating in identifying the house by name or number. Nevertheless, in other situations, remaining orientated in space involves a more implicit reliance on understanding the spatial layout of the environment, recognizing scenes or cues, and integrating this knowledge in existing spatial representations. There is evidence that this type of spatial memory is impaired following right TLs. First, using the Everyday Memory Questionnaire with patients who had undergone unilateral TLs, Miotto et al. (2000) found that those with right lesions showed a significantly higher rating than did controls or left-lesion patients on the item concerned with "getting lost or turning in the wrong direction on a journey." Second, a recent study by Feigenbaum and Morris (2003a) looked directly at the ability of left- and right-TL patients to remember routes in a building. They led patients in circular route round a building (within the main building of the Institute of Psychiatry, London) and then required the patients to replicate the route. Despite the fact that this type of navigation can be augmented by verbal encoding, it was the right-TL patients who showed significant impairment.

CUE GUIDANCE VERSUS SPATIAL MEMORY

The preceding section illustrates the association between visuospatial memory impairment and right unilateral temporal lobe lesions. Further studies have sought to distinguish the visual from the spatial components of memory in which visual refers to pattern or object memory and spatial specifically to location. As indicated previously, cue guidance may depend only on the visual aspect of memory. The distinction may reflect a more fundamental neuroanatomical dissociation between visual and spatial processing. Both animal and human studies support the presence of two visual pathways, a *ventral* pathway that specializes in object perception, running from the occipital to the temporal lobe, and a *dorsal* route, which is concerned with spatial perception and manipulation and runs from the occipital to the parietal lobe (Ungerleider & Mishkin, 1982). In nonhuman primates, for example, ventral lesions produce impairments in discriminating between forms, patterns, and objects, whereas dorsal lesions impair the ability to determine the spatial relations between objects (De Renzi, 1982; Morris & Morton, 1995). Figure 10.4 illustrates how these two separate pathways converge on the hippocampal formation, including the hippocampus and parahippocampus. An additional caveat is that objects or patterns in humans may give rise to verbal or semantic codes, and these may form quite separate memory representations (Paivio, 1971).

Visual versus spatial memory was explored initially in patients with unilateral temporal lobectomies in a landmark experiment by Smith and Milner (1981). They showed patients an array of toys, laid out on a blank piece of paper. Initially, participants were asked to price the toys, which

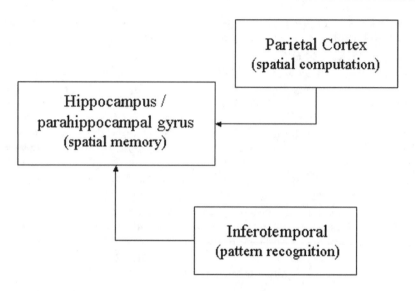

FIG. 10.4.   Convergence of dorsal route (via parietal cortex) and ventral route (via inferotemporal cortex) on the hippocampus.

was an incidental learning task. Subsequently, they were asked to recall the objects and then indicate the original location of the objects during the incidental learning task. The test of memory was repeated again after 24 hr. It was found that both right- and left-TL groups showed impairment in object recall and recognition but only after the 24-hr delay. Only the right-TL patients were impaired on memory for location, and this deficit occurred at both delays. Additionally, the extent of spatial memory impairment was found to be associated with the amount of hippocampal removal.

Subsequent studies have replicated the spatial memory impairment using filled or unfilled delay to show that the outcome was not the result of encoding difficulties, in view of the fact that no delay produced no deficit (Smith & Milner, 1989). One way of interpreting these data for the objects, however, is that both the left and right temporal lobe are involved in object memory. The objects may have been encoded verbally, as their label or name, and visually, as their appearance; respectively, left and right TL may have produced impairments in these two types of memory presentations.

This finding appears to dissociate spatial from other types of memory, visual or verbal. Further support for this dissociation has come through an adaptation of the Smith and Milner (1981) technique by Nunn et al. (1999) using temporal titration. Here, the issue addressed is the extent to which separable representations may be formed in right hippocampal formation relating to object versus spatial location, given that the right TL results in impairments in both. One way to approach this issue is to vary the retention intervals between studying objects and testing memory so as to match between groups on one type of memory and then see whether a difference in the other type of memory occurs. This implies a differential forgetting rate, and hence, separable representations. Nunn et al. (1999) again used 16 objects on a static spatial array. Through pilot work they determined an appropriate delay to match for recall and recognition of the objects, in this case 1 hr for the left-TL group, 2 hr for the right-TL group, and 3 hr for the controls. With this matching technique they found impairment in spatial recall only in the right-TL group. A further aspect of the study was to conduct an analysis of the patient lesions, as described previously. The degree of removal of hippocampal, parahippocampal, and remaining cortical areas in the temporal lobe revealed a correlation between hippocampal removal and spatial memory impairment.

As indicated previously, the method of using objects is complicated by the fact that the objects can be labeled verbally, hence a verbal code can support memory for them. To avoid this difficulty, Nunn et al. (1998) applied a similar technique but substituted line drawings for the objects based on stimuli developed by Jones-Gotman (1986; see Fig. 10.5). Although it is pos-

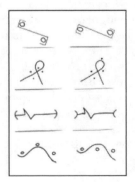

FIG. 10.5. Line drawings used in the experiment by Nunn, Polkey, and Morris (1998). The top panel shows the drawings presented in a spatial layout. The bottom panel shows the recognition memory pairings of drawings. From "Selective spatial memory impairment after right unilateral temporal lobectomy." by J. A. Nunn, C. E. Polkey, and R. G. Morris, 1998, *Neuropsychologia,* *36,* 837–848. Copyright 1998 by Elseyier. Reprinted with permission.

sible to attach verbal labels to these drawings to test memory for them, Nunn et al. (1998) controlled for this possibility using a recognition memory paradigm in which features of the objects were changed slightly as distractor items (see Fig. 10.5). Without advanced knowledge of the distractor items, it would not be possible to use initial verbal labels to discriminate them from the original objects. The titration technique was again used, with a 2-hr delay for the left-TL and control groups and a 1-hr delay for the right-TL group. Recall (drawing) performance matched recognition, but there remained impairment in recalling object locations. The same lesion analysis was conducted on these patients, and this showed significant correlations only in the right-TL group between hippocampal and parahippocampal removal and spatial recall impairment.

In summary, these three studies have shown that in relation to the placement of an object, the spatial component can be dissociated from the visual or verbal. The dissociation occurs behaviorally in the sense that performance is differentiated on the basis of task manipulation. It also occurs neuronally in the sense that the object or pattern memory deficit does not appear to be associated specifically with hippocampal removal in any of the studies; the spatial deficit is only associated with the right TL or the extent of removal of the hippocampus or parahippocampal gyrus on the right (see also Postma, Kessels, & van Asselen, chap. 7, this volume).

COGNITIVE MAPPING

The term *cognitive mapping* as introduced by Tolman (1948) is now commonly used to indicate the internal representation of spatial information. It also implies using Euclidean geometry and a form of mental trigonometry to encode spatial relations between landmarks. As indicated previously, the neurophysiological underpinning of cognitive maps was strongly supported by the discovery of place cells in the rodent hippocampus (Nadel, 1991; O'Keefe & Nadel, 1978), and elucidation of the properties of such cells, combined with computational modeling, has provided further support (Burgess et al., 1999; O'Keefe & Burgess, 1996).

The existence of mapping facilitates allocentric spatial memory, the ability to determine spatial location independent of the body axis. This is a critical feature of the animal paradigms used to investigate mapping and spatial memory in general, for example, the Olton Maze (Olton, Becker, & Handelmann, 1979) and the Morris Water Maze (Morris et al., 1982). In these tasks, the animal is immersed in the spatial environment. In contrast, studies of spatial memory impairment associated with focal lesions in humans have initially used desktop tasks with static spatial arrays placed in front of the participant. This includes, for example, the investigations cited previously by Smith (1989), Smith and Milner (1981), and by Nunn et al. (1999, 1998).

In recent years, the emphasis has shifted toward allocentric tasks, either using computer simulations of three-dimensional space or immersing the participant in a spatial environment and requiring allocentric memory processing. Such tasks may draw on a range of computational facilities to do with movement and space, thus invoking a larger network of neural computational modules (see Fig. 10.6). For example, in addition to the ventral route providing pattern recognition and parietal encoding spatial location, systems involved in bodily orientation and integrating this with spatial encoding are invoked. These include cingulate input relating to self-motion, thalamic and vestibular inputs that code head direction and movements, and parietal lobe processing concerned with movement.

The experiments described in the following section illustrate how this has been investigated using human analogues of animal maze tasks, helping to draw the link between animal and human memory. This is an impor-

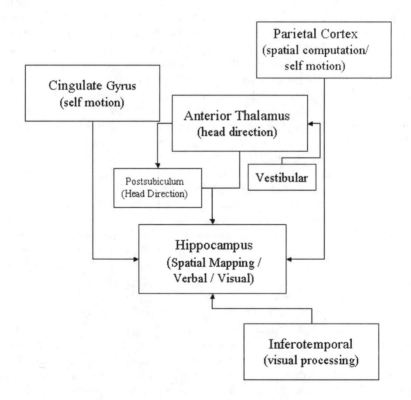

FIG. 10.6. Computational modules concerning during allocentric spatial processing and their inputs to the hippocampus.

tant area of research because the extent to which the findings from animal work can be generalized to humans has not yet been addressed. The concept of an allocentric spatial mapping system involving the hippocampus is a well-developed theory in research based on rodents, but how well does this apply to humans? To what extent do the same functions share the neural substrate as established through extensive animal experimentation?

Human Analogues of the Olton Maze

In his laboratory, Morris and colleagues have conducted a series of studies using human analogues of the Olton (Olton et al., 1979) Maze to explore allocentric memory. In the original radial arm maze, there is a central platform and eight radiating arms that the animal has to traverse in search of food, remembering not to go back to previously successful locations (Jarrard, 1991; Olton et al., 1979). To do this task, the rodent has to use extramaze cues, looking above the maze to see landmarks around them.

In a computerized analogue of this test, called the *rotate task*, Feigenbaum et al. (1996) used a visual display unit to present a large graphically represented "disc" with the appearance of a gramophone turntable. This disc has a number of specified location points signified by small circles rendered onto it. The participant has to search these circles in turn to find a target one, success signalled by the circle changing color. The disc then rotates, and the participant has to search for another target location, remembering not to go back to the previous one. A series of searches followed until all the locations had been targets, with the disc rotating between each searches by either 90° or 180°. Because of the rotation of the disc, the locations cannot be encoded in relation to the body axis, hence the allocentric nature of the task. Feigenbaum et al. (1996) investigated patients who had undergone the TL operation and found a robust impairment in the right-TL group only.

A potential criticism of this task is that the participant can solve the task in an egocentric sense by mentally rotating the configuration of circles for each trial (Taube, 1996). Although this may be possible, it would require additional computation and may not be the most efficient strategy to solve the task. Additionally, right-TL patients have convincingly been shown to have normal mental rotation abilities in different studies (Abrahams et al., 1997; Feigenbaum et al., 1996; Worsley et al., 2001). Thus, the spatial memory deficit is not easily explained in terms of egocentric spatial processing.

Nevertheless, an additional problem with this type of task is that the participant may view the array of circles as gestalt or pattern and use the local geometry of the pattern to guide their memory (see Uttal & Chiong, chap. 6, this volume). This type of memory may rely on the type of processing that encodes the categorical and coordinate relations when perceiving objects (Kosslyn, Flynn, Amsterdam, & Wang, 1990). To minimize this type of configural memory, other studies have invoked movement, with participants moving around a spatial array or setting and having to remember locations. In some sense, this movement makes tasks in human studies more akin to those in animal studies.

Abrahams et al. (1997) incorporated movement into a study aimed at distinguishing between spatial working memory and reference memory as introduced Olton et al. (1979) in animal research. The working memory concept suggests that the hippocampus holds and manipulates information pertinent to the current context, with spatial location encoded as a type of event or context (see Sholl & Fraone, chap. 4, this volume). According to this view, the rodent in a radial maze relies on working memory to traverse the arms of the maze to obtain food rewards, remembering not to go back to previously successful ones. In contrast, reference memory is where information remains constant across trials and therefore is independent of time or context. To test this construct, certain arms are left unbaited across trials, and the animal has to learn which ones to avoid because they never result in reward. Studies using the radial arm maze have been used to support the distinction between the two types of memories, with hippocampal lesions affecting working memory (see Jarrard, 1991).

Translating this into a human paradigm, Abrahams et al. (1997) arranged nine containers in a circular array, each lidded (see Fig. 10.7). For each trial, four objects were placed in four of the containers and the lids repositioned. To incorporate movement and test allocentric memory, the participant had to move round the array after the objects had been placed. They then had to indicate which containers had objects in them and also identify out of a pictorial array of the objects which of them had been placed in the containers. For the distinction between working and reference memory, respectively, two containers were different on each next trial and two were always the same. Similarly, two objects were always different and two the same.

This test was administered to left- and right-TL patients. In terms of the spatial memory test, the right-TL group only were found to be impaired on both the working and reference components, suggesting that there was a generalized deficit not specific to working memory as indicated by rodent work (but see Jarrard, 1991). Object recognition memory impairment was seen in both left- and right-TL groups, and this was restricted to learning the trial invariant (i.e., reference memory) objects.

This result accords with an allocentric memory deficit restricted to patients with right temporal lobe lesions but with both hemispheres contributing to object recognition memory. Abrahams et al. (1997) also tested groups of left and right MTS patients on the Olton Maze analogue. As indicated previously, the patients have focal hippocampal lesions and therefore test the hypothesis of hippocampal involvement more directly. The same pattern was replicated with these patients, with a generalized spatial memory restricted to right MTS and object recognition memory with both left and right MTS. As a follow-up to this study, Abrahams et al. (1999) obtained a new MTS sample and did volumetric MRI, with measurements of the hippocampus, the parahippocampus, and the remaining temporal lobe. This

FIG. 10.7.   Allocentric memory procedure used by Abrahams, Pickering, Jarosz, Cox, and Morris (1999) and Abrahams, Pickering, Polkey, and Morris (1997). The experimenter places objects in four of the bins. The participant then moves around the table and has to point to the bins that have objects in them (hidden by lids) and then identify the objects that have been hidden in a recognition memory procedure.

sample showed the same pattern of memory performance, thus replicating the original finding. Additionally, reduced right hippocampal volume was found to correlate with spatial memory impairment, but there were no significant correlations relating to object recognition.

This finding is strongly suggestive of specific right hippocampal involvement in allocentric memory, partly because the degree of impairment was not increased in the TL sample. Hence, the additional cortical tissue did not appear to be contributing to supporting spatial memory function. Furthermore, the Abrahams et al. (1999, 1997) studies have shown the same dissociation between spatial and object memory as the studies by Smith and Milner (1981, 1989) and Nunn et al. (1999, 1998). Across studies, there is also strong evidence that the distinction between working and reference memory does not hold up well for humans, with no dissociation being found for spatial memory in three patient samples.

The tasks just described have the advantage of involving movement in space, hence the similarity with animal studies. They also rely on room cues to provide landmark cues necessary for spatial memory. Nevertheless, non-specific cues are difficult to control and use of strategy in relation to these cues may confound attempts at investigating allocentric memory. For example, in the Abrahams et al. (1999, 1997) container task, a participant might code a particular location in relation to scratch marks on the container combined with proximity to a room cue. To gain more control of the spatial environment, Morris and coworkers (Recce & Morris, 2002; Morris, Parslow, & Recce, 2000) have used immersive virtual reality to construct a different human analogue of the Olton Maze.

This procedure is called the *shell task* and constructed using The World Tool kit, creating a virtual environment as illustrated by Fig. 10.8. The visual image was presented through a head mounted display and a Polhemus FasTrak sensor was used to track head position and hence coordinate the changing visual display with the movement of the head. A virtual room (2 × 2 m) was constructed in which the participant could move about. In the center of the room was a circular virtual table, and on this was a set on concentrically arranged up turned shells. This arrangement was similar in kind to the container task used by Abrahams et al. (1999, 1997) and designed to be analogous to the arms of the Olton Maze. The object of the task was to move around the table and inspect shells in turn to find one with a blue cube underneath. To inspect the shell, the participant would simply stand in front of it and say "lift," and the shell could appropriately disappear to reveal whether there was a cube underneath it. Once a cube had been found, the cube was moved to a different hidden location. The participant had then to search for this new location while avoiding going back to a previously successful one. There was a series of searches until all the shells used had been the target location.

A feature of this type of task is that humans are good at developing strategies to reduce the memory load. To some extent, this is reduced by the procedure of having the target location move around in a pseudorandom fashion as opposed to the original Olton procedure in which the animal may be simply able to explore the baited arms in an easy sequence (Olton et al., 1979). To reduce further the use of strategy, it was arranged that on each search only a subset of shells could be inspected: those color coded green. Each time the target location was found, this set changed, therefore disrupting any systematic search path across searches. Additionally, the difficulty of the task was varied by the number of shells used (and hence target locations). After practice trials, there were four "games" with four shells and

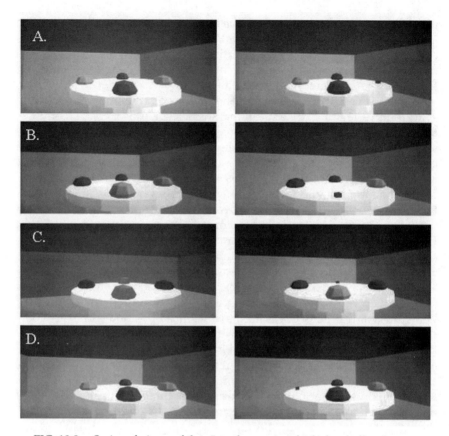

FIG. 10.8.   Series of views of the virtual room in which the shell task was administered (in this illustration at the four-shell level). To illustrate the task, the table is seen from a static viewpoint. The left panels show the array at the start of each search. The right panels show the shells removed to reveal the target blue cube. The darker shells are those that cannot be 'inspected' in a particular trial. Panel sets A through D represent a series of searches in which the cube has been hidden under all four shells in turn.

then three with six shells, the most difficult level. For each level, only half the number of shells could be inspected in each search.

The task was applied to left- and right-TL patients and matched controls. The main measure for the task is the number of times the participant goes back to a previously successful shell in a series of searches. Figure 10.9 shows the error rate for the different trials. With only four shells, the error rate is comparatively low and did not differentiate the groups. In the last trial with four shells, the difficulty of the task is mini-

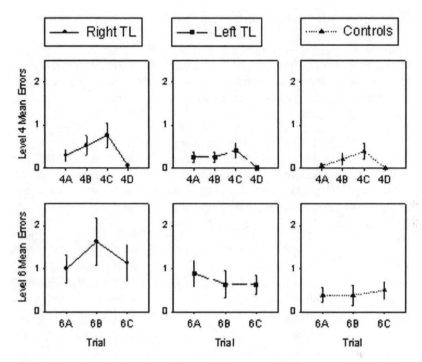

FIG. 10.9. Graph showing right and left temporal lobectomy (TL) partici-pants at two levels of difficulty on the shell task. Data for separate trials (Level 4, A, B, C, and D and Level 6, A, B, and C) are given.

mized by making one of the available choices (two shells were color coded green) the previous target location. In this case, the participant simply had to select the shell that had not just been the target. The mini-mal errors in all three groups provided evidence that the participants thoroughly understood the nature of task before moving on to the more difficult six-shell problems. Here there was a clear differentiation of groups, with the right-TL performance close to chance responding and the left-TL performance showing no deficit.

In summary, these three tasks all showed a specific impairment in allocentric memory associated with lesions to the right temporal lobe; in the Feigenbaum et al. (1996) rotate task, the right TL showed an impairment and this was also true for the Abrahams et al. (1999, 1997) container task and the Recce and Morris (2002) shell tasks. Additionally, the Abrahams et al. (1999, 1997) studies showed that the deficit was just as great when le-sions were restricted to the hippocampal formation and that the deficit was dissociable from impairments in object recognition memory.

Human Analogues of the Morris Water Maze

The other main animal paradigm is the Morris Water Maze in which a rodent has to swim around a circular pool in search of a hidden platform (Morris et al., 1982). The animal has to return to this platform from a different entry point in the pool using room cues to guide navigation. Bilateral hippocampal lesions severely impair performance on this task (Morris et al., 1982).

A human analogue of this maze was developed by Feigenbaum, Polkey, and Morris (2003b) for use with the unilateral TL patients. As shown in Fig. 10.10, this consists of an upturned visual display unit (VDU) fitted with a touch sensitive screen. In the center of the screen is the representation of a circular pool. The participants are instructed to search for a hidden platform by moving their finger from a starting point around the pool. Surrounding the pool are a number of landmarks, for example, a picture of a beach ball or a towel. Place learning is measured as the length of path the participant takes to find the platform over several trials. In this task, there was an egocentric condition in which the participant stood in the one place and the landmarks would arbitrarily move around such that they could not be used to locate the hidden platform. This was contrasted with an allocentric memory condition in which the platform moved around the screen

FIG. 10.10.   Layout used in the Feigenbaum and Morris (2003) human analogue of the Morris Water Maze. The participant searches around the representation of the circular pool, responding using a touch sensitive screen.

in between trials but was in a fixed position in relation to the landmarks. The participant also moves around the VDU in between trials in a pseudorandom fashion. Both left- and right-TL patients showed no impairment on the egocentric condition, learning the location as well as the control group. For the allocentric condition, there was a substantial impairment in learning in the right-TL group, with lengthy path segments that failed to reduce significantly over learning trials. The left-TL group were also impaired but with a less robust impairment.

These findings suggest a specifically allocentric deficit, suggesting that this type of process shows differential hippocampal formation involvement. Such a conclusion has been supported by a functional MRI (fMRI) study using another type of Morris water maze analogue designed recently by Parslow and Morris and called the *arena task* (Parslow et al., 2003). It was again designed to investigate differential patterns of neuronal activation associated with either egocentric or allocentric memory function as in the Feigenbaum et al. (2003) experiment. It consists of a virtual reality circular arena with walls rendered with abstract patterns (see Fig. 10.11). The participant can move around the arena using a joystick. They "enter" the arena and then have to move to a pole in the distance. When the pole is reached, the participants' movements are "locked" and then, after a delay interval, they have to reenter the arena. In this case, the pole has disappeared, and they have to navigate to the position of the pole from memory. The two main conditions were as follows:

1. In the egocentric memory condition, the participant reenters the arena at the same point and has to move toward the position of the pole, encoded in relation to the participant's body. To prevent the use of the arena walls being used as cues, the walls of the arena are rotated.
2. In the allocentric memory condition, participants reenter the arena and have to move toward the position of the pole using the patterns from the arena wall to guide them.

For both conditions, brain activity was sampled while the participants were moving to the pole (encoding) and while they were using their memory to attempt to move back to the pole location (retrieval). For each phase, fMRI sampling of neural activity was taken for 30 s. A third control condition was constructed by presenting participants with an amalgam of the arena wall patterns, again for 30 s, to determine neural activation associated only with visual processing.

For both the egocentric and allocentric conditions, the main areas of activation reflect the activity of a network of neural centers that represent different aspects of the task (see Fig. 10.12). Activation of the visual cortex was seen reflecting low-level visual analysis involved in processing the incoming visual information. Parietal lobe activation was seen,

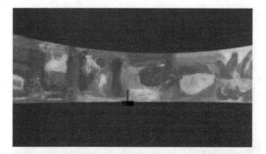

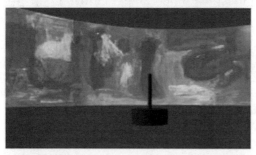

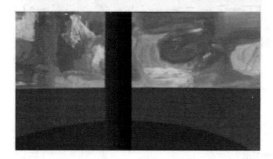

FIG. 10.11.   A view of the virtual reality arena task showing the pole in the distance. The participant uses a joystick to move toward the pole at the encoding stage of the experiment. A series of views are shown with the participant approaching the pole.

which can be interpreted as being due to the processes involved in encoding location and guiding movement to the pole. There was also thalamic activation, and this may be associated with bodily orientation to the target location. At retrieval, the same pattern of activation is seen, but this time there was prefrontal activation, which may reflect mnemonic retrieval processes (Nyberg et al., 1996). However, for the egocentric condition, no hippocampal or parahippocampal activation was seen at either encoding or retrieval. In the allocentric condition, there was clear activation in these regions at encoding only, and this was bilateral in nature (see Fig. 10.12). In contrast, in the visual control condition, only visual cortical activation was seen, with no areas of activation that relate specifically to spatial processing.

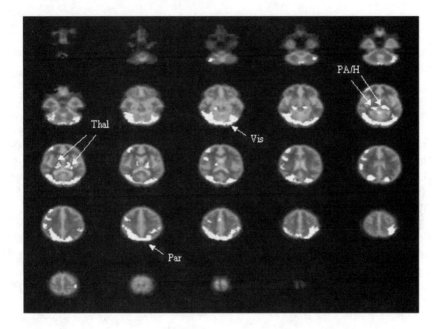

FIG. 10.12. The pattern of activation comparing the encoding phase of the allocentric condition to a rest condition. PA/H = parahippocampal/hipocampal; Thal = thalamic; Vis = visual cortex; Par = parietal cortex.

A notable aspect of the Parslow et al. (2003) study is that hippocampal formation activation was seen only at the encoding phase and only with allocentric memory. This activation is clearly in the posterior region of the hippocampus. Allocentric encoding requires computation of the spatial interrelationship between the patterns on the arena walls and the vectors that link these to the position of the pole. Hence, it is likely that this type of processing is sufficient to exceed a level of activation which is detected by fMRI measurement. Previous studies have linked posterior activation to topographical memory (Ghaëm et al., 1997) or memory for location for objects (Johnsrude, Owen, Crane, Milner, & Evans, 1999; Maguire, Burgess, et al., 1998; Maguire, Frith, et al., 1998). Additionally, the studies of object place memory by Nunn et al. (1999, 1998) indicate that correlations between spatial memory impairment and degree of hippocampal removal in the TL operation are mainly due to variations in removal of posterior hippocampus. Again, as has been pointed out, it is dorsal hippocampal lesions in rodents—analogous to the posterior hippocampus in humans—that produce spatial memory impairment.

PATH INTEGRATION

Cognitive mapping provides a means by which an animal can orientate itself in space using distal cues. In contrast, by means of path integration it is possible to maintain orientation in the absence of distal cues by using perception of motion using ideothetic cues (Loomis et al., 1999). Additionally, directional references (such as the direction of the sun) can aid orientation during path integration. To use these sources of information, it is proposed that the animal integrates outward-bound vectors (directions and distances) to update position with reference to the starting point. This could occur either continuously using moment-to-moment changes or by integrating the information at the end of a series of movements (Gallistel, 1990).

Different types of ideothetic cues can potentially provide the information necessary for path integration. The vestibular system is sensitive to acceleration and deceleration, both linear and angular. Somatosensory perception can also provide movement information, for example, proprioception relating to the joints, tendons, and muscles. Finally, there is the possibility of using stored motor commands in the form of efference copies, which indicates the movements that are in process based on motoric output. The relative importance of these ideothetic cues in perceiving rotations and distances has been examined in humans (Glasauer, Amorim, Vitte, & Berthoz, 1994; Israel & Berthoz, 1989; Loomis et al., 1999; Metcalfe & Gresty, 1992).

Support for the hippocampal formation involvement in path integration comes from a variety of findings relating to animal studies. Firstly, there are a series of studies of rodents in which the hippocampal formation has been lesioned and path integration investigated directly. This includes experiments by Whishaw and colleagues (Masswinkel, Jarrard, & Whishaw, 1999; Whishaw, Cassel, & Jarrard, 1995; Whishaw & Gorney, 1999; Whishaw & Tomie, 1997) with Fornix-Fimbria or hippocampal lesions showing that the rodents fail to return to hidden locations using self-motion cues while swimming, foraging, or following a scented string. Additionally, it has been found that place fields are not dependent on the visibility of landmarks, suggesting that place cells can detect that the animal has moved into a spatial location based on information coming from ideothetic sources (Muller & Kubie, 1987; Markus, Barnes, McNaughton, Gladden, & Skaggs, 1994).

In humans, a preliminary study of the effects of hippocampal formation lesions was conducted by Worsley et al. (2001) in which patients with unilateral TL were tested on path integration abilities. Worsley et al. adapted a procedure used by Loomis et al. (1993) to explore path integration in people with visual impairments. The experiments took place in a large room and involved participants being led along a predetermined path by the experimenter and then having to return to a starting place. To force reliance on ideothetic cues, the participant is blindfolded and thus cannot use visual cues to determine position. In the main condition, the participant is led along two outward-bound paths and then has to return to the start, the whole configuration making a triangle. Movement is monitored by placing a light on the participant's head and tracking the movement of the light using two cameras that provide position coordinates (see Fig. 10.13). By varying the distance and direction of the two legs, it is possible to administer a number of trials to measure path integration ability. A series of paths made by a participant is shown in Fig. 10.14.

The Worsley et al. (2001) study included two control tasks: first, distance estimation, in which the participant was led forward a certain distance then turned and instructed to walk the same distance. Second, turn estimation was tested, requiring the participant to move two paces forward and then turn a particular angle. They then were required to reproduce the turn immediately. Both left- and right-TL patients were unimpaired on either task, suggesting the basic abilities to encode distances and turns were unimpaired.

In contrast, there was a clear impairment in the path integration in the right-TL patients as measured by the distance between the final position and the starting position. This deficit was found to relate to the direction that the participants went in on the homing run rather than the distance traveled.

The path integration deficit was also compared to a further condition, which required participants to remember routes. The purpose of this condition was to test the ability to hold in memory a particular route, again established on the basis of idiothetic cues. The participant moved along two legs of a triangle and then had to reproduce these movements from memory. Again, the right-TL patients only were impaired, and again, the tendency was to make errors with turns rather than distances. Of note, the deficit observed on this task did not correlate with the path integration deficit, implying that the two impairments were dissociated.

In conclusion, path integration impairment was observed in right TL independent of the ability to judge distances or turns or to remember routes. This is the first study of this type implicating the human hippocampus in path integration and suggesting contiguity across species. The result is also supported by a very recent study replicating the findings of impairment in patients with medial TLs (Philbeck et al., 2002). Additionally, impairments in path integration may be specific to hippocampal circuitry rather than other regions of the brain. For example, Philbeck, Behrmann, Black, and Ebert (2000) also reported data showing that patients with right posterior parietal lesions have intact spatial updating following locomotion, despite the spatial manipulation impairments associated with parietal lobe damage.

An issue of interpretation is whether the deficit resulted from inaccurate accumulation of integration of the vector information or storing the final outcome of computation, the homing vector. There is evidence that outbound distances can be held separately (Berthoz et al., 1999), with integra-

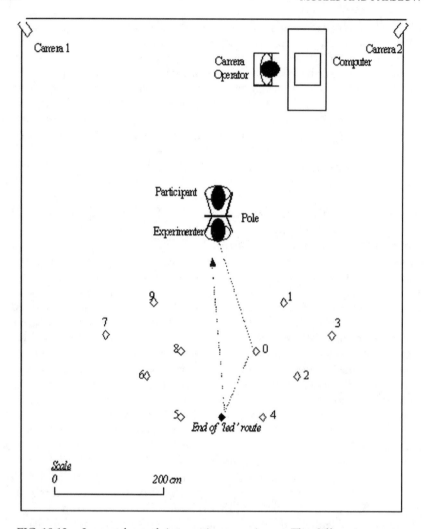

FIG. 10.13.   Layout for path integration experiment. The different num-
bered floor points provide the outward-bound vector target positions. The
participant is led by the experimenter along two outward-bound vectors
and then has to return to the start.

tion happening at the end. The fact that only directional information was
degraded in the right-TL patients might indicate impairment during final
integration in which there was a problem computing this information
rather than the distance. Further studies are needed to explore the nature of
these deficits using converging methods of measurement and exploring the

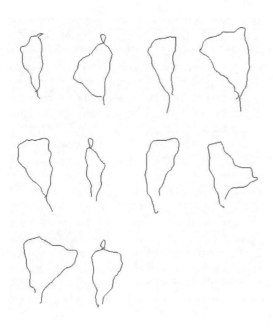

FIG. 10.14. Examples of different path integration trajectories as recorded by the head tracking device.

relative contribution of different self-motion cues, including vestibular and somatosensory processing.

DISCUSSION

These studies follow on from previous ones in that they demonstrate clearly a role for the human hippocampal formation in spatial orientation. First, they show that the spatial element of visuospatial memory can be dissociated from other forms of memory, both at a behavioral and neuronal level. Second, they show that tasks that involve allocentric memory or orientation to spatial stimuli independent of the body axis are consistently sensitive to hippocampal lesions and also result in specific hippocampal or parahippocampal activation. Finally, they indicate a role for the human hippocampus in path integration, with preliminary evidence that this may be separable from route reproduction.

The studies we reviewed also give some hint to localization of spatial memory within the hippocampal formation. The initial finding of spatial memory impairment associated with right TL does not provide sufficient specificity to locate the critical region within the anterior temporal lobe. However, a number of findings help to narrow down the possibilities. This includes the specific correlation between the extent of hippocampal removal and spatial memory function as measured by Nunn et al. (1999, 1998). Also, there are findings by Abrahams et al. (1999, 1997) that there is extensive spatial memory impairment in patients with MTS in which damage appears to be restricted to the hippocampus; this was verified by structural MRI, with a correlation between extent of right hippocampal removal and allocentric memory impairment. Because the level of deficit matched that found in patients with unilateral TLs, this finding suggests further damage or removal of extrahippocampal tissue has no additional effect on spatial memory. Thus, it can be inferred that the hippocampus plays a central role in spatial memory function.

A further finding relates to the involvement of the right hemisphere in spatial memory, supported strongly by the association between spatial memory impairment and right unilateral TLs. This result has been replicated many times across different paradigms, although in many studies there are trends for the left-TL patients to show impairment, and a bilateral result was observed in one of the studies reviewed previously (Feigenbaum et al., 2003). An interpretation of this finding is that where left-hemisphere effects are found, the task in some way is invoking verbal encoding, important for task performance. For example, in route finding, a series of spatial operations can be recoded into verbal format for memory purposes and decoded to aid performance. This possibility can be ruled out by careful design of experiments that produce task demands that mean the participant does not benefit significantly from using a verbal strategy. Nevertheless, because many studies implicate the right hemisphere, this should be taken as indicating right hippocampal involvement specifically.

This is clearly a difference between species because a similar result has not been observed in infrahumans. Hemispheric specialization is seen across a number of domains of cognitive functions, including language, attention, emotional processing, and visuospatial function; therefore, it would not be an unusual finding if it applied to spatial memory. An obvious interpretation is the right hippocampal system has specialized in spatial memory, just as the right parietal lobe may play a dominant role in visual attention. However, an alternative explanation can be considered in relation to the inputs into the hippocampal formation. If the primary inputs are via the right hemisphere, then a lesion of the hippocampus will effectively prevent entry of spatial information into the memory system. One way of exploring this distinction is to compare the results of functional neuroimaging studies versus the results of brain lesion studies. In the former, left-hippocampal, in addition to right-hippocampal, activation is frequently observed, hinting at bilateral spatial representation; additionally, direct comparison between left and right activations are very rarely reported (Aguirre et al., 1996; Burgess et al., 2001; Maguire, Burgess, et al., 1998; Maguire, Frith, et al., 1998). This distinction will need to be tested by further study and possibly by exploring spatial memory function in which the inputs from the right hemisphere are lesioned through brain damage.

As well as providing support for the right hippocampus specializing in spatial memory, whether relating to inputs into the system or representation, the research provides some evidence for distinctions between different types of spatial memory. As sets of experiments have progressed from those using flat desktop arrays to those involving immersion in a three-dimensional environment, this has enabled studies to test the relative involvement of egocentric or allocentric memory function. Also, the procedures have become more akin to everyday spatial orientation demands whether people are active within their environment. Preliminary evidence suggests a preferential hippocampal role for the human hippocampus in allocentric memory, with robust deficits seen (e.g., Morris et al., 2000) and direct comparisons between the two types revealing a significant difference (Feigenbaum et al., 2003) both in terms of patient deficits and also in the degree of hippocampal activation.

This could be interpreted as the hippocampus either having a larger role in spatial mapping or responding to the larger computational demands required in integrating vectors relating to multiple distal landmarks. Indeed, this debate applies to nonhumans in which it is possible to argue that the apparent specialization of the hippocampal formation reflects the computational characteristics that the animal has to use (Gluck & Myers, 1996; McClelland & Goddard, 1996; Treves & Rolls, 1991). Nevertheless, the existence of place cells in rodents and view cells in nonhuman primates provides fairly convincing evidence for a specialized system. Clearly, cellular recording in humans using paradigms similar to the ones either used to explore view cells or those described in this review would shed further light on this issue.

In conclusion, the findings presented here are consistent with those from other species in that the human hippocampal formation is involved in spatial memory. Many other questions remain unresolved, including the nature of the representation and whether this differs from other related species; the extent to which involvement of specific hippocampal regions or related structures can be teased apart given the relatively blunt instrument of investigating naturally occurring brain lesions in humans; or the measurement problems associated with functional neuroimaging. Despite these methodological difficulties, substantial knowledge in this field has been gained by the construction of immersive or real-world spatial environments, which nevertheless incorporate experimental control.

REFERENCES

Abrahams, S., Pickering, A., Jarosz, J., Cox, T., & Morris, R. G. (1999). Spatial working memory impairment correlates with hippocampal sclerosis. *Brain and Cognition, 41,* 39–65.

Abrahams, S., Pickering A., Polkey, C. E., & Morris R. G. (1997). Spatial memory deficits in patients with unilateral damage to the right hippocampal formation. *Neuropsychologia, 35,* 11–24.

Aguirre, G. K., Detre, J. A., Alsop, D. C., & D'Esposito, M. (1996). The parahippocampus subserves topographical learning in man. *Cerebral Cortex, 6,* 823–829.

Angeli, S. J., Murray, E. A., & Mishkin, M. (1993). Hippocampectomized monkeys can remember one place but not two. *Neuropsychologia, 31,* 1021–1030.

Appleyard, D. (1970). Styles and methods of structuring in a city. *Environment and Behavior, 2,* 100–117.

Babb, T. L., & Brown, W. J. (1987). Pathological findings in epilepsy. In J. Engel, Jr. (Ed.), *Surgical treatment of the epilepsies* (pp. 511– 540). New York: Raven:

Berthoz, A., Amorim, M., Gasauer, S., Grasso, R., Takei, Y., & Viaud-Delomon, I. (1999). Dissociations between distance and direction during locomotion. In R. Golledge (Ed.), *Wayfinding behavior: Cognitive mapping and other spatial processes* (pp. 328–348). Baltimore: Johns Hopkins University Press.

Bruton, C. J. (1988). *The neuropathology of temporal lobe epilepsy* (Maudsley Monograph No. 31). Oxford, England: Oxford University Press.

Burgess, N., Jeffery, K. J., & O'Keefe, J. (Ed.). (1999). *The hippocampal and parietal foundations of spatial cognition.* New York: Oxford University Press.

Burgess, N., Maguire, E. A., Spiers, H. J., & O'Keefe, J. (2001). A temporoparietal and prefrontal network for retrieving the spatial context of lifelike events. *Neuroimage, 14,* 439–453.

De Renzi, E. (1982). *Disorder of space exploration and cognition.* New York: Wiley.

Feigenbaum, J. D., & Morris, R. G. (2003a). *Real life route replication in patients after unilateral temporal lobectomies.* Manuscript in preparation.

Feigenbaum, J. D., & Morris, R. G. (2003b). *Allocentric versus egocentric spatial memory after temporal lobectomy in humans.* Manuscript submitted for publication.

Feigenbaum, J. D., Polkey, C. E., & Morris, R. G. (1996). Deficits in spatial working memory after unilateral temporal lobectomy in man. *Neuropsychologia, 34,* 163–176.

Feigenbaum, J. D., Polkey C. E., & Morris, R. G. (2003). *Allocentric versus egocentric working memory after temporal lobectomy in man.* Manuscript in preparation.

Frank, A. U., Campari, I., & Formentini, U. (1992). *Theories and methods of spatiotemporal reasoning in geographic space.* Berlin: Springer-Verlag.

Gallistel, C. R. (1990). *The organization of learning.* Cambridge, MA: Bradford.

Ghaëm, O., Mellet, E., Crivello, F., Tzourio, N., Mazoyer, B., Berthoz, A., & Denis, M. (1997). Mental navigation along memorized routes activates the hippocampus, precuneus and insular. *Neuroreport, 8,* 739–744.

Glasauer, S., Amorim, M. A., Vitte, E., & Berthoz, A. (1994). Goal directed linear locomotion in normal and labyrinthine-defective subjective subjects. *Experimental Brain Research, 98,* 323–335.

Gluck, M. A., & Myers, C. E. (1996). Integrating behavioral and physiological models of hippocampal function. *Hippocampus, 6,* 643–653.

Goldstein, L. H., & Polkey, C. E. (1993). Short-term cognitive changes after temporal lobectomy or unilateral amygdalo-hippocampectomy for the relief of temporal lobe epilepsy. *Journal of Neurology, Neurosurgery and Psychiatry, 53,* 135–140.

Graydon, R., Nunn, J., & Morris, R. G. (2001). Memory outcome and magnetic resonance imaging measured resection in unilateral temporal lobectomy. *Epilepsy and Behaviour, 2,* 140–151.

Israel, I., & Berthoz, A. (1989). Contributions of the otoliths to the calculation of linear displacement. *Journal of Neurophysiology, 62,* 247–263.

Jarrard, L. E. (1991). On the neural basis of the spatial mapping system: Hippocampus vs. hippocampal formation. *Hippocampus, 1,* 236–239.

Johnsrude, I. S., Owen, A. M., Crane, J., Milner, B., & Evans, A. C. (1999). A cognitive activation study of memory for spatial relationships. *Neuropsychologia, 37,* 829–841.

Jones-Gotman, M. (1986). Memory for designs: the hippocampal contribution. *Neuropsychologia, 24,* 193–203.

Kosslyn, S. M., Flynn, R. A., Amsterdam, J. B., & Wang, G. (1990). Components of high-level vision: A cognitive neuroscience analysis and accounts of neurological syndromes. *Cognition, 34,* 203–277.

Loomis, J. M., Klatzky, R. L., Golledge, R. G., Cicinelli, J. G., Pellegrino, J. W., & Fry, P. A. (1993). Nonvisual navigation by blind and sighted: Assessment of path integration ability. *Journal of Experimental Psychology: General, 122,* 73–79.

Loomis, J. M., Klatzky, R. L., Golledge, R. G., & Philbeck, J. W. (1999). Human navigation by path integration. In R. Golledge (Ed.), *Wayfinding behavior: Cognitive mapping and other spatial processes* (pp. 125–151). Baltimore: Johns Hopkins University Press.

Maguire, E. A., Burgess, N., Donnett, J. G., Frackowiak, R. S. J., Frith, C. D., & O'Keefe, J. (1998). Knowing where and getting there: A human navigational network. *Science, 280,* 921–924.

Maguire, E. A., Frith, C. D., Burgess, N., Donnett, J. G., & O'Keefe, J. (1998). Knowing where things are: Parahippocampal involvement in encoding object relations in virtual large-scale space. *Journal of Cognitive Neuroscience, 10,* 61–76.

Margerison, J. H., & Corsellis, J. A. N. (1966). Epilepsy and the temporal lobes: A clinical electroencephalographic and neuropathological study of the brain in epilepsy with particular reference to the temporal lobes. *Brain, 89,* 499–450.

Markus, E. J., Barnes, C. A., McNaughton, B. L., Gladden, V. L., & Skaggs, W. E. (1994). Spatial information content and reliability of hippocampal CA1 neurons: Effects of visual input. *Hippocampus, 4,* 410–421.

Masswinkel, H., Jarrard, L. E., & Whishaw, I. Q. (1999). Hippocampectomized rats are impaired in homing by path integration. *Hippocamus, 9,* 553–561.

McClelland, J. L., & Goddard, N. H. (1996). Considerations arising from a complementary learning systems perspective on hippocampus and neocortex. *Hippocampus, 6,* 654–665.

McNaughton, B. L., Barnes, C. A., Gerrard, J. L., Gothard, K., Jung, M. W., Kneirm J. J., Kudrimoti, H., Qin, Y., Skaggs, W. E., Suster, M., & Weaver, K. L. (1996). Deciphering the hippocampal polyglot: The hippocampus as a path integration system. *Journal of Experimental Biology, 199,* 173–185.

Metcalfe, T., & Gresty, M. A. (1992). Self-controlled reorienting movements in response to rotational displacements in normal subjects and patients with labyrinthine disease. *Annals of the New York Academy of Sciences, 656,* 695–698.

Miotto, E. C., Feigenbaum, J. D., & Morris, R. G. (2000). Everyday executive, attention and memory dysfunction in patients with focal frontal and temporal lesions. *Neuropsychological Assessment, 1,* 54–65.

Morris, R. G. M., Garrud, P., Rawlins, J. N. P., & O'Keefe, J. (1982). Place navigation in rats with hippocampal lesions. *Nature, 297,* 681–683.

Morris, R. G., & Morton, N. (1995). The dissociation between visuospatial working memory and mental transformation. In R. Campbell & M. Conway (Eds.), *Broken memories: Neuropsychological case studies* (pp. 170–194). London: Blackwell.

Morris, R. G., Parslow, D., & Recce, M. D. (2000). Using immersive virtual reality to test allocentric spatial memory impairment following unilateral temporal lobectomy. *ICDVRAT, 3,* 189–196.

Moser, E., Moser, M. B., & Andersen, P. (1993). Spatial learning impairment parallels the magnitude of dorsal hippocampal lesions, but is hardly present following ventral lesions. *Journal of Neuroscience, 13,* 3916–3925.

Muller, R. U., & Kubie, J. L. (1987). The effect of changes in the environment on the spatial firing of hippocampal complex-spike cells. *Journal of Neuroscience, 7,* 1951–1968.

Nadel, L. (1991). The hippocampus and space revisited. *Hippocampus, 1,* 221–229.

Nunn, J. A., Graydon, F. J. X., Polkey, C. E., & Morris, R. G. (1999). Differential spatial memory impairment after right temporal lobectomy demonstrated using temporal titration. *Brain, 122,* 47–59.

Nunn, J. A., Polkey, C. E., & Morris, R. G. (1998) Selective spatial memory impairment after right unilateral temporal lobectomy. *Neuropsychologia, 36,* 837–848.

Nyberg, L., McIntosh, A. R., Cabeza, R., Habib, R., Houle, S., & Tulving, E. (1996). General and specific brain regions involved in encoding and retrieval of events: What, where and when. *Proceedings of the National Academy of Sciences, USA, 93,* 11280–11285.

O'Keefe, J. (1976). Place units in the hippocampus of the freely moving rat. *Experimental Neurology, 51,* 78–109.

O'Keefe, J., & Burgess, N. (1996). Geometric determinants of the place fields of hippocampal neurons. *Nature, 381,* 425–428.

O'Keefe, J., & Nadel, L. (1978). *The Hippocampus as a cognitive map.* Oxford, England: Clarendon.

Olton, D. S., Becker, J. T., & Handelmann, G. E. (1979). Hippocampus, space and memory. *Behaviour and Brain Science, 2,* 315–365.

Olton, D. S., Walker, J. A., & Gage, H. (1978). Hippocampal connections and spatial discrimination. *Brain Research, 139,* 295–308.

Parslow, D. M., Rose, D., Brooks, B., Fleminger, S., Giampietro, V., Brammer, M. J., Williams, S., Gray, J. A., Gasston, D., Andrew, C., Vythelingum, N., Ioannou, G., Simmons, A., & Morris, R. G. (2003). *Viewpoint independent spatial memory activation of the hippocampal formation measured using fMRI.* Manuscript submitted.

Paivio, A. (1971). *Imagery and verbal processes.* New York: Holt, Reinhart & Winston.

Philbeck, J. W., Behrmann, M., Black, S. E., & Ebert, P. (2000). Intact spatial updating during locomotion after right posterior parietal lesions. *Neuropsychologia, 38,* 950–963.

Philbeck, J. W., Behrmann, M., Brown, S., Richter, K., Levy, L., & Potolicchio, S. J. (2002). Human path integration deficits after right medial temporal lobectomy. *Journal of Cognitive Neuroscience, C114* (Supp. S), 94.

Polkey, C. E. (1987). Anterior temporal lobectomy at the Maudsley Hospital London. In J. Engle (Ed.), *Surgical treatment of the epilepsies* (pp. 641–645). New York: Raven.

Recce, M., & Morris, R. G. (2002). *Immersive virtual reality exploration of spatial memory impairment in patients with unilateral damage to the right hippocampal formation.* Manuscript in preparation.

Rolls, E. T. (1999). Spatial view cells and the representation of place in the primate hippocampus. *Hippocampus, 9,* 467–480.

Rolls, E. T., & O'Mara, S. M. (1995). View-responsive neurons in the primate hippocampal complex. *Hippocampus, 5,* 409–424.

Smith, M L. (1989). Memory disorders associated with temporal-lobe lesions. In L. Squire (Ed.), *Handbook of neuropsychology* (Vol. 3, pp. 91–106). New York: Elsevier Science.

Smith, M. L., & Milner, B. (1981). The role of the right hippocampus in the recall of spatial location. *Neuropsychologia, 19*, 781–795.

Smith, M. L., & Milner, B. (1989). Right hippocampal impairment in the recall of location: Encoding deficit or rapid forgetting? *Neuropsychologia, 27*, 71–82.

Taube, J. S. (1996). Commentary on "Space and the Hippocampal Formation in Humans." *Brain Research Bulletin, 40*, 487–490.

Tolman, E. C. (1948). Cognitive maps in rats and men. *Psychological Review, 56*, 144–155.

Treves, A., & Rolls, E. T. (1991). What determines the capacity of autoassociative memories in the brain. *Network, 2*, 371–397.

Ungerleider, L. G., & Mishkin, M. (1982). Two cortical visual systems. In D. Ingle, M. Goodale, & R. Mansfield (Eds.), *Analysis of visual behavior* (pp. 549–589). Cambridge, MA: MIT Press.

Whishaw, I. Q., Cassel, J. C., & Jarrard, L. E. (1995). Rats with fimbria-fornix lesions display a place response in a swimming pool: A dissociation between getting there and knowing where. *Journal of Neuroscience, 15*, 5779–5788.

Whishaw, I. Q., & Gorney, B. (1999). Path integration absent in scent-tracking fimbria-fornix rats: Evidence for hippocampal involvement in "sense of direction" and "sense of distance" using self-movement cues. *Journal of Neuroscience, 19*, 462–467.

Whishaw, I. Q., & Tomie, J. A. (1997). Piloting and dead reckoning dissociated by fimbria-fornix lesions in a rat food carrying task. *Behavioural Brain Research, 89*, 87–89.

Wilson, M. A., & McNaughton, B. L. (1993). Dynamics of the hippocampal ensemble code for space. *Science, 261*, 1055–1058.

Worsley, C. L., Recce, M., Spiers, H. J., Marley, J., Polkey, C. E., & Morris, R. G. (2001). Path integration following temporal lobectomy in humans. *Neuropsychologia, 39*, 452–464.

IV

Remembering Where in Artificial Media and From Alternative Perspectives

As mentioned in the prologue, the final group of chapters is concerned with memory for spatial relations arising from experience other than a traveler's normal view of the environment. In chapter 11 (this volume), Dan Montello, David Waller, Mary Hegarty, and Tony Richardson discuss some of the critically important issues in spatial memory as they apply to spatial knowledge acquired from real, virtual, and cartographic displays. Both virtual environments and maps qualify as artificial media for providing spatial information, and maps provide an alternative to the environmental view that a typical traveler sees. In chapter 12 (this volume), Mark Blades, Christopher Spencer, Beverly Plester, and Kathryn Desmond report studies concerned with the development of the ability to establish correspondence between overhead views and everyday experience of the environment, a long controversial issue in developmental psychology and geography. In this case, aerial photographs represent an artificial media providing an alternative perspective. Cleverly, this research team examined toy play as a link between aerial views of real environments and the child's everyday experience with small objects. The volume concludes with chapter 13 in which Amy Shelton presents a neuroscientific analyses of the effects of perspective during spatial learning. In addition to providing an informative link to Robin Morris and David Parslow's chapter 10 (this volume) in its consideration of both virtual displays and overhead perspectives, it binds the other chapters in this section.

11

Spatial Memory of Real Environments, Virtual Environments, and Maps

Daniel R. Montello, Mary Hegarty,
and Anthony E. Richardson
University of California—Santa Barbara

David Waller
Miami University

SPATIAL MEMORY OF REAL ENVIRONMENTS, VIRTUAL ENVIRONMENTS, AND MAPS

As people move about the environment, they acquire knowledge about patterns of their own movement and about spatial relations among places in the world. This knowledge is encoded and stored in memory, allowing people to find the places again in an efficient manner and to communicate the locations to others. As they sit, stand, and travel in environments, people acquire spatial knowledge "directly" via perceptual–motor interaction with the world. But spatial knowledge is also acquired "indirectly" via external representations of the world and its spatial layout. We refer to these direct and indirect ways of learning spatial relations in the world as alternative sources for knowledge acquisition. For both theoretical and practical reasons, it is interesting to ask how the spatial knowledge acquired through different sources is similar and how it is different. To what degree are memory content, structure, and process similar or different when based on different sources, and why?

In this chapter, we review research on how people remember spatial relations in the environment as a function of the source through which the knowledge is acquired. We focus on knowledge of spatial properties (location, direction, distance, etc.) of large-scale environments that "contain" people and in which people locomote (Montello, 1993). Although it is difficult to delimit this range of scales precisely, it includes something like the space of rooms up to the space of large cities or perhaps even small countries. It is significant that such spaces often require people to integrate information (such as views of scenes) over considerable time periods as they move about and gain perceptual access to new parts of the environment. Our concern is not primarily with spatial relations in molecules, table-top arrays, or hand gestures, nor with spatial relations in the solar system. However, people acquire spatial knowledge about environments from representations at other scales; notably, people learn about environments from maps, and so we do discuss maps in this chapter as sources of environmental spatial knowledge.

People acquire spatial knowledge via several different sources (reviewed by Montello & Freundschuh, 1995). One may first distinguish direct from indirect sources. Direct sources are non-symbolic; they involve apprehension of spatial knowledge directly from the environment via sensorimotor experience in that environment. All other sources may be termed indirect, or symbolic (Gibson's [1979] term was "mediated"). They are symbolic because they transmit spatial information by exposing people to external representations or simulations of the environments to which they refer. Indirect sources include static pictorial representations, such as maps and pictures (3-D models of environments may be included here, as they are still primarily about the 2 dimensions of the earth surface). Also included are various dynamic pictorial representations, such as movies and animations. This class would include dynamic computer graphics, which are commonly called "virtual reality" or "virtual environments" when the viewer controls movement through the simulated environment. Finally, language, spoken or written (even sung—Chatwin, 1987), provides an important indirect source for learning spatial knowledge.

In this chapter, we consider research and theory on the nature of spatial memory resulting from learning via three specific sources:

1. Direct experience, particularly standing and walking,
2. Flat and static maps, and
3. Virtual environments of both the desktop and immersive varieties.

The first two sources are very common ways by which people learn space; all three are of great interest to researchers currently and over the last several decades. To begin, different sources lead to variations in spatial memory because of the different information they make available for encoding into memory. The sources do not provide exactly the same information about space, and they do not provide information in exactly the same format. Because of this, spatial memories from different sources must vary somewhat, at least in content. But do the three sources lead to different memory structures and processes? To answer we briefly review a framework for understanding memory structure and processes; we also consider empirical methods for studying memory, including their limitations. We then turn to two major issues in the research literature concerning environmental spatial memory structure and process: orientation specificity, and the distinction between route and survey knowledge. We finish the chapter with a set of conclusions about spatial memory as a function of the source by which it was acquired; we also consider some other approaches to the question of how spatial memory might vary as a function of the source from which it was acquired.

A primary concern of memory researchers during the last couple decades has been the conceptual and empirical characterization of different memory systems. Distinctions have been considered between procedural and declarative memory, episodic and semantic memory, implicit and explicit memory, and so on (e.g., Schacter & Tulving, 1994). These distinctions have hardly been considered in research on environmental spatial memory (Anooshian & Siegel, 1985, and Golledge & Stimson, 1997, provide rare examples). We do not believe the issues of orientation specificity and route-survey knowledge map well onto the concerns of general memory researchers. For example, route knowledge is sometimes described as procedural and/or implicit but in fact is often said at other times to consist of explicit knowledge of which landmarks follow which landmarks along a route, not just the procedural ability to actually follow the route. Similarly, I may know the direction straight back to the campsite either implicitly or explicitly. For this reason, we do not attempt in this chapter to characterize environmental spatial knowledge from different sources with respect to some of the common distinctions among types of memory systems made by general memory researchers.

CHARACTERISTICS OF THE SOURCES

Wilma is about to land at the airport in Santa Barbara, where she will start her freshman year at the University of California. Wilma is from Northern California, however, and she has never been to the Santa Barbara area before. She knows almost nothing about the layout of the area beyond an impression of the general appearance of the campus she acquired from looking at the university web site and a few plausible assumptions about the typical layout of medium-sized California cities. As her plane descends toward the airport, Wilma sees a chain of mountains to one side of the urban area and the glimmering Pacific Ocean to the other. She mistakenly infers, as many visitors do, that the mountains sit to the east of the city because the ocean view must be to the west; Wilma has never learned to interpret the sun's position carefully enough to realize her mistaken assumption. In any case, the beautiful surroundings captivate her more than a concern with the cardinal orientation of her new home. She does notice that the airport itself lies about a minute or two (which must be at least a few miles) beyond the largest urban area she sees; passengers around her are saying it's the actual city of Santa Barbara. Just before touching down, she also sees a cluster of buildings along the ocean cliffs that look like the picture of the campus she saw on the university web site. After she deplanes, she can still see some of the buildings on the campus. She realizes that the airport is very near the campus, and that both are right next to the ocean. For a moment, she wonders if her college dormitory window might even give her an ocean view. As she leaves the airport in a taxi, Wilma notes the pattern of the roads that lead from the airport to the campus and realizes that she could have walked there if she had been without luggage. Although the trip from the airport to campus is not long, it is rather indirect. But Wilma maintains a sense of the location of the campus relative to the airport because she can continue to see both places from the window of the taxi as she rides along. Wilma begins to develop knowledge of the spatial layout of her new home.

Wilma's first day in Santa Barbara demonstrates the spatial cognitive challenges and opportunities facing a person encountering a new place for the first time. She is exposed to information about the spatial layout via pictures, verbal comments, directly experienced views from different perspectives, and visual and proprioceptive perceptions of her own movement. Perceptual information is combined with prior expectations and initial assumptions in order to shape the spatial memories she is developing. Notably, Wilma is like the rest of us in that her spatial memories are based on a variety of sources of information, not just direct experience but various indirect experiences as well. As we noted above, the various direct and indirect sources provide somewhat different information about space, in somewhat different formats. Furthermore, within each class of sources such as direct experience, maps, and virtual environments, there are specific variants that may lead to different spatial memories because of characteristic differences in the information they make available for encoding into memory.

Types of Direct Experience, Maps, and Virtual Environments

Environments may be experienced directly in various ways—variations that pertain both to the sensory systems and the motor systems involved. For most people, vision is probably the main sensory modality for acquiring spatial knowledge at environmental scales, insofar as it affords apprehension of the most precise information at the greatest distances. But spatial information in directly experienced environments is acquired via other sensory modalities, especially the vestibular senses (linear and angular acceleration information), kinesthesis (limb position, force, and movement), and audition. In specialized situations, other sensory modalities, such as tactile pressure or temperature senses (wind or sun directions can be detected) may contribute to the apprehension of spatial properties. Perspective varies too. One may view a place statically from a single perspective or from several perspectives. Given a single, static perspective, one may view a place while standing in the street, or from the window of a tall building or airplane. Different modes of locomotion are used to get around the environment. One may locomote by crawling, walking, or running; one may locomote with mechanical aids such as bicycles, cars, or planes. Mechanically-assisted direct experience, such as riding in a car, must surely lead to the acquisition of different knowledge than does unassisted experience, such as walking (though no research demonstrates this definitively, to our knowledge).

As an indirect pictorial source of spatial knowledge, cartographic maps may take a variety of forms that could have implications for the knowledge that results from them. First, maps vary in scale. Smaller-scale maps show larger areas of the earth, such as continents or the whole planet; larger-scale maps show smaller areas of the earth, such as cities or neighborhoods. Besides the amount of earth surface depicted at different scales, smaller-scale maps tend strongly to be more generalized—they depict fewer features, in less detail, and more schematically. For example, rivers and roads are depicted as meandering more on larger-scale maps. A second relevant distinction is the difference between reference and thematic maps. Reference maps attempt to show perceptible features of the earth surface and relatively stable entities to be found there (lakes, mountains, cities, roads). They are meant to be more general-purpose, and they therefore attempt to depict information as accurately and completely as they can at a particular scale. Thematic maps are statistical maps; they attempt to show the spatial distribution of one or a few variables on the earth's surface, variables that may not be directly perceptible in the environment at all (e.g., disease rates). Thematic maps are specific in purpose and may reduce spatial detail to a minimum, though reference maps such as those designed for subway navigation (or those people sketch to give directions) may also be highly schematic, distorting and simplifying spatial properties such as metric distance. Third, although maps are usually thought of as flat and static, they may represent relief as in a 3-D model or change over time as in an animation. Fourth, maps often depict the earth surface from directly overhead, using a vertical perspective, but they sometimes depict from an oblique perspective. Vertical-perspectives are often orthogonal, showing all areas as if from directly overhead; oblique perspectives nearly always depict a single point-of-view so that more distant features are smaller and occluded. Perspective is part of the larger issue of projection, the particular geometrical or mathematical approach taken to making a flat picture from the spherical earth surface. Projection determines which spatial properties are distorted, and how, at various locations on the map (all flat maps distort spatial properties to some degree). Although we usually think of maps as visual displays, they may be designed for the tactile or even the auditory modalities. For most people, prototypical maps include small-scale reference maps (e.g., a map of the United States showing cities, rivers, and state boundaries) and medium- or large-scale navigation maps (see Vasiliev et al., 1990; Warren, 1995). Spatial cognition research has involved both of these types of maps, but has also included many studies with very large-scale and highly schematized map-like graphics (e.g., Fig. 11.1). Our review below focuses on these types of maps, though thematic maps and various types of non-map graphics do present spatial information (e.g., Hegarty & Just, 1993; Lloyd, 1988).

Virtual environments (VEs) also take a variety of forms that have implications for knowledge acquisition. VEs are interactive, real-time, 3-D graphical displays—computer-created simulations of places or environments that change appropriately in response to locomotion or other motor behaviors by users (active control). Virtual displays always include a first-person perspective, as if being viewed through the eyes (or heard through the ears, etc.) of someone moving through the space. The visual appearance of the simulated environment looks somewhat like what one

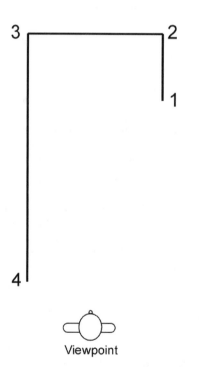

FIG. 11.1. Typical pathway used in orientation-specificity research by Levine, Presson, McNamara, Sholl, and others. (Adaptation of collaborative research—year not applicable.)

would see in a real environment, and of course, the detail and faithfulness of this visual realism continues to increase with improvements in computer technology, etc. But this apparent realism is not very great in some virtual displays of today, and by itself, even great visual realism of this type would not qualify a display to be dubbed "virtual" (a photograph is almost never called "virtual"). Even given these definitional constraints, however, there are a variety of virtual systems that appear realistic to different degrees and in different ways. Just as it is important to characterize variations in the ways that environments are directly experienced and in the types of maps, it is important for our purposes to characterize aspects of different virtual systems.

Different VEs include desktop displays, projected displays, caves, augmented realities, and fully immersive systems. Displays created by these systems vary in their size, their coverage of the visual field, and the sensory and motor systems they involve. A desktop VE presents the environment on a flat CRT screen before a stationary observer. Locomotion is usually accomplished through the use of a joystick or keyboard, which provide different efference copy and proprioceptive feedback from that provided by head or whole-body movement. Vestibular information provided from head and body rotations is unavailable. These types of VE are most similar to slide and video presentations. They differ from slides/videos in that they allow for active control of locomotion by the observer, but they also present the observer with images generally lower in fidelity than a slide or video. Another type of VE interface that affords a more direct form of interaction with the environment uses head-mounted displays (HMDs) and tracking systems to update head orientation, allowing the navigator to look around during travel. However, most of these systems do not track rotation of the entire body, which may or may not affect the way people acquire spatial knowledge from them. Instead, body rotation and translation is accomplished through a secondary manner such as using keyboard, mouse, or pointing with a data glove. These types of systems provide proprioceptive information regarding head orientation but do not provide such information regarding body heading. The most sophisticated VE systems allow for complete head and body tracking, allowing the observer to translate and rotate in space as they would in a real environment and producing interaction most similar to real navigation. These VEs are referred to in the literature as immersive or fully immersive VEs.

Information the Sources Provide for Encoding

Our review of various types of direct experience, maps, and virtual environments makes it clear that spatial knowledge will vary as a function of its source, at least in content. That is because different sources provide somewhat different information about environments. Montello and Freundschuh (1995) differentiated the sources they listed in terms of eight characteristics by which the sources differ in the way they present information to people. First, some sources present information in a dynamic stream, others present it in static snapshots; also, information about dynamic process may be presented statically or dynamically (compare arrows on maps to animations). Another difference is that sources such as maps present information in a way that supports relatively simultaneous pickup of information (though scanning a map requires eye movement and takes place over time, e.g., Dobson, 1979); most direct and virtual presentations require sequential pickup and integration of information over considerable time periods, though VEs can be designed to allow obstructions to turn invisible. Related to this, sources vary in the viewing perspective they provide, whether from a vertical perspective (a "bird's-eye view"), a horizontal or terrain-level perspective, or some oblique perspective in between. A fourth characteristic that differentiates the sources concerns the abstractness of their symbols (MacEachren, 1995). The need to interpret symbols clearly differentiates indirect sources like maps from direct sources (and many VEs) in the first place. However, among different indirect sources, there are variations in the degree to which symbols are iconic—Robinson & Petchenik (1976) called it mimetic—perceptually resembling what they stand for, versus arbitrary, not resembling what they stand for. Maps usually show distances in a very iconic way, for example, insofar as a distance between places in the world that is twice as far as another is shown as twice as far on the map (this is actually only approximately true on most maps, and is never perfectly true everywhere on any map because of the inevitable distortions of projection). In contrast, other map symbols represent quite arbitrarily; the hypsometric color changes that represent elevation changes do not particularly resemble different elevations (the very dry and low Death Valley is very green on such a map). Another characteristic that differentiates sources concerns whether a source is at the same or a different spatial scale than the environment, thus perhaps requiring scale translation for its comprehension; again, maps and direct experience provide the strongest contrast here, though desktop VEs typically display the environment on a small computer monitor. A sixth characteristic is the precision of the spatial knowledge presented (and represented) by a source. Spatial language is well known to represent spatial information quite imprecisely most of the time ("meet me next to the fountain"). Most maps present spatial information rather precisely; unfortunately this precision is frequently spurious, as when subway maps show precise distances that are not intended to be interpreted as such. A seventh characteristic differentiating sources for acquiring spatial knowledge is that they differ with respect to their inclusion of detail, some of which may be irrelevant to spatial problem-solving.

It is clear the various sources provide different information to be encoded into memory, and will thus lead to the acquisition of different quantities and qualities of spatial knowledge. They offer sensorimotor access to information in different ways and supply information varying in precision, accuracy, and completeness. Some sources make explicit what others only suggest and still others simply do not provide. It is difficult if not impossible to learn the layout of very large spaces from direct experience alone, for example, unless that direct experience comes from the window of an airplane; maps are normally the only way most people ever gain access to this information. And because maps present distorted spatial relationships, especially at small scales (large areas), people who learn from them will learn distorted spatial relationships (e.g., Saarinen, Parton, & Billberg, 1996). Furthermore, different sources require more or less in the way of symbolic transformations to be made in order to understand the information they provide (e.g., some require scale translation and some do not). Such transformations are psychologically nontrivial and are definitely not carried out in the same way or to the same end by all people (e.g., Liben, 1999). Taken together, these considerations make it evident that spatial memories will not be identical when based on different sources.

The Role of Body Movement.   For our purposes, one of the most significant variations in the spatial information the sources provide for encoding into memory may concern whether the source involves locomotion of the body and its concomitant proprioceptive sensing. Kinesthetic and vestibular sensing, and efferent copy from actively-controlled movements, provide information about the spatial pattern of one's own movement through the environment—information which people (and other animals) use to perform *path integration*, to update knowledge of their location relative to a starting location and surrounding features based on perceived body speed and direction (Loomis, Klatzky, Golledge, & Philbeck, 1999). Map use, by itself, does not involve locomotion, directly experiencing environments often does. VEs do not involve (real) locomotion if they are of the desktop variety, though they do communicate movement via optic flow. Some immersive systems do, although a completely mobile virtual system that allows for a full range and extent of locomotory movements is quite rare at the present time (no behavioral-science research has been reported with such a system yet).

Research supports the contribution of proprioception, particularly vestibular sensing, to updating one's knowledge of location (Potegal, 1982; Rieser, Guth, & Hill, 1986). Gale, Golledge, Pellegrino & Doherty (1990) had participants learn routes by walking or by watching a video. They found that walkers were better able to re-travel the route than were the video watchers, suggesting the value of proprioceptive and/or efferent information. Taking a neuroscience approach to the question of what proprioception adds to spatial learning, Péruch et al. (1999) compared the navigation performance of control participants and patients who underwent surgery because of unilateral defects in their vestibular systems.

Within days after the operations, the vestibular patients made shortcuts and retraced routes with greater error than did the controls.

A study by Klatzky et al. (1998) produced clear evidence of the contributions of vestibular sensing to spatial learning. They had participants travel along two legs of a triangular path depicted in a virtual environment. One group of participants actually walked the path while viewing the appropriate optic flow for translations along the legs and rotations at the turn, shown through an HMD. At the end of the second leg, participants turned their bodies to face the origin location, which was unmarked. These participants were quite accurate facing toward the origin and varied their facing directions appropriately for paths with turns of varying angular size. Two other groups of participants did not actually locomote, but only viewed the appropriate optic flow through the HMD. One of these groups, however, was rotated on a chair as they saw the simulated rotation at the turn in the path. They received vestibular information about the turn, in other words, and their performance facing toward the origin was only a little worse than the group who actually walked the paths. The third group also did not actually locomote, nor were they rotated in their chair; they only saw rotational optic flow. They thus received no vestibular information about the turn. Their performance facing toward the origin was much worse than the first two groups, and got much worse as the actual turn size increased. This last group turned to face the origin as if they were still facing in their initial heading. Thus, visual information alone without concomitant body rotation was not sufficient to induce egocentric updating, at least with respect to body rotations (see also Bakker, Werkhoven, & Passenier, 1999; Chance, Gaunet, Beall, & Loomis, 1998).

A recent study has found strong evidence that brings into question the importance of proprioceptive information in learning environmental layout. Waller, Loomis, and Steck (2001) had participants learned a 1-mile (1.6 km) route in one of three ways. One group viewed the environment normally from the front seat of a car driven by the experimenter. A second group sat in a lab room and viewed a video of the route recorded through the front window of the car. A third group also learned the route from the video, but they viewed it while sitting in the back seat of the car as the video was being shot (they could not see the route directly from the car). The second and third groups, therefore, received identical visual information about the route but only the third group received proprioceptive information about the route. Results showed more accurate memory for directions and distances by the first group, but no difference between the second and third groups. In other words, the vestibular information provided by body movement while sitting in the car did not enhance spatial-knowledge acquisition over and above viewing the video. This surprising result suggests that the proprioceptive information available while riding in a car added little or nothing to spatial learning, at least given the scale and pattern of this particular route. Waller, Loomis, and Steck (2001) interpreted their results as indicating that vestibular information does not much facilitate learning spaces this large, and pointed out that previous findings (like those reviewed above) were typically confined to rooms or building-size spaces. It remains likely that the kinesthetic and efferent information available during actively-controlled and non-mechanically-assisted locomotion, such as when walking, would improve spatial learning (Waller, Loomis, & Haun, in press).

QUALITIES OF MEMORY REPRESENTATION: STRUCTURES AND PROCESSES

In this section, we discuss structures and processes of memory that result from different sources of spatial knowledge about the environment. Most research attention has focused on two qualities of spatial memory representations that may vary across sources of spatial knowledge. The first is *orientation specificity*. An orientation-specific memory representation is stored in memory and accessed preferentially in a single orientation; an *orientation-free* representation would be equally accessible in any orientation . The second quality concerns the distinction between *route* and *survey* knowledge. Route knowledge is knowledge of a sequence of places or landmarks connected by locomotion patterns. It is "string-like" or one-dimensional. Survey knowledge is knowledge of a layout of places or landmarks and their direct spatial interrelationships (distances, directions). It is "maplike" or two-dimensional, and not restricted to spatial interrelationships along routes that have been traveled.

It is important to note that memory representations themselves cannot be directly observed behaviorally—they must be inferred from performance on tasks that depend on the stored representations. In a typical situation, a person learns the layout of an environment from some experience, such as walking in the environment, viewing a map, or interacting with a virtual rendition of the environment. Based on perceptual and encoding processes, one or more representations of that environment are stored in memory. This internal representation can include not only properties directly perceived but also properties inferred from perceived information. At some later time the person performs a task (outcome measure), such as wayfinding or giving verbal directions, that relies at least in part on his or her stored representation of the environment. The performance of this task may or may not involve some transformation of the internally stored representation, i.e., some additional inferences. It is in fact difficult to determine to what extent a person's performance on a given outcome measure directly reflects the stored memory representation as opposed to transformations of that representation made in response to task demands.

One method that has been used to infer qualities of internal representations is the measurement of response time in addition to accuracy on outcome measures. If two tasks require different amounts of the same transformation of the stored representation, then they should take different amounts of time to perform. For example, orientation-specific representations are inferred from *alignment effects*. After viewing a map with west at the top, for example, people store a representation of the map in memory that also has west at the top. When this memory is accessed, the top is assigned by default to the forward direction of view in the environment (Levine, Jankovic, & Palij, 1982, called it "forward-up equivalence"). Questions about directions on the map will be answered most quickly and accurately when they are phrased from this preferred perspective, for example, "point to the town hall from the courthouse, as if you were facing west." When people have to answer questions about directions between places on a map from a perspective other than that stored in memory, the response is slower and/or less accurate. In our example, that would be pointing between places as if you were facing east (or any other direction than west). The extra time and/or error when pointing from an imagined perspective other than the learned orientation is the alignment effect.

Another method of reducing ambiguity about qualities of internal representations is to observe performance over several measures. For example, route knowledge may be sufficient to perform some spatial tasks well, such as route re-traveling. It may not be sufficient to perform other spatial tasks well, such as pointing directly to nonvisible features in the environment. If a person can re-travel a route well but performs at chance level on a pointing task, it could be concluded the person has only an internal route representation. In reality, however, the pattern of performance over different measures is rarely as clear as this. For example, suppose a person can re-travel a route well, and his or her pointing accuracy is above chance but much less than perfect. This pattern of performance would result if the person had acquired some imprecise survey knowledge. However it would also result if the person could eliminate some possible pointing directions on the basis of route knowledge alone. Therefore the nature of the internal representation is ambiguous in this case. Detailed simulations of specific models for route (or survey) knowledge could address the question of the qualities of spatial representations necessary to support particular levels of accuracy and precision in observed behaviors, but very little of this work has been done (e.g., Dawson, Boechler, & Valsangkar-Smyth, 2000; Montello & Frank, 1996).

Researchers must therefore be cautious in assuming that a specific outcome measure necessarily reflects a particular type of internal representation. For example, the ability to draw a map of an environment has sometimes been viewed as evidence for an internal survey representation. However, although a map is a survey representation of an environment, a relatively accurate map can be drawn from an internal route representation that is quantitatively scaled, such that integration of the layout of segments and turns of the route occurs when the route representation is externalized in the drawing process. In such a case, the "survey knowledge" was not stored in memory but was created by inference during recall and task performance. Similarly, pointing to nonvisible locations is often viewed as a measure of survey knowledge. However, pointing from one's self to a landmark requires not only knowledge of the layout of the surrounds, but also knowledge of one's location and heading in the surrounds; it requires one's survey representation to be "egocentrically-oriented" (some other measures, such as sketch maps, do not require this). One's failure to point accurately could result from being misoriented (i.e. misrepresenting one's current heading), even with a perfect internal representation of the configuration of the environment. Thus, while patterns of performance over a number of different outcome measures (including accuracy and response time) can provide insights into the nature of people's internal representations, researchers must always be mindful that an internal representation might be transformed in response to task demands.

Orientation Specificity

Back on campus, Wilma has gotten out of her taxi and is walking back to her dormitory. She thinks she can find the dorm, even though this is her first visit to the campus, because she spent several minutes before she left home studying the campus map she received with her registration material. Wilma knows her dorm is near the most prominent landmark on campus, Storke Tower, and she also remembers that the dorm is below and to the left of the tower on the map. As she walks, she pictures the campus map in her mind. As is common with maps, the campus map is designed with north to the top, and Wilma's image is also oriented this way. She begins walking to left of the tower, but she gets confused for a few moments when she realizes she is walking south. She regains her sense of orientation and changes her walking direction, knowing that her dorm should be to the other side of the tower. Thus, Wilma clears up her encounter with the orientation specificity of spatial memories derived from maps.

   Wilma experienced the effects of orientation specificity because her memory based on the campus map was recalled in the same orientation in which it was viewed. Maps, and memory images of maps, are accessed in a particular orientation. When the map information is used in an ongoing navigation task, it must generally be coordinated with the orientation of the local surrounds—the person's heading as she locomotes through the environment. The most common way to do this is to assume that "up" on the map is "forward" in the surrounds (Shepard & Hurwitz, 1984). When this assumption is not true, as in Wilma's case, either errors of movement from being misoriented or extra response time attempting to fix orientation, or both, result.

   The question of the orientation specificity of spatial memory, including how it may differ for knowledge derived from different sources, has been a particularly active area of spatial-cognition research in the last couple of decades. The phenomenon of orientation specificity for memory representations was demonstrated by Evans and Pezdek (1980), who showed people a series of depictions of the names of three U.S. states. Participants were asked to judge whether these depictions portrayed the true spatial relationships among the three states. Evans and Pezdek found that people's times to perform this task were closely related to the degree to which the stimuli were rotated away from the canonical north-up orientation of a U.S. map. This suggested that the relative locations of these states were stored in memory in a preferred orientation—the orientation typically seen on a map—and that recognizing alternate orientations required additional mental processing, which took time. These observations are consistent with a conceptualization of memory for map-acquired geographic information as a depictive image constructed in working memory of a previously viewed map. When tasks demand it, the contents of such an imagined map are scanned, rotated, or otherwise transformed much as a real map would be. Of course, the underlying long-term memory code could be a set of propositions (e.g., Pylyshyn, 1981), as long as the propositions contained information that resulted in their expression in working-memory with a preferred orientation. Regardless of the underlying memory structures and processes, the findings of Evans and Pezdek, along with a host of subsequent studies (Boer, 1991; Levine, Marchon, & Hanley, 1984; MacEachren, 1992; Presson & Hazelrigg, 1984), have made the orientation specificity of memories for map-acquired knowledge one of the most robust phenomena in spatial cognition.

Evans and Pezdek (1980) also examined the orientation specificity of spatial memories derived from direct experience rather than maps. Although they found that memories for the relative locations of U.S. states were stored with a preferred orientation, they also reported that memory for the relative locations of frequently visited campus buildings showed little or no such orientation specificity. People answered questions about the configurations of campus buildings equally quickly regardless of the orientation in which the depictions were presented. Evans and Pezdek suggested that no particular orientation for the campus buildings was preferred in memory because, as is common for directly experienced places, their locations had been viewed in the environment from multiple perspectives. Thus, spatial information can be accessed more flexibly from memories of directly experienced spaces than from those of maps.

The idea that memory for large spaces is orientation free was most persuasively argued by Presson and his colleagues, especially Presson, DeLange, & Hazelrigg (1989). Like Evans and Pezdek, Presson et al. noted that direct experience of a space typically involves viewing it in multiple orientations, whereas maps are generally learned in only one orientation. In other words, the distinction between map learning and direct experience is commonly confounded by the ways in which these different sources of information are learned. To eliminate this confound, Presson et al. controlled the manner in which people learned spatial information from maps and direct experience. They asked participants to study several simple spatial layouts like those used by Levine et al. (1984) (see Fig. 11.1). Presson et al. presented the layouts at different sizes, referring to them either as maps of a larger environment or as paths in the environment itself. Importantly, participants were shown each layout from a single perspective only. This control allowed Presson et al. to focus on differences between learning from maps and direct experience independent of the effect of learning from multiple perspectives. A single trial went as follows: After viewing the layout, participants were blindfolded, and taken to the location on the path and faced in the heading specified by the test question. They were either walked or pushed in a wheelchair along a meandering route to get to the test location; Presson et al. did this to try to ensure that participants would answer from memory only—not from an updated perception of their new location and heading. After arriving at the test location, participants were asked to make judgments of relative directions based on their memories of the layouts (e.g., "You are at Location 1, and Location 2 is directly behind you. Point to Location 4"). Consistent with past results, the investigators found that when people learned about the space by viewing a small display (2×2 ft), their judgments of relative directions revealed large alignment effects; they were more accurate when the judgment involved imagining a view aligned with the perspective during study (i.e. the question involved a facing direction that was up on the display) than when it involved a view that was misaligned. However, Presson et al. found that when people learned about the space by viewing a large display (12×12 ft), their judgments of relative directions revealed much smaller alignment effects that did not reach statistical significance.

Presson et al.'s (1989) finding of an attenuated alignment effect with large displays added an intriguing wrinkle to Evans and Pezdek's (1980) contention that the source of spatial knowledge affects the way in which it is stored in memory. Presson et al.'s results suggested that orientation-free performance was not necessarily related to learning an environment from multiple perspectives, as Evans and Pezdek had suggested. Because memories for large spaces viewed from only a single perspective appeared to be orientation free, Presson et al. suggested that the nature of the learning medium itself—not the manner in which it is used—affects the way that spatial knowledge is represented in memory. Specifically, Presson et al. conjectured that a large space that surrounds the viewer and affords navigation (an *environment*) will be encoded in terms of the relationships among the objects in the environment, not in terms of the relationships between the viewer and the objects in the environment. Because it is not viewer-centered, this *allocentric* way of coding environments is orientation free and does not produce alignment effects when accessed. In contrast, spaces learned from symbolic sources such as maps will be remembered in relation to the viewer, like pictures. Because they are coded in terms of the viewer, such *egocentric* memories are orientation specific and produce large alignment effects when accessed. Presson and his colleagues regarded this distinction between directly experienced spaces and symbolically-experienced spaces as critical to understanding spatial memory, and suggested that these different ways of learning were processed by two separable memory systems. They coined the phrases "primary" and "secondary" learning to describe this distinction (Presson & Hazelrigg, 1984; Presson & Somerville, 1985).

The lack of alignment effects for large displays reported by Presson et al. (1989) proved difficult to replicate. Notably, a series of studies by McNamara and his colleagues (Diwadkar & McNamara, 1997; Roskos-Ewoldsen, McNamara, Shelton, & Carr, 1998; Shelton & McNamara, 1997, 2001) has repeatedly found sizeable and statistically significant alignment effects with spatial arrays as large as those used by Presson et al. (1989). Roskos-Ewoldsen et al. (1998) tried to replicate Presson et al. (1989) closely, comparing performance on small and large paths like that in Figure 1. Unlike Presson et al.'s participants, however, those tested by Roskos-Ewoldsen et al. were wheeled to a center location, facing in the heading from which the paths had initially been viewed. Half were wheeled directly and half were wheeled along a very circuitous route. These researchers found alignment effects for both small and large displays, in both errors and response times.

Research by Sholl and her colleagues (Sholl & Bartels, 2002; Sholl & Nolin, 1997) and by ourselves (Waller, Montello, Richardson, & Hegarty, 2002) has also helped clarify the reasons for the variations in the results of different researchers. First, we point out in Waller et al. (2002) that some previous work purporting to show that large spaces are stored in an orientation-free manner in memory, such as the research by Presson and his colleagues, failed to include measures of response times; alignment effects are often revealed in pointing error but are sometimes reflected in slower responses that are just as accurate. A second consideration concerns whether participants are actually disoriented in the testing room—whether they are aware of their headings in the surrounds. If participants in fact maintain orientation (update) while traveling to a location that corresponds to the location and heading of test questions, as in the work of Presson and his colleagues, questions misaligned with the initially viewed perspective of the layout will not be misaligned with the updated representation. Presson et al. (1989) did not check how disoriented participants actually were; Roskos-Ewoldsen et al. (1998) suggested that Presson et al.'s participants may not have been effectively disoriented. Alternatively, if participants update while traveling to a location that corresponds to the initial heading from which the paths had been viewed, as in Roskos-Ewoldsen et al., questions misaligned with the initially viewed perspective of the layout will still be misaligned with the updated representation. Roskos-Ewoldsen et al. empirically verified that participants who were wheeled directly to the test location were able to point to a particular wall of the room 60% of the time. But even participants who were wheeled circuitously were able to point to the wall 39% of the time, which is statistically greater orientation than chance at 25% (N = 66). To the degree that they had maintained orientation, participants would show alignment effects because they were answering misaligned questions from a misaligned heading. (Sholl & Bartels [2002] offer the interesting hypothesis that updating participants will be exposed to multiple "virtual" views of the path layout as they are circuitously moved about. Such imagined views of the path, according to these authors, would constitute the kind of multiple exposures that Evans and Pezdek [1980] had argued produces orientation-free memory).

Alternatively, if people do become thoroughly disoriented while traveling to the test location (as intended by the several researchers who have used circuitous blindfolded transport), people will be located and facing as required by the test question but will be unaware of this. Test questions will not be aligned or misaligned with the orientation of the person's working-memory representation because they have no oriented representation of their heading—they are disoriented. In such a case, according to Waller et al. (2002), all questions will be answered with nearly the same speed and accuracy. This will be less quickly and accurately than aligned questions, and more quickly and accurately than misaligned questions, are answered by a person who is oriented to the surrounds. In fact, orientation specificity is still revealed in this situation: A persistent influence of the learned perspective in disoriented participants results in alignment effects, though they are significantly weaker than those found with oriented participants who stay at the initial viewing location. Consistent with this, the alignment effects reported by Roskos-Ewoldsen et al. (1998) were smaller in both time and error (though not significantly) among participants who were wheeled circuitously than among those who were wheeled directly.

It thus appears that spatial memories based on single views are stored in an orientation-specific manner, whether based on maps or environments. Viewing spaces from multiple perspectives during learning will lead to an attenuation or elimination of alignment effects. This is true whether the source of spatial knowledge is directly experienced environments (Evans & Pezdek, 1980) or cartographic maps (MacEachren, 1992). There are two possible explanations for the fact that memory based on multiple views shows attenuated alignment effects. One is that learning spatial knowledge from multiple views leads to the creation of orientation-free representations. A second explanation suggests that even spatial memories acquired from multiple views are in fact orientation specific, whether based on direct experience or on maps. But when people are exposed to multiple views, they store multiple orientation-specific representations. Tasks that demand the adoption of a given perspective on the space either activate a previously experienced view that is aligned with the question, or they lead to interpolation between separate views that were previously experienced. Although not completely resolved yet, most contemporary evidence favors the hypothesis that spatial memories based on multiple views are stored in multiple orientation-specific representations, at least during early stages of learning (Diwadkar & McNamara, 1997).

However, even if spaces of all sizes are stored in an orientation-specific manner, there are still ways that knowledge sources at different scales may lead to differences in memory for space, though they may not be fundamental structural differences. In all three of Presson et al.'s (1989) experiments, participants produced much larger alignment effects (in error) with small displays than with large displays. Roskos-Ewoldsen et al. (1998) also found smaller alignment effects with circuitously-wheeled participants on large than on small displays, though the 11° difference was nonsignificant. Whether participants maintain or lose their orientations to the surrounds during circuitous transport to test locations, it remains the case that memories based on viewed displays of different sizes may be accessed somewhat differently. This may be a greater persistence of remembered views from small displays, or a lesser tendency to update within knowledge based on small displays. These possibilities await further research.

Orientation Specificity in VEs

To the degree that the distinction between primary and secondary spaces is important for understanding the nature of spatial memory, then knowledge derived from experience with virtual environments presents an interesting case. VEs have an intrinsically dual nature. On one hand, VEs are typically shown on small-scale display devices such as computer monitors or HMDs that are capable of being viewed entirely from one perspective. In this sense, VEs may be perceived as presenting a series of small-scale pictures to an observer who remains outside of the display. On the other hand, these display devices, particularly those with HMDs, can give a user the impression of being surrounded by a large-scale environment—they can induce *presence*. The dual nature of VEs is that they are at once representations of environments and environments in themselves. Researchers have noted that VEs might be regarded more as primary than secondary sources of spatial information (Liben, 1997; Wilson, 1997), yet this potential clearly relates to the quality of the VE system. For example, immersive VEs that surround the user with perceptual information and preserve natural means of interacting with space may be much more engaging and likely to be treated as a "primary" spaces than are desktop VEs.

In the last few years, several studies have examined the orientation specificity of spatial memories derived from experience in VEs. Despite wide differences in the quality of the VEs used, ranging from relatively simple desktop systems (e.g., Albert, Rensink, & Beusmans, 2000; Christou & Bülthoff, 1999; Richardson et al., 1999; Rossano et al., 1999) to more advanced systems that employ motion tracking and head-mounted displays (Miller, Clawson, & Sebrechts, 1999; Clawson, Miller, Knott, & Sebrechts,

1998), most studies have found evidence that memory for spatial information that is learned from a VE is orientation specific. For example, Christou and Bülthoff (1999) asked participants to explore a detailed computer model of a building, searching for several prominent landmarks. The position and orientation of the participants' viewpoint during the search was continuously recorded. This enabled the experimenters subsequently to show participants three kinds of images from the environment that they had learned:

1. Views of the landmarks they had actually seen,
2. Views of the landmarks that were oriented differently from what they had seen, and
3. Views that were mirror images of what they had seen.

The results clearly showed that participants were faster and more accurate in recognizing views that were previously seen than those that were not. Memories for these landmarks were stored simply as experienced views. These memories thus had a preferred orientation—that of the viewpoint during learning. Several other studies have also shown a preferred orientation for memories of VE spaces. In some cases, the preferred orientation is the one that was experienced at a particular location in the simulated space while it was explored (Albert et al., 2000; Clawson et al., 1998; Miller et al., 1999). In other studies, the preferred orientation appears to be one that is aligned with the initial view of the participant during learning (Richardson et al., 1999; Rossano et al., 1999); that is, people learning a complex environment from a VE sometimes use the orientation of the initial segment as a preferred orientation for the storage of spatial information for the rest of the layout. And some evidence suggests, like the findings of Evans and Pezdek (1980), that when people are given multiple views of a virtual environment, such as might occur during extended free exploration, alignment effects weaken (Rossano & Moak, 1998).

Survey vs. Route Knowledge

Returning once more to the story of Wilma's first day at UCSB, we find that she has unpacked her luggage at her dorm room. Now she wants to get a bite to eat, so she heads out of her room to walk over to the University Center where restaurants are located on campus. Wilma does not remember seeing this building on the campus map, but she does remember walking past it soon after getting out of the taxi. For a moment, she considers which way to walk. She knows she could probably backtrack along the route she walked to her dorm, but she also knows that may not be the shortest way. As she thinks about the route, Wilma imagines a sequence of views she had along her walk and specifically remembers a couple of turns she took to get to the dorm. But she does not feel confident that she can remember the entire route well enough to try and take a shortcut to the University Center. Instead, she decides to backtrack, but she will pay attention to the turns in her walk and the landmarks she will see along the way so she can start to figure out the direct spatial relationships among places on the campus. In this manner, Wilma will continue to acquire not just knowledge of specific routes between places, but an understanding of the two-dimensional configuration of the campus.

Wilma's knowledge of the route she walked is essentially a temporally connected linear series of views and movements, but she aspires to learn a more two-dimensional understanding of spatial layout so she can travel more efficiently from place to place. This is the distinction between route and survey knowledge, which has a long history in the spatial-cognition literature (reviewed by Montello, 1998). The distinction has in fact been conceptualized in somewhat different ways by various researchers, and it is thus difficult to draw conclusions about whether a person has route or survey representations stored in memory. Route knowledge is typically defined as an internal representation of the procedures necessary for finding one's way from place to place. This is sometimes conceptualized as a set of stimulus-response pairs, or a sequence of landmarks, with little or no intervening distance information, and perhaps imprecise turn instructions (ahead, left, right). Route representations are thought to be highly constrained and rigid, allowing wayfinding only along known pathways, typically in only one direction (e.g., Kuipers, 1978). Although they may be efficient for rapidly navigating well-known, unchanging environments, their fixed, sequential nature makes route representations impractical for creating novel paths or shortcuts, or for navigating in a changing environment. Most models of route knowledge suggest it contains little quantitative information about distances and directions. However, some researchers allow route knowledge to include quantitative information about distances and directions, as long as it is restricted to the "string-like" space of the route, and not the space across or between routes. In contrast, survey representation (or "configurational knowledge") is a more flexible form of spatial knowledge. Often conceived of as a "map in the head," survey representations allow direct access to quantitative spatial relationships, such as distances and directions between arbitrary locations in an environment—not solely those locations between which one has traveled. This way of representing information facilitates spatial inference and can be more accurate over longer distances (Thorndyke & Hayes-Roth, 1982; Sholl, 1993). Another aspect of the route-survey distinction of concern to some researchers is the perspective of the representation. Route knowledge is thought to be horizontal, from the terrain-level perspective of a traveler; survey knowledge is thought to be vertical, from a bird's-eye or orthogonal perspective (the latter is without a single viewpoint, but as if from directly above at all points). Clearly, though, one may know or not know the direction to a nonvisible target whether one accesses that from memory as if seeing through walls or as if floating above the space.

One factor that should facilitate attaining survey knowledge is familiarity—the amount of exposure one has to an environment. It is commonly thought that survey representations that are acquired by direct experience require time to develop. This view was put forth in a highly influential work by Siegel and White (1975), who synthesized much of the then-existing research on large-scale spatial representations in memory. They posited a "main sequence" of changes in mental representations of environmental space over time, from knowledge of landmarks, to knowledge of routes, to survey knowledge. Siegel and White suggested this sequence occurs both ontogenetically, from birth to adulthood, and microgenetically, from first to later exposures to a new environment over the course of time. This developmental hypothesis has been widely influential (Montello, 1998, called it the "dominant framework"), so that survey knowledge has usually been thought to be predicated on more rudimentary forms of spatial knowledge, such as knowledge of routes and landmarks.

Yet some evidence has raised questions about the degree to which survey knowledge requires comprehensive familiarity with an environment. Several investigators have concluded that survey knowledge can be formed quickly (Montello & Pick, 1993), even upon one's initial exposure to an environment (Holding & Holding, 1989). There is no question that over small areas, people can and do extract quantitative information about distances and directions (much of this evidence is reviewed by Montello, 1998). For instance, Loomis et al. (1993) demonstrated that blindfolded people can keep track of the distance and direction back to their start location with nonrandom accuracy after short walks including one or more turns (see also Sadalla and Montello, 1989). There is some evidence that survey knowledge can develop rapidly even in very large, complex environments. For example, Montello and Pick (1993) led participants twice along a complex route (approximately 500 meters with 15 to 20 turns) inside and outside of a large building. The accuracy with which participants were later able to point to the locations on this route led the researchers to conclude that at least some participants had formed survey knowledge of the area in less than half an hour. This and similar results have led many theorists either to discount the status of landmarks, routes, and survey knowledge as distinct entities, or at least to discount their status as a strict developmental sequence, instead considering them as more-or-less independent forms of spatial representations that develop concurrently (Foley & Cohen, 1984; Hanley & Levine, 1983; Montello, 1998; Schmitz, 1997). Of course, the finding that some people can quickly acquire survey knowledge from navigating large spaces does not mean that familiarity with the environment does not play an important role in establishing survey knowledge. Many contemporary investigators would agree that although it may be neither necessary nor sufficient for acquiring survey knowledge, familiarity with an environment does facilitate it.

In addition to familiarity, two other factors—field of view and the allocation of attention—have also been linked to the acquisition of survey knowledge. Using concepts from J. J. Gibson (1979), Sholl (1996) noted that a person's peripheral vision is instrumental in extracting the invariant spatial structure of an environment and proposed that peripheral vision is thus necessary for acquiring survey knowledge. Sholl examined this hypothesis by having participants learn an environment either naturally or with goggles that limited their field-of-view (restricted to the central 5°). When subsequently tested on their knowledge of the environment, participants in the full-vision group pointed between locations with patterns of error that were unrelated to the complexity of the route that connected the locations, suggesting to Sholl that they had formed survey knowledge. Participants who learned with the limited field-of-view apparently did not acquire much survey knowledge. Sholl concluded that when peripheral vision is unavailable, survey knowledge cannot be acquired. A wide field-of-view is thus necessary for developing a survey representation of a space.

The allocation of attention has also been linked to the acquisition of survey knowledge. There is some evidence that survey knowledge does not arise automatically, even after adequate exposure, but that it requires conscious attention to the environment during learning. In a series of studies, Lindberg and Gärling examined the degree to which conscious, effortful attention was required in order to learn the spatial characteristics of an environment (Lindberg & Gärling, 1981, 1983). In one experiment, Lindberg and Gärling (1981) asked people to walk through the corridors of a building, along paths of varying complexity. Participants were stopped periodically during the trip and asked to point and to estimate their distances to a previously passed location. One group of participants was required to perform a concurrent backward-counting task as they learned the environment. Another group had no such concurrent task and was thus able to devote more of their central, controlled processing to maintaining their orientation and learning the environment. Lindberg and Gärling (1981) found that while all participants were able to acquire knowledge about the routes that they had walked, those participants who were engaged in a secondary task during learning were less able to keep track of where the learned locations were. While these findings are often interpreted to mean that people acquire route knowledge more automatically than survey knowledge, some recent evidence by Allen and Willenborg (1998) suggests that route knowledge requires some conscious effort to acquire as well.

The two factors of attention and field of view may in fact be related. Sholl has speculated that the mechanism by which attention to a secondary task, such as backward counting, interferes with the acquisition of survey knowledge involves a functional restriction of one's field of view. She suggests that a secondary task usurps cognitive resources that might otherwise be used to process visual information from the periphery (see also Miura, 1990; Williams, 1982). Regardless of whether attention or field of view represents the more fundamental underlying mechanism, it appears likely that both influence the acquisition of survey knowledge.

Route and Survey Knowledge from Real World Navigation and Maps.
Maps can be considered artifacts that facilitate the acquisition of survey knowledge—they eliminate the need for familiarity. They explicitly and immediately provide a survey representation of the global structure of an environment, and reveal spatial relationships that may not have been realized from direct experience. Unlike directly experienced environments, which surround people and are viewed while locomoting, maps provide a "survey overview" of an area, depicting quantitative spatial relations among places and features. The power of maps to depict survey relationships becomes especially important in the case of "gigantic" spaces such as countries and continents (Montello & Golledge, 1999); without maps, people would probably never come to realize the shapes of large earth features and their spatial interrelations.

Although we may think of maps as providing a replacement for extended direct experience, it was suggested some time ago that survey knowledge from a map is not equivalent to survey knowledge gained from direct experience. A classic study by Thorndyke and Hayes-Roth (1982) pointed to some differences between spatial knowledge learned from maps and from direct experience. The researchers compared performance by two groups of participants on tasks that required either route or survey knowledge of a large building. The first group consisted of people who had worked in the building for some time, from one month to two years, and had presumably learned the layout directly by traveling around its hallways (called "navigation" learners). The second group of participants had never visited the building; they learned its layout by studying a map of it for approximately one hour. Participants estimated straight-line distances directly between places in the building and route distances along corridors. Consistent with the idea that maps provide direct access to survey relationships, map learners estimated straight-line and route distances equally accurately, whereas navigation learners estimated route distances more accurately than straight-line distances. Map learners were less accurate than navigation learners in pointing to targets from various places in the building, but were more accurate in placing targets on a map of the building. Thorndyke and Hayes-Roth (1982) concluded that studying a map allows people to acquire survey knowledge of the environment, knowledge they can use to estimate straight-line distances by simple recall processes, such as image scanning, without the need for more complex inferences. Map learners make more errors in pointing to nonvisible targets because they must translate the vertical perspective of the map to a horizontal one. In contrast, navigation learners develop primarily knowledge of routes connecting places in the building. This allows route distances to be recalled without complex inferences, though simple manipulations such as adding up lengths of separate segments may be required. Navigation learners must use more complex inferential processes to determine straight-line distances from route knowledge.

The ability of people to acquire survey knowledge of complex environments through direct experience may also be limited by the complexity of the layout. Moeser (1988) studied the cognitive-mapping performance of participants who had worked in a hospital building with a complex configuration. In one experiment, participants were nurses who had either 4 or 25 months of experience in the building. Moeser asked these nurses to draw sketch maps of the layout of four floors. Analyses showed that none of the sketch maps bore close resemblance to the actual layout and that over 50% of the objects depicted on them were located in error. In another experiment, a different group of nurses who had worked in the building were compared to a group of participants who had never visited the building but learned it by studying a map. Map learners memorized the layout of the floors and were tested until they could place all of the names of items in their correct location on a floorplan. Map learners were then given a guided tour of each floor, following their progress with a map. This guided tour confounded participants' map knowledge with direct experience, limiting the comparison between the two groups. Nevertheless, Moeser's results illustrated the efficacy of map experience. Map learners were substantially more accurate than the nurses at pointing to targets (though they also estimated route distances more accurately). Even after two years of working in the building, nurses (who had presumably never seen a floorplan) had very poor survey knowledge of the extremely complex building layout. Moeser's findings demonstrate the power of maps to provide survey spatial information (see also Lloyd, 1989). They also suggest that maps may even be necessary for survey-knowledge acquisition if the environment is very complex.

When the layout of an environment is easier to apprehend, differences between map and direct-learning experience may diminish. Richardson et al. (1999) had participants learn the layout of two floors of a university building. Each floor consisted of three corridors; the corridors on each floor overlapped. Map and direct learners were given equal amounts of exposure—approximately 10 minutes. Results showed that both groups performed relatively accurately, and that there was no difference in error pointing between landmarks for the map and direct learners. There was also no difference between groups in their ability to estimate route distances; however, the map learners performed better at straight-line distance estimation. These findings suggest that for initial learning of a relatively simple environment, survey knowledge formed from a map may be quite similar to that formed from direct experience.

Route and Survey Knowledge From Virtual Environments.   Unlike maps, which represent environments with abstract symbols, VEs represent them by iconic simulation. As Hunt and Waller (1999) point out, simulations of environments, in general, do not require that users consciously interpret spatial information to the degree that is required by more abstract representations of environments. Thus, VEs and other environmental simulations such as slideshows, 3-D models, and motion pictures, offer users a more naturalistic medium in which to acquire spatial information, and potentially allow users to devote less cognitive effort to learning spatial information than required by maps. In the decades preceding the advent of VE technology, several studies investigated spatial knowledge derived from a variety of less technologically sophisticated simulations, such as photographs or movies. Much of this research illustrated how readily people can learn spatial information from relatively impoverished sources, and how people use schemata to organize their mental representations of space. It also showed that real-world spatial cognition can be effectively studied using environmental simulations, though questions remained about aspects of the simulations that might not simulate direct experience accurately. In particular, these earlier simulations generally lacked whole-body movement, active control of simulated locomotion, and a full field-of-view. As discussed above, these aspects may have implications for the acquisition of survey knowledge. The shortcomings of earlier simulations are overcome to a large degree by features that VEs offer: interactivity, and in some systems, immersion and whole-body movement. By allowing users to interact in real time with an environment that apparently surrounds them, some investigators have claimed that VEs have the potential to be more effective than previous simulated environments, both at enabling people to learn about spaces and in enabling researchers to understand human spatial cognition in the real world (see, for example, Loomis, Blascovich, & Beall, 1999; Wilson, 1997).

There is now ample evidence that people are capable of acquiring route knowledge from experience in VEs. For example, Ruddle, Payne, & Jones (1997) examined people's spatial representations formed from desktop VEs by replicating Thorndyke and Hayes-Roth's (1982) classic study. Ruddle et al. had participants learn the layout of the same floorplan as in Thorndyke and Hayes-Roth's original study. After nine daily learning trials, participants showed similar levels of distance estimation, pointing, and navigation ability as did participants who navigated the real-world building in Thorndyke and Hayes-Roth's original study. Ruddle et al. concluded that, given sufficient experience, people are able to learn the spatial characteristics of a VE in much the same way that they learn from the real world. Similar research by other investigators has reached the same conclusions, especially with respect to the use of VEs to acquire route knowledge (Bliss, Tidwell, & Guest, 1997; Waller, Knapp, & Hunt, 2001; Witmer, Bailey, Knerr, & Parsons, 1996).

The degree to which VEs enable users to acquire survey knowledge is currently less clear. From a theoretical point of view, there are several reasons to believe that people may have difficulty acquiring survey knowledge by navigating in VEs. In the first place, many people have difficulty

acquiring survey knowledge in the real world. For VEs that attempt to simulate the real-world faithfully, one would expect that survey knowledge acquisition from a VE would be at least as effortful and time consuming as in
the real-world. As we have seen, the acquisition of survey knowledge is
typically considered to require the learner's attention. We have also argued
that VEs, inasmuch as they are simulations of environments, demand fewer
conscious cognitive resources to interpret them. Perhaps it is because VEs
elicit relatively little conscious effort in their interpretation that they do not
lend themselves to acquiring survey knowledge. Moreover, VEs can place
additional demands on users that are not present in the real world that may
make acquiring survey knowledge even more difficult. For example, many
of today's VE interfaces are arbitrary or unintuitive (e.g., clicking a mouse
to move forward), and require a navigator to enlist conscious cognitive resources in order to use them. The effort required to use a VEs interface will
thus likely detract from the acquisition of survey knowledge (see Waller,
2000). Additionally, we have seen that survey knowledge acquisition may
require a wide field-of-view. Yet current VE systems do not typically offer
very wide fields-of-view because they are computationally expensive. If
survey knowledge acquisition is indeed facilitated through stimulation of
one's peripheral vision, then current VE systems may make survey knowledge acquisition more difficult than it is in the real world. And as we reviewed above, the lack of whole-body movement, particularly body
rotations, found in many VE systems, may impede the acquisition of directional knowledge. In this regard, even systems that respond to head rotations may be a considerable improvement over systems that utilize only a
keyboard or joystick.

Despite the potential difficulties that VEs may have in enabling the acquisition of survey knowledge, a handful of studies have suggested that it
is possible, especially when the spaces depicted are relatively small or simple in layout (Colle & Reid, 2000; Richardson et al., 1999; Rossano et al.,
1999; Waller et al., 2001; Witmer, Sadowski, & Finkelstein, 2002). For example, the study by Richardson et al. (1999), discussed above, included a third
group of participants who learned the two-storied building from a desktop
VE, in addition to the map and walk groups. Participants did not differ in
either their distance- or pointing-estimation accuracy within the same
floor, suggesting that similar types of spatial knowledge had been acquired
among the groups. However, VE learners performed the worst on direction
and distance estimates that required an integrated understanding of the
two floors. Sketch maps by these participants suggested that they fared
much worse than the other two groups in reconciling the relative vertical
orientations of the two floors because they were confused about the body
rotations they took while "climbing" the virtual stairs between the floors.
This points to the special difficulty of combining separate "pieces" of environments into an integrated representation, as suggested for decades by
theory and data on the acquisition of spatial knowledge (Montello & Pick,

1993; Siegel and White, 1975), particularly in desktop systems when people do not actually turn their bodies during "locomotion." Such pieces might be separate floors, as in the example, or rooms, neighborhoods, route segments, and so on. Colle and Reid (2000) also demonstrated the difficulty people have learning configural relationships among multiple rooms in a desktop VE.

SUMMARY AND CONCLUSIONS

Knowledge of spatial relations in the environment is acquired and stored in memory for later retrieval and use. Memory representations are based on direct sensorimotor experience in environments but also on indirect sources such as maps, language, and virtual displays. It is both interesting and practically useful to ask how spatial memory based on different sources is similar and how it is different. To begin, sources of spatial knowledge present information differently. Directly experienced environments may be sensed through vision, audition, proprioception, or other senses to lesser extents. They may be viewed statically or dynamically during locomotion, and they may be experienced with or without the aid of machines like cars or planes. Likewise, maps vary in scale, whether they are reference or thematic maps, degree of schematicity, dimensionality, perspective and projection, and other ways. Virtual environments also take a variety of forms, including desktop, augmented, and immersive systems. These variations lead to characteristic differences in at least the content of memory based on different sources, because they provide different information for encoding into memory.

Especially noteworthy is the fact that different sources involve body movement in different ways and to different degrees. Sources that depend on whole-body locomotion provide proprioceptive and efferent information and take advantage of updating systems that allow mobile organisms to integrate movement information so as to maintain orientation. While several studies point to the role of body movement in spatial-knowledge acquisition, an important recent study suggest limits to the role of vestibular sensing at environmental scales. Ongoing research in a variety of labs will undoubtedly help clarify this in the near future.

Although the sources certainly lead to characteristic differences in the content of memory, it is not clear that they affect memory structures and processes more fundamentally beyond that. Two issues have been central to the question of whether memory structures and processes vary with spatial knowledge sources. The first concerns *orientation specificity*, whether spatial memory representations are stored and accessed preferentially in a particular orientation, usually the orientation from which a spatial layout was viewed during learning. Given the totality of the data, the most plausible hypothesis is that spatial memory, whether derived from maps, VEs, or direct experience, and whether it represents large or small spaces, is stored with a preferred orientation. This is particularly evident when one includes measures of response time as well as measures of response error. Most contemporary research finds little support for the notion that the medium through which spatial information is learned affects the orientation specificity of memory, though some evidence remains that body movement and spatial memory may not interact in exactly the same way for spaces of all sizes. The preferred orientation observed is typically that of the viewer's perspective during learning, suggesting that spatial memory is commonly stored by means of an egocentric *(viewpoint-dependent)* reference system. Other work has shown that the structure of the environment (Shelton & McNamara, 2001; Werner & Schmidt, 1999) and the structure of the learned spatial layout itself (Mou & McNamara, 2002) can affect the reference systems used to store spatial relationships. An intriguing possibility for future research is that speakers of languages without egocentric spatial terms might think about space in fundamentally different ways (Levinson, 1996) and would not show egocentric orientation specificity.

A second issue central to the question of whether memory structures and processes vary with spatial knowledge sources concerns the distinction between *route* and *survey* knowledge. Route knowledge is conceived to be more one-dimensional, less quantitative, and less flexibly accessible; survey knowledge is the opposite. In fact it is difficult to evaluate the validity of the route-survey distinction, and whether sources lead differentially to one or the other, insofar as the concepts have not been clearly and consistently defined in the literature. Conceptual and empirical arguments clearly support the special ability of maps to support the formation of survey knowledge, particularly over brief time periods of minutes or hours. At the same time, maps do not facilitate the acquisition of route knowledge the way direct travel does (albeit as reflected in a person's ability to follow routes in the real world). Evidence also supports the acquisition of survey knowledge from direct and virtual experience, and suggests the likely roles of familiarity, field-of-view, and attentional allocation in facilitating its acquisition. The precise nature of survey knowledge from direct and virtual experiences is not the same as that from maps, however, and individuals appear to differ greatly in their abilities to acquire survey knowledge (Hegarty, Montello, Richardson, & Ishikawa, 2000). These too are issues for ongoing and future research.

We restricted our focus in this chapter to the sources of direct experience, maps, and virtual environments. As mentioned above in the section on route and survey knowledge, research on spatial memory has been conducted on a variety of indirect sources besides maps and VEs, including still photographs (Allen, Siegel, & Rosinski, 1978; Hock & Schmelzkopf, 1980; Moar & Carleton, 1982), scale models (Allen et al., 1996; Hunt & Roll, 1987), and videos and movies (Goldin & Thorndyke, 1982; Hooper, 1981). Language in particular is an important source for spatial learning about which researchers are quite interested (Bloom, Peterson, Nadel, & Garrett,

1996). Language generally presents spatial information much more abstractly than do direct experience or virtual environments, and even maps present most *spatial* information fairly iconically.

Finally, it must be stressed that spatial memory from different sources is similar in many ways (for reviews, see McNamara, 1992; Tversky, 1997, 2000). Whatever its source, spatial knowledge stored in memory reveals both random and nonrandom patterns of error and distortion. Any measure of spatial knowledge will reflect error because of simple ignorance about the spatial facts in question. In addition, spatial memory is *schematic*. Shapes become more symmetric and regular over time, remembered as being more like familiar or typical shapes. Turns and angles are remembered as being straighter or more nearly like right angles, an *orthogonality* bias that holds for map-learned and directly experienced spatial knowledge (Sadalla & Montello, 1989; Tversky, 1981), and, we can assume, virtually-acquired knowledge. *Regionalization* effects, the subjective partitioning of environmental knowledge into pieces, characterize all sources too (Allen et al., 1978; Franklin, Henkel, & Zangas, 1995; Gale & Golledge, 1982; Hirtle & Mascolo, 1986). Furthermore, the fact is that spatial memory is often, perhaps usually, based on multiple learning sources (Tversky, 1993). How multiple sources are integrated, or otherwise reconciled, is a critical issue that has been researched only a little (e.g., Ruddle, Payne, & Jones, 1999; Taylor & Tversky, 1992). Taken further, the interaction of different sources may be reflected in ways that experience with one source can change the way knowledge from other sources is encoded and stored. A recent and intriguing case in point is discussed by Uttal (2000), who proposes that training and experience in the use of maps changes the way spatial knowledge acquired from direct experience is conceptualized and stored in memory. Similarly, we can also ask how the increasing use of videogames and more sophisticated virtual environments will change the way people think about and remember space and place. An intriguing possibility is that the "supernatural" capabilities of VEs (instantaneously transporting people, zooming in and out of different scales, etc.) might be used to enhance spatial learning in new ways (Darken & Sibert, 1996; Pausch, Burnette, Brockway, & Weiblen, 1995; Ruddle, Howes, Payne, & Jones, 2000).

REFERENCES

Albert, W. S., Rensink, R. A., & Beusmans, J. M. (2000). Learning relative directions between landmarks in a desktop virtual environment. *Spatial Cognition & Computation, 1,* 131–144.

Allen, G. L., Kirasic, K. C., Dobson, S. H., Long, R. G., & Beck, S. (1996). Predicting environmental learning from spatial abilities: An indirect route. *Intelligence, 22,* 327–355.

Allen, G. L., Siegel, A. W., & Rosinski, R. R. (1978). The role of perceptual context in structuring spatial knowledge. *Journal of Experimental Psychology: Human Learning and Memory, 4,* 617–630.

Allen, G. L., & Willenborg, L. J. (1998). The need for controlled information process-ing in the visual acquisition of route knowledge. *Journal of Environmental Psychol-ogy, 18*, 419–427.

Anooshian, L. J., & Siegel, A. W. (1985). From cognitive to procedural mapping. In C. J. Brainerd & M. Pressley (Eds.), *Basic processes in memory development: Progress in cognitive development research* (pp. 47–101). New York: Springer-Verlag.

Bakker, N. H., Werkhoven, P. J., & Passenier, P. O. (1999). The effects of proprioceptive and visual feedback on geographical orientation in virtual envi-ronments. *Presence: Teleoperators and Virtual Environments, 8*, 36–53.

Bliss, J. P., Tidwell, P. D., & Guest, M. A. (1997). The effectiveness of virtual reality for administering spatial navigation training to firefighters. *Presence: Teleoperators and Virtual Environments, 6*, 73 –86.

Bloom, P., Peterson, M. A., Nadel, L., & Garrett, M. F. (1996). *Language and space.* Cambridge, MA: MIT Press.

Boer, L. (1991). Mental rotation in perspective problems. *Acta Psychologica, 76*, 1–9.

Chance, S. S., Gaunet, F., Beall, A. C., & Loomis, J. M. (1998) Locomotion mode af-fects the updating of objects encountered during travel: The contribution of ves-tibular and proprioceptive inputs to path integration. *Presence: Teleoperators and Virtual Environments, 7*, 168–178.

Chatwin, B. (1987). *The songlines.* New York: Viking.

Christou, C. G., & Bülthoff, H. H. (1999). View dependence in scene recognition after active learning. *Memory & Cognition, 27*, 996–1007.

Clawson, D. M., Miller, M. S., Knott, B. A., & Sebrechts, M. M. (1998). Navigational training in virtual and real buildings. *Proceedings of the 42nd Annual Meeting of the Human Factors and Ergonomics Society*, 1427–1431.

Colle, H. A., & Reid, G. B. (2000). The room effect: Exploring paths and rooms in a desktop virtual environment with objects grouped categorically and spatially. *Ecological Psychology, 12*, 207–229.

Darken, R. P., & Sibert, J. L. (1996). Navigating large virtual spaces. *International Journal of Human-Computer Interaction, 8*, 49–71

Dawson, M. R. W., Boechler, P. M., & Valsangkar-Smyth, M. (2000). Representing space in a PDP network: Coarse allocentric coding can mediate metric and nonmetric spatial judgements. *Spatial Cognition and Computation, 2*, 181–218.

Diwadkar, V. A., & McNamara, T. P. (1997). Viewpoint dependence in scene recogni-tion. *Psychological Science, 8*, 302–307.

Dobson, M. W. (1979). Visual information processing during cartographic commu-nication. *The Cartographic Journal, 16*, 14–20.

Evans, G. W., & Pezdek, K. (1980). Cognitive mapping: Knowledge of real-world distance and location. *Journal of Experimental Psychology: Human Memory and Learning, 6*, 13–24.

Foley, J. E., & Cohen, A. J. (1984). Mental mapping of a megastructure. *Canadian Jour-nal of Psychology, 38*, 440–453.

Franklin, N., Henkel, L. A., & Zangas, T. (1995). Parsing surrounding space into re-gions. *Memory & Cognition, 23*, 397–407.

Gale, N., & Golledge, R. G. (1982). On the subjective partitioning of space. *Annals of the Association of American Geographers, 72*, 60–67.

Gale, N., Golledge, R. G., Pellegrino, J. W., & Doherty, S. (1990). The acquisition and integration of route knowledge in an unfamiliar neighborhood. *Journal of Envi-ronmental Psychology, 10*, 3–25.

Gibson, J. J. (1979). *The ecological approach to visual perception.* Boston: Houghton Mifflin.

Goldin, S. E., & Thorndyke, P. W. (1982). Simulating navigation for spatial knowledge acquisition. *Human Factors, 24,* 457–471.

Golledge, R. G., & Stimson, R. J. (1997). *Spatial behavior: A geographic perspective.* New York: Guilford.

Hanley, G. L., & Levine, M. (1983). Spatial problem solving: The integration of independently learned cognitive maps. *Memory & Cognition, 11,* 415–422.

Hegarty, M., & Just, M. A. (1993). Constructing mental models of machines from text and diagrams. *Journal of Memory and Language, 32,* 717–742.

Hegarty, M., Montello, D. R., Richardson, A. E., & Ishikawa, T. (2000, November). *Individual differences in spatial abilities in large- and small-scale space.* Paper presented at the annual meeting of the Psychonomic Society, New Orleans, LA.

Hirtle, S. C., & Mascolo, M. F. (1986). Effect of semantic clustering on the memory of spatial locations. *Journal of Experimental Psychology: Learning, Memory, and Cognition, 12,* 182–189.

Hock, H. S., & Schmelzkopf, K. F. (1980). The abstraction of schematic representations from photographs of real-world scenes. *Memory &Cognition, 8,* 543–554.

Holding, C. S., & Holding, D. H. (1989). Acquisition of route network knowledge by males and females. *The Journal of General Psychology, 116,* 29–41.

Hooper, K. (1981). The use of computer-controlled video disks in the study of spatial learning. *Behavior Research Methods & Instrumentation, 13,* 77–84.

Hunt, E., & Waller, D. (1999). *Orientation and wayfinding: A review.* (ONR technical report N00014-96-0380). Arlington, VA: Office of Naval Research.

Hunt, M. E., & Roll, M. K. (1987). Simulation in familiarizing older people with an unknown building. *Gerontologist, 27,* 169–175.

Klatzky, R. L., Loomis, J. M., Beall, A. C., Chance, S. S., & Golledge, R. G. (1998). Spatial updating of self-position and orientation during real, imagined, and virtual locomotion. *Psychological Science, 9,* 293–298.

Kuipers, B. (1978). Modeling spatial knowledge. *Cognitive Science, 2,* 129–153.

Levine, M., Jankovic, I. N., & Palij, M. (1982). Principles of spatial problem solving. *Journal of Experimental Psychology: General, 111,* 157–175.

Levine, M., Marchon, I., & Hanley, G. L. (1984). The placement and misplacement of you-are-here maps. *Environment and Behavior, 16,* 139–157.

Levinson, S. C. (1996). Frames of reference and Molyneux's question: Cross-linguistic evidence. In P. Bloom, M. A. Peterson, L. Nadel, & M. F. Garrett (Eds.), *Language and space* (pp. 109–169). Cambridge, MA: MIT Press.

Liben, L. S. (1997). Children's understanding of spatial representations of place: Mapping the methodological landscape. In N. Foreman & R. Gillet (Eds.), *A handbook of spatial research paradigms and methodologies, Vol. 1: Spatial cognition in the child and adult* (pp. 41–83). Hove, England: Lawrence Erlbaum Associates, Inc.

Liben, L. S. (1999). Developing an understanding of external spatial representations. In I. E. Sigel (Ed.), *Development of mental representation: Theories and applications.* Mahwah, NJ: Lawrence Erlbaum Associates, Inc.

Lindberg, E., & Gärling, T. (1981). Acquisition of locational information about reference points during blindfolded and sighted locomotion: Effects of a concurrent task and locomotion paths. *Scandinavian Journal of Psychology, 22,* 101–108.

Lindberg, E., & Gärling, T. (1983). Acquisition of different types of locational information in cognitive maps: Automatic or effortful processing. *Psychological Research, 45,* 19–38.

Lloyd, R. (1988). Searching for map symbols: The cognitive processes. *The American Cartographer, 15,* 363–377.

Lloyd, R. (1989). Cognitive maps: Encoding and decoding information. *Annals of the Association of American Geographers, 79,* 101–124.

Loomis, J. M., Blascovich, J. J., & Beall, A. C. (1999). Immersive virtual environment technology as a basic research tool in psychology. *Behavior Research Methods, Instruments & Computers. Psychonomic Society, 31,* 557–564.

Loomis, J. M., Klatzky, R. L., Golledge, R. G., Cicinelli, J. G., Pellegrino, J. W., & Fry, P. A. (1993). Nonvisual navigation by blind and sighted: Assessment of path integration ability. *Journal of Experimental Psychology: General, 122,* 73–91.

Loomis, J. M., Klatzky, R. L., Golledge, R. G., & Philbeck, J. W. (1999). Human navigation by path integration. In R. G. Golledge (Ed.), *Wayfinding behavior : cognitive mapping and other spatial processes* (pp. 125–151). Baltimore: Johns Hopkins Press.

MacEachren, A. M. (1992). Learning spatial information from maps: Can orientation specificity be overcome? *Professional Geographer, 44,* 431–443.

MacEachren, A. M. (1995). *How maps work: Representation, visualization, and design.* New York: Guilford.

McNamara, T. P. (1992). Spatial representation. *Geoforum, 23,* 139–150.

Miller, M. S., Clawson, D. M., & Sebrechts, M. M. (1999). Long-term retention of spatial knowledge acquired in virtual reality. In *Proceedings of the 43rd Annual Meeting of the Human Factors and Ergonomics Society,* 1243–1246.

Miura, T. (1990). Active function of eye movement and useful field of view in a realistic setting. In R. Groner, G. d'Ydewalle, & R. Parham (Eds.), *From eye to mind: Information acquisition in perception, search, and reading* (pp. 119–127). Amsterdam: North-Holland.

Moar, I., & Carleton, L. R. (1982). Memory for routes. *Quarterly Journal of Experimental Psychology, 34A,* 381–394.

Moeser, S. D. (1988). Cognitive mapping in a complex building. *Environment and Behavior, 20,* 21–49.

Montello, D. R. (1993). Scale and multiple psychologies of space. In A. U. Frank & I. Campari (Eds.), *Spatial information theory: A theoretical basis for GIS* (pp. 312–321). Berlin: Springer-Verlag.

Montello, D. R. (1998). A new framework for understanding the acquisition of spatial knowledge in large-scale environments. In M. J. Egenhofer & R. G. Golledge (Eds.), *Spatial and temporal reasoning in geographic information systems* (pp. 143–154). New York: Oxford University Press.

Montello, D. R., & Frank, A. U. (1996). Modeling directional knowledge and reasoning in environmental space: Testing qualitative metrics. In J. Portugali (Ed.), *The construction of cognitive maps* (pp. 321–344). Dordrecht, The Netherlands: Kluwer Academic.

Montello, D. R., & Freundschuh, S. M. (1995). Sources of spatial knowledge and their implications for GIS: An introduction. *Geographical Systems, 2,* 169–176.

Montello, D. R., & Golledge, R. G. (1999). *Scale and Detail in the Cognition of Geographic Information* (Report of Specialist Meeting of Project Varenius). Santa Barbara, CA: University of California at Santa Barbara, NCGIA.

Montello, D. R., & Pick, H. L. (1993). Integrating knowledge of vertically-aligned large-scale spaces. *Environment and Behavior, 25,* 457–484.

Mou, W., & McNamara, T. P. (2002.) Intrinsic frames of reference in spatial memory. *Journal of Experimental Psychology: Learning, Memory, & Cognition, 28,* 162–170.

Pausch, R., Burnette, T., Brockway, D., & Weiblen, M. E. (1995, July). *Navigation and locomotion in virtual worlds via flight into hand-held miniatures.* Paper presented at the ACM SIGGRAPH '95.

Péruch, P., Borel, L., Gaunet, F., Thinus-Blanc, C., Magnan, J., & Lacour, M. (1999). Spatial performance of unilateral vestibular defective patients in nonvisual versus visual navigation. *Journal of Vestibular Research, 9,* 37–47.

Potegal, M. (1982). Vestibular and neostriatal contributions to spatial orientation. In M. Potegal (Ed.), *Spatial abilities: Development and physiological foundations* (pp. 361–387). New York: Academic.

Presson, C. C., DeLange, N., & Hazelrigg, M. D. (1989). Orientation specificity in spatial memory: What makes a path different from a map of the path? *Journal of Experimental Psychology: Learning, Memory, & Cognition, 15,* 887–897.

Presson, C. C., & Hazelrigg, M. D. (1984). Building spatial representations through primary and secondary learning, *Journal of Experimental Psychology: Learning, Memory, and Cognition, 10,* 716–722.

Presson, C. C., & Somerville, S. C. (1985). Beyond egocentrism: A new look at the beginnings of spatial representation. In H. Wellman (Ed.), *Children's searching: The development of search skill and spatial representation* (pp. 1–22). Hillsdale, NJ: Lawrence Erlbaum Associates, Inc..

Pylyshyn, Z. W. (1981). The imagery debate: Analogue media versus tacit knowledge. *Psychological Review, 87,* 16–45.

Richardson, A. E., Montello, D. R., & Hegarty, M. (1999). Spatial knowledge acquisition from maps and from navigation in real and virtual environments. *Memory & Cognition, 27,* 741–750.

Rieser, J. J., Guth, D. A., & Hill, E. W. (1986). Sensitivity to perspective structure while walking without vision. *Perception, 15,* 173–188.

Robinson, A. H., & Petchenik, B. B. (1976). *The nature of maps: Essays toward understanding maps and mapping.* Chicago: The University of Chicago Press.

Roskos-Ewoldsen, B., McNamara, T. P., Shelton, A. L., & Carr, W. S. (1998). Mental representations of large and small spatial layouts are orientation dependent. *Journal of Experimental Psychology: Learning, Memory, & Cognition, 24,* 215–226.

Rossano, M. J., & Moak, J. (1998). Spatial representations acquired from computer models: Cognitive load, orientation specificity and the acquisition of survey knowledge. *British Journal of Psychology, 89,* 481–497.

Rossano, M. J., West, S. O., Robertson, T. J., Wayne, M. C., & Chase, R. B. (1999). The acquisition of route and survey knowledge from computer models. *Journal of Environmental Psychology, 19,* 101–115.

Ruddle, R. A., Howes, A., Payne, S. J., & Jones, D. M. (2000). The effects of hyperlinks on navigation in virtual environments. *International Journal of Human-Computer Studies, 53,* 551–581.

Ruddle, R. A., Payne, S. J., & Jones, D. M. (1997). Navigating buildings in 'desk-top' virtual environments: Experimental investigations using extended navigational experience. *Journal of Experimental Psychology: Applied, 3,* 143–159.

Ruddle, R. A., Payne, S. J., & Jones, D. M. (1999). The effects of maps on navigation and search strategies in very-large-scale virtual environments. *Journal of Experimental Psychology: Applied, 5,* 54–75.

Saarinen, T. F., Parton, M., & Billberg, R. (1996). Relative size of continents on world sketch maps. *Cartographica, 33,* 37–47.

Sadalla, E. K., & Montello, D. R. (1989). Remembering changes in direction. *Environment and Behavior, 21,* 346–363.

Schacter, D. L., & Tulving, E. (1994). *Memory systems.* Cambridge, MA: MIT Press.

Schmitz, S. (1997). Gender-related strategies in environmental development: Effects of anxiety on wayfinding in and representation of a three-dimensional maze. *Journal of Environmental Psychology, 17,* 215–228.

Shepard, R. N., & Hurwitz, S. (1984). Upward direction, mental rotation, and discrimination of left and right turns in maps. *Cognition, 18,* 161–193.

Shelton, A. L., & McNamara, T. P. (1997). Multiple views of spatial memory. *Psychonomic Bulletin & Review, 4,* 102–106.

Shelton, A. L., & McNamara, T. P. (2001). Systems of spatial reference in human memory. *Cognitive Psychology, 43,* 274–310.

Sholl, M. J. (1993, November). *The effect of visual field restriction on spatial knowledge acquisition.* Paper presented at the annual meeting of the Psychonomic Society, Washington, DC.

Sholl, M. J. (1996). From visual information to cognitive maps. In J. Portugali (Ed.), *The construction of cognitive maps* (pp. 157–186). Netherlands: Kluwer.

Sholl, M. J., & Bartels, G. P. (2002). The role of self-to-object updating in orientation-free performance on spatial-memory tasks. *Journal of Experimental Psychology: Learning, Memory, and Cognition, 28,* 422–436.

Sholl, M. J., & Nolin, T. L. (1997). Orientation specificity in representations of place. *Journal of Experimental Psychology: Learning, Memory, & Cognition, 23,* 1494–1507.

Siegel, A. W., & White, S. H. (1975). The development of spatial representations of large-scale environments. In H. W. Reese (Ed.), *Advances in child development and behavior* (Vol. 10, pp. 9–55). New York: Academic.

Taylor, H. A., & Tversky, B. (1992). Descriptions and depictions of environments. *Memory & Cognition, 20,* 483–496.

Thorndyke, P. W., & Hayes-Roth, B. (1982). Differences in spatial knowledge acquired from maps and navigation. *Cognitive Psychology, 14,* 560–589.

Tversky, B. (1981). Distortions in memory for maps. *Cognitive Psychology, 13,* 407–433.

Tversky, B. (1993). Cognitive maps, cognitive collages, and spatial mental models. In A. U. Frank & I. Campari (Eds.), *Spatial information theory: A theoretical basis for GIS* (pp. 14–24). Berlin: Springer-Verlag.

Tversky, B. (1997). Memory for pictures, environments, maps, and graphs. In D. Payne & F. Conrad (Eds.), *Intersections in basic and applied memory research* (pp. 257–277). Mahwah, NJ: Lawrence Erlbaum Associates, Inc.

Tversky, B. (2000). Remembering spaces. In E. Tulving & F. I. M. Craik (Eds.), *The Oxford handbook of memory* (pp. 363–378). Oxford: Oxford University Press.

Uttal, D. H. (2000). Seeing the big picture: Map use and the development of spatial cognition. *Developmental Science, 3,* 247–264.

Vasiliev, I., Freundschuh, S., Mark, D. M., Theisen, G. D., & McAvoy, J. (1990). What is a map? *The Cartographic Journal, 27,* 119–123.

Waller, D. (2000). Individual differences in spatial learning from computer-simulated environments. *Journal of Experimental Psychology: Applied, 6,* 307–321.

Waller, D., Knapp, D., & Hunt, E. (2001). Spatial representations of virtual mazes: The role of visual fidelity and individual differences. *Human Factors, 43,* 147–158.

Waller, D., Loomis, J. M., & Haun, D. B. M. (in press). Body-based senses enhance knowledge of directions in large-scale environments. *Psychonomic Bulletin & Review.*

Waller, D., Loomis, J. M., & Steck, S. (2001, November). *Inertial cues do not facilitate large-scale spatial learning.* Paper presented at the annual meeting of the Psychonomic Society, Orlando, FL.

Waller, D., Montello, D. R., Richardson, A. E., & Hegarty, M. (2002). Orientation specificity and spatial updating of memories for layouts. *Journal of Experimental Psychology: Learning, Memory, & Cognition, 28,* 1051–1063.

Warren, D. H. (1995). Maps and landscapes: Modes of spatial representation. *Geographical Systems, 2,* 255–266.

Werner, S., & Schmidt, K. (1999). Environmental reference systems for large-scale spaces. *Spatial Cognition & Computation, 1,* 447–473.

Williams, L. J. (1982). Cognitive load and the functional field of view. *Human Factors, 24,* 683–692.

Wilson, P. N. (1997). Use of virtual reality computing in spatial learning research. In N. Foreman & R. Gillet (Eds.), *A handbook of spatial research paradigms and methodologies, Vol. 1: Spatial cognition in the child and adult* (pp. 181–206). Hove, England: Lawrence Erlbaum Associates, Inc.

Witmer, B. G., Bailey, J. H., Knerr, B. W., & Parsons, K. C. (1996). Virtual spaces and real world places: Transfer of route knowledge. *International Journal of Human-Computer Studies, 45,* 413–428.

Witmer, B. G., Sadowski, W. J., & Finkelstein, N. M. (2002). VE-based training strategies for acquiring survey knowledge. *Presence: Teleoperators and Virtual Environments, 11,* 1–18.

12

Young Children's Recognition and Representation of Urban Landscapes
From Aerial Photographs and in Toy Play

Mark Blades and Christopher Spencer
University of Sheffield

Beverly Plester
Coventry University

Kathryn Desmond
University of Sheffield

A person's representation of the environment, or cognitive map, is derived from two sources: from direct experience (e.g., by moving through an environment) or from indirect experience of the environment (e.g., from maps). There will be contexts in which direct experience is the predominant source, for instance, a person who has lived in and traveled through the same town all their lives may only refer to a map to find a particularly obscure place. In other contexts, both direct and indirect knowledge will be important—for example, when visiting a new city for the first time, most people would use a map or a guidebook.

As Liben (2001) said with reference to maps, "spatial representations help us think" (p. 45), and we argue following that representations are important for several reasons. They provide information about the location of places, and therefore, they are an important aid for planning actions and behavior. Furthermore, the structure of representations also structures the way that people think about space (Gattis, 2001; Uttal, 2000). In this way, both the information and the spatial structures that people learn from representations become part of their memory for the environment, in other words, part of their cognitive maps.

Despite the role of representations in the formation of cognitive maps, almost all the research into adults' cognitive maps has focused on assessing adults' recall of very familiar environments or in studying how they encode new environments from direct experience (Kitchin & Blades, 2002). Only a little attention has been given to how adults encode information from indirect sources, such as route directions and written descriptions (Ferguson & Hegarty, 1994; Taylor & Tversky, 1992; Tversky, 2000) or cartographic and sketch maps (Blades, Ungar, & Spencer, 1999; Kitchin & Blades, 2002). That research has shown that the nature of the source may influence the spatial information that is encoded (see Montello, Waller, Hegarty, & Richardson, chap. 11, this volume). For example, cognitive maps based on information learned from a plan or a map may sometimes be orientation specific (Rossano, Warren, & Kenan, 1995) or may include more accurate configurational relations (Moeser, 1988). Nonetheless, information from an indirect source can often be as effective as information from direct experience in contributing to spatial knowledge (Richardson, Montello, & Hegarty, 1999), and sometimes indirect sources are the only available information about areas that are too large to experience directly (MacEachren, 1995).

Researchers who have investigated the cognitive maps of children have also focused on what children know from direct experience of the environment. There are long-established frameworks for the study of children's cognitive maps in large environments such as towns and cities (e.g., Piaget & Inhelder, 1956; Siegel & White, 1975), and there is now a large literature on how children develop cognitive maps from direct experience. This literature has been reviewed elsewhere (e.g., Blades, 1997; Kitchin & Blades, 2002; Matthews, 1992; Spencer, Blades, & Morsley, 1989). Rather less attention has been paid to the role of indirect experience in the formation of children's cognitive maps.

There has been much research into kindergarten children's understanding of spatial representations such as models and maps. For example, children might be shown a model of a room in which a location is pointed out, and then they are asked to find the same location in the actual room that the model represents (DeLoache 1989, 2000; Loewenstein & Gentner, 2001). Or children might be given a map showing a route through a maze set up in a school playground (Blades & Spencer, 1994; Bremner & Andreasen, 1998). However, these studies have only limited relevance to cognitive maps because the experimental environments are temporary ones in which the child only has limited experience. Nonetheless, they have demonstrated that, at least in small spaces, kindergarten children do have some appreciation of models and maps as representations. Otherwise, there has been little research into how children derive spatial knowledge from indirect sources.

Uttal (2000) argued that as children learn about maps, it helps them to learn about the world around them. He suggested that maps provide a cognitive tool that can contribute to novel ways of thinking about space. For example, maps are usually small-scale symbolic representations that reduce the salience of individual features, and in this way, a map user may focus more on the relations between features and the context of the features than on the features themselves. In other words, using maps may lead to thinking about space in new ways that can be applied even when the child is not looking at a map, and in turn, this might contribute to children's encoding and representation of environments that are directly experienced (Uttal & Wellman, 1989). The argument that maps contribute to the development of children's spatial reasoning that in turn contributes to the development of their cognitive maps is an important one and requires more research (Uttal, 2000). Nonetheless, it is an appealing idea that as children become more familiar with representations of environments, they become better at encoding environments themselves.

Although Uttal (2000) concentrated on discussing the potential influence of maps, Blades (2000) pointed out that other representations such as pictures, models, and aerial photographs may all contribute to children's cognitive maps. This contribution could come about in at least two ways. First, as Uttal (2000) suggested, they may encourage new ways of thinking about space. Second, if a representation is of an area that has also been experienced directly (e.g., a map of the child's home area), the information on the map may provide additional knowledge about the features in that area and their relations.

We also take these arguments a step further by pointing out that understanding representations at all must depend on having some prior environmental knowledge. The features shown on a map will have little meaning to anyone who is not familiar with either the specific environment portrayed in the map or familiar with similar environments. An alternative way to put this argument is to say that there will be a continual interaction between a child's understanding of real space and their understanding of represented space. Some understanding of real space is necessary to interpret a map, and the interpretation of maps may contribute to a better encoding of real spaces.

In this chapter, we discuss several studies that have been carried out to investigate young children's understanding of aerial photographs and studies in which young children were asked to make a model town. The aerial photographs that were used were mostly of large urban spaces, usually showing several blocks. Interpreting an aerial photograph relies on children having some understanding of the type of features that might be present in a photograph and the vocabulary to identify and describe them. In other words, such interpretation depends on some existing knowledge about the world. In the same way, if children can make a model town, they have to rely on their knowledge of towns, whether from direct or indirect experience.

UNDERSTANDING AERIAL PHOTOGRAPHS

There is no reason to think that young children would show a spontaneous understanding of an aerial photograph when they are shown one for the first time. Aerial photographs are small-scale representations of the world, and information and detail that is readily apparent on the ground is lost in a photograph. They typically portray the world from directly above so that even tall and significant buildings on the ground appear as nothing more than small rectangles, and if they are black and white photographs, any color cues are lost as well. Nonetheless, Blaut (1991) put forward a theory that he called "natural mapping" and suggested that very young children have the ability to understand aerial photographs and simple maps without prior experience of them.

Blaut's (1991) natural mapping theory has generated much debate (e.g., Blaut, 1997; Liben & Downs, 1997). Without going into the details of this debate, we summarize two issues that have been raised. First, Blaut's (1991) proposal that very young children have an almost innate and unlearned ability to appreciate spatial representations has been disputed. There is no evidence to support this strong view of children's abilities. A more modest view would be the one summarized in the previous section, that by kindergarten age, children have had much experience of familiar environments, and this knowledge might contribute to their understanding of representations.

The second issue is related to the nature of understanding. What do children need to do to demonstrate an understanding of representations like an aerial photograph? We have already pointed out that young children do have some understanding of representations like models and simple maps, but this understanding has only been demonstrated in spaces no larger than a small room or part of a playground. An aerial photograph typically includes a much larger landscape.

In most studies with aerial photographs, children are shown a photograph and asked to name as many features as they can see, or alternatively, specific features are pointed out and the children are asked to name those (Blades et al., 1998; Spencer, Harrison, & Darvizeh, 1980; Stea & Blaut, 1973). An additional method used in one or two studies has been to ask children to walk or "drive" between two places on the photograph by drawing a route between those places (Blaut, McCleary, & Blaut, 1970). If the children draw an appropriate route that follows paths or roads and does not go across buildings or boundaries, this has been taken as a demonstration that they treat the photograph as a representation of a three-dimensional space and appreciate the constraints of moving through such a space.

In the earlier studies with aerial photographs, some researchers have found that young children were able to name numerous features correctly on the photographs and took this as a clear indication of the children's success (Blaut et al., 1970; Stea & Blaut, 1973). Other researchers have focused less on what children reported accurately and more on their errors. For example, Liben and Downs (1991) pointed out that some children who labeled some features correctly also described other features very inaccurately, for instance, saying that they saw people, bugs, or snowflakes in a small scale photograph where such features, even if they existed, would have been impossible to see. Such a finding suggests that even when children name some features appropriately, they may have only a limited appreciation of the photograph as a landscape because they are willing to say that a building and a bug are equally visible in the same picture. If this is the case, it would mean that children are only interpreting individual features in a piecemeal fashion and do not recognize the photograph as a coherent representation at a consistent scale. We refer to the type of errors just described as *scale errors*. The presence of such errors in a child's description of an aerial photograph would be evidence that they do not understand the nature of the photograph.

Young Children's Interpretation of Aerial Photographs

In one of the first studies, Sowden, Blades, Spencer, and Blaut (1996) looked at young children's responses when they were asked to name features on an aerial photograph. Sowden et al. showed twenty 4-year-olds a 1:1300 black and white vertical aerial photograph of a city center (Sheffield, UK).

The children were shown the photograph and asked to say what they could see in it, and they were prompted with neutral questions ("What else can you see?") until they stopped mentioning features. After this, the interviewer pointed to several features (houses, tower block, roundabout, etc.) and asked the children to name those features. Then the interviewer pointed out two houses that were some way apart on the photograph and asked children to pretend that they lived at one house and that their friend lived at the other. They were asked to draw a route on the photograph from their house to their friend's. Appropriate routes between the two houses involved a number of turns.

Sowden et al. (1996) found that the children were able to name an average of five features correctly and that three fourths of the children drew an appropriate route between the two houses. They drew the route along the roads and did not go across buildings or boundaries. These results imply that the children had some understanding that the photograph represented an urban landscape with roads, houses, buildings, and so on.

As discussed previously, Liben and Downs (1991) found that some young children labeled some features inappropriately given the scale constraints of the representation. Sowden et al. (1996) had therefore expected some of the children in their study to make such scale errors. Contrary to this expectation, Sowden et al. found that children rarely made errors; 13 of the 20 children made no errors at all, and none made more than three errors. Most of these errors were children giving an incorrect label to a feature (e.g., saying that a roundabout was a pond), which even though it was inaccurate still referred to a landscape feature that would have been possible at the scale of the photograph. There were only one or two scale errors (e.g., referring to a roundabout as a football). This type of error was so rare that there was no evidence that children were identifying features piecemeal without considering the overall context of the photograph.

Lack of Errors in Free Responses to Aerial Photographs

The small number of errors in Sowden et al. (1996) was an important finding, but it was based on a small sample. Therefore, Blades, Spencer, Patel, and Mannion (1999) repeated the study using the same photograph but with a larger number of children from a wider age range. Four groups of 20 children aged 3.5 years, 4 years, 4.5 years, and 5 years were asked about the photograph using a similar procedure as Sowden et al. First the children were asked for free responses and encouraged to name as many features as possible. The children were scored as correct for any appropriately labeled features. Their incorrect responses were divided into the following categories:

1. *Misinterpretations* were when a response was not correct but was still a reference to an aerial view of a landscape feature (e.g., pond for roundabout).
2. *Shape errors* were when children referred only to the shape of a feature (e.g., circle for roundabout).
3. *Scale errors* were when children referred to an item of inappropriate scale (e.g., football for roundabout).
4. *Other errors* were when children gave answers that could not be classified (e.g., "the place where cows go").

There were very few shape or other errors, and therefore, we focus on the incorrect misinterpretations and the scale errors. The percentage of responses that were correct and the percentage that were misinterpretations and scale errors are shown in Table 12.1. Most of the identifications made in free response were correct, and when children did make an error, they still referred to some aspect of a landscape (the misinterpretation category). Blades, Spencer, et al. (1999) found that the children rarely made scale errors, and this confirmed the findings from Sowden et al. (1996) and did not support Liben and Downs's (1991) suggestion that young children make a large number of these errors.

In a second part to the experiment, Blades, Spencer, et al. (1999) pointed out eight features (houses, road, roundabout, trees, cars, church, tower

TABLE 12.1

Percentage of Children's Responses That Were Correct, Misinterpretations, or Scale Errors in the Free Response Phase of Blades, Spencer, et al. (1999)

Age (Years)	Correct (%)	Incorrect	
		Misinterpretations (%)	Scale Errors (%)
3.5	70	16	2
4.0	72	18	3
4.5	72	18	1
5.0	88	5	3

block, and football ground) in random order for each child and asked the children to name them. The children's responses were classified as before. The children were generally successful: 5-year-olds had 69% correct; 4.5-year-olds had 61% correct; 4-year-olds had 47% correct; and 3.5-year-olds had 44% correct. When the children were unable to give a correct answer, their most frequent response was to say "don't know." The few errors were misinterpretations, and again, the children very rarely made scale errors.

The children were also asked to perform other tasks with the photographs, including a route task (as described previously), and more than half the children in each age group did this without drawing over buildings or barriers. Then at the end of the experiment, the children were each given 10 model cars (each a few millimeters long) that were approximately the same scale as the photograph and were asked to place the cars wherever they liked on the picture. Nearly all the children placed all the cars in appropriate places on the photograph (i.e., on roads, in car parks, next to houses). Almost none of the cars were placed across features or on top of buildings.

There is no doubt that in the Blades, Spencer, et al. (1999) study, the children treated the aerial photograph as a view of the landscape, and they were able to describe many of its features with accuracy and consistency. The most striking result from both Sowden et al. (1996) and from Blades, Spencer, et al. (1999) was the near absence of scale errors. Although other researchers have placed much emphasis on such errors as evidence that young children do not interpret an aerial photograph as a coherent representation, Blades, Spencer, et al. and Sowden et al. found no support at all for the frequency of errors reported by previous researchers.

Although Blades, Spencer, et al. (1999) and Sowden et al. (1996) found that children rarely made scale errors, also note that the aerial photograph used in those studies was 1:1300, and this was a much larger scale than the photographs used by researchers who reported frequent scale errors. It might be assumed that children would have greater difficulty identifying features on a smaller scale photograph, and this difficulty may, in some way, have contributed to the frequency of scale errors found by other researchers. To address this question directly, Craddock (2001) compared children's feature identifications on a photograph that was presented at different scales.

Lack of Errors in Specific Questioning About Aerial Photographs

To investigate the effects of scale, Craddock (2001) used a black and white vertical view of Evanston, Illinois (see Fig. 12.1). This was shown to children in the United Kingdom who were, of course, unfamiliar with the area.[1] There were four age groups of 20 children (aged 4, 5, 6, and 7 years), and half the children in each age group saw the photograph at scale 1:1150 and half were shown it at scale 1:4200.

Twelve features were chosen for feature identification. These features included two buildings, two paths, a road, a crossroads, three intersecting roads, a garden, a park, a baseball pitch, tennis courts, and a rail station. Craddock (2001) assumed that some of these features were unambiguous (e.g., the roads), but others were chosen to be difficult or ambiguous features. For example, some features had distinctive two-dimensional patterns (one of the buildings was an "H" shape, one path looked like a snake, and the three intersecting roads appeared as a triangle), and other features were difficult to interpret (the tennis courts, and for UK children, the baseball pitch). By choosing such features, Craddock expected to increase the likelihood of errors.

The interviewer pointed to the 12 features in random order and asked the children to identify each one. Children were allowed to say "don't know" if they could not name a feature. Overall performance was good, and three fourths of the children's responses were correct. The 4-year-olds (with a mean score of 60% correct) were poorer than the three older groups who all performed similarly (with mean scores between 72% and 85% correct). Contrary to Craddock's (2001) prediction, there was no difference in performance on the small-scale and the large-scale photograph because all four age groups performed equivalently with the two different scales.

If children did not give a correct response, they nearly always said "didn't know." Errors were classified in the same way as in Blades, Spencer, et al. (1999), described previously. The most common errors were misrepresenta-

---

[1]A parallel study, using the same photograph, has been carried out by David Uttal in the United States.

FIG. 12.1.   Vertical aerial photograph of Evanston, Illinois, used in
Craddock (2001). The photograph shown to children was black and white.

tions when children labeled a feature incorrectly but did refer to another possible landscape feature of an appropriate scale. Overall, only 4% of the children's responses were scale errors, and half of these were the result of confusion about the tennis courts. All age groups, particularly the youngest, found it hard to identify this feature and many referred to them as "windows" (presumably from the appearance of lines marking the courts). Otherwise, scale errors were rare and not associated with any one feature. The results from Craddock (2001) therefore confirmed and supported the previous findings.

Throughout these studies, researchers have found that children from 4 years of age do offer sensible and appropriate interpretations of features on aerial photographs. Incorrect responses such as scale errors are rarely made, and therefore, little or no evidence that children look at an aerial photograph in a piecemeal way was found. Instead, we suggest that at least from 4 years of age children can look at a photograph and describe individual features in a coherent way, and they do so without making many inappropriate errors.

A lack of scale errors does not necessarily mean that children understand an aerial photograph as a representation—they may just be very good at identifying individual features without much understanding of the spatial relations between those features and without much appreciation that the photograph represents an actual landscape. Therefore, two series of studies were carried out to find out if young children can use an aerial photograph as a representation.

In one set of studies, Shevelan (2001) showed kindergarten children a large model landscape that was about 18 square ft., and included a lake, several roads, car parks, numerous houses and buildings, and many landscape features. The model landscape was set up on a table, and children were given the opportunity to examine it. In effect, they had an oblique view of the model as they walked round it. Then they were shown a small-scale color, vertical, aerial photograph of the model (see Fig. 12.2).

Despite the different perspective and the different scale, all the children spontaneously recognized that the model and the photograph were the "same." Places were pointed out on the photograph (e.g., the soccer pitch, a specific building), and children were asked to find the same place on the model. Young children had no difficulty completing this task. In other words, they could appreciate the correspondence between the photograph and the model. This is to say that they treated the photograph as a representation. To test this understanding further, Plester, Richards, Blades, and Spencer (2002) went on to ask children to use an aerial photograph in a real environment.

Using Aerial Photographs in Real Environments

In a recent study, Plester et al. (2002) asked 30 kindergarten children (aged between 4 years, 7 months and 5 years, 6 months) to carry out several tasks with an aerial photograph of their school and its immediate environment.

FIG. 12.2.   Vertical aerial photograph of the model landscape used in Shevelan (2001). The photograph shown to children was in color. Photograph by Leonard Hetherington.

Two aerial photographs were used, and children saw one or the other. One photograph was a color vertical view (scale 1:1100; see Fig. 12.3), and one was a color oblique view that was judged to be equivalent because the central features were the same dimensions on both photographs (see Fig. 12.4).

Children were taken to the middle of their playground where they were shown one of the aerial photographs aligned with the environment. The children were first asked what they saw in the picture in the photograph, and they were able to identify an average of more than six features.

Then they were asked, "Where do you think is the place in the picture? Where do you think this is a picture of?" Responses were scored as correct if children mentioned "school," "here," the name of the church, or the specific name of any other building in the photograph. Two children (with the vertical photograph) identified the locale immediately. If children did not recognize the locale straight away, the experimenter pointed to specific features in a predetermined order (church, school, nursery, houses adjacent to the playground, and nearby car park) and each time asked, "What do you think this is in real life?" If a child did not respond, the experimenter pointed out the feature and then asked about the next one. Children needed an average of three such prompts before they recognized the space and were slightly quicker at recognizing the locale from the oblique photograph than from the vertical photograph.

After children had identified the locale, five further features were pointed to on the photograph (a wall, a tool shed, a fence, a specific tree, and a climbing frame), and the children were asked to point to those features in the environment. Children were typically able to identify three of them, although half the children using the oblique photograph were able to identify four or five of the features. The children were then asked to point out on the photograph where they were standing (at the center), and all but three of them were able to do this. Then they walked to two other places and were asked to point these out on the photograph, and they were correct on nearly half these trials.

The young children in Plester et al. (2002) demonstrated a good ability to interpret the aerial photographs. The children were not perfectly correct on every task, and the structured nature of the tasks provided them with an optimal context for interpreting the photograph. Nonetheless, it must be remembered that these 4- and 5-year-old children had had no previous experience of looking at or using aerial photographs and that they had never been asked to identify a familiar place from an aerial view. Given their lack of previous experience, these children demonstrated a remarkable ability to recognize the correspondence between their own view and an aerial view of the same landscape. The children were slightly quicker at recognizing the locale when looking at the oblique photograph, but otherwise, performance with the vertical and oblique photographs were similar. In other words, children were able to integrate their own knowledge of the environment with an unfamiliar view of it.

FIG. 12.3.   Vertical aerial photograph of children's school and its vicinity used in Plester, Richards, Blades, and Spencer (2002). The photograph shown to children was in color, and was 8 inches x 10 ½ inches.

FIG. 12.4.   Oblique aerial photograph of children's school and its vicinity used in Plester, Richards, Blades, and Spencer (2002). The photograph shown to children was in color, and was 8 inches x 10 ½ inches.

Children may have been slightly better with the oblique photographs because such photographs provide the child with a perspective that shows the sides of buildings (see Fig. 12.4). In earlier studies, researchers have also found that children were better at naming features on oblique, compared to vertical, photographs (Blades, Hetherington, Spencer, & Sowden, 1997). We assume that in such views some features will be easier to recognize than when the same buildings are viewed from directly above and children are presented with the perspective showing only the unfamiliar roof of a feature. This is not surprising because the side view of features in an oblique view reduces any ambiguity in interpretation.

Taken together, the experiments described previously show that young children have a good ability to recognize aerial photographs. Earlier studies (mostly with older children) had demonstrated that children could look at an aerial photograph and name individual features that they selected themselves (Blaut et al., 1970; Stea & Blaut, 1973), but the studies we discuss here have shown that young children can also name ambiguous features that are specifically pointed out to them (e.g., Craddock, 2001). This understanding goes beyond just identifying features because young children can use an aerial photograph as a representation (Shevelan, 2001) and can use photographs in real world contexts (Plester et al., 2002).

As all the children in these studies were untrained, we assume that their performance would have been better still with more practice and experience, and this has clear implications for geographical education. There seems no reason why kindergarten children should not be introduced to geographical work through the medium of aerial photographs, and those photographs do not need to be limited to pictures of rooms or small layouts but can be views of real landscapes. As we pointed out in the first part of this chapter, representations of space can contribute to adults' cognitive maps of familiar areas because information gained from maps can be integrated with information learned from direct experience. We suggest that it is likely that even young children's knowledge of their locality could be enhanced if they have the opportunity to experience it through representations, and this is an aspect of children's environmental cognition that requires new research.

For adults, representations of space are essential when the environment itself cannot be experienced directly. Compared to adults, children have much more restricted direct experience of the world around them, and therefore, representations of space might be particularly important as children develop concepts of large spaces that are beyond their own direct experience, and we consider this next.

MODELING LANDSCAPES IN TOY PLAY

Although aerial photographs might provide children with information, we can assume that young children rarely if ever see such photographs. However, as Blaut and Stea (1974) argued, children do experience environmental representations through toy play. Blaut and Stea (1974) suggested that in the course of toy play young children will

> Assemble a set of landscape-feature toys, like houses, cars, trees, into a map-like model of a macro-environment or geographic region—defined as a region which is too large to be perceived as a whole from a single earthbound vantage point and which, therefore, requires a cognitive map for comprehension. (p. 5)

Blaut and Stea (1974) gave 3- to 6-year-olds a set of toy houses, buildings, cars, trees, and pasteboard strips painted to look like roads. The children were first asked to make a "street corner" using two of the roads and with help from the experimenters. Then they were asked to play with all the toy items on a sheet of white paper, but they were not given any specific instructions other than to play with the toys.

Blaut and Stea (1974) found that the children, including the youngest, made layouts that included connected street segments with toy items placed appropriately, and they argued that these reflected realistic land-scapes. If so, this result suggests that very young children can represent street patterns and buildings. Blaut and Stea referred to the toy layouts as representations of the children's cognitive maps, and this implied that the layouts were the outcome of direct experience in urban environments. Given the necessarily limited range of toy items that the children were given, we assume that children would have been unable to model a specific environment, and instead, their layouts are more likely to have reflected a general appreciation or schema of what an urban layout should be like.

Blades and Banham (1990) found evidence of environmental schemas in other contexts. Blades and Banham showed 4-year-olds a model of a kitchen layout that included 10 items of toy furniture (e.g., chairs, table, sink unit, washing machine, refrigerator) but did not include a stove. Children were told that they would be asked to reconstruct the kitchen from memory and asked to learn the model as well as possible. They had as long as they liked to learn the layout, and when they felt confident the items were removed from the kitchen and placed in a pile with a large number of other pieces of toy furniture (e.g., beds, armchairs, bookshelves, a dressing table, a bath). Children were asked to reconstruct the kitchen layout from memory. Most were able to do this very accurately; they rarely included non-kitchen items, and most of the furniture was put back in the correct places. However, nearly two thirds of the children incorrectly included the cooker in their reconstructions. In other words, their recall of the model in-cluded both the specific information they had learned from direct experi-ence of the layout and their general knowledge about what is typically found in a kitchen.

If young children are able to develop environmental schemas, this might have contributed to their success when Blaut and Stea (1974) asked them to model an urban landscape. In the same way, if children already have the concept of a typical urban environment, this may contribute to their inter-pretation of aerial photographs. Taken together the results from Blaut and Stea and from the studies with aerial photographs suggest that young chil-dren have a good ability to represent or interpret representations of the larger environment. Is this surprising? As we noted previously, it is un-likely that young children have had any previous experience of aerial pho-tographs before they are asked to use them in the course of an experiment, and therefore, their ability to talk about such photographs as landscapes might be unexpected.

However, children's ability to make toy layouts might be less unex-pected because most children of kindergarten age will be familiar with models of landscape features (houses, buildings, trees, and so on). More specifically, children often have experience of commercially produced "play mats" that are printed with road and town layouts. They may have LEGO® and other town layouts, as well as particular toy representations (e.g., farm sets, zoo sets, and rail layouts). Interaction with all these representations of real environments might, as Blaut and Stea (1974) suggested, contribute to young children's ability to make landscape models.

Blaut and Stea's (1974) study is the only one we know that has tested very young children's ability to make a model landscape. However, Dijkink and Elbers (1980) carried out a similar study with older children. Dijkink and Elbers asked 7-, 9- and 12-year-olds to make a model of a city. The children were given a board with roads, a rail track, and a river painted on it and model buildings that included representations of old and new houses, shops, city center buildings, factories, and farms. Dijkink and Elbers found that some of the youngest children in their study were poor at making a coherent representation of a city because they showed a lack of structure and did not place similar elements together so that, for example, farms, factories, and old and new houses were placed anywhere on the board. The poor performance of some of the 7-year-olds in Dijkink and Elbers' study is in marked contrast to the results reported by Blaut and Stea from much younger children. For this reason, we carried out a replication of Blaut and Stea's research.

Can 3- and 4-Year-Olds Represent Landscapes in Toy Play?

Thirty-two 3- and 4-year-old children (with a mean age of 4 years) were tested individually. A large sheet of plain white paper was laid out on the floor and on one corner of the paper there was a pile of toy items. These included buildings, trees, vehicles, and cardboard pieces painted with road markings. The items were pointed out to the children, but otherwise the only instruction was, "Why don't you play with these on here [indicating the paper]?" If the child was hesitant, various neutral prompts were used (e.g., "see what you can make"), but at no point were any suggestions given about what the child should make. Children were allowed as long as they liked to play with the toys, and they were filmed while doing so.

A third of the children did nothing with the items other than rearrange them in the pile on the corner. The remaining children did place the items on the paper, but they showed little planning in the way they placed items. Although most of the children put a road piece on the paper first, only 8 children laid out all the road pieces before placing other items (although not all these children connected the pieces; sometimes they were just placed individually on the paper). About half the children took the nearest item from the pile and placed it on the paper, and usually did not move it again. These children gave the impression of randomly picking up and placing items with no regard to making a layout. The other half of the children did select items from the pile, but there was little difference between their layouts and the layouts made by the children who were placing items apparently randomly.

We used the following categories to classify the performance of the 32 children. The categories were "non-starters" who were children who just played with the toys in the pile without attempting to make a layout.

"Grouping" was when children placed all the buildings together, all the trees together, and all the cars together. Children in this category would typically make a row of all the buildings (sometimes putting those with the same colored roofs together), or all the trees in a line, or place all the cars in a line on a single road piece. These groups would often be on distinct areas of the paper. "Ambiguous" was when children did not group similar items together but spread them out over the paper; however, they did so with little coherence. For instance, children might put one or two road pieces together but not connect all of them. Or they might place some buildings and trees next to a road piece as if to begin a model but then put the rest of the items anywhere on the paper. The other category was "geographical" when children placed all or most of the items in a way that could represent a town.

Almost all the children were classified in the first two categories (non-starters or grouping). Four were categorized as making ambiguous layouts, but only one made a model that could be said to be a representation of a town. These results did not support the findings from Blaut and Stea (1974) because we found little evidence that 3- to 4-year-olds spontaneously used the toy items to make a layout that could be described as a landscape.

In both our study and in Blaut and Stea's (1974) study, the children were given minimum instructions. However, in Blaut and Stea the children had been given preliminary practice in which they were asked to make a "street corner" and this procedure may have given the children a cue about using the toys to make a landscape. Therefore, we repeated our first experiment with a further group of 31 3- and 4-year-olds. In the second experiment, the procedure was exactly the same as in the first study, but we gave the children explicit instructions to "make a place where people live, like a town or a city." Despite the explicit nature of the instructions, the results from the second experiment were very similar to those of the first experiment, and only 6 children made a geographical layout.

We repeated the experiment a third time with 14 of the children who had taken part in the second study. Again we used the explicit instructions, but this time we laid out a few road pieces in a simple grid pattern before the children were given the remainder of the items. We thought that the provision of a partial layout might encourage the children to complete a geographical layout. The children in this experiment were more likely to connect their road pieces to the ones that had already been placed, and this provided some with a better framework in which to place the buildings. Nonetheless, only one child produced a layout that could be classified as geographical.

The results of these studies showed that only a very small proportion of 3- to 4-year-olds made a toy layout that could be called a representation of a landscape. Almost all the children placed the items either in an arbitrary manner across the paper, with little or no connection between elements, or they just placed items of a similar kind together in rows or groups. When we carried out similar studies with 5- and 6-year-olds, we found that less than half the children made geographical layouts.

It is possible that making the instructions even more explicit (e.g., asking the children to make a specific place they knew) or providing more context (e.g., giving the children toy people and asking them to make a town for those people) might have prompted more landscape models.[2] Nonetheless, our results stand in contrast to Blaut and Stea (1974) who suggested that children as young as 3 could spontaneously represent places in the course of toy play.

As we noted at the beginning of this section, young children are familiar with "play mats" and with many toy layouts, and they may play with these in their own homes or in kindergarten. The obvious assumption from this sort of play would be that children are either reflecting what they have already learned about the environment from direct experience or that playing with the toys may contribute to children's awareness of spatial relations. This assumption seemed to be supported by Blaut and Stea's (1974) early findings. However, given our recent experiments, we would suggest caution in thinking that toy play necessarily leads to geographical understanding in very young children. The 3- and 4-year-olds in our studies showed little spontaneous ability to make a model that reflected a coherent representation of an environment.

CONCLUSIONS

The main part of this chapter has been a description of research with aerial photographs. This research has shown that young children are good at identifying features on aerial photographs (Craddock, 2001) and that this ability goes beyond just labeling items in a picture because kindergarten children can treat an aerial photograph of a landscape as a representation of that landscape (Plester et al., 2002; Shevelan, 2001).

Previous researchers have shown that even younger children can treat models and maps of small spaces as representations (Blades & Spencer, 1994; DeLoache, 1989), but these demonstrations of representational understanding have been carried out in limited spaces. We found that within 1 or 2 years of first understanding simple representations such as a model of a room, children can demonstrate an understanding of aerial photographs as representations of large environmental spaces. This reflects rapid development in children's understanding of spatial representations during the preschool and very early school years. We assume that this development is an untrained one because young children do not receive experience or practice in the use of aerial photographs. This finding provides some support for Blaut's (1991) theory of natural mapping in the sense that young children do not need specific training in looking at aerial photographs to under-

---

[2]We are grateful to Gary Allen for the suggestions about other ways to prompt young children's model making and the potential importance of seeing transformations of perspective.

stand them as representations of the environment. However, the results from the toy play experiments have different implications for any theory that stresses early mapping competence.

In contrast to the findings from the aerial photograph studies, the toy play research does not provide any support for Blaut's (1991) theory of natural mapping. The emphasis of that theory is on young children's ability to map the world around them. However, in the previously mentioned studies, the 4-year-olds' lack of modeling and the poor performance of 5- and 6-year-olds showed that children do not have a natural ability to represent the world through toy play. Blaut (1991) suggested that understanding aerial photographs might not only develop from the child's own experience of looking down at the world (e.g., from any high vantage point or from being lifted and carried) but also from the opportunity to look down on models of the world in the course of toy play. This implies that modeling through toy play should either be a precursor for understanding aerial photographs or at least be an equivalent development. However, as we have pointed out, we found that interpreting aerial views is achieved well before the age when children can make representations in play.

Although this research was not designed to address Uttal's (2000) theory directly, our findings can be considered in the context of his theory. Uttal suggested that learning about maps may contribute to the way that children think about the space around them. If so, children's understanding of representations will precede their ability to make model layouts. Creating a realistic layout involves an explicit awareness of typical spatial relations between features, and children may need experience of recognizing such relations (e.g., from maps and photographs) before they are able to model them.

This leaves open the question of how untrained children come to understand representations like aerial photographs. At present, we can only speculate on the answer to this question. One possibility is that as young children's travel experience increases, they gain a better understanding of large spaces, and this contributes to their ability to interpret aerial photographs. A second possibility is that children do experience different views of the world, including aerial views, through media such as television, film, and picture books. Children may even see transformations of perspective from ground level to aerial views (e.g., as planes take off or as cartoon characters fly) and these experiences may contribute to their understanding of aerial photographs.[2] After all, young children do not seem to be discomforted when watching cartoons or films that include scenes showing the landscape from above. This is an issue that can be investigated empirically by studying children's interpretations of such scenes. As yet, these possibilities are only speculations, but the rapid development in children's understanding of landscape representations is an aspect of cognitive development that deserves more research.

ACKNOWLEDGMENTS

We are grateful for awards (SBR–9423865 and BCS–9906604) from the National Science Foundation (United States) to Jim Blaut, David Stea, Christopher Spencer, and Mark Blades and for an Economic and Social Research Council (United Kingdom) scholarship to Caroline Shevelan, which supported several of the studies discussed in this chapter. Others were supported by grants from Barnsley College, Coventry University, and the University of Sheffield. This research was inspired by the original work of Jim Blaut and David Stea and is better for the constant support, argument, and debate provided by Jim Blaut, who was always convinced that young children make good geographers.

REFERENCES

Blades, M. (2000). Young children's understanding of indirect sources of spatial information. *Developmental Science, 3*, 265–266.

Blades, M., & Banham, J. (1990). Children's memory in an environmental learning task. *Journal of Environmental Education and Information, 9*, 119–131.

Blades, M., Blaut, J., Davizeh, Z., Elguea, S., Sowden, S., Soni, D., Spencer, C., Stea, D., Surajpauli, R., & Uttal, D. (1998). A cross-cultural study of young children's mapping abilities. *Transactions of the Institute of British Geographers, 23*, 269–277.

Blades, M., Hetherington, D., Spencer, C., & Sowden, S. (1997, April). *Can young children recognize aerial photographs?* Paper presented to the biennial meeting of the Society for Research in Child Development, Washington, DC.

Blades, M., & Spencer, C. (1994). The development of children's ability to use spatial representations. *Advances in Child Development and Behavior, 25*, 157–199.

Blades, M., Spencer, C., Patel, H., & Mannion, A. (1999, April). *Young children's identification of landmarks on aerial photographs.* Paper presented to the biennial meeting of the Society for Research in Child Development, Albuquerque, NM.

Blades, M., Ungar, S., & Spencer, C. (1999). Map using by adults with visual impairments. *Professional Geographer, 51*, 539–553.

Blaut, J. M. (1991). Natural mapping. *Transactions of the Institute of British Geographers, 16*, 55–74.

Blaut, J. M. (1997). The mapping abilities of young children. Children can. *Annals of the Association of American Geographers, 87*, 152–158.

Blaut, J. M., McCleary, G. S., & Blaut, A. S. (1970). Environmental mapping in young children. *Environment and Behavior, 2*, 335–349.

Blaut, J. M., & Stea, D. (1974). Mapping at the age of three. *Journal of Geography, 73*, 5–9.

Bremner, J. G., & Andreasen, G. (1998). Young children's ability to use maps and models to find ways in novel spaces. *British Journal of Developmental Psychology, 16*, 197–218.

Craddock, S. (2001). *Young children's abilities to use aerial photographs as simple maps.* Master's thesis, University of Sheffield, Sheffield, England.

DeLoache, J. (1989). The development of representation in young children. *Advances in Child Development and Behavior, 22*, 1–39.

DeLoache, J. (2000). Dual representation and young children's use of scale models. *Child Development, 71*, 329–338.

Dijkink, G., & Elbers, E. (1980). The development of geographic representation in children. Cognitive and affective aspects of model-building behaviour. *Tijdschrift voor Economische en Sociale Geografie, 72*, 2–16.

Ferguson, E. L., & Hegarty, M. (1994) Properties of cognitive maps constructed from texts. *Memory and Cognition, 22,* 455–473.

Gattis, M. (Ed.). (2001). *Spatial schemas and abstract thought.* Cambridge, MA: MIT Press.

Kitchin, R. M., & Blades, M. (2002). *The cognition of geographic space.* London: Tauris.

Liben, L. S. (2001). Thinking through maps. In M. Gattis (Ed.), *Spatial schemas and abstract thought* (pp. 45–77). Cambridge, MA: MIT Press.

Liben, L. S., & Downs, R. (1991). The role of graphic representations in understanding the world. In R. M. Downs, L. S. Liben, & D. S. Palermo (Eds)., *Visions of aesthetics, the environment and development: The legacy of Joachim F. Wohlwell.* Hillsdale, NJ: Lawrence Erlbaum Associates, Inc.

Liben, L. S., & Downs, R. (1997). Can-ism and Can'tianism: A straw child. *Annals of the Association of American Geographers, 87,* 159–167.

Loewenstein, J., & Gentner, D. (2001). Spatial mapping in preschoolers: Close comparisons facilitate far mappings. *Journal of Cognition and Development, 2,* 189–219.

MacEachren, A. M. (1995) *How maps work. Representation, visualization and design.* New York: Guilford.

Matthews, M. H. (1992). *Making sense of place: Children's understanding of large-scale environments.* Hemel Hempstead, England: Harvester Wheatsheaf.

Moeser, S. D. (1988). Cognitive mapping in a complex building. *Environment and Behavior, 20,* 21–49.

Piaget, J., & Inhelder, B. (1956). *The child's conception of space.* London: Routledge & Kegan Paul.

Plester, B., Richards, J., Blades, M., & Spencer, C. (2002). Young children's ability to use aerial photographs as maps. *Journal of Environmental Psychology, 22,* 29–47.

Richardson, A. E., Montello, D. R., & Hegarty, M. (1999). Spatial knowledge acquisition from maps, and from navigation in real and virtual environments. *Memory and Cognition, 27,* 741–750.

Rossano, M. J., Warren, D. H., & Kenan, A. (1995). Orientation specificity: How general is it? *American Journal of Psychology, 108,* 359–380.

Shevelan, C., (2001). *The effects of materials, complexity and knowledge on three- to six-year olds' ability to relate a spatial representation to a referent space.* Unpublished doctoral dissertation, University of Sheffield, Sheffield, England.

Siegel, A. W., & White, S. (1975). The development of spatial representation of large scale environments. *Advances in Child Development and Behavior, 10,* 9–55.

Sowden, S., Stea, D., Blades, M., Spencer, C., & Blaut, J. (1996). Mapping abilities of four-year-old children in York, England. *Journal of Geography, 95,* 107–111.

Spencer, C., Blades, M., & Morsley, K. (1989). *The child in the physical environment.* Chichester, England: Wiley.

Spencer, C. P., Harrison, N., & Darvizeh, Z. (1980). The development of iconic mapping ability in young children. *International Journal of Early Childhood, 12,* 57–64.

Stea, D., & Blaut, J. M. (1973). Some preliminary observations on spatial learning in school children. In R. M. Downs and D. Stea (Eds.), *Image and environment* (pp. 226–234). Chicago: Aldine.

Taylor, H. A., & Tversky, B. (1992). Spatial mental models derived from survey and route descriptions. *Journal of Memory and Language, 31,* 261–292.

Tversky, B. (2000). Level and structure of spatial knowledge. In R. Kitchin & S. Freundschuh (Eds.), *Cognitive mapping, past, present and future* (pp. 24–43). London: Routledge.

Uttal, D. (2000). Seeing the big picture: Map use and the development of spatial cognition. *Developmental Science, 3,* 247–264.

Uttal, D., & Wellman, H. M. (1989). Children's mental representation of spatial information acquired from maps. *Developmental Psychology, 25,* 128–138.

Putting Spatial Memories Into Perspective:
Brain and Behavioral Evidence for Representational Differences

Amy Lynne Shelton
Johns Hopkins University

Spatial memory is a complex phenomenon that holds a unique position in human cognition at the crossroads of low-level perceptual processing (e.g., perception of depth cues and three-dimensional structure) and high-level constructive processes (e.g., integration over successive views). One can observe behaviors that can best be described as relying on spatial memory in other primates (Rolls, 1991), rats (Cho & Kesner, 1996; Olton & Samuelson, 1976), and even honey bees (Collett & Cartwright, 1983), yet human navigation and spatial memory seem intuitively difficult to characterize fully. The goal of this chapter is to address this issue by exploring how evidence from studies of the brain, in conjunction with behavioral results, can elucidate the multifaceted nature of human spatial cognition.

Understanding spatial cognition in humans has benefited from a long tradition of single unit recording and lesion studies in the brains of other animals. These studies have provided a wealth of information about what areas of the brain might be important to spatial cognition and how the neurons in those regions operate at the electrophysiological level. Observations of individuals with brain damage have further informed researchers about areas of the brain that participate in spatial cognition by identifying how injuries to particular brain regions produce deficits in performance on spatial tasks. However, these studies provide limited insight into how networks of areas might work together in the intact human brain during spatial learning and memory. With the advent of neuro-imaging techniques such as event-related potentials, positron emission tomography (PET), functional magnetic resonance imaging (fMRI), and magnetoencephalography, it became possible for researchers to study the intact human brain in action. As computer presentation and virtual reality technology have evolved, the exploration of spatial learning and memory in the functioning human brain has been realized.

KEY QUESTION: DIFFERENCES IN SPATIAL LEARNING

Spatial memory is often addressed as if it relies on one type of memory representation. For example, comparisons are often made between deficits in spatial processing compared to deficits in object processing (Ettlinger, 1990) or in verbal processing (e.g., Langdon & Warrington, 2000; Maguire & Cipolotti, 1998). Similarly, the neurophysiological literature has differentiated processing streams for object-based information and information about positions in space in the delineation of the "what" and "where" pathways (Mishkin, Ungerleider, & Macko, 1983). Like the neurophysiological and neuropsychological studies, much of the initial neuroimaging of spatial cognition focused on the differences between spatial processing and nonspatial processing. For example, differences have been proposed for spatial versus verbal processing (e.g., Frisk & Milner, 1990; Milner, 1971; Smith, Jonides, & Koeppe, 1996) or for spatial versus object processing (e.g., Courtney, Petit, Maisog, Ungerleider, & Haxby, 1998; Courtney, Ungerleider, Keil, & Haxby, 1996; Postle, Stern, Rosen, & Corkin, 2000).

Although spatial versus nonspatial distinctions have played a major role in understanding spatial processing, there is a tendency to assume that spatial information is a unitary concept. In the world, however, spatial experiences come in a wide variety. Spaces vary in scale from small spaces (e.g., tabletops) to large spaces (e.g., an entire continent). Space can be structured artificially through the application of geometric principles, as in a well-planned building, or structured naturally through the effects of weather and wildlife on the terrain, as in a forest preserve. Moreover, spatial learning for a given environment can occur in many different ways (see Montello, Waller, Hegarty, & Richardson, chap. 11, this volume). For example, we as humans learn a great deal about the environments of everyday life by navigating within our surroundings. When we are in an unfamiliar setting, we might use a map to help us learn where things are located. We can also learn from verbal or text descriptions of space. This type of spatial information can take the form of someone giving us directions (e.g., "Turn left onto Amarillo Ave. You will see a school on your right ...") or the form of someone describing a spatial array (e.g., "In the living room of my apartment, there is a large window on the south-facing wall, a small couch lines the wall under the window, with two end tables on either side ..."). For a given environment (a new campus, for instance), one can learn about the spatial layout from one or more of these sources. Given this wide variety of experiences one can have with a spatial environment, an important consideration for spatial memory is the degree to which different spatial learning conditions influence the representation of space in memory.

The goal of this chapter is to look at the convergence of behavioral and brain data on an understanding of how different types of spatial information are represented in the brain. The primary argument is that memory representations of space vary as a function of the specific experience(s) one has with the space. To address this question requires careful consideration of (a) the behavioral evidence for subsequent memory effects due to different types of spatial learning, (b) current understanding of the brain mechanisms that might underlie spatial representation in general, and (c) the convergence of brain and behavioral data to develop a more comprehensive understanding of how different representations might map onto the structures and functions of the brain.

BEHAVIORAL EVIDENCE FOR EFFECTS OF SPATIAL LEARNING ON REPRESENTATION

One well-established example of how changing spatial learning conditions affects spatial memory is the demonstration of orientation dependence in the mental representation of spatial arrays (see McNamara & Valiquette, chap. 1, this volume). When a spatial array of objects is learned from a specific subset of possible viewpoints, subsequent memory performance varies as a function of the particular views learned (Diwadkar & McNamara, 1997; Roskos-Ewoldsen, McNamara, Shelton, & Carr, 1998; Shelton & McNamara, 1997, 2001a). For example, cover the right panel of Fig. 13.1,

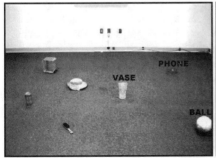

FIG. 13.1.   Two different views of a floor display like those used in Roskos-Ewoldsen, McNamara, Shelton, and Carr (1998) and Shelton and McNamara (1997, 2001a).

look at the object display in the left panel, and attempt the following judgments: (a) imagine you are at the ball facing the phone; point to the vase; and (b) imagine you are at the ball facing the vase; point to the phone. Now, cover the left panel, look at the right panel, and answer the same questions.

When participants were asked to learn displays like these from a single perspective and then make judgments like those just mentioned from memory, results revealed that they could make judgments better when the test orientation corresponded to the learned view (Roskos-Ewoldsen et al., 1998; Shelton & McNamara, 2001a). In other words, participants would find judgment A easier than judgment B if they learned the display from the view in the Fig. 13.1 left panel, whereas they would find judgment B easier than judgment A if they learned the display from the view in the Fig. 13.1. right panel. Moreover, the orientations with which people were fastest and most accurate could be manipulated by changing the number and locations of the learned views relative to the larger environmental context (Shelton & McNamara, 2001a). Together, these results demonstrate a simple example of how one aspect of experience (viz., orientation) can affect the representation and/or retrieval of spatial information.

Changing the viewing orientation represents one type of change in the spatial learning experience, but it does not speak to the representational consequences of more drastic changes such as differences between map learning and navigational learning. Maps generally provide spatial information in a holistic form (often using abstract symbols), allowing the observer to see the entire environment at once or through visual scanning. Alternatively, navigation provides the observer with successive views from within the space. Access to the global structure of the environment is indirect; that is, it must be constructed by integrating the information available in the successive views. Comparisons of memory for an environment learned through navigation and through map reading have produced different behavioral consequences (e.g., Moeser, 1988; Streeter, Vitello, & Wonsiewicz, 1985; Thorndyke & Hayes-Roth, 1982). Thorndyke and Hayes-Roth (1982) compared people who learned a building by navigating in it to people who learned solely from a map. They found that the two different groups varied in performance on tests of spatial memory. However, participants in these studies differed not only in the type of perspective (map or navigation) but also in the amount of time spent learning. The navigation learning took place over extended time periods, whereas map learning was done in a limited number of sessions.

Several studies have investigated differences analogous to the differences between navigation and map learning by controlling the exposure time. One approach has been to present participants with text descriptions of environments written from either the route or survey perspective (e.g., Ferguson & Hegarty, 1994; Langer, Keenan, Wetzel, Jacques-Griffin, & Chiszar, 1996; Perrig & Kintsch, 1985; Taylor & Tversky, 1992; Tversky, 1991). Route texts (navigation) describe an environment sequentially, as if the reader were taking a walking (or driving) tour of the space (e.g., "As you enter the market, there is a policeman to your left and a lamppost to your right …"). Survey texts (maplike) describe the environment in terms of the spatial organization and use cardinal directions (e.g., "In the center of the market, there are four booths, one facing in each direction. The cheese stand is in the north-facing booth …"). People's ability to answer inference questions about route and survey level information after each type of text provides insight into the consequences of these different sources of spatial information.

Using route and survey text descriptions, Perrig and Kintsch (1985) found that participants could make either route or survey inferences when they learned an environment from a survey description, whereas participants were impaired on survey inferences (compared to route inferences) when they learned the environment from a route description. In contrast, Taylor and Tversky (1992; see also Tversky, 1991) found that both route and survey descriptions of fictional environments led to equivalent performance on route and survey inferences, suggesting no subsequent memory difference. The results of these direct comparisons of route and survey text are therefore inconclusive with respect to differential memory representations.

Shelton and McNamara (in press) compared route and survey learning in both the visual and textual realm. To better approximate navigation and map learning, visual displays were created using desktop virtual reality. The virtual environments paralleled the environments in Taylor and Tversky's (1992) text descriptions, and movies were made from a route perspective (ground-level observer walking in space) and from a survey perspective (aerial perspective panning over the space). Participants studied the environments in one of four learning conditions: route text, route visual, survey text, or survey visual. Following the learning, all participants were tested on scene recognition of scenes from both the route and survey perspectives. Results indicated that recognition was faster when the environment was studied and tested in the same perspective than when the perspective changed between study and test. The same-perspective facilitation was equivalent for route and survey learning, producing a symmetrical interaction for study by test type. Moreover, this facilitation occurred following both the visual and text presentation, suggesting that it was not due entirely to the visual similarity of the study and test information.[1] Instead, these results suggest that route and survey information were encoded differently in the brain, supporting distinct representations for these two types of spatial information.

Together, the results of the behavioral work make a strong case for subsequent memory effects due to differences in the spatial learning perspec-

---

[1]The only visual information provided in the text conditions consisted of images of individual landmarks. These images were taken from a perspective intermediate to the route and survey visual perspectives. As such, the visual information in the route and survey text conditions was identical.

tive. In turn, this supports the claim that different spatial learning experiences lead to differences in the underlying memory representations. However, what do these behavioral differences tell researchers about the nature of the relation between learning from the route perspective and learning from the survey perspective? Early speculations about spatial learning and development have suggested that route knowledge was a precursor to survey knowledge (Appleyard, 1969, 1970; Evans, Marrero, & Butler, 1981; Millar, 1994; Siegel & White, 1975; but see Taylor, Naylor, & Chechile, 1999), but these studies focused on the underlying knowledge constructs rather than the sources of learning. Studies of route and survey information as sources of spatial information tell a different story. As noted previously, different information appears to be available in memory when an environment is learned through navigation compared to maps (Moeser, 1988; Thorndyke & Hayes-Roth, 1982). However, the symmetrical interaction between study and test perspective in scene recognition (Shelton & McNamara, in press) suggests that route and survey information during spatial learning do not appear to be hierarchically related. Instead, route and survey perspectives appear to reflect two different types of spatial information, perhaps two of many.

BRAIN AREAS ASSOCIATED WITH SPATIAL PROCESSING

One approach to interpreting the behavioral differences resulting from different types of spatial learning is to consider what brain areas might be associated with spatial processing and how different types of spatial information might engage those areas (see Morris & Parslow, chap. 10, this volume). From animal studies and observations of humans with brain injuries, three primary regions of interest have been identified as participating in spatial learning and memory: the parietal cortex, the hippocampal formation, and the retrosplenial cortex.

Neurons in subregions of the parietal cortex in nonhuman primates respond selectively to locations of objects in space (Colby & Goldberg, 1999; Hyvarinen & Poranen, 1974; Mountcastle, Lynch, Georgopoulos, Sakata, & Acuna, 1975). In humans, damage to the inferior portion of the posterior parietal cortex is associated with spatial neglect, a syndrome in which patients tend to ignore the half of a stimulus or display contralateral to the side of the lesion (Critchley, 1953; Robertson & Marshall, 1993). Although neglect has generally been characterized as a deficit in attention to a particular region of space or part of an object, the spatial nature of the impairment strongly supports the role of the parietal cortex in spatial processing and representation. Furthermore, ample evidence points to the posterior parietal and temporal regions being critically involved in object-location memory (see Postma, Kessels, & van Asselen, chap. 7, this volume).

In the rat hippocampus, neurons have been shown to respond selectively when the navigating rat was in a particular location in space (e.g.,

McNaughton, Barnes, & O'Keefe, 1983). The discovery of these "place cells" lead to the conclusion that the hippocampal region plays a role in the encoding and/or storage of cognitive maps (O'Keefe & Nadel, 1978). Likewise, in nonhuman primates, neurons have been identified that fire selectively when a monkey views a stimulus in a particular location in space. These "spatial view cells," like place cells in rats, support the role for the hippocampus in spatial learning and navigation (Rolls, 1999). Furthermore, damage to the hippocampus and nearby structures has been shown to impair spatial navigation and memory performance in rats (Morris, Garrud, Rawlins, & O'Keefe, 1982; Warburton, Baird, Morgan, Muir, & Aggleton, 2001), nonhuman primates (Zola-Morgan & Squire, 1985, 1986), and humans (Smith & Milner, 1981; Warrington & Baddeley, 1974).

The retrosplenial cortex, a region deep in the parietal cortex, provides an important pathway to the hippocampus in the rat (Chen, Lin, Barnes, & McNaughton, 1994; Chen, Lin, Green, Barnes, & McNaughton, 1994; Cho & Sharp, 2001). Temporary inactivation of the rat's retrosplenial cortex has been shown to cause changes in the place-cell properties of hippocampal neurons, suggesting that the two regions may cooperate in the path integration necessary for successful navigation (Cooper & Mizumori, 2001). In humans, this area likely corresponds to the posterior cingulate/retrosplenial cortex (Brodmann Areas 23/29/30). Damage to this brain region has been shown to impair spatial problem solving, including the acquisition of novel routes and navigation in familiar environments (Maguire, 2001).

Together, these brain regions are thought to be components of a spatial processing network, and differences in the properties of these regions suggest different roles for the different regions (for review, see Burgess, Jeffery, & O'Keefe, 1999). For example, it has been proposed that the hippocampal place cells are representing the environment in an allocentric, or environmentally centered, reference frame (O'Keefe & Nadel, 1978). Alternatively, the parietal cortex uses egocentric reference frames, with different subregions encoding information according to retinal-centered, head-centered, or arm-centered locations (e.g., Colby & Goldberg, 1999). This variety of reference frames may be related to the specific roles of these subregions in detecting and/or remembering locations for specific actions such as reaching and grasping or eye movements. To understand how these different functions might work together in spatial learning and memory requires an exploration of these areas operating concurrently.

Neuroimaging provides a way to explore multiple regions of the brain working together in the intact brain. For spatial memory, the results of a number of studies have been largely consistent with the expectations set forth by the neurophysiology and neuropsychological findings identifying a network of brain regions involved in human spatial memory (Fig. 13.2). In addition to the three primary areas identified by neurophysiology/ neuropsychology (hippocampus, parietal cortex—postcentral gyrus and precuneus—and posterior cingulate/retrosplenial cortex), regions of the

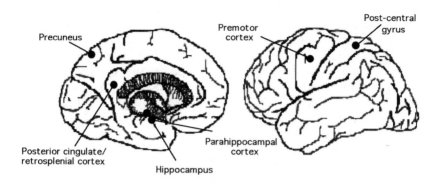

FIG. 13.2.   Medial (left) and lateral (right) views of the brain showing areas that have been identified as important for human navigational memory.

premotor and parahippocampal cortices appear to participate in human spatial processing (Aguirre & D'Esposito, 1997; Aguirre, Zarahn, & D'Esposito, 1998; Epstein & Kanwisher, 1998; Ghaëm et al., 1997; Maguire et al., 1998, Maguire, Frackowiak, & Frith, 1997; Mesulam, Nobre, Kim, Parrish, & Gitelman, 2001).

The research paradigms used to identify this spatial processing network have generally contrasted memory for spatial navigation and memory for individual objects or landmarks. For example, Maguire et al. (1997) compared taxi drivers' memories for specific routes through a familiar town with memories for specific landmarks in the same environment. Results revealed that the right hippocampus, bilateral parahippocampal cortex, and bilateral precuneus were more active during the spatial (route-recollection) task than during the object (landmark-recollection) task. Similarly, when participants were asked to mentally imagine navigating a previously learned route versus mentally imagining static landmarks, activation was observed in the left hippocampus, precuneus, and insula (Ghaëm et al., 1997). When participants were explicitly instructed to explore a virtual environment at the route level, a similar network of areas were identified for such exploration, including the parahippocampal cortex, precuneus, and posterior cingulate (Aguirre et al., 1998). The parahippocampal cortex has also been associated with memory for scenes when compared to memory for individual objects (Epstein & Kanwisher, 1998). Despite some variability in the left–right location across studies, these results provide support for a hippocampal-parietal network of brain regions for spatial learning and memory.

Although not all of the previous studies explicitly required navigation, the scenes and memories that were tested typically took the form of route-level information. As such, these results provide evidence for a spatial processing network for route-based spatial information distinct from object information, but they do not speak directly to the role of this network in processing, representing, and/or retrieving different types of spatial information.

DIFFERENTIATION IN THE BRAIN WITHIN SPATIAL PROCESSING

If different types of spatial information are represented differently in the brain, then it is reasonable to consider whether these representations are the product of distinct neural mechanisms for encoding and retrieving these different perspectives. The behavioral dissociation could be the associated with recruitment of different brain areas for encoding different types of information or differential activation within the same spatial processing network. Mounting evidence from neurophysiology and neuropsychology already suggests that multiple representations and multiple frames of reference across different brain areas are used to represent space (Colby & Goldberg, 1999; Halligan & Marshall, 1991; Marshall & Halligan, 1995; Weiss et al., 2000). In addition, the literature on topographical disorientation, a disorder marked by difficulties in dealing with large-scale space, has suggested that deficits can occur to very specific aspects of spatial processing (Aguirre & D'Esposito, 1999). For example, a patient might show route navigation impairment with intact map drawing and landmark identification (Suzuki, Yamadori, Hayakawa, & Fujii, 1998). The evidence suggests that a given spatial memory likely has separable components, but how do different types of spatial learning tap into these components, engage the associated brain regions, and interact with their particular representations of space?

Appealing to the behavioral distinction between route and survey perspectives, neuroimaging studies have begun to identify different neural correlates associated with these two different types of spatial information. Mellet et al. (2000) compared a group of individuals who learned the spatial layout of a park from navigating in the environment (route learning) and a second group who learned the park from a map (survey learning). After the learning phase, PET scans were conducted on participants in each group while they were asked to mentally "replay" either the route (mental navigation) or the map (mental map) from the learning phase. Both types of mental exploration were compared to rest scans during which participants laid in the dark with eyes closed. Results revealed that both the mental navigation and the mental map activated a number of regions relative to rest. Most notably, both conditions activated the right hippocampus (cf. Morris & Parslow, chap. 10, this volume). When directly compared, mental navigation showed greater activation in the bilateral parahippocampal cortex, left posterior cingulate, and left precuneus. These areas were not activated for the mental map relative to rest, suggesting that these regions, previously identified in the spatial processing network, were specific to remembering the mental navigation or route-level information. The mental map condition also showed areas of exclusive activation but in regions not typically associated with spatial processing (right superior temporal gyrus, precentral sulcus, and Hechl's gyrus). These results indicated that retrieving information from route learning recruited some of the spatial processing areas that retrieval from survey learning did not engage, suggesting that indeed these two types of information were previously encoded/represented differently.

One advantage of neuroimaging studies is the ability to look at the brain when there is no behavior to observe, as is the case with encoding. Investigating the brain activation during encoding provides insights into the processes that produce the memory representations, allowing speculation about the neural mechanisms underlying subsequent performance differences. Although encoding through navigation in physical environments is not currently possible with neuroimaging, navigation in virtual environments provides a tool for exploring the visual elements of navigation. In a study of visual route and survey encoding (Shelton & Gabrieli, 2002), participants were scanned using fMRI while they learned two different virtual environments, one from the route perspective (Fig. 13.3 top-left) and one from the survey perspective (Fig. 13.3 top-right). Using virtual environments, participants repeatedly watched movies of the two environments (route and survey perspective)[2] interspersed with blocks of fixation (rest). When either type of encoding was compared to rest, a number of brain areas were activated, but the critical question was whether differential activation was observed for route and survey encoding.

The results suggested that survey encoding engaged a specialized subset of areas activated by the route encoding, with greater activation in certain areas within that subset. These areas of greater activation included the bilateral fusiform gyrus, inferior temporal gyrus, and the posterior part of the superior parietal cortex. As shown in Fig. 13.3 bottom-left, these areas overlapped completely with areas that were activated by route encoding relative to fixation. As shown in Fig. 13.3 bottom-right, this was not true for areas that were more active for route encoding than for survey encoding. In addition to the areas that overlapped between route and survey encoding, route encoding activated the bilateral posterior hippocampus and parahippocampal cortex, the bilateral posterior cingulate and precuneus, the bilateral postcentral gyrus, and a region of the left medial frontal cortex.[3] Notably, these regions correspond to the key regions in the spatial processing network and again appear to be exclusive to route level spatial information.

---

[2]These conditions replicated the visual conditions of Shelton and McNamara (in press).

[3]Route encoding showed greater activation than survey encoding in more anterior portions of the parietal cortex and the cuneus, which also showed activation in survey encoding relative to fixation.

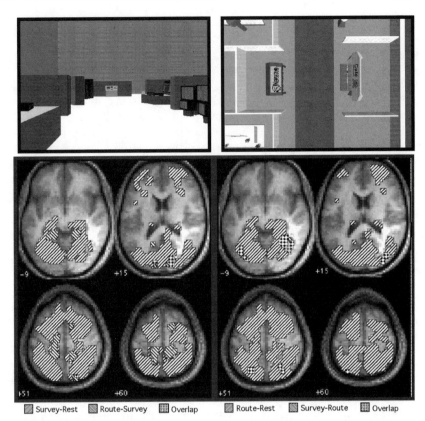

Survey-Rest   Route-Survey   Overlap   Route-Rest   Survey-Route   Overlap

FIG. 13.3. Top panel shows examples of route and survey visual stimuli: (top-left) still image of a virtual convention center taken from the route perspective and (top-right) still image of a virtual market square taken from the survey perspective. Bottom panel shows a qualitative summary of the results from Shelton and Gabrieli (2002). Bottom-left shows areas of greater activation for route encoding than for survey encoding overlapping very little with areas that were positively activated by survey encoding. Bottom-right shows areas of greater activation for survey encoding than for route encoding overlapping entirely with areas that were positively activated by route encoding. (Activation maps shown at liberal thresholds, $p < .005$ uncorrected, to decrease Type II error in evaluating overlap.)

Taken together, the results from encoding and retrieval suggest that although there are regions common to route and survey information in the brain, the regions of the spatial processing network may be engaged much more in route-based learning and memory than in survey learning. During retrieval, both perspectives appeared to recruit the hippocampus (Mellet et al., 2000), but this region appeared to be exclusively activated by route information during encoding. The presence of hippocampal activation during survey retrieval is not surprising given evidence for hippocampal activation in more general retrieval tasks (hippocampal role in memory discussed following; see also Stark & Squire, 2000a, 2000b). What is notable is the strong activation of this and related regions in route-level encoding and retrieval, with little or no activation in these regions for the survey encoding relative to a baseline of fixation.

IMPLICATIONS FOR SPATIAL MEMORY

The literature on spatial cognition spans a wide variety of questions and methods. Behavioral studies have expanded researchers' understanding of spatial cognition in terms of what people can do and how they perform under a number of conditions. Likewise, neuroimaging studies have provided considerable insight into the brain regions that subserve spatial processing. When taken together, the results begin to tell a story about the way in which the brain processes different types of spatial information. As expected from the behavioral data, route and survey information can be distinguished in the brain. However, the symmetry of the behavioral data was not associated with symmetry in the brain results. First, these two types of spatial information do not appear to be subserved by largely separable networks. Instead, it appears that survey knowledge recruits a specialized subset of the route-processing network. In isolation, this might be viewed as support for a hierarchical relationship between route and survey learning analogous to Siegel and White's (1975) proposed hierarchy for route and survey knowledge constructs. However, other aspects of the results speak to the behavioral dissociation. Based on neuroimaging findings, facilitation of scene recognition performance has different neural mechanisms for route and survey encoding. The facilitation of survey recognition following survey learning was associated with greater recruitment of areas activated by both types of encoding. In contrast, the facilitation of route recognition following route learning was associated with the recruitment of additional areas. Although this supports a hierarchical relationship between route and survey information in terms of the network of brain areas involved, the increased activation in shared regions for survey information suggests some survey-specific specialization.

Another critical finding in the comparison of route and survey information was the nature of the shared brain regions. Regions of overlap for the two types of encoding were generally outside the areas of the spatial processing network identified previously. Rather than supporting more general spatial cognition, this set of regions might be more aptly named the *navigation network*, specialized for route-level knowledge. This new distinction raises questions about the components of route-level information and why they might engage these particular regions.

A number of psychological properties distinguish route- and survey-level information. For example, the route perspective requires monitoring of local position and orientation, whereas the survey perspective is global and external to the space. In studies of near (peripersonal) and far (extrapersonal) space, dorsal visuomotor regions of parietal and premotor cortices have been associated with experiences and deficits in peripersonal space (e.g., Halligan & Marshall, 1991; Weiss et al., 2000). Navigation is an immersive experience and may involve more processing of peripersonal space than other types of spatial learning.

Similarly, the medial temporal lobe structures (hippocampus and parahippocampal cortex) play an important role during navigation (Maguire et al., 1997), but initial evidence suggests that the contributions of this region to survey or map-like encoding are more limited (Shelton & Gabrieli, 2002). How does this fit with the characterization of the hippocampus as a locus for cognitive maps (e.g., O'Keefe & Nadel, 1978)? First, it has been suggested that the hippocampus may not be requisite for more remote spatial memories (Rosenbaum et al., 2000), questioning whether the hippocampus is actually representing memory for space or playing some other role in spatial learning. One speculation based on the discrepancy between route and survey activation in this region is that hippocampal structures play a more specific cognitive mapping role in extracting or building cognitive maps from limited spatial information. In this proposed role, the hippocampal structures would participate more in route encoding because route encoding requires more "map building" than survey encoding. In the survey perspective, the global information is more direct. There would be much less need to build a cognitive map when many of the cognitive map elements are readily available in the visual presentation. Further research on the global structure of the survey perspective may help evaluate this hypothesis for a more specific cognitive mapping function.

An alternative interpretation of the medial temporal lobe as a navigation-specific brain area lies in the more general role of the medial temporal lobe in memory processes. It is widely known that damage to the hippocampus can produce profound memory impairments, extending beyond spatial memory (Scoville & Milner, 1957; Stark & Squire, 2000c). In addition, research on place cells in rats has demonstrated that rat hippocampal neurons encode both spatial and nonspatial aspects of an experience (e.g., Wood, Dudchenko, & Eichenbaum, 1999). One suggestion has been that the hippocampus is not representing a spatial map but rather providing a memory space in which episodes are associated (Eichenbaum, Dudchenko, Wood, Shapiro, & Tanila, 1999). Navigation requires participants to link sequential steps together. Extracting the global structure of the space requires the appropriate sequential links. The need for such sequential integration is much less with a map or survey perspective because much of the global environment is readily available from the visual information. For example, the continuation of a boundary and its relation to adjacent boundaries does not have to be inferred from turns in space but can be seen visually. This latter integration may lead to much less associative processing (i.e., less mnemonic demand).

Whether the hippocampal region is responsible for storing a cognitive map or for a more general memory process, it clearly participates in spatial memory processes. Differentiating the role of this region (as well as other regions) in different types of spatial encoding and retrieval provides two routes for future research and interpretation. First, it has opened the door for scrutinizing these alternatives more closely. Second, it has provided grounding for thinking about the different psychological processes that might contribute to different types of spatial learning. As more research is brought to bear on these issues, it will lend greater specificity to the functions of brain areas and help to constrain theories of spatial cognition.

CONCLUSIONS

The emphasis of this chapter has been on finding source-specific regions for spatial memory processing. However, the flip side to this issue is the question of centralized spatial processing. Are there regions that are activated across different types of spatial information? The answer is likely "yes," given a number of observations. First, although route and survey information were distinguishable in memory, there were also a number of brain areas that were activated by both route and survey information during encoding (Shelton & Gabrieli, 2002) and retrieval (Mellet et al., 2000). Second, there is evidence that spatial information from different modalities is integrated in the brain (Andersen, 1997; Banati, Goerres, Tjoa, Aggleton, & Grasby, 2000; Calvert, 2001; Frassinetti, Pavani, & Làdavas, 2002). Indeed, behavioral studies suggest that not only can different sources of spatial memory be integrated but may even be confused in memory (Shelton & McNamara, 2001b). Brain regions responsible for such cross-modal integration likely subserve more general spatial processing. Given the consummate goal of developing a comprehensive understanding of spatial learning and memory, the identification and characterization of such regions is just as critical as distinguishing source-specific regions.

Cognitive psychology and cognitive neuroscience have only begun to scratch the surface of understanding the complex world of spatial cognition in the brain. Efforts to isolate different experiences have been fruitful, but they only represent part of the spatial learning picture. For example, when starting at a new college campus, one might consult a campus map to learn the general layout before ever stepping foot on campus. Then, on arrival, one is faced with navigating the new terrain using the information learned from the map along with the new information about the actual appearance of landmarks and paths, the number of paces between different buildings, and the changing sounds around the campus. Along the way, one might consult one of the "you-are-here" maps placed strategically about the campus to verify (or correct) one's perceived location. All of these different sources provide information about spatial layout, and they may be used implicitly or explicitly to learn the environment. Together, they will eventually allow the sensation of effortless navigation in a familiar environment.

From this example, it should be clear that the distinction between navigation and map learning is but one distinction in broader tapestry of spatial cognition. Differences between visual and tactile spatial experience, visual and text-based learning, learning with and without proprioceptive inputs, or even active versus passive learning may influence how information is encoded in and later retrieved from memory. Behavioral evidence has already demonstrated that performance on spatial memory tasks can be contingent on our experiences with space. Using neuroimaging in conjunction with these observed behaviors provides an opportunity to explore the neurological grounding for claims about spatial processing, contributing both detail and constraint to theoretical interpretations. The results of such endeavors are likely to provide better understanding of the brain as well as more robust models of human spatial cognition.

REFERENCES

Aguirre, G. K., & D'Esposito, M. (1997). Environmental knowledge is subserved by separable dorsal/ventral neural areas. *Journal of Neuroscience, 17*, 2512–2518.

Aguirre, G. K., & D'Esposito, M. (1999). Topographical disorientation: A synthesis and taxonomy. *Brain, 122*, 1613–1628.

Aguirre, G. K., Zarahn, E., & D'Esposito, M. (1998). Neural components of topographical representation. *Proceedings of the National Academy of Science USA, 95*, 839–846.

Andersen, R. A. (1997). Multimodal integration for the representation of space in the posterior parietal cortex. *Philosophical Transactions of the Royal Society of London B, Biological Sciences, 352*, 1421–1428.

Appleyard, D. (1969). Why buildings are known. *Environment and Behavior, 1*, 131–156.

Appleyard, D. (1970). Styles and methods of structuring a city. *Environment and Behavior, 2*, 100–118.

Banati, R. B., Goerres, G. W., Tjoa, C., Aggleton, J. P., & Grasby, P. (2000). The functional anatomy of visual-tactile integration in man: A study using positron emission tomography. *Neuropsychologia, 38*, 115–124.

Burgess, N., Jeffery, K. J., & O'Keefe, J. (Ed.). (1999). *The hippocampal and parietal foundations of spatial cognition*. Oxford, England: Oxford University Press.

Calvert, G. A. (2001). Crossmodal processing in the human brain: Insights from functional neuroimaging studies. *Cerebral Cortex, 11*, 1110–1123.

Chen, L. L., Lin, L. H., Barnes, C. A., & McNaughton, B. L. (1994). Head-direction cells in the rat posterior cortex, II. Contributions of visual and ideothetic information to the directional firing. *Experimental Brain Research, 101*, 24–34.

Chen, L. L., Lin, L. H., Green, E. J., Barnes, C. A., & McNaughton, B. L. (1994). Head-direction cells in the rat posterior cortex, I. Anatomical distribution and behavioral modulation. *Experimental Brain Research, 101*, 8–23.

Cho, J., & Sharp, P. E. (2001). Head direction, place, movement correlates for cells in the rat retrosplenial cortex. *Behavioral Neuroscience, 115,* 3–25.

Cho, Y. H., & Kesner, R. P. (1996). Involvement of entorhinal cortex or parietal cortex in long-term spatial discrimination memory in rats: Retrograde amnesia. *Behavioral Neuroscience, 110,* 436–442.

Colby, C. L., & Goldberg, M. E. (1999). Space and attention in parietal cortex. *Annual Review of Neuroscience, 22,* 319–349.

Collett, T. S., & Cartwright, B. A. (1983). Eidetic images in insects: Their role in navigation. *Trends in Neurosciences, 6,* 101–105.

Cooper, B. G., & Mizumori, S. J. Y. (2001). Temporary inactivation of the retrosplenial cortex causes a transient reorganization of spatial coding in the hippocampus. *Journal of Neuroscience, 21,* 3986–4001.

Courtney, S. M., Petit, L., Maisog, J. M., Ungerleider, L. G., & Haxby, J. V. (1998, February 27). An area specialized for spatial working memory in human frontal cortex. *Science, 279,* 1347–1351.

Courtney, S. M., Ungerleider, L. G., Keil, K., & Haxby, J. V. (1996). Object and spatial visual working memory activate separate neural systems in human cortex. *Cerebral Cortex, 6,* 39–49.

Critchley, M. (1953). *The parietal lobes.* London: Arnold.

Diwadkar, V. A., & McNamara, T. P. (1997). Viewpoint dependence in scene recognition. *Psychological Science, 8,* 302–307.

Eichenbaum, H., Dudchenko, P., Wood, E., Shapiro, M., & Tanila, H. (1999). The hippocampus, memory, and place cells: Is it spatial memory or a memory space? *Neuron, 23,* 209–226.

Epstein, R., & Kanwisher, N. (1998, April 9). A cortical representation of the local visual environment. *Nature, 392,* 598–601.

Ettlinger, G. (1990). "Object vision" and "spatial vision": The neuropsychological evidence for the distinction. *Cortex, 26,* 319–341.

Evans, G. W., Marrero, D. G., & Butler, P. (1981). Environmental learning and cognitive mapping. *Environment and Behavior, 13,* 83–104.

Ferguson, E. L., & Hegarty, M. (1994). Properties of cognitive maps constructed from texts. *Memory & Cognition, 22,* 455–473.

Frassinetti, F., Pavani, F., & Làdavas, E. (2002). Acoustical vision of neglected stimuli: Interaction among spatially converging audiovisual inputs in neglect patients. *Journal of Cognitive Neuroscience, 14,* 62–69.

Frisk, V., & Milner, B. (1990). The role of left hippocampal region in the acquisition and retention of story content. *Neuropsychologia, 28,* 349–359.

Ghaëm, O., Mellet, E., Crivello, F., Tzourio, N., Mazoyer, B., Berthoz, A., & Denis, M. (1997). Mental navigation along memorized routes activates the hippocampus, precuneus, and insula. *Neuroreport, 8,* 739–744.

Halligan, P. W., & Marshall, J. C. (1991, April 11). Left neglect in near but not far space in man. *Nature, 350,* 498–500.

Hyvarinen, J., & Poranen, A. (1974). Function of the parietal area 7a as revealed from cellular discharges in alert monkeys. *Brain, 97,* 673–692.

Langdon, D., & Warrington, E. K. (2000). The role of left hemisphere in verbal and spatial reasoning tasks. *Cortex, 36,* 691–702.

Langer, P., Keenan, V., Wetzel, J., Jacques-Griffin, J., & Chiszar, D. (1996). Memorial representations as a product of feedback and text variants. *Psychological Reports, 78,* 803–813.

Maguire, E. A. (2001). The retrosplenial contribution to human navigation: A review of lesion and neuroimaging findings. *Scandinavian Journal of Psychology, 42,* 225–238.

Maguire, E. A., Burgess, N., Donnett, J. G., Frackowiak, R. S. J., Frith, C. D., & O'Keefe, J. (1998, May 8). Knowing where and getting there. A human navigation network. *Science, 280,* 921–924.

Maguire, E. A., & Cipolotti, L. (1998). Selective sparing of topographical memory. *Journal of Neurology, Neurosurgery, and Psychiatry, 65,* 903–909.

Maguire, E. A., Frackowiak, R. S. J., & Frith, C. D. (1997). Recalling routes around London: Activation of the right hippocampus in taxi drivers. *Journal of Neuroscience, 17,* 7103–7110.

Marshall, J. C., & Halligan, P. W. (1995, February 9). Seeing the forest but only half the trees? *Nature, 373,* 521–523.

McNaughton, B. L., Barnes, C. A., & O'Keefe, J. (1983). The contributions of position, direction, and velocity to single unit activity in the hippocampus of freely-moving rats. *Experimental Brain Research, 52,* 41–49.

Mellet, E., Bricogne, S., Tzourio-Mazoyer, N., Ghaëm, O., Petit, L., Zago, L., Etard, O., Berthoz, A., Mazoyer, B., & Denis, M. (2000). Neural correlates of topographic mental exploration: The impact of route versus survey learning. *NeuroImage, 12,* 588–600.

Mesulam, M. M., Nobre, A. C., Kim, Y.-H., Parrish, T. B., & Gitelman, D. R. (2001). Heterogeneity of cingulate contributions to spatial attention. *NeuroImage, 13,* 1065–1072.

Millar, S. (1994). *Understanding and representing space: Theory and evidence from studies with blind and sighted children.* Oxford, England: Clarendon.

Milner, B. (1971). Interhemispheric differences in the localization of psychological processes in man. *British Medical Bulletin, 27,* 272–277.

Mishkin, M., Ungerleider, L. G., & Macko, K. A. (1983). Object vision and spatial vision: Two cortical pathways. *Trends in Neuroscience, 6,* 414–417.

Moeser, S. D. (1988). Cognitive mapping in a complex building. *Environment and Behavior, 20,* 21–49.

Morris, R. G., Garrud, P., Rawlins, J. N., & O'Keefe, J. (1982, June 24). Place navigation is impaired in rats with hippocampal lesions. *Nature, 297,* 681–683.

Mountcastle, V. B., Lynch, J. C., Georgopoulos, A., Sakata, H., & Acuna, C. (1975). Posterior parietal association cortex of the monkey: Command functions for operation within extrapersonal space. *Journal of Neurophysiology, 38,* 871–908.

O'Keefe, J., & Nadel, L. (1978). *The hippocampus as a cognitive map.* Oxford, England: Clarendon.

Olton, D. S., & Samuelson, R. J. (1976). Remembrance of places passed: Spatial memory in rats. *Journal of Experimental Psychology: Animal Behavior Processes, 2,* 97–116.

Perrig, W., & Kintsch, W. (1985). Propositional and situational representations of text. *Journal of Memory and Language, 24,* 503–518.

Postle, B. R., Stern, C. E., Rosen, B. R., & Corkin, S. (2000). An fMRI investigation of cortical contributions to spatial and nonspatial visual working memory. *NeuroImage, 11,* 409–423.

Robertson, I. H., & Marshall, J. C. (Eds.). (1993). *Unilateral neglect: Clinical and experimental studies.* Hove, England: Lawrence Erlbaum Associates.

Rolls, E. (1991). Functions of the primate hippocampus in spatial processing and memory. In J. Paillard (Ed.), *Brain and space* (pp. 353–375). Oxford, England: Oxford University Press.

Rolls, E. T. (1999). Spatial view cells and the representation of place in the primate hippocampus. *Hippocampus, 9,* 467–480.

Rosenbaum, R. S., Priselac, S., Köhler, S., Black, S. E., Gao, F., Nadel, L., & Moscovitch, M. (2000). Remote spatial memory in an amnesic person with extensive bilateral hippocampal lesions. *Nature Neuroscience, 3,* 1044–1048.

Roskos-Ewoldsen, B., McNamara, T. P., Shelton, A. L., & Carr, W. (1998). Mental representations of large and small spatial layouts are orientation dependent. *Journal of Experimental Psychology: Learning, Memory and Cognition, 24,* 215–226.

Scoville, W. B., & Milner, B. (1957). Loss of recent memory after bilateral hippocampal lesions. *Journal of Neurology, Neurosurgery, & Psychiatry, 20,* 11–21.

Shelton, A. L., & Gabrieli, J. D. E. (2002). Neural correlates of encoding space from route and survey perspectives. *Journal of Neuroscience. 22,* 2711–2717.

Shelton, A. L., & McNamara, T. P. (1997). Multiple views of spatial memory. *Psychonomic Bulletin and Review, 4,* 102–106.

Shelton, A. L., & McNamara, T. P. (2001a). Systems of spatial reference in human memory. *Cognitive Psychology, 43,* 274–310.

Shelton, A. L., & McNamara, T. P. (2001b). Visual memories from nonvisual experiences. *Psychological Science, 12,* 343–347.

Shelton, A. L., & McNamara, T. P. (in press). Orientation and perspective dependence in route and survey learning. .*Journal of Experimental Psychology: Learning, Memory, and Cognition*

Siegel, A. W., & White, S. H. (1975). The development of spatial representations of large-scale environments. In H. W. Reese (Ed.), *Advances in child development and behavior* (pp. 9–55). New York: Academic.

Smith, E. E., Jonides, J., & Koeppe, R. A. (1996). Dissociating verbal and spatial working memory using PET. *Cerebral Cortex, 6,* 11–20.

Smith, M. L., & Milner, B. (1981). The role of right hippocampus in the recall of spatial location. *Neuropsychologia, 19,* 781–793.

Stark, C. E. L., & Squire, L. R. (2000a). fMRI activity in the medial temporal lobe during recognition memory as a function of study-test interval. *Hippocampus, 10,* 329–337.

Stark, C. E. L., & Squire, L. R. (2000b). Functional magnetic resonance imaging (fMRI) activity in the hippocampal region during recognition memory. *Journal of Neuroscience, 20,* 7776–7781.

Stark, C., & Squire, L. (2000c). Recognition memory and familiarity judgments in severe amnesia: No evidence for a contribution of repetition priming. *Behavioral Neuroscience, 114,* 459–467.

Streeter, L. A., Vitello, D., & Wonsiewicz, S. A. (1985). How to tell people where to go: Comparing navigational aids. *International Journal of Man-Machine Studies, 22,* 549–562.

Suzuki, K., Yamadori, A., Hayakawa, Y., & Fujii, T. (1998). Pure topographical disorientation related to dysfunction of the viewpoint dependent visual system. *Cortex, 34,* 589–599.

Taylor, H. A., Naylor, S. J., & Chechile, N. A. (1999). Goal-specific influences on the representation of spatial perspective. *Memory & Cognition, 27,* 309–319.

Taylor, H. A., & Tversky, B. (1992). Spatial mental models derived from survey and route descriptions. *Journal of Memory and Language, 31,* 261–292.

Thorndyke, P. W., & Hayes-Roth, B. (1982). Differences in spatial knowledge acquired from maps and navigation. *Cognitive Psychology, 14,* 560–589.

Tversky, B. (1991). Spatial mental models. In G. H. Bower (Ed.), *The psychology of learning and motivation* (pp. 109–145). San Diego, CA: Academic.

Warburton, E. C., Baird, A., Morgan, A., Muir, J. L., & Aggleton, J. P. (2001). The conjoint importance of the hippocampus and anterior thalamic nuclei for allocentric spatial learning: Evidence from a disconnection study in rats. *Journal of Neuroscience, 21,* 7323–7330.

Warrington, E. K., & Baddeley, A. D. (1974). Amnesia and memory for visual location. *Neuropsychologia, 12,* 257–263.

Weiss, P. H., Marshall, J. C., Wunderlich, G., Tellmann, L., Halligan, P. W., Freund, H.-J., Zilles, K., & Fink, G. R. (2000). Neural consequences of acting in near versus far space: A physiological basis for clinical dissociations. *Brain, 123,* 2531–2541.

Wood, E. R., Dudchenko, P. A., & Eichenbaum, H. (1999, February 18). The global record of memory in hippocampal neuronal activity. *Nature, 397,* 613–616.

Zola-Morgan, S., & Squire, L. (1985). Mesial temporal lesions in monkeys impairs memory on a variety of tasks sensitive to human amnesia. *Behavioral Neuroscience, 99,* 22–34.

Zola-Morgan, S., & Squire, L. (1986). Memory impairment in monkeys following lesions limited to the hippocampus. *Behavioral Neuroscience, 100,* 155–160.

Author Index

A

Abrahams, S., 150, 153, *157*, 217, 222, 228–231, 233, 242, *234*, *244*
Acredolo, L. P., 25, 28, *38*, 44, *61*, 130, 131, *141*
Acuna, C., 314, *325*
Adelstein, T. B., 144, *157*
Aggleton, J. P., *96*, *99*, *158*, 215, 322, *323*, *326*
Agid, Y., 154, *158*, *159*
Aglioti, S., 178, *185*
Aguirre, G. K., 15, 16, *22*, *96*, 218, 242, *244*, 316, 317, *323*
Albert, W. S., 268, 269, *279*
Alberts, D. M., 199, *212*
Allamano, N., 70, *96*
Allen, G. L., 44, 50, *61*, 93, 95, 121, *121*, 129, 130, *142*, 272, 278, *279*, *280*
Alpert, N. M., 176, *187*
Alsop, D.C., 218, *244*
Amorim, M.-A., 164, 171, 172, *185*, 238, *244*
Amsterdam, J. B., 228, *245*
Anand, S., 177, 178, 181, 182, *185*
Andersen, P., 222, *246*
Andersen, R. A., 15, *22*, 322, *323*
Anderson, A. K., 11, *23*, *186*
Anderson, D. I., *38*
Anderson, J. R., 102, *121*
Anderson, N. H., 202, *212*
Andreasen, G., 288, *307*
Andrew, C., *246*
Angeli, S. J., 35, *38*, 217, *244*
Anooshian, L. J., 44, *61*, 253, *260*
Appleyard, D., 218, *244*, 314, *323*
Ashburner, J., *39*
Atkinson, R. C., 67, *95*
Awh, E., 74, 75, 83, *95*, *97*, *100*, *160*

B

Babb, T. L., 222, *244*

Baddeley, A., 59, *61*, 67, 69–71, 75, *95*, *96*, 101, 103, 107, 118, 120, *121*, *122*, 147, 153, *157*, 315, *326*
Bailey, J. H., 275, *285*
Baillargeon, R., 25, 30, *38*, *40*
Bailleux, C., 120, *122*
Baird, A., 315, *326*
Bakker, N. H., 260, *280*
Balin, J. H., 128, *141*
Ballard, D., *96*
Banati, R. B., 322, *323*
Banham, J., 302, *307*
Barbu, R., *38.*
Barnes, C. A., 92, *97*, 238, *245*, 315, *323*, *325*
Barr, D. J., 128, *141*
Barrett, A., *23*, *62*, 146, *158*
Bartels, G. P., 266, 267, *284*
Bartlett, F. C., 12, *22*
Bartsch, K., 26, *38*
Baylis, G. C., 146, *157*
Beall, A. C., 164, *185*, *187*, 260, 275, *280–282*
Beck, S., 93, *95*, 121, *121*, *279*
Becker, J. T., 226, *246*
Behrmann, M., 239, *246*
Belliveau, J. W., *186*
Benton, A. L., xiv, *xviii*
Benvenuti, F., 178, *188*
Berch, D., 114, *121*
Berlie, J., 198, 199, *213*
Berthoz, A., *23*, 164, *188*, 238, 239, *244*, *245*, 324, *325*
Beusmans, J. M., 268, *279*
Bhalla, M., 15, 24, 41, 56, 58, *61*, *62*, 178, *188*
Bialystock, E., 128, *142*
Biegler, R., 192, 203, *212*
Billberg, R., 259, *283*
Bishop, D. V. M., 107, *121*, *122*
Bjorklund, D., 115, *121*, *123*
Black, S. E., *160*, 239, *246*, *325*
Blades, M., 130, 131, *141*, 196, *214*, 288–294, 296, 299, 300, 302, 305, *307*, *308*
Blascovich, J. J., 275, *282*

329

Subject Index